CRITICAL THINKING

LEARN THE TOOLS
THE BEST THINKERS USE

CONCISE EDITION

Richard Paul
Linda Elder

PEARSON
Prentice
Hall

Upper Saddle River, New Jersey
Columbus, Ohio

Library of Congress Cataloging-in-Publication Data

Paul, Richard.

    Critical thinking : learn the tools the best thinkers use / Richard Paul,
Linda Elder. — Concise ed.

      p. cm.

    Includes bibliographical references and index.

    ISBN 0-13-170347-1

    1. Critical thinking—Study and teaching (Higher)   2. Academic
achievement.   I. Elder, Linda.   II. Title.

LB2395.35.P38 2006

370.15'2—dc22   2005014358

Vice President and Publisher: Jeffery W. Johnston
Executive Editor: Sande Johnson
Editorial Assistant: Susan Kauffman
Production Editor: Holcomb Hathaway
Design Coordinator: Diane C. Lorenzo
Cover Designer: Jeff Vanik
Cover Photo: Corbis
Production Manager: Pamela D. Bennett
Director of Marketing: Ann Castel Davis
Marketing Manager: Amy Judd
Compositor: Carlisle Communications, Ltd.
Cover Printer: Phoenix Color Corp.
Printer/Binder: R. R. Donnelley & Sons Company

Pearson Education Ltd.   Pearson Education Canada, Ltd.
Pearson Education Australia Pty. Limited   Pearson Educación de Mexico, S.A. de C.V.
Pearson Education Singapore Pte. Ltd.   Pearson Education–Japan
Pearson Education North Asia Ltd.   Pearson Education Malaysia Pte. Ltd.

15 14 13 12 11
ISBN: 0-13-170347-1

CONTENTS

Chapter 2

DISCOVER THE PARTS OF THINKING   11

Chapter 3

DISCOVER UNIVERSAL STANDARDS
FOR THINKING   43

Chapter 4

REDEFINE GRADES AS LEVELS OF
THINKING AND LEARNING   73

Chapter 5

LEARN TO ASK THE QUESTIONS THE
BEST THINKERS ASK   83

Chapter 6

DISCOVER HOW THE
BEST THINKERS LEARN   103

Chapter 7

THE BEST THINKERS READ CLOSELY AND WRITE SUBSTANTIVELY   133

Chapter 8

BECOME A FAIR-MINDED THINKER   189

Chapter 9

DEAL WITH YOUR IRRATIONAL MIND   213

Chapter 10

THE STAGES OF CRITICAL THINKING DEVELOPMENT: *AT WHAT STAGE ARE YOU?*   257

Appendices

PREFACE

You are what you think. That's right. Whatever you are doing right now is determined by the way you are thinking. Whatever you feel—all your emotions—are determined by your thinking. Whatever you want—all your desires—are determined by your thinking. If your thinking is unrealistic, it will lead you to many disappointments. If your thinking is overly pessimistic, it will deny you due recognition of the many things in which you should properly rejoice.

Test this idea for yourself. Identify some examples of your strongest feelings or emotions. Then identify the thinking that is correlated with those examples. For example, if you *feel* excited about college, it is because you *think* that good things will happen to you in college. If you dread going to class, it is probably because you think it will be boring or too difficult.

In a similar way, if the quality of your life is not what you would wish it to be, it is most likely because it is tied to the way you think about your life. If you think about it positively, you will feel positively about it. If you think about it negatively, you will feel negative about it.

For example, suppose you came to college with the view that college was going to be a lot of fun, that you were going to form good friendships with fellow students who would respect and like you, and, what is more, that your love life would become interesting and exciting. And let's suppose that hasn't happened. If this were the thrust of your thinking, you now would feel disappointed and maybe even frustrated (depending on how negatively you have interpreted your experience).

For most people, thinking is subconscious, never explicitly put into words. For example, most people who think negatively would not say of themselves, "I have chosen to think about myself and my experience in a negative way. I prefer to be as unhappy as I can make myself."

The problem is that when you are not aware of your thinking, you have no chance of correcting it if it is poor. When thinking is subconscious, you are in no position to see any problems in it. And, if you don't see any problems in it, you won't be motivated to change it.

Since few people realize the powerful role that thinking plays in their lives, few gain significant command of it. Most people are in many ways victims of their thinking; that is, they are *hurt* rather than *helped* by it. Most people are their own worst enemy. Their thinking is a continual source of problems, preventing them from recognizing opportunities, keeping them from exerting energy where it will do the most good, poisoning relationships, and leading them down blind alleys.

Or consider your success as a student in college. The single most significant variable in determining that success is the quality of your thinking. If you think well when you study, you will study well. If you think well when you read, you will read well. If you think well when you write, you will write well. And if you study well, read well, and write well, you will do well in college. Certainly your instructors will play a role in your learning. Some of them will do a better job than others of helping you learn. But even the best teachers cannot get into your head and learn for you. Even the best teachers cannot think for you, read for you, or write for you. If you lack the intellectual skills necessary for thinking well through course content, you will not be successful in college.

Here is the key question we are putting to you in this book. If the quality of a person's thinking is the single most significant determinant of both happiness and success—as it is—why not discover the tools that the best thinkers use and take the time to learn to use them yourself? Perhaps you will not become proficient in all of them, but for every tool you learn, there will be a payoff.

This book will alert you to the tools the best thinkers use and will exemplify the activities and practice you can use to begin to emulate them. You will then have your destiny as a thinker in your own hands. The only thing that will determine whether you become a better and better thinker is your own willingness to practice. Here are some of the qualities of the best thinkers.

- **The best thinkers think about their thinking.** They do not take thinking for granted. They do not trust to fate to make them good in thinking. They *notice* their thinking. They *reflect* on their thinking. They act upon their thinking.

- **The best thinkers are highly purposeful.** They do not simply act. They know why they act. They know what they are about. They have clear goals and clear priorities. They continually check their activities for alignment with their goals.

- **The best thinkers have intellectual "tools" that they use to raise the quality of their thinking.** They know how to express their thinking clearly. They know how to check it for accuracy and precision. They know how to keep focused on a question and make sure that it is relevant to their goals and purposes. They know how to think beneath the surface and how to expand their thinking to include insights from multiple perspectives. They know how to think logically and significantly.

- **The best thinkers distinguish their thoughts from their feelings and desires.** They know that wanting something to be so does not make it so. They know that one can be unjustifiably angry, afraid, or insecure. They do not let unexamined emotions determine their decisions. They have "discovered" their minds, and they examine the way their minds operate as a result. They take deliberate charge of those operations. (See Chapter 1.)

- **The best thinkers routinely take thinking apart.** They "analyze" thinking. They do not trust the mind to analyze itself automatically. They realize that the art of analyzing thinking is an art one must consciously learn. They realize that it takes knowledge (of the parts of thinking) and practice (in exercising control over them). (See Chapter 2.)

- **The best thinkers routinely evaluate thinking—determining its strengths and weaknesses.** They do not trust the mind to evaluate itself automatically. They realize that the automatic ways that the mind evaluates itself are inherently flawed. They realize that the art of evaluating thinking is an art one must consciously learn. They realize that it takes knowledge (of the universal standards for thinking) and practice (in exercising control over them). (See Chapter 3.)

Each chapter concentrates on one dimension of the "thinking" tools the best thinkers use. Each provides you with insights it is in your interest to acquire. Each can help you discover the power of your own mind and of your potential to think systematically about your thinking.

This book, as a whole, introduces you to the tools of mind that will help you reason well through the problems and issues you face, whether in the classroom, in your personal life, or in your professional life. If you take these ideas seriously, and practice using them, you can take command of the thinking that ultimately will command the quality of your life.

ACKNOWLEDGMENTS

We would like to thank the following reviewers, who read and commented on the manuscript in earlier forms: Bruce Bloom, DeVry University; Stephen Felder, University of California at Irvine; Stephen Kopp, Ohio University; George Nagel, Ferris State University; Paige Wilmeth, University of Hawaii; and Connie Wolfe, Surrey Community College.

DEDICATION

To all those who use their thinking to expose hypocrisy and self-deception, and work to create—what is now but a dream within a dream—a just and humane world.

ACKNOWLEDGMENT

A special acknowledgment is due to Gerald Nosich—dedicated thinker, exemplary scholar, lifelong friend and colleague.

INTRODUCTION

The mind is its own place and in itself can make a hell of heaven or a heaven of hell.

John Milton, *Paradise Lost*

There are many ways to articulate the concept of critical thinking, just as there are many ways to articulate the meaning of any rich and substantive concept. But, as with any concept, there is an *essence* to critical thinking that cannot be ignored. In this introduction we introduce the essence of critical thinking. We begin to unfold its complexities. We begin to show you its relevance to your life. Then we will ask you to articulate your understanding of critical thinking, to demonstrate that you are beginning to make it your own.

A START-UP DEFINITION OF CRITICAL THINKING

Let us consider a "start-up" definition of critical thinking:

> Critical thinking is the art of thinking about thinking while thinking in order to make thinking better. It involves three interwoven phases: It analyzes thinking;[1] it evaluates thinking;[2] it improves thinking.[3]

To think critically, you must be willing to examine your thinking and put it to some stern tests. You must be willing to take your thinking apart (to see it as something

---

[1] By focusing on the parts of thinking in any situation—its purpose, question, information, inferences, assumptions, concepts, implications, and point of view.

[2] By figuring out its strengths and weaknesses: the extent to which it is clear, accurate, precise, relevant, deep, broad, logical, significant, and fair.

[3] By building on its strengths while reducing its weaknesses.

constructed out of parts). You must be willing to identify weaknesses in your thinking (while recognizing whatever strengths it may have). And, finally, you must be willing to reconstruct your thinking creatively to make it better (overcoming the natural tendency of the mind to be rigid, to want to validate one's current thoughts rather than improving them).

> The best thinkers pay close attention to thinking. They analyze it. They evaluate it. They improve it.

To think critically, you develop high standards for your thinking. You learn how to step back from it and make it meet those standards. This book will help you see how to act upon your thinking in this important and disciplined way, how to drag your thinking out into the light of day, take it apart, see it for what it is, and make it better.

HOW SKILLED ARE YOU AS A THINKER?

> The best thinkers use their ability to think well in every dimension of their lives.

There is nothing more practical than sound thinking. No matter what your circumstance or goals, no matter where you are or what problems you face, you are better off if you are in control of your thinking. As a student, shopper, employee, citizen, lover, friend, parent—in every realm and situation of your life—good thinking pays off. Poor thinking, in contrast, inevitably causes problems, wastes time and energy, and engenders frustration and pain.

Critical thinking is the disciplined art of ensuring that you use the best thinking you are capable of in any set of circumstances. The general goal of thinking is to figure out some situation, solve some problem, answer some question, or resolve some issue. We must all make sense of the world in which we live. How well or poorly we do this is crucial to our well-being.

Whatever sense we make of things, we have multiple choices to make. We need the best information to make the best choices. We need to figure out: What is really going on in this or that situation? Does so-and-so really care about me? Am I deceiving myself when I believe that. . . ? What are the likely consequences of failing

EXHIBIT I.1 *Critical thinkers use theories to explain how the mind works. Then they apply those theories to the way they live every day.*

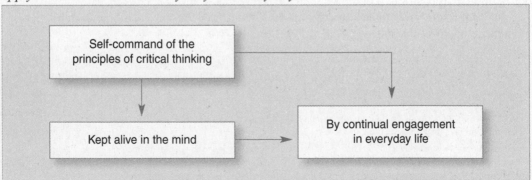

to . . . ? If I want to do . . . , what is the best way to prepare? How can I be more successful in doing . . . ? Is this my biggest problem, or do I need to focus my attention on that? Successfully responding to questions such as these is the daily work of thinking.

Nothing you can do will guarantee that you will find the complete truth about anything, but there is a way to get better at it. Excellence of thought and skill in thinking are real possibilities. To maximize the quality of your thinking, however, you must learn how to become an effective critic of your thinking. And to become an effective critic of your thinking, you have to make *learning about thinking* a priority.

Consider for a minute all of what you have learned in your life: about sports, money, friendship, anger and fear, love and hate, your mother and father, nature, the city you live in, manners and taboos, human nature and human behavior. Learning is a natural and inevitable process. We learn in many directions. One direction in which learning is *not* natural is inward learning—self-knowledge, knowledge of the workings of our own mind, of how and why we think as we do.

Begin by answering these—rather unusual—questions: What have you learned about how you think? Did you ever *study* your thinking? What information do you have, for example, about the intellectual processes involved in how your mind thinks? More to the point, perhaps, what do you really know about how to analyze, evaluate, or reconstruct your thinking? Where does your thinking come from? How much of it is of high quality? How much of it is of poor quality? How much of your thinking is vague, muddled, inconsistent, inaccurate, illogical, or superficial? Are you, in any real sense, in control of your thinking? Do you know how to test it? Do you have any conscious standards for determining when you are thinking well and when you are thinking poorly? Have you ever discovered a significant problem in your thinking and then changed it by a conscious act of will? If someone asked you to teach him or her what you have learned about thinking thus far in your life, would you have any idea what that was or how you learned it?

> The best thinkers make the study of thinking second nature.

If you are like most people, the honest answers to these questions run along the lines of: "Well, I suppose I don't know much about my thinking or about thinking in general. I suppose in my life I have more or less taken my thinking for granted. I don't really know how it works. I have never studied it. I don't know how I test it, or even if I *do* test it. It just happens in my mind automatically."

Serious study of thinking, serious thinking about thinking, is rare in human life. It is not a subject in most schools. It is not a subject taught at home. But if you focus your attention for a moment on the role that thinking is playing in your life, you may come to recognize that everything you do or want or feel is influenced by your thinking. And if you become persuaded of that, you will be surprised that humans show so little interest in thinking. What is more, if you start to pay attention to thinking in a manner analogous to the way a botanist observes plants, you will be on your way to becoming a truly exceptional person. You will begin to notice what few others notice. You will be the rare person who is engaged in discovering what human thinking is about. You will be the rare person who knows how and why he or she is thinking, the rare person skilled in assessing and improving how he or she thinks.

Some things you will eventually discover are: All of us, somewhere along the way, have picked up bad habits of thinking. All of us, for example, make generalizations when we don't have the evidence to back them up, allow stereotypes to influence our thinking, form some false beliefs. tend to look at the world from one fixed point of view, ignore or attack points of view that conflict with our own, fabricate illusions and myths that we subconsciously confuse with what is true and real, and think deceptively about many aspects of our experience. As you discover these problems in your thinking, we hope you will begin to ask yourself some key questions: Is it possible for me to learn to avoid bad habits of thought? Is it possible for me to develop good habits of thought? Is it possible for me to think at a high, or at least *higher,* level?

These are problems and questions that few discover or ask. Nevertheless, every major insight you gain into good or bad thinking can enhance your life significantly. You can begin to make better decisions. You can gain power, important power that you presently lack. You can open up new doors for yourself, see new options, minimize significant mistakes, maximize potential understandings. If you're going to live your life as a thinker, why not get good at thinking about thinking?

I.1 *Think for Yourself*

BEGINNING TO THINK ABOUT YOUR THINKING

See if you can identify any discovery you made about your thinking before you started to read this book. If you can't think of any, write out your best explanation as to why not. If you do think of something, explain what you learned about your thinking.

GOOD THINKING REQUIRES HARD WORK

There is a catch—there almost always is. To make significant gains in the quality of your thinking, you will have to engage in a kind of work that most humans find unpleasant, if not painful: intellectual work. This is the price you have to pay if you want the gain. One doesn't become a skillful critic of thinking overnight any more than one becomes a skillful basketball player or dancer overnight. To become a student of thinking, you must be willing to put the work into thinking that skilled improvement requires. When thinking of what physical conditioning requires, we say, "No pain, no gain!" In this case, it would be more precise to say, "No intellectual pain, no *intellectual* gain!"

This means you must be willing to practice special "acts" of thinking that are, initially at least uncomfortable, and sometimes challenging and difficult. You have to learn to do "moves" with your mind analogous to what accomplished athletes learn to do through practice and feedback with their body. Improvement in thinking, then, is similar to improvement in other domains of performance in which progress is a product of sound theory, commitment, hard work, and practice. Although this book will point the way to what you need to practice to become a skilled thinker, it cannot provide you with the internal motivation to do the required work. This must come from you. You must be willing, as it were, to be the monkey who comes down from the trees and starts to observe your fellow monkeys in action. You must be willing to examine mental films of your own monkeying around, as well.

Let's now develop further the analogy between physical and intellectual development. This analogy, we believe, goes a long way, and provides us with just the right prototype to keep before our minds. If you play tennis and you want to play better, there is nothing more advantageous than to look at some films of excellent players in action and then painstakingly compare how they, in comparison to you, address the ball. You study their performance. You note what you need to do more of, what you need to do less of, and you practice, practice, practice. You go through many cycles of practice/feedback/practice. Your practice heightens your awareness of the ins and outs of the art. You develop a vocabulary for talking about your performance. Perhaps you get a coach. And slowly, progressively, you improve. Similar points could be made for ballet, distance running, piano playing, chess playing, reading, writing, parenting, teaching, studying, and so on.

One major problem, however, is that all the activities of skill development with which we are typically familiar are visible. We could watch a film of the skill in action. But imagine a film of a person sitting in a chair *thinking*. It would look like the person was doing nothing. Yet, increasingly, workers are being paid precisely for the thinking they are able to do, not for their physical strength or physical activity. Therefore, though most of our thinking is invisible, it represents one of the most important things about us. Its quality, in all likelihood, will determine whether we will become rich or poor, powerful or weak. Yet we typically think without explicitly noticing how we are doing it. We take our thinking for granted.

For example, important concepts, such as love, friendship, integrity, freedom, democracy, and ethics, are often unconsciously twisted and distorted in common life and thought. Our subconscious interest is often in getting what we want, not in describing ourselves or the world truly and honestly.

In any case, most of our concepts are invisible to us, though implicit in our talk and behavior. So is much of our thinking. We would be amazed, and sometimes shocked, if we were to see all of our thinking displayed for us on a large screen.

To develop as a thinker, you must begin to think of your thinking as involving an implicit set of structures—concepts being one important set—whose use can be improved only when you begin to take the tools of thinking seriously. You develop as a thinker when you explicitly notice what your thinking is doing and when you become committed to recognizing both strengths and weaknesses in that thinking. You develop as a thinker as you build your own "large screen" on which to view your thinking.

Critical thinking, then, provides the tools of mind you need to think through anything and everything that requires thought—in college and in life. As your intellectual skills develop, you gain instruments that you can use deliberately and mindfully to better reason through the thinking tasks implicit in your short- and long-range goals. There are better and worse ways to pursue whatever you are after. Good thinking enables you to maximize the better ways and minimize the worse.

EXHIBIT I.2 *Critical thinking is the way we should approach everything we do.*

CRITICAL THINKING ≠ Something you add onto everything else

Rather

CRITICAL THINKING = The way you do everything you do

The way you shop, teach, learn, vote, relate, evaluate, and so on

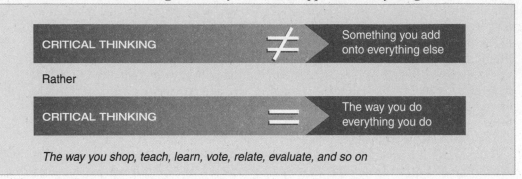

I.2 *Think for Yourself*

UNDERSTANDING THE IMPORTANCE OF CONCEPTS

See if you can think of a time in which you "misused" an important concept. Hint: Think of an idea that you commonly use in your thinking, such as friendship, trust, truthfulness, or respect. Have you ever implied you were someone's friend but acted against that person (such as gossiping behind that person's back)? Write out or orally explain your answer.

Only by applying the fundamentals to a wide range of human problems can one begin to appreciate their power and usefulness. Think of it this way. If we were coaching you in tennis, we would remind you again and again to keep your eye on the ball. Could you imagine saying to your coach, "Why do I have to keep my eye on the ball? I already did that once." The same logic applies to the principles of skilled thinking. If you want to be proficient, you have to redirect your eyes to the fundamentals, again and again and again.

EXHIBIT I.3 *Why is critical thinking so important? (A more elaborated "definition.")*

The Problem:

Everyone thinks. It is our nature to do so. But much of our thinking, left to itself, is biased, distorted, partial, uninformed, or downright prejudiced. Yet the quality of our life and that of what we produce, make, or build depends precisely on the quality of our thought. Shoddy thinking is costly, both in money and in quality of life. Excellence in thought, however, must be systematically cultivated.

DEFINING CRITICAL THINKING

Critical thinking is that mode of thinking—about any subject, content, or problem—in which the thinker improves the quality of his or her thinking by skillfully analyzing, assessing, and reconstructing it. Critical thinking is self-directed, self-disciplined, self-monitored, and self-corrective thinking. It presupposes assent to rigorous standards of excellence and mindful command of their use. It entails effective communication and problem-solving abilities, as well as a commitment to overcome one's native egocentrism and sociocentrism.

To analyze thinking:

Identify its

purpose

question

information

conclusion(s)

assumptions

implications

main concept(s)

point of view

To assess thinking:

Check it for

clarity

accuracy

precision

relevance

depth

breadth

significance

logic

and fairness

The Result

A well-cultivated critical thinker:

- raises vital questions and problems, formulating them clearly and precisely
- gathers and assesses relevant information, using abstract ideas to interpret it effectively

- comes to well-reasoned conclusions and solutions, testing them against relevant criteria and standards

- thinks open-mindedly within alternative systems of thought, recognizing and assessing, as need be, their assumptions, implications, and practical consequences

- communicates effectively with others in figuring out solutions to complex problems.

I.3   *Think for Yourself*

BEGINNING TO CONSIDER PROBLEMS IN THINKING

Exhibit I.3 shows that a big part of "the problem" critical thinking addresses is that "much of our thinking, left to itself, is biased, distorted, partial, uninformed, or downright prejudiced." Make a list of five significant problems in human life. Then see if you can identify the problems in *thinking* that lead to those problems. Be as specific as possible.

THE CONCEPT OF CRITICAL THINKING

The concept of critical thinking reflects an idea derived from roots in ancient Greek. The word *critical* derives etymologically from two Greek roots: *kriticos* (meaning "*discerning judgment*") and *kriterion* (meaning "*standards*"). Etymologically, then, the word implies the development of "discerning judgment based on standards." In *Webster's New World Dictionary,* the relevant entry for *critical* reads: "characterized by careful analysis and judgment" and is followed by: "Critical, in its strictest sense, implies an attempt at objective judgment so as to determine both merits and faults." Considering these definitions together, then, critical thinking may be appropriately defined as

> thinking explicitly aimed at well-founded judgment, utilizing appropriate evaluative standards in an attempt to determine the true worth, merit, or value of something.

Critical thinking, then, has three dimensions: an analytic, an evaluative, and a creative component. As critical thinkers, we analyze thinking in order to evaluate it. We evaluate it in order to improve it.

In other words, critical thinking is the *systematic monitoring of thought with the end of improvement.* When we think critically, we realize that thinking must not be accepted at face value but must be analyzed and assessed for its *clarity, accuracy, relevance, depth, breadth,* and *logic.* We recognize that all reasoning occurs within *points of view* and frames of reference, that all reasoning proceeds from some *goals and objectives* and has an *informational base,* that all data when used in reasoning must be *interpreted,* that interpretation involves *concepts,* that concepts entail *assumptions,* and that all basic inferences in thought have *implications*. Because problems in thinking can occur in any of these dimensions, each dimension must be monitored.

When we think critically, we realize that in every domain of human thought, it is possible and important to question the parts of thinking and the standards for thought. Routine questioning in the critical mind looks something like this:

> Let's see, what is the most fundamental issue here? From what point of view should I approach this problem? Does it make sense for me to assume this? What may I reasonably infer from these data? What is implied in this graph? What is the fundamental concept here? Is this information consistent with that information? What makes this question complex? How could I check the accuracy of these data? If this is so, what else is implied? Is this a credible source of information? And so forth.

With intellectual language such as this in the foreground, one can come to recognize fundamental critical thinking "moves" that can be used in reasoning through any problem or issue, class or subject. To help you learn the language of critical thinking and to apply it on a regular basis to your learning and your life is a primary objective of this book. With the analytic and evaluative tools of critical thinking, you can learn how to raise the quality of your thinking.

I.4 *Think for Yourself*

BEGINNING TO THINK ABOUT YOUR THINKING

Consider your thinking in personal relationships, in dealing with friends, in relating to romantic partners, in sports, as a reader, as a writer, as a listener to lectures, as an employee, in planning your life, in dealing with your emotions, and in figuring out complex situations. Complete these statements:

1. Right now, I believe my thinking across all domains of my life is of _____ quality. I base this judgment on _____.

2. In the following areas, I think very well:
   a. _____
   b. _____
   c. _____

3. In the following areas, my thinking is okay, not great, but not terrible either:
   a. _____
   b. _____
   c. _____

4. In the following areas, my thinking is probably poor:
   a. _____
   b. _____
   c. _____

EXHIBIT I.4 *Critical thinking applies to everything about which we think.*

Critical Thinking About:

Teaching and learning	Well-being	Speaking
Creativity	Listening	Politics
Emotions	Medicine	Religion
Intuition	Writing	Problem solving
Habits	Nursing	Reading

BECOME A CRITIC OF YOUR THINKING

One of the most important things you can do for yourself is to begin the process of becoming a critic of your thinking. You do this not to negate or "dump on" yourself but, instead, to improve yourself, to begin to practice the art of skilled thinking and lifelong learning. To do this, you must discover your thinking, see its structure, observe its implications, and recognize its basis and vantage point. You must come to recognize that, through commitment and daily practice, you can make foundational changes in your thinking. You need to learn about your bad habits of thought and about what you are striving for: good habits of thought. At whatever level you think, you need to recognize that you can learn to think better. Creative improvement is the end for which critical thinkers strive.

EXHIBIT I.5 *Critical thinking adds a second level of thinking to ordinary thinking. The second level analyzes, assesses, and improves our ordinary thinking.*

Second-order thinking is first-order thinking raised to the level of conscious realization (analyzed, assessed, and reconstructed).

First-order thinking is spontaneous and nonreflective. It contains insight, prejudice, truth and error, good and bad reasoning, indiscriminately combined.

ESTABLISH NEW HABITS OF THOUGHT

Most of us get through school by modifying our thinking the hard way—through trial and error. Most of us have little help in learning how to become a critic of our thinking. We develop few tools for working on our thinking. The result is that we use our native capacities to think in a largely unconscious fashion. We develop some good habits of thought and many poor habits of thought. The productive and unproductive habits of mind become intermixed and hard to disentangle. We learn without a clear sense of the ideal in thinking. We are not clear about our goals as thinkers. We treat each class like a new set of tasks to complete mechanically. We fail to learn important ideas that enable us to learn how to learn better and better.

To learn at a deeper level, you need to get powerful leverage on learning. You need a clearer perspective on what you should be striving to achieve, and you need powerful tools for upgrading your thinking and learning.

Critical thinking works. It is practical. It will enable you to be more successful, to save time and energy, and to experience more positive and fulfilling emotions. It is in your interest to become a better critic of your own thinking: as a student, scholar, parent, consumer, and citizen, and in other roles as well. If you are not progressively improving the quality of your life, you have not yet discovered the true power of critical thinking. We hope this book will serve as an impetus for this shift. Good thinking works—for everyone.

I.5   *Think for Yourself*

CHANGING YOUR HABITS

Have you ever changed a habit as a result of your conscious effort and planning? What do you have to do to change a habit? Is it easy? If not, why not? What do you think you would have to do to change your habits of thought? Write out your answer or explain orally.

DEVELOP CONFIDENCE IN YOUR ABILITY TO REASON AND FIGURE THINGS OUT

No matter how well or poorly you have performed in school or in college, it is important to realize that the power of the human mind, *the power of your mind,* is virtually unlimited. But, if any of us are to reach our potential, we must take command of the workings of our minds. No matter where we are as thinkers, we can always improve.

As young children going through school, we usually get the impression that those students who are the quickest to answer questions, the quickest to turn in their papers, the quickest to finish tests are the "smartest" students. Those students who fall into this category often define themselves as "smart," and therefore as *better* than other students. They consequently often become intellectually arrogant. On the contrary, those students who struggle often see themselves as inferior, as incapable. And these students often give up on learning. They don't see that the race is to the tortoise, not the hare.

The fact is that standard measures of intelligence often impede learning. The point is that, whatever you have learned or mislearned about what it means to learn, you can now begin in earnest to develop your own mind, to take command of it. Critical thinking provides the tools for you to do just that. And it levels the playing field for all students. Some of the best thinkers in the world—thinkers who are like Albert Einstein, Charles Darwin, and Isaac Newton—are not the quickest thinkers. They are thinkers who plod along, who ask questions, who pursue important ideas, who put things together in their minds, who figure things out for themselves, who create connections among important ideas. They are people who believe in the power of their own minds. They are people who appreciate the struggle inherent in substantive learning and thinking.

Consider how Darwin (1958) articulated his own struggles with learning:

> I have as much difficulty as ever in expressing myself clearly and concisely; and this difficulty has caused me a very great loss of time, but it has had the compensating advantage of forcing me to think long and intently about every sentence, and thus I have been led to see errors in reasoning and in my own observations or those of others.

In pursuing intellectual questions, Darwin relied upon perseverance and continual reflection, rather than memory and quick reflexes.

> I have no great quickness of apprehension or wit. . . . My power to follow a long and purely abstract train of thought is very limited. . . . My memory is extensive, yet hazy. . . . So poor in one sense is my memory, that I have never been able to remember for more than a few days a single date or line of poetry. . . . I have a fair share of invention, but not, I believe, in any higher degree. . . . I think that I am superior to the common run of man in noticing things which easily escape attention, and in observing them carefully. . . . I have had the patience to reflect or ponder for any number of years over any unexplained problem. (p. 55)

Einstein (Clark, 1984), for his part, performed so poorly in school that when his father asked his son's headmaster what profession his son should adopt, the answer was simply, "It doesn't matter; he'll never make a success of anything." He showed no signs of being a genius, and as an adult denied that his mind was extraordinary: "I have no particular talent. I am merely extremely inquisitive" (p. 27).

The best thinkers are those who systematically and carefully reason their way through problems. They ask questions when they don't understand. They don't allow other people to define their level of intelligence. They don't allow intelligence tests or other standardized tests to define their level of intelligence. They realize that, no matter how difficult or easy it is for them to "remember" facts for tests, the real work of learning requires perseverance and commitment. The real work of learning requires skills of mind that you can develop, if and when you decide to. Learning these skills of mind is precisely what this book is all about.

Remember, the race is to the tortoise, not the hare. Be the tortoise.

EXHIBIT I.6 *Critical thinking: an elaborated definition.*

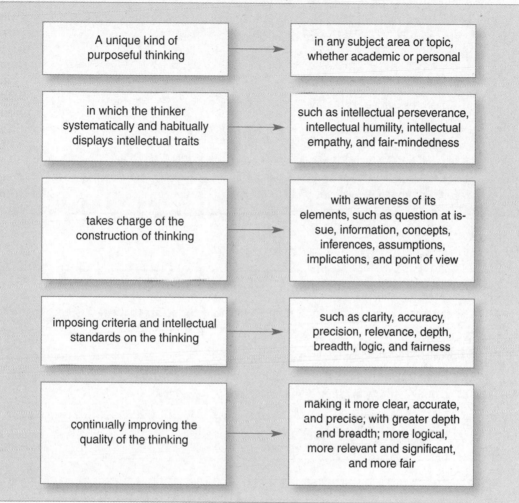

A unique kind of purposeful thinking	→ in any subject area or topic, whether academic or personal
in which the thinker systematically and habitually displays intellectual traits	→ such as intellectual perseverance, intellectual humility, intellectual empathy, and fair-mindedness
takes charge of the construction of thinking	→ with awareness of its elements, such as question at issue, information, concepts, inferences, assumptions, implications, and point of view
imposing criteria and intellectual standards on the thinking	→ such as clarity, accuracy, precision, relevance, depth, breadth, logic, and fairness
continually improving the quality of the thinking	→ making it more clear, accurate, and precise; with greater depth and breadth; more logical, more relevant and significant, and more fair

I.6   *Think for Yourself*

HOW DO YOU SEE YOURSELF AS A THINKER?

Think back to your previous school or college experience. Which pattern have you typically fallen into?

1. The quick student to whom teachers typically are drawn, because you can answer the factual questions they think are important.

2. The student who has difficulty remembering facts so that learning has been more difficult for you.

3. The student who does pretty well because, though you are not the quickest at remembering facts and answering factual questions, you still have a pretty good memory so you have performed adequately in school.

4. A different pattern entirely.

Complete these statements:

1. Given the categories outlined above, I would say that I am the following "type" of student: _____

2. I have/have not typically struggled in school/college because . . .

3. I generally see myself as capable/incapable as a student because . . .

4. To the extent that I see myself as incapable as a student, I can begin to change this view of myself by realizing . . .

I.7 *Think for Yourself*

ARTICULATE YOUR UNDERSTANDING OF CRITICAL THINKING

Read through this introduction again, highlighting the points that relate directly to the definition of critical thinking. Then complete these statements:

1. To me, critical thinking means:

_____

2. In other words (this should be at least four or five sentences):

_____

_____

_____

_____

_____

3. I can apply critical thinking to my life in the following ways:

_____

_____

_____

_____

_____

HOW THE MIND CAN DISCOVER ITSELF

All humans have a human mind, but most humans uncritically assume that their minds will take care of themselves and, in their "normal" operations, function well. The best thinkers do not make this assumption. Rather, the best thinkers recognize that humans use their minds most effectively when they understand them. They also come to realize that humans are not just thinking creatures. They have an emotional life as well—they have feelings and form desires. The best thinkers come to understand that the mind has three distinctive functions—thinking, feeling, and wanting—and that they influence, and are influenced by, one another. The goal of this chapter is to lay a foundation for understanding what we, as aspiring critical thinkers, need to know about how human minds function—with a view to using that knowledge in our own lives.

RECOGNIZE THE MIND'S THREE BASIC FUNCTIONS

The mind has three basic functions: thinking, feeling, and wanting.

1. The function of *thinking* (the thinking mind) is to create meaning—to make sense of the events of our lives, sorting them into named categories and finding patterns in our experience. The thinking mind continually tells us: "This is what is going on. This is what is happening. Notice this and that." It is the part of the mind that figures things out—the intellect.

2. The function of *feeling* (the feeling mind) is to monitor or evaluate the meanings created by the thinking function—it evaluates how positive and negative the events of our life are, given the meaning we ascribe to them. It continually creates feelings and emotions that reflect thoughts. The emotion-forming

EXHIBIT 1.1 *The three basic functions of the mind are intricately interrelated.*

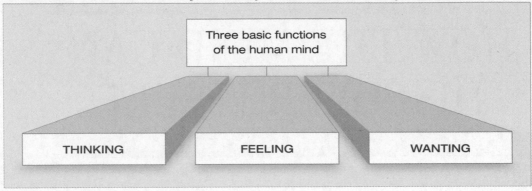

EXHIBIT 1.2 *Thinking is the part of the mind that figures out what is going on. Feelings tell us whether things are going well or poorly for us. The wanting part of the mind propels us forward or away from action.*

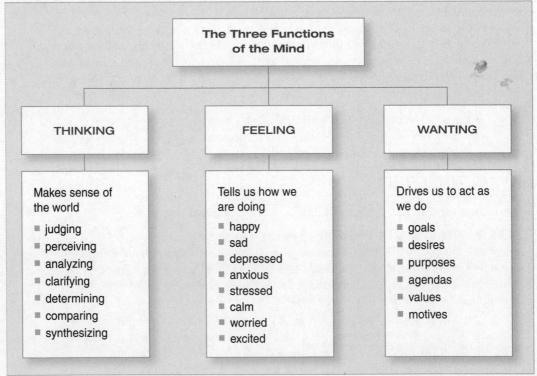

dimension of the mind continually reads what the intellect is telling us and forms emotions to match those thoughts. Most of the feelings that the mind forms are either positive or negative. They tell us either: "Things are going well for you!" or "Things are not going well for you!" When our thoughts are both positive and negative, then so are the corresponding emotions.

3. The function of *wanting* (the desiring mind) allocates energy to action, in keeping with our ideas of what is desirable and possible. It continually tells us: "This is what is worth getting. Go for it!" Or, conversely, it says: "This is not worth getting. Don't bother."

Looked at this way, our mind is continually communicating three kinds of things to us: (1) thoughts about what is going on in our life; (2) feelings (positive or negative) about those events; and (3) desires to pursue, driving us in one direction or another (in the light of 1 and 2). What is more, there is an intimate, dynamic interrelation between thoughts, feelings, and desires. As we have said, each is continually influencing the other two (see Exhibit 1.3). When, for example, we *think* we are being threatened, we *feel* fear, and we *want* to flee from or attack whatever we think is threatening us. When we *think* a subject we are required to study has no relationship to our lives and values, we *feel* bored by instruction in it and develop a negative *motivation* with respect to it. The thinking mind, the feeling mind, and the desiring mind are, ultimately, one mind, not three—one mind performing three functions.

ESTABLISH A SPECIAL RELATIONSHIP TO YOUR MIND

It should now be clear that everyone lives in an intimate relationship to his or her mind—at least unconsciously. We *are* our minds. The best thinkers make that unconscious relationship *conscious* and *deliberate*. All of our activity is a product of inward ideas of who and what we are, ideas of what we are experiencing (from moment to moment), of where we are going (our future), and of where we have come from (our past). In addition, all of these ideas are in a state of continual interplay with our emotions and feelings. Emotions and feelings function as ongoing evaluators of the quality of our lives and circumstances. For every positive thought the mind "believes," the mind automatically generates a positive emotion to fit it. Conversely, for every negative thought, the mind automatically generates a negative emotion.

The best thinkers recognize that it is in their interest to be aware of and in command of the functions of their own minds (see Exhibit 1.4). The reasons are simple. It is easy and natural for the human mind to form false, misleading, or deceptive thoughts. If we notice the continual interrelationships among the three functions of our mind, we will learn something that we can use to our advantage. Then we can begin to exercise command over our own mind's functions. Let's look into this idea more closely.

We experience joy, happiness, frustration, pain, confusion, desire, passion, and indifference because we give a meaning to every situation we experience. We think about the situation in a particular way, and we connect it to feelings we experienced in

EXHIBIT 1.3   *Thinking, feeling, and wanting are interwoven. Where there is one, the other two are present as well. These three functions continually interact and influence one another in a dynamic process.*

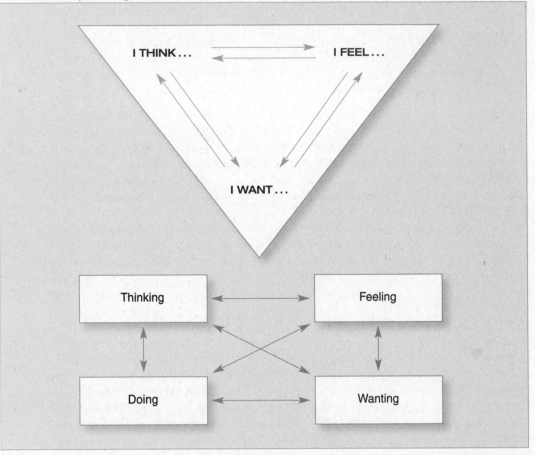

similar or related circumstances (or what seem to be similar circumstances). The meaning we create can be grounded in insight, objective reality, a fantasy, or even a dysfunctional interpretation of reality. Two people in the same situation may react completely differently, with one person experiencing pain and frustration while the other experiences curiosity and excitement.

Consider two students faced with the task of improving their writing ability. The first may experience difficulty, confusion, and frustration, and may ultimately give up. This person gives a negative meaning to the task of learning to improve her writing, defining it as a situation destined for failure. Because she *thinks* that learning to write should be easy, she *feels* frustrated when it is difficult. On the other hand, another person in the same situation may experience learning to write better as a challenge, as exciting, even exhilarating, not because he has writing skills that she does not but, rather, because he brings a different mind-set to the task. He *thinks* that

EXHIBIT 1.4   *We change undesirable feelings and desires by changing the thinking that is leading to them.*

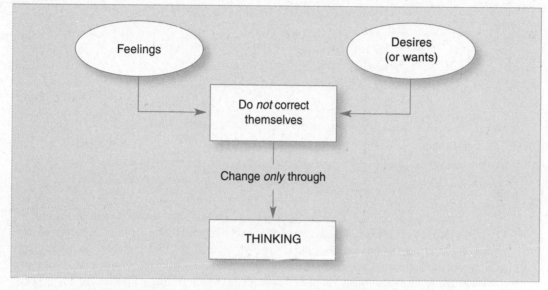

learning to write should be difficult, that it should take considerable time, that it involves rewriting and rewriting and rewriting yet again if it is to be of high quality. Hence he *feels* challenged and excited.

The actual task at hand is precisely the same. But the difficulty or ease with which a person handles the challenge, the decision to take up the challenge or avoid it altogether, and ultimate success or failure are determined fundamentally by the way the person interprets the situation through *thinking*. Different emotions and different actions follow from these differences in thought.

Instructors do not always consider the ways students will respond emotionally to classes. The result can be that students dislike school and learning. Students themselves can take control of the situation and avoid coming to "hate school" by taking command of their own thinking and learning. For example, when we are force-fed math in a way that ignores our emotional response, we typically end up with a bad case of "math hatred" or "math phobia." For the rest of our life we avoid anything mathematical. We may view mathematics as unintelligible, as just a bunch of formulas, unrelated to anything important in our life, or we may view ourselves as "too dumb" to understand it.

If, however, we take command of our thinking in our classes, we carefully analyze the content in our classes to determine what is most important for us to learn. We are self-motivated no matter how boring the class in itself may seem. We see ourselves as being capable of learning anything we put our minds to. When we feel frustrated during the learning process, we are intellectually persistent. When we feel confused, we realize that we need to ask questions so we can better understand what we are learning. We are not afraid to say, "I don't understand." We realize that the best thinkers are those who can differentiate that which they understand and that which they do not.

> The best thinkers
> are masters of
> their minds,
> of their thoughts,
> of their feelings
> of their desires.

EXHIBIT 1.5   *By taking command of our thinking, we can take command of all three functions of the mind.*

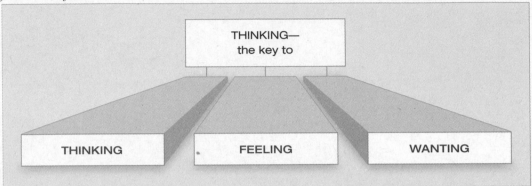

When we understand the interrelated roles of thoughts, feelings, and motivation—when we see that for every feeling we experience, a related thought process exists that motivates us to take some action—we can begin to analyze the thoughts underlying our emotions and desires (see Exhibit 1.5). If you are bored in class, you can ask yourself: "What is the thinking in my mind that is leading to this feeling of boredom?" If you are uninterested in what you are learning, you can ask yourself: "What is the thinking that influences me not to want to learn this? What exactly is the value of learning this? Is this something I need to learn, that will be useful to me? If so, what do I need to do to learn it?"

1.1   *Think for Yourself*

UNDERSTANDING THE RELATIONSHIP BETWEEN THE THREE FUNCTIONS OF THE MIND

Think of a situation you were in recently where you experienced a negative emotion such as anger, frustration, depression, insecurity, or fear.

1. Write out in detail what was going on in the situation and how you felt in the situation.
2. Now try to figure out the thinking you were doing that led to the negative feeling. Write out the thinking in detail.
3. Then write how your thinking and feeling affected your behavior. (In other words, given the thinking and feeling, what were you motivated to do?)

CONNECT ACADEMIC SUBJECTS TO YOUR LIFE

One challenge you face as a student is to learn to approach your classes with a fuller understanding of how your emotional life influences your learning for good or ill. Interestingly, your emotions can aid or hamper your learning, your goals can facilitate or limit your insights.

EXHIBIT 1.6   *Your thinking controls every part of your life. But do you control your thinking?*

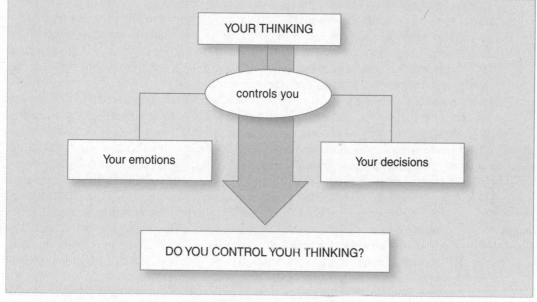

If you typically don't learn at a deep level, you need to observe the thoughts, emotions, and desires that keep you from learning deeply. You must generate the thoughts and desires that motivate you to discover the powerful thinking created and defined by academic disciplines. You need to discover rational thought: the power of sound reasoning. You need to experience nonegocentrical thinking. You need to value bringing ideas, emotions, and will power together as you learn.

When we discover, for example, that historical thought frees us from the egocentric stories we tend to build our lives upon, that sociological thought frees us from the domination of peer groups, that philosophical thought frees us to reason comprehensively about the direction and values embedded in our lives, and that economic thought enables us to grasp powerful forces that are defining the world we are inhabiting—when we truly recognize these forms of power, we are motivated to study and internalize these subjects more deeply.

> The best thinkers know that learning is both an intellectual and an emotional task.

LEARN BOTH INTELLECTUALLY AND EMOTIONALLY

As humans, we spend most of our time thinking about what we personally want or value. Our emotional life keeps us focused on the extent to which we are successfully achieving our personal values. The subjects we take in college contribute to our educational growth only insofar as we are able to relate what we are studying to our personal lives. If we are to personally value literature, for example—and hence to be motivated to read literature for its own sake—we must discover the relevance of literary insights to our life.

When we see connections between the issues and problems that the characters in stories face and the issues and problems we face, literature comes alive to us. The characters we read about live in our minds. We identify with them. We puzzle with them, suffer with them, triumph with them. And we learn, as it were, the lessons they learn.

When academic content seems important to us, we value it. We are motivated to learn more, to figure out more, to "study" more. If we want to motivate ourselves—and it is no one else's responsibility but ours—we have to seek out connections between the academic content we study and our emotions and values.

As a student, then, only you can build or create motivation in your life. If learning becomes sheer drudgery to you and you don't see value in it, you will put it off to the last minute and look for short-cuts (like cramming) that typically substitute short-term memorization for long-term internalization. The thinking that then guides your study habits is, "If I can get by through cramming, why should I work hard to internalize this (worthless) stuff?" Your life, though still emotionally significant to you, becomes intellectually barren. As intellectual drudgery, your classes cannot help but be emotionally boring. You live within emotions that you don't intellectually analyze, on the one hand, and on the other, your intellectual life becomes an alienated set of rituals by which you take notes (that mean little to you), cram for exams (that provide you with no insights), and crank out papers (that are mainly a patchwork of the thoughts of others).

> "Education is not the filling of a pail. It is the lighting of a fire."
>
> William Butler Yeats

One key to the integration of intellectual and emotional learning is found in the insight that each academic discipline represents a powerful mode of thinking that can contribute to your development as a thinker. Until you discover this insight as a result of actually working your way into the thinking of one or more disciplines, though, you are unlikely to be strongly motivated by it. For example, until you experience the power of historical thinking, you will not value historical thinking. On the other hand, if you do not value historical thinking in the first place, you will not be motivated to learn it.

This is the vicious circle that often prevents the uneducated from becoming educated. Those who are uneducated typically do not value education. But until we value education, we will not put the time, energy, and work into the deep learning that alone provides us with an education. It is your challenge to struggle with this dilemma. Will you be able to sufficiently value the work of learning to discover the power of academic subjects and disciplines to which college classes expose you? Or will you, like many students before you, simply become a "survivor" of college?

> The best thinkers are passionate about learning. They are not thinking machines.

In some sense, all knowledge is personal, as no knowledge would exist without people having that knowledge. In the long run, we acquire only the knowledge we value. We internalize only that information that seems essential to what we want and what we think is important. It is up to each one of us to decide when, where, and how we learn.

The more emotionally powerful connections you can make between what you study and what you value in life, the easier it will be to learn. Seek out the most basic concepts in the disciplines that you study. Express those concepts in the most nontechnical manner you can. Relate those concepts to the most fundamental goals in the discipline. Relate those goals to your goals. The tools of this book can make possible the transition to higher-order thinking and learning. You, however, must summon the energy, the emotional reserves, to do the *intellectual* work required.

1.2   *Think for Yourself*

CONNECTING COURSE CONTENT TO WHAT YOU THINK IS IMPORTANT

Select one of your courses and write out the most fundamental, most significant concept in the course. Then make a list of ways in which you can use this idea in your life. Next, make a list of important questions that thinkers within the field of study might ask. Write out your answers or explain them orally.

DISCOVER THE PARTS OF THINKING

I t should now be clear to you that becoming a skilled thinker is like becoming skilled in basketball, ballet, or in playing the saxophone—it requires the development of basic intellectual skills, abilities, and insights. In this chapter we begin to focus on these skills.

The best thinkers recognize that there are parts to thinking, that the only way to ensure that we are thinking well is by taking command of these parts. This chapter focuses on how to take thinking apart—how to *analyze* it by examining its parts. The next chapter focuses on the *assessment* of thinking: how to apply intellectual standards to the parts of thinking to decide whether your thinking   or someone else's—is of high quality.

We begin with a brief discussion of *reasoning,* the mental process the mind uses to make sense of whatever we seek to understand.

THINKING IS EVERYWHERE IN HUMAN LIFE

The words *thinking* and *reasoning* are often used in everyday life as synonyms. *Reasoning,* however, has a more formal flavor. This is because it highlights the intellectual dimension of thinking.

Reasoning occurs whenever the mind draws conclusions on the basis of reasons. We draw conclusions whenever we make sense of things. So, whenever we think, we reason. Usually we are not aware of the full scope of reasoning in our lives.

We begin to reason from the moment we wake up in the morning. We reason when we figure out what to eat for breakfast, what to wear, whether to stop at the store on the way to school or work, whether to go with this or that friend to lunch. We reason while we drive, as we interpret the oncoming flow of traffic, react to the decisions of other drivers, and speed up or slow down.

EXHIBIT 2.1 *Critical thinkers routinely apply the intellectual standards to the elements of reasoning in order to develop intellectual traits. The standards are covered in Chapter 3; the intellectual traits, in Chapter 8.*

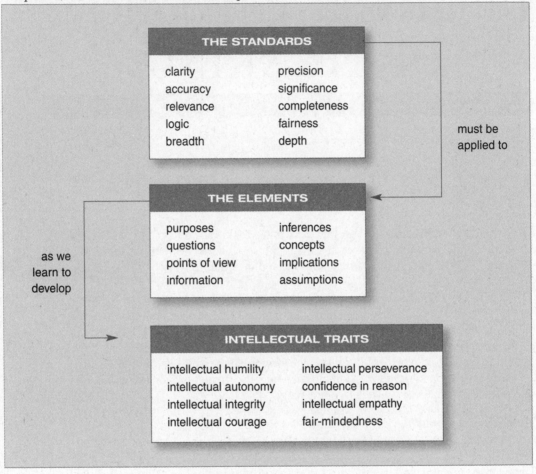

One can draw conclusions, then, about everyday events or, really, about anything at all: about poems, microbes, people, numbers, historical events, social settings, psychological states, character traits, the past, the present, the future.

To reason well, we must scrutinize the process we are using, by asking ourselves: What are we trying to figure out? What information do we need? Do we have that information? How could we check it for accuracy? The less conscious we are of how we are thinking, the easier it is to make some mistake or errors. To maximize your learning, try to approach your classes so that you are not only noticing but also analyzing and evaluating your reasoning.

2.1 *Think for Yourself*

BECOMING MORE AWARE OF THE ROLE OF REASONING IN YOUR LIFE

Make a list of all the things you did today. Then, for each act, figure out the thinking that led you to do, or guided you while doing, the act. (Remember that most of your thinking is unconscious.) For example, when you left your house this morning, you may have stopped at the store for food. This act makes no sense unless you somehow had come to the conclusion that you needed some food. Then, while at the store, you bought certain items. This action resulted from the tacit conclusion you came to that you needed some items and not others.

Realize that every time you make a decision, that decision represents a view or conclusion you reasoned to. For each action you identify, answer these two questions:

1. What exactly did I do?
2. What thinking is presupposed in my behavior?

Write out your answers or explain orally.

THE PARTS OF THINKING

The elements of thought also can be called the *parts of thinking* or the *fundamental structures of thought*. We will use these expressions interchangeably. The elements or parts of reasoning are those essential dimensions of reasoning that are present whenever and wherever reasoning occurs—regardless of whether we are reasoning well or poorly. Working together, these elements shape reasoning and provide a general framework for thought.

When you become adept at identifying the elements of your reasoning, you will be in a much better position to recognize flaws in your thinking, by locating problems in this or that part. This ability is essential to critical thinking. The ability to identify the elements of reasoning, then, is an important ability in critical thinking.

Reasoning is a process whereby one draws conclusions on the basis of reasons. On the surface, reasoning seems somewhat simple, as if it has no component structures. Looked at more closely, however, you can see that it is really a set of interrelated intellectual processes. Some of these may occur subconsciously, without your awareness. It is useful to practice making conscious what is subconscious in your thinking. Then you can better understand what's going on beneath the surface of your thought. In this chapter we introduce you to ways to make your thinking more conscious.

A First Look at the Elements of Thought

Let us begin by looking at the parts of thinking as they stand in an interrelated set. It is possible to name them in just one, somewhat complex, sentence:

Whenever you reason,

you do so in some circumstances,

EXHIBIT 2.2 *The parts or elements of reasoning are always present in human thinking.*

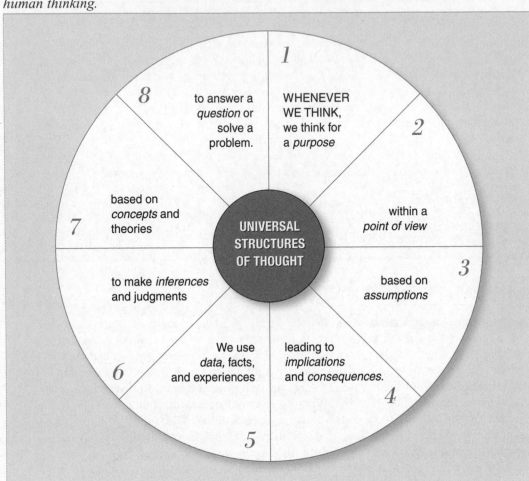

EXHIBIT 2.3 *Critical thinkers understand the importance of taking thinking apart in order to analyze it for flaws.*

Critical thinkers routinely → *take their thinking apart*

making some inferences (that have some implications and consequences)

based on some reasons or information (and assumptions)

using some concepts,

in trying to settle some question (or solve some problem)

for some purpose

within a point of view.

If you like, you can put it in two sentences:

Whenever you are *reasoning*,

you are trying to accomplish some *purpose*,

within a *point of view*,

using concepts or ideas.

You are focused on some issue, *question*, or problem,

using *information*

to come to *conclusions*,

based on *assumptions*,

all of which has *implications*.

Let us now examine, at least provisionally, each of these crucial concepts. We will be using them throughout this book. It is essential that they become a comfortable part of your own critical thinking vocabulary. As you read these initial explanations, see if you can explain them in your own words and give examples from your own experience.

By *reasoning*, we mean *making sense of something by giving it some meaning in one's mind*. Virtually all thinking is part of our sense-making activities. We hear scratching at the door and think, "It's the dog." We see dark clouds in the sky and think, "It looks like rain." Some of this activity operates at a subconscious level. For example, all of the sights and sounds around me have meaning for me without my explicitly noticing that they do. Most of our reasoning is unspectacular. Our reasoning tends to become explicit to us only when someone challenges it and we have to defend it ("Why do you say that Jack is obnoxious? I thought he was quite pleasant."). Throughout life, we begin with a goal or purpose and then figure out what to do to achieve that goal. Reasoning is what enables us to come to these decisions using ideas and meanings.

By *reasoning having a purpose*, we mean that *when humans think about the world, we do not do so randomly but, rather, in line with our goals, desires, needs, and values*. Our thinking is an integral part of a patterned way of acting in the world, and we act, even in simple matters, with some set of ends in view. To understand someone's thinking—including your own—you must understand the functions it serves, what it is about, the direction it is moving, and the ends that motivate it. Most of the time, what we are "after" in our thinking is not obvious to us. Raising our goals and desires to the level of conscious awareness is an important part of critical thinking.

EXHIBIT 2.4   *If you understand the parts of thinking, you can ask the crucial questions implied by those parts.*

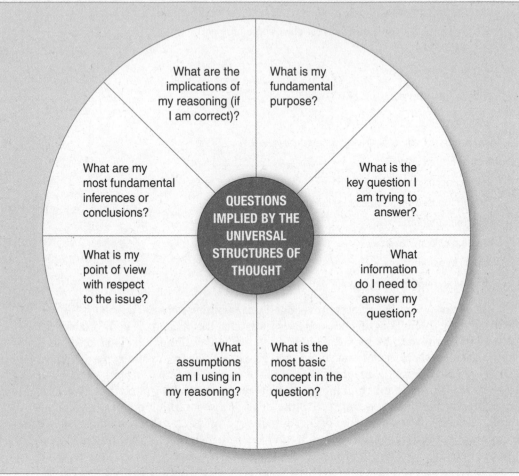

By *reasoning within a point of view,* we mean that *our thinking has some comprehensive focus or orientation.* Our thinking is focused *on* something *from* some angle. We can change either what we focus on or the angle of our focus. We often give names to the angle from which we are thinking about something. For example, we could look at an issue politically or scientifically, poetically or philosophically. We might look at a problem conservatively or liberally, religiously or secularly. We might view a question from a cultural or a financial perspective, or both. Once we understand how people are approaching a question or topic (what their comprehensive perspective is), we are usually much better able to understand the whole of their thinking.

By *using concepts and theories in reasoning,* we mean the *general categories or ideas by which we interpret, classify, or group the information we use in our thinking.* For example, in this book the concepts of critical thinking and uncritical thinking are important. Everything in this book can be classified as an attempt to explain one or the other of these two important ideas. Each of these ideas is explained, in turn, by means of other ideas. Thus, the concept of thinking critically is explained by reference to other concepts, such as "intellectual standards for thought." Each subject discipline (chemistry, geology, literature, math, and so forth) develops its own set of concepts or technical vocabulary to facilitate its thinking. Every sport requires a vocabulary of concepts that enables those who are trying to understand or master the game to make sense of it. Try to explain baseball to someone without using these ideas: *strike, ball, shortstop, inning, at bat, hit, run, safe, out, bunt.* To play the game, we must interpret everything we do in it by means of concepts such as these. The rules would not make sense without them; the game would be incomprehensible.

By *reasoning through some question, issue, or problem,* we mean that *when we think about the world in line with our goals, desires, needs, and values, we often face questions we need to answer, problems we need to solve, and issues we need to resolve.* Therefore, when we find ourselves confronting a difficulty, it makes sense to say, "What is the question we need to answer?" or, "What is the problem we need to solve?" or, "What is the issue we need to resolve?" To improve our ability to think well, it is important to learn how to phrase the questions, problems, and issues we need to deal with in a clear and distinct way. If we change the question, we change the criteria we have to meet to settle it. If we modify the problem, we need to modify how we are going to solve the problem. If we shift the issue, new considerations become relevant to its resolution.

By *using information in our reasoning,* we mean *using some set of facts, data, or experiences to support our conclusions.* Whenever someone is reasoning, it makes sense to ask, "Upon what facts or information are you basing your reasoning?" The factual basis for reasoning can be important. For example, in a newspaper ad (*New York Times,* November 22, 1999) the following pieces of information were used to support an argument against capital punishment:

- "Since the death penalty was reinstated by the Supreme Court in 1976, for every seven prisoners who were executed, one prisoner awaiting execution was found to be innocent and released."

- "At least 381 homicide convictions have been overturned since 1963 because prosecutors concealed evidence of innocence or presented evidence they knew to be false."

- "A study by the U.S. General Accounting Office found racial prejudice in death sentencing . . .: killers of whites were proportionally more likely to be executed than were killers of blacks."

- "Since 1984, 34 mentally retarded people have been executed."

Can you see how information such as this—if true—gives strength to the reasoning? People who hold the opposing position would, of course, advance information of their own to try to challenge or counter this information. Check your facts! Check your data! These are important critical-thinking axioms.

By *coming to conclusions* we mean *figuring out something new on the basis of something we believe we already know.* When we do this, we *make inferences.* For example, if you walk right by me without saying hello, I might come to the conclusion (make the inference) that you are angry with me. If the water kettle on the stove begins to whistle, I come to the conclusion (make the inference) that the water in it has started to boil. In everyday life, we are continually making inferences (coming to conclusions or making judgments about people, things, places, and events).

By *reasoning based on assumptions* we mean *using beliefs we take for granted to figure something else out.* Thus, if you infer that since a candidate is a Republican, he will support a balanced budget, you assume that all Republicans support a balanced budget. If you infer that foreign leaders presented in the news as "enemies" or "friends" of the United States are in fact enemies or friends, you assume that the news is always accurate in its presentation of the character of foreign leaders. If you infer that someone who invites you to her apartment after a party "to continue this interesting conversation" is really interested in you romantically or sexually, you might be assuming that the only reason for going to someone's apartment late at night after a party is to pursue a romantic or sexual relationship. All reasoning has some basis in the assumptions we make (but usually are unaware of).

By the *implications of reasoning* we mean that which follows from our thinking— *that to which our thinking is leading us.* If you say to someone that you "love" him, you *imply* that you are concerned with his welfare. If you make a promise, you *imply* that you intend to keep it. If you call a country a "democracy," you *imply* that the political power is in the hands of the people at large (as against in the hands of a powerful minority). If you call yourself a "feminist," you *imply* that you are in favor of the political, social, and economic equality of the sexes. We often test the credibility of people by seeing if they are true to the implications of their own words. "Say what you mean and mean what you say" is a sound principle of critical thinking (and of personal integrity, for that matter).

An Everyday Example: Jack and Jill

Let's now look at and then analyze a disagreement that might arise in everyday life— in this case, between lovers who come to different conclusions about a situation they both experienced. Suppose Jack and Jill, who are in a romantic relationship, go to a party, during which Jack spends most of the evening talking with Susan. On their way back, Jack, sensing that Jill is upset, asks, "What's wrong?"

After some hesitation, Jill says, "I didn't appreciate your spending the whole night flirting with Susan!"

Jack: Flirting . . . flirting, I was *not* flirting!

Jill: What would you call it?

Jack: Being friendly. I was being *friendly.*

Jill: When a guy spends the whole evening focused on one girl, sits very close to her, looks at her in a romantic way, and periodically touches her in supposedly casual ways, he is engaged in what can only be called *flirting.*

Jack: And when a girl spends her whole evening watching everything her boyfriend does, collecting evidence as if preparing for a trial, a boyfriend who has always been faithful to her, she is engaged in what can only be called *paranoia.*

Jill: Paranoid! How dare you call me that!

Jack: Well, how else can I describe your behavior? You're obviously distrustful and in-
        secure. You're accusing me without a good reason for doing so.

Jill: Don't act like this is the only time you have ever flirted. I have heard that you
        played the field before we got together.

Jack: And I have heard about your possessiveness and jealousy from your friends. I
        think you need to deal with your own problems before you attack me. If you ask
        me, I think you need counseling.

Jill: You're nothing but a typical male. You gauge your manhood on how many girls
        you can conquer. You're so focused on getting strokes for that male ego of yours
        that you can't see or admit what you're doing. If you aren't willing to change, I
        don't see how we can have a relationship!

Jack: I don't see how we can have a relationship either—not because I am unfaithful,
        but because *you are paranoid.* And unless I get an apology, I'm out of here!

Analysis of the Example

Now let's analyze this exchange using the elements of thought.

- **Purpose.** Both Jack and Jill presumably seek a successful romantic relationship.
  That is their implied shared goal.

- **Problem.** They see a problem or issue standing in the way, a problem they
  conceptualize differently. To Jack, the problem is, "When is Jill going to deal
  with her paranoia?" To Jill, the problem is, "When is Jack going to take
  responsibility for his flirtatious behavior?"

- **Assumptions.** Jack is assuming that he is not self-deceived in his motivation with
  respect to Susan and other women. Jack also is assuming that he is competent to
  identify paranoia in another person's behavior. Further, he is assuming that a
  woman could not behave in the way that Jill is without being paranoid. Jill is
  assuming that Jack's behavior is not compatible with ordinary friendliness. Both
  of them assume that what they have heard about the other is accurate. Both
  assume themselves to be justified in their own behavior in the situation.

- **Information.** The information in the situation includes everything Jack actually
  said and did at the party. Other relevant facts include Jack's behavior toward
  other women in the past. Additional facts include Jill's behavior toward former
  boyfriends and any other facts that bear on whether she is acting out of insecurity
  or "paranoia."

- **Concepts.** There are four key concepts in the reasoning: *flirtation, friendliness,
  paranoia,* and *male ego.*

- **Conclusions.** Jack's and Jill's inferences (conclusions) about the situation derive
  from the same behavior in the same circumstance, but they clearly see the
  behavior differently. To Jack, his behavior is to be understood as merely
  "friendly." To Jill, Jack's behavior can be understood only as "flirtation."

- **Implications.** Both Jack and Jill imply by their reasoning that the other person is entirely to blame for any differences between them regarding Jack's behavior at the party. Both seem to imply that the relationship is hopeless.

- **Point of view.** Both Jack and Jill may be seeing the other through the bias of a gender-based point of view. Both see themselves as a victim of the other. Both see themselves as blameless.

Given what we know about the dispute, it is not possible for us to assess who is correct and to what extent. To decide whose interpretation of the situation is more plausible, we would need more facts. There are subtle but observable behaviors that might lead us to conclude that Jill is correct and that Jack was behaving flirtatiously—if we could verify them. Or, if we heard the conversation firsthand, we might decide that Jill's response is unjustified.

How the Parts of Thinking Fit Together

The trick to learning the elements of thought is to express them in a number of different ways until their interrelationships begin to become intuitive to you. For example, you might think of the parts of reasoning as analogous to the parts of the human body. They are all present, whether we are healthy or not. Like the parts of the body, the parts of thought function interdependently. One way to express those interrelationships is that

- our purpose affects the manner in which we ask *questions;*
- the manner in which we ask *questions* affects the *information* we gather;
- the *information* we gather affects the way we *interpret* it;
- the way we *interpret* information affects the way we *conceptualize* it;
- the way we *conceptualize* information affects the *assumptions* we make;
- the *assumptions* we make affect the *implications* that follow from our thinking;
- the *implications* that follow from our thinking affect the way we see things, our *point of view.*

2.2 *Think for Yourself*

THINKING THROUGH THE ELEMENTS OF YOUR REASONING

Select an important conclusion that you have reasoned to—for example, your decision to go to college. Identify the circumstances in which you made that decision and some of the inferences you made in the process (about the costs, advantages, etc.). State the likely *implications* of your decision; the consequences it has had, and will have, in your life; the *information* you took into account in deciding to go to college; the way you expressed the *question* to yourself; and the *way you looked at your life* and your future (while reasoning through the question). See if you can grasp the interrelationships of all of these elements in your thinking. Don't be surprised if you find this task difficult.

In the remainder of this chapter, we will give a more detailed account of each of the elements of reasoning. We will direct special attention to the distinction between inferences and assumptions, as we find that initially students often have difficulty distinguishing these two. Once you become comfortable differentiating these two elements, the others tend to fall into place much more readily. Throughout this book, we will shed more light on all of the elements. There is even an entire chapter on one of them: the question.

Periodically put down the book and see if you can elaborate on the elements of thought in your own words, using your own examples. By doing this you will make the concepts your own. You must *talk* ideas, *write* ideas, and *think* ideas into your system if you want to learn them.

THE RELATIONSHIP BETWEEN THE ELEMENTS

Because the elements do not exist in isolation but in relation to each other, it is important not to think of the distinctions between them as *absolute*. The distinctions are always a *relative* matter. For example, if our *purpose* is to figure out how to spend less money, the *question* we have to figure out is, "What can I do to ensure that I spend less money?" The question is a virtual reformulation of the purpose. What is more, the point of view might be expressed as "viewing my spending habits to determine how to decrease my expenditures." This seems a virtual reformulation of purpose and question. The point is that it is important to recognize an intimate overlap among all of the elements by virtue of their interrelationship. At times, formulating some of the elements explicitly may seem redundant. Don't give way to this feeling. With practice, you will come to recognize the analytic power of making the distinctions explicit.

THE ELEMENTS OF THOUGHT

The Best Thinkers Think to Some Purpose

British scholar Susan Stebbing once wrote a book entitled *Thinking to Some Purpose* (1939) on the importance of purpose in thinking. In it, she said: "To think logically is to think relevantly to the purpose that initiated the thinking: all effective thinking is directed to an end." We agree. All thinking pursues a purpose. We do not think without having something we are trying to accomplish, without having some aim in view. As we've already observed, when humans think about the world, we do not do so randomly but, rather, in line with our goals, desires, needs, and values. Our thinking is an integral part of a patterned way of acting in the world, and we act, even in simple matters, with some end in view. To understand someone's thinking—including our own—we must understand the functions it serves, what it is about, the direction it is moving, the purposes that make sense of it.

Often, what we are "after" in our thinking is not obvious. Becoming more aware of our own and others' goals and desires is an important part of critical thinking. Though we always have a purpose in thinking, we are not always fully aware of that purpose. We may have some vague idea of it. Perhaps we have not clearly come to terms with our purpose. For example, you might be in college for the purpose of getting a degree, but you may not have analyzed exactly why you are seeking a degree. You may be going to college simply because all your friends are going. In this case, you have not thought seriously about your purpose. We are much more likely to achieve an end when we know exactly what we are trying to achieve.

One problem with human thinking is that we sometimes pursue contradictory ends. We might want to become educated and also want to avoid doing any intellectual work. We might want others to love us but not behave in loving ways toward them. We might want people to trust us but behave in ways that undermine trust. Our stated purpose might be simply what we would like to believe we are aiming toward. Our real purpose, however, might be one that we would be ashamed to admit. We might think we want to get into medical school to help and care for people, when our actual purpose may be to make a lot of money, gain prestige and status, and be admired by others. We must be careful, therefore, not to assume that our purposes are consistent with one another or that the purposes we tell ourselves and others are our actual purposes.

Furthermore, the purposes we pursue influence and are influenced by our point of view—the way we see the world. Our purposes shape how we see things, and how we see things shapes what we seek. Each person formulates his or her purpose from a given point of view, which is determined by the context of his or her own experience. To understand our goals and objectives, then, we should consider the perspectives from which we see the world or some situation in it.

A hairdresser, for example, because of her perspective, might be more concerned with personal appearance than most janitors would be. Looking good and helping others to look good are more intimately connected with her view of herself and the world. An orthodontist would naturally think much more about teeth and their appearance than most other people would. Having straight teeth would naturally seem more significant to her than it might to, say, most professional football players. The orthodontist's purpose in promoting straight teeth arises out of her perspective or point of view.

2.3 *Think for Yourself*

IDENTIFYING YOUR PURPOSES

To begin to see how important purpose is in thinking, try the following activity. First, make a list of five fundamental goals you have. Then comment on how these goals shape your thinking. Fill in the blanks:

"One of my purposes is _____.

I can achieve this purpose best by _____."

Second, identify five things that you think about a lot. Then comment on how those things are tied to your fundamental purposes. For example, if you spend a considerable amount of time thinking about people with whom you would like to explore a relationship, one of your purposes is probably to find a meaningful relationship. Or if you spend a lot of time thinking about your future, one of your purposes might be to figure out how you can prepare yourself to succeed.

The Best Thinkers Take Command of Concepts

Concepts are like the air we breathe. They are everywhere. They are essential to our life. But we rarely notice them. Yet only when we have conceptualized a thing in some way can we think about it. Nature does not give us, or anyone else, instruction in how things are to be conceptualized. We must create that conceptualization, alone or with others. Once it is conceptualized, we integrate a thing into a network of ideas (as no concept stands alone).

Humans approach virtually everything in our experience as something that can be "decoded" or given meaning by the power of our mind to create a conceptualization and to make inferences on the basis of it—hence, to create further conceptualizations. We do this so routinely and automatically that we don't typically recognize ourselves as engaged in these processes. In our everyday life we don't first experience the world in "concept-less" form and then deliberately place what we experience into categories so as to make sense of things. Rather, it is as if things are given to us with their name inherent in them. So we see trees, clouds, grass, roads, people, children, sunsets, and so on and on. We apply these concepts intuitively, as if the names belong to the things by nature, as if we had not created these concepts in our own minds.

To develop as a critical thinker, you must come to terms with this human power of mind—to create concepts through which we see and experience the world—for it is precisely this capacity of which you must take charge if you are to take command of your thinking. You must become the master of your own conceptualizations. You must develop the ability to mentally "remove" this or that concept from the things named by the concept, and try out alternative ideas. As general semanticists often say: "The word is not the thing! The word is not the thing!" If you are trapped in one set of concepts (ideas, words), you can think of things in only one way. Word and thing become one and the same in your mind.

To figure out the proper use of words, the proper way to conceptualize things, events, situations, emotions, abstract ideas, it is important to first achieve a true command of the uses of words. For example, if you are proficient in the use of the English language, you recognize a significant difference in the language between *needing* and *wanting,* between *having judgment* and *being judgmental,* between *having information* and *gaining knowledge,* between *being humble* and *being servile,* between *stubbornness* and *having the courage of your convictions.* Command of distinctions such as these, and many others, in the language has a significant influence upon the way you interpret your experience. People who do not have this command confuse these important discriminations and distort the important realities they help us to distinguish.

2.4   *Think for Yourself*

TESTING YOUR UNDERSTANDING OF BASIC CONCEPTS

To the extent that you have a sound command of the English language, you should be able to state the essential differences between related but distinguishably different realities that are marked by words or expressions in our language. To the extent that you can, you are conceptualizing the ideas labeled with these words in keeping with educated use. In this activity you will test your ability to do this. What follows is a set of related words, each pair illustrating an important distinction marked by our language. For each set, working with a partner, discuss your understanding of each concept pair, emphasizing the essential and distinguishing difference. Then write down your understanding of the essential difference between each word pair.

After you have done this for each pair of words, look them up in the dictionary and discuss whether your understanding of the difference between the words is close to what the dictionary tells you. (We recommend the *Webster's New World Dictionary*.)

1. clever/cunning
2. power/control
3. love/romance
4. believe/know
5. socialize/educate
6. selfish/self-motivated
7. friend/acquaintance
8. anger/rage
9. jealousy/envy

In learning to speak our native language, we learn thousands of concepts. When properly used, these concepts enable us to make legitimate inferences about the objects of our experience. Unfortunately, nothing in the way we ordinarily learn to speak a language forces us to use concepts carefully or prevents us from making unjustifiable inferences in using them.

Often we misuse or confuse ideas because of our indoctrination into a social system, resulting in a distortion of our experience. As critical thinkers, we must continually distinguish the concepts and ideas implicit in our social conditioning from the concepts and ideas implicit in the natural language we speak. For example, people from many different countries and cultures speak the same natural language. The peoples of Canada, Ireland, Scotland, England, Australia, Canada, and the United States all speak English. By and large, they implicitly share (to the extent that they are proficient in the language) the same set of concepts (codified in the 23 volumes of the *Oxford English Dictionary*). Nevertheless, the people in these countries are not socially conditioned in the same way.

What is more, a person from China or Tibet could learn to speak the English language fluently without in any sense sharing in the same social conditioning. Because of this, natural languages (French, German, English, Swahili, or Hindi are examples) are repositories of concepts that, by and large, are not to be equated with the concepts implicit in the social indoctrination of any social or cultural group speaking the language. This is a difficult insight to gain, but it is a powerful and essential one.

Let's take for example the concept of *capitalism*. In the United States, most people are socially conditioned to believe that our form of economic system, capitalism, is superior to any other. We often call it "free enterprise." We assume that no country can be truly democratic unless it has an economic system similar to ours. Furthermore, we assume that the major opposing systems, socialism and communism, are wrong, or enslaving, or even evil (the "Evil Empire"). We are encouraged to think of the world in these ways by movies, the news media, schooling, political speeches, and many other cultural influences. People who grow up in the United States typically internalize different concepts, beliefs, and assumptions about ourselves and the world than they would had they grown up in China or Iran, for example.

Lexicographers (dictionary makers), however, do not include these socially implied meanings and psychological associations in the definitions they provide. The term *communism* is not defined as "an economic system that enslaves the people." The word *capitalism* does not have the definition, "an economic system essential to a democratic society." Instead, they give the foundational meanings of the words.

Nevertheless, because we are socialized to believe that we, as a people, are *free, reasonable, just, and caring,* we assume that our behavior matches what these words imply. Words often substitute, in human life, for the realities named by them. Fundamental contradictions or inconsistencies in our life, then, go unquestioned. This is part of the self-deceptive tendencies to which the human mind is prone.

Critical thinkers learn how to strip off surface language and consider alternative ways to talk and think about things. For example, when we think sociocentrically, we become trapped in the world view of our peer group and society with little or no conscious awareness of what it would be to rationally decide upon alternative ways to conceptualize situations, persons, and events. Most people are awed by social rituals and the trappings of social authority, status, and prestige. They live their life, as it were, on the surface. As a critical thinker, you will learn how to think sociologically, and thus how to recognize when your ideas are controlled by social rituals, social expectations, and taboos.

The Best Thinkers Assess Information

It is impossible to reason without using some set of facts, data, or experiences upon which to base one's thinking. For a critical thinker, finding trustworthy sources of information and carefully interpreting experience are important goals. We must be vigilant about the sources of information we use. We must also be analytically critical of the meanings we give to our experiences. Experience may be the best teacher, but biased experience supports bias, distorted experience supports distortion, self-deluded experience supports self-delusion. We therefore must not think of our experience as sacred in any way but, instead, as one important dimension of thought that must, like all others, be critically analyzed and assessed.

The mind can take in information in three distinctive ways: (1) by memorizing factoids, or *inert information* (which is not understood well enough to be used by the mind), (2) by mislearning or partially learning information, or accepting illogical beliefs (which then leads to *activated ignorance*), and (3) by bringing significant ideas accurately into the mind (which then leads to *activated knowledge)*.

Inert Information

By *inert information,* we mean *taking into the mind information that, though memorized, we do not understand*—despite the fact that we may think we do. For example, during their schooling, many people take in a lot of information about democracy that leads them to believe they understand the concept. Often, much of the information they internalize consists of empty verbal rituals and superficial processes. For example, many children learn in school that "democracy is government of the people, by the people, for the people." This catchy phrase often sticks in their mind. It leads them to think they understand what democracy means. Most of them, however, do not translate this into any practical criteria for assessing the extent to which democracy does or does not exist in any given country. Most people could not intelligibly answer any of the following questions:

1. What is the difference between a government *of* the people and a government *for* the people?
2. What is the difference between a government *for* the people and a government *by* the people?
3. What is the difference between a government *by* the people and a government *of* the people?
4. What exactly is meant by "the people"?

Thus, students often do not think about information they memorize in school sufficiently to transform it into something truly meaningful in their mind. Much human information is, in the mind of the humans who "possess" it, merely empty words (inert or dead in the mind). Critical thinkers try to clear the mind of inert information by recognizing it as such and transforming it, through analysis, into something meaningful.

2.5 *Think for Yourself*

SEARCHING FOR INERT INFORMATION

Think about information you were taught in school or at home. In particular, look for information you may have repeated often on command, to see if it qualifies for what we are calling *inert information*. For example, consider the Pledge of Allegiance, slogans within subject fields, memorized bits and pieces of content, and sayings you have often heard but probably not thought much about. See how many candidates for inert information you can locate. Test each one by asking: Can I explain it or use it effectively? If not, it is likely to be inert information in your mind. Be prepared to report what you find to your classmates. If you do not find this sort of information, don't assume that you are free of inert information.

Activated Ignorance

By *activated ignorance,* we mean *taking into the mind, and actively using, information that is false, though we mistakenly think it to be true.* The philosopher René Descartes came to believe that animals have no feelings but are simply robotic machines. Based on this activated ignorance, he performed painful experiments on animals and interpreted their cries of pain as mere noises.

Through activated ignorance, some people believe that they understand things, events, people, and situations that they do not. Acting on their false ideas, illusions, and misconceptions often leads to needless waste, pain, and suffering. Sometimes activated ignorance is the basis for massive actions involving millions of people (think of the consequences of the Nazi idea that Germans were the master race and Jews an inferior race). Sometimes it is an individual misconception acted on only by one person in a limited number of settings. But, wherever activated ignorance exists, it is dangerous.

It is essential, therefore, that we question our beliefs, especially when acting upon them has significant potential implications for the harm, injury, or suffering of others. It is reasonable to suppose that everyone has *some* beliefs that are, in fact, a form of activated ignorance. Eliminating as many such beliefs as we can is a responsibility we all have. Consider automobile drivers who are confident they can drive safely while they are intoxicated. Consider the belief that smoking does not have any significant negative health effects.

It is not always easy to identify what is and is not activated ignorance. The concept of activated ignorance is important regardless of whether we determine whether information we come across is false or misleading. Keep in mind definitive cases of activated ignorance so you have a clear idea of it, and be vigilant in determining what information to accept and what information to reject. Most people who act harmfully as a result of activated ignorance probably do not even realize that they are causing the suffering of others (remember Descartes!). Ignorance treated as the truth is no trivial matter.

2.6 *Think for Yourself*

IN SEARCH OF ACTIVATED IGNORANCE

Think about what you have been taught in school or at home. Seek what you once believed to be true but since have found to be false or even harmful. For example, you might have picked up some activated ignorance from your peer group as you were growing up. Think of things you learned "the hard way." See how many candidates for activated ignorance you can find. Test each one by asking: Did I think this was true at one time, and now know it to be false? Be prepared to report to your classmates what you find. If you do not find any examples of activated ignorance, don't assume that you are free of it. Consider why you are having trouble finding it.

Activated Knowledge

By *activated knowledge,* we mean *taking into the mind, and actively using, information that is not only true but that, when insightfully understood, leads us to more and more knowledge.*

Consider the study of history, for example. Many students do no more than memorize isolated statements in their history textbook so as to pass exams. Some of these statements—the ones they *don't understand* and cannot explain—become part of the students' battery of inert information. Other statements—the ones they *misunderstand* and *wrongly explain*—become part of their battery of activated ignorance. Much of the information, of course, they simply forget shortly after the exam.

What is much more powerful, from a critical-thinking perspective, is understanding the logic of historical thinking as a way of understanding the logic of history. When we understand the basic ideas in history and its study, the ideas become a form of activated knowledge. They enable us to discover new historical knowledge by thinking through previous historical knowledge.

For example, we might begin by understanding the basic agenda of historical thinking: *to construct a story or account of the past that enables us to better understand the present and make rational plans for the future.* Once we understand this, it becomes obvious that we already engage in historical thinking in our daily life. We begin to see the connection between thinking within the subject of history and thinking in everyday life situations. For example, once we see the basic logic of historical thinking, we can hardly help noticing that all humans create their own stories in the privacy of their mind. They use this story to make sense of the present, in the light of their conception of the past, and make plans for the future, given their understanding of the present and past. Most of us do not think of ourselves as doing this, however.

If we reflect on this process, we might become aware of the similarity between historical thinking and ordinary, everyday "gossip." When people gossip, they create a story about events in someone's recent past and pass on that story to others. If we reflect further on the logic of history, we might also notice that every issue of a daily newspaper is produced by a kind of thinking analogous to historical thinking. In both cases someone is constructing accounts of the past and presenting those accounts as a way of making sense of events.

Further reflection on the logic of history should lead us to ask ourselves questions such as, "In creating an account of some time period, approximately what percentage of what actually took place finds its way into any given historical account?" This should lead us to discover that for any given historical period, even one as short as a day, countless events take place. By implication, any historical account contains only a tiny percentage of the total events within any given historical period. This should lead us to discover that historians must regularly make value judgments to decide what to include in, and what to exclude from, their accounts. Upon further reflection, it should become apparent to us that there are different possible stories and accounts that highlight different patterns in the events themselves—for example, accounts that highlight "high-level" decision makers ("great person" accounts), in contrast to accounts that highlight different social and economic classes (social and economic histories). It then should be apparent to us that the specific questions that any given historical thinker asks depend on the specific agenda or goal of that thinker.

It also should be apparent that:

- The historical questions that are asked determine which data or events are relevant.
- One and the same event can be illuminated by different conceptualizations (for example, different political, social, and economic theories about people and social change).
- Different historians make different assumptions, which influence the way they put their questions and the data that seem most important to them.
- When a given historian identifies with a given group of people and writes a historical account of this group, the historian often highlights the positive characteristics of those people and the negative characteristics of those with whom they are or were in conflict.

Through "discoveries" and insights such as these—which we must think through for ourselves to truly grasp them as knowledge—our view of history is transformed. They enable us to begin to "see through" historical texts. They also lead us to value historical thinking, as its significance in everyday life becomes clear to us. They make more and more transparent to us our own history and our use of history. And they enable us to see how the manner in which we "see" history determines how we interpret historical information and the effect of our use of history on the world and human welfare.

Activated knowledge, then, is knowledge that we gain by reflecting on the seminal—most basic—ideas in a field. When we apply activated knowledge to our experience, it enables us to infer, by implication, further and further knowledge. Activated knowledge is potential in every legitimate human discipline. We begin with basic information about the most basic ideas and goals of a field. Grounded in basic concepts and principles, we are able to experience the power of thought, knowledge, and experience working in unison. A habit of studying to learn to seek the logic of things is one of the most powerful ways to begin to discover activated knowledge. It is one of the most important keys to making lifelong learning an essential ingredient in one's life.

2.7   *Think for Yourself*

SEARCHING FOR ACTIVATED KNOWLEDGE

Identify some ideas you were taught in school or at home. Seek what you learned so deeply and well that you were able to build further knowledge upon it. One possibility might be found in a sport that you took seriously, learning the basic moves of the game and the fundamental principles underlying those moves.

Don't be surprised if you conclude that you have not yet developed activated knowledge. This does not mean you don't know many things that are true. Rather, it means that you have not yet learned how to master basic principles to use as instruments in your thinking and learning. Be prepared to report what you find to your classmates.

2.8   *Think for Yourself*

IN SEARCH OF THE FACTS

SOME KEY QUESTIONS TO ASK

One of the most important skills in critical thinking is that of evaluating information. This skill begins with recognizing that information and fact (information and verification) are not the same thing. It also means recognizing that everything presented as fact or as true is not, and that the setting in which information is asserted, as well as the prestige of the person or group asserting it, is no guarantee of accuracy or reliability. Consider the following very helpful maxim: *An educated person is one who has learned that information almost always turns out to be at best incomplete and very often false, misleading, fictitious, mendacious—just dead wrong.*

Careful professionals use a wide variety of safeguards in the disciplines in which they work. It is not possible to learn these safeguards separately from an actual study of the disciplines. However, it is possible to develop a healthy skepticism about information in general, especially about information presented in support of a belief that serves the vested interests of a person or group. This skepticism is given in the regular asking of key questions about information presented to us:

- To what extent could I test the truth of this claim by direct experience?
- To what extent is believing this consistent with what I know to be true or have justified confidence in?
- How does the person who advances this claim support it?
- Is there a definite system or procedure for assessing claims of this sort?
- Does the acceptance of this information advance the vested interest of the person or group asserting it?
- Does the person asserting this information seem uncomfortable with having it questioned?

These questions, both singly and as a group, are no panacea. Their effectiveness depends on how we follow up on them. Used with good judgment, they help us reduce the number of mistakes we make in assessing information. They will not prevent us from making mistakes. Practice asking the above questions when information is presented to you as true and important.

2.9 *Think for Yourself*

ASSESSING INFORMATION (PROVISIONALLY)

Assess the following claims—that is, decide whether you think they are true or false. Explain your reasoning.

1. A friend of yours claims that astrology is accurate because he has used it to figure out why people he knew were behaving in a certain way. He also claims that you can use it to predict people's behavior (such as deciding who to marry or not marry).

2. You hear someone say, "Science should use statements from the Bible to help assess scientific findings because anything that contradicts the Bible (the word of God) must be false."

3. You read about a person who is reported to have returned from the dead as the result of a resuscitation after a heart attack. The person says there is definitely a spirit world because he met a spirit while he was dead.

4. A friend of yours claims that the universe is run on spiritual principles, citing the fact that once, when he was alone in the desert, the universe gave him a mantra (a chant).

5. You hear a woman say that no man can truly understand a woman because there is no way, as a man, he can have the experience of a woman.

The Best Thinkers Distinguish Between Inferences and Assumptions

As we have said, the elements of reasoning interrelate. They continually influence and are influenced by one another. We will now focus on the crucial relationship between two of the elements: inferences and assumptions. Learning to distinguish inferences from assumptions is an important skill in critical thinking. Many confuse the two elements. Let us begin with a review of the basic meanings:

1. Inference. An inference is a "step" of the mind, an intellectual act by which one concludes that something is true in light of something else's being true, or seeming to be true. If you come at me with a knife in your hand, I probably would infer that you mean to do me harm. Inferences can be accurate or inaccurate, logical or illogical, justified or unjustified.

2. Assumption. An assumption is something we take for granted or presuppose. Usually it is something we previously learned and do not question. It is part of our system of beliefs. We assume our beliefs to be true and use them to interpret the world about us. If you believe that it is dangerous to walk late at night in big cities and you are staying in Chicago, you will infer that it is dangerous to go for a walk late at night. You take for granted your belief that it is dangerous to walk late at night in big cities. If your belief is a sound one, your assumption is sound. If your belief is not sound, your assumption is not sound. Beliefs, and hence assumptions, can be unjustified or justified, depending upon whether we do or do not have good reasons for them. Consider this example: "I heard a scratch at the door. I got up to let the cat in." My inference was based on the assumption (my prior belief) that only the cat makes that noise, and that he makes it only when he wants to be let in.

EXHIBIT 2.5   *Humans routinely draw conclusions in situations. Those conclusions are based on assumptions that usually operate at an unconscious level.*

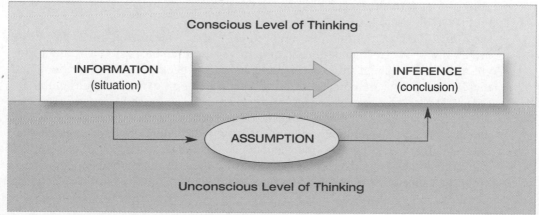

We humans naturally and regularly use our beliefs as assumptions and make inferences based on those assumptions. We must do so to make sense of where we are, what we are about, and what is happening. Assumptions and inferences permeate our lives precisely because we cannot act without them. We make judgments, form interpretations, and come to conclusions based on the beliefs we hold.

If you put humans in any situation, they naturally try to make sense of it, to give it some meaning. People make inferences automatically to gain understanding and as a basis for action. We see dark clouds and infer rain. We hear the door slam and infer that someone has arrived. We see a person's frowning face and infer that the person is angry. If a friend is late, we infer that she is being inconsiderate. We meet a tall guy and infer that he is good at basketball, an Asian and infer that she will be good at math. We read a book and interpret what the various sentences and paragraphs—indeed what the whole book—is saying. We listen to what people say and make a series of inferences as to what they mean. We make inferences so quickly and automatically that we notice them as such only when we make a special effort to do so.

As we write, we make inferences as to how readers will interpret and respond to what we are writing. We make inferences as to the clarity of what we are saying, about what needs further explanation, about what needs to be exemplified or illustrated. Many of our inferences are justified and reasonable, but some are not.

As always, an important part of critical thinking is bringing what is subconscious in our thought to the level of conscious awareness. This requires the skill of identifying and reconstructing the inferences we make so that the various ways in which we interpret our experiences through our inferences become more and more clear to us. This skill enables us to separate our experiences into two categories: We learn to distinguish the *raw data* of our experience from our *interpretations of those data,* from the inferences we are making about them. By becoming aware of your own inferences, you will be able to see that these inferences are heavily influenced by your point of view (beliefs) and the assumptions you have made about people and situations. This insight allows you to broaden your outlook, to see situations from more than one point of view, and hence to become more open-minded.

Often different people make different inferences because they bring different points of view to situations. They see the "data" differently. To put it another way, they have different assumptions about what they see. For example, if two people see a man lying in a gutter, one might infer, "There's a drunken bum." The other might infer, "There's a man in need of help." These inferences are based on different assumptions about the conditions under which people end up in gutters, and these assumptions are connected to each person's point of view about human behavior. The first person assumes, "Only drunks are to be found in gutters." The second person assumes, "People lying in the gutter are in need of help." The first person may have developed the point of view that people are fundamentally responsible for what happens to them and ought to be able to take care of themselves. The second may have developed the point of view that the problems people have are often caused by forces and events beyond their control. The reasoning of these two people, in terms of their inferences and assumptions, could be characterized in the following way:

Person One

Situation: A man is lying in the gutter.

Inference: That man's a bum.

Assumption: Only bums lie in gutters.

Person Two

Situation: A man is lying in the gutter.

Inference: That man is in need of help.

Assumption: Anyone lying in the gutter is in need of help.

To increase your critical thinking skills, begin to notice the inferences you make, the assumptions you are basing those inferences on, and the point of view about the world you are developing. The exercise below will give you practice in noticing your inferences and discovering the assumptions that led to them.

2.10 *Think for Yourself*

DISTINGUISHING BETWEEN INFORMATION, INFERENCES, AND ASSUMPTIONS

As thinkers, it is important that we be able to distinguish among information, inferences, and assumptions. Whenever we are in a situation, we naturally make inferences. We come to conclusions about the situation or give it meaning through our interpretations. And these inferences result from the assumptions we made or are making. For example:

- If it were 12:00 noon, what might you infer? (It's time for lunch.)
- If there are black clouds in the sky? (It's probably going to rain.)
- If Jack comes to school with a bump on his head? (He probably got hit.)
- If there are webs in the corners of the ceiling? (Spiders made them.)
- If Jill is in the eighth grade? (She is probably 13 or 14 years old.)
- If it were 12:00 noon and you inferred that it was time for lunch, what did you assume? (That whenever it is 12 noon, it is time for lunch.)
- If there are black clouds in the sky and you inferred that it's probably going to rain, what did you assume? (That it usually rains when there are black clouds in the sky.)
- If Jack comes to school with a bump on his head and you inferred that he must have been hit, what did you assume? (That the only time you develop a bump on the head is when you are hit.)

In the following activity, we will provide you with situations (information). Imagine what someone might infer (rightly or wrongly) in the situation. A range of inferences is possible, depending on the beliefs of the person in the situation. Write down what you think someone might infer. Then, think of an assumption that would lead someone to make that inference. The assumption will be a general belief that would lead the person to make the inference. We have provided two examples to help you begin.

INFORMATION (SITUATION)	POSSIBLE INFERENCE THAT ONE MIGHT MAKE	ASSUMPTION LEADING TO THE INFERENCE
1. You see a woman in a wheelchair.	She must have a sad life.	All people in wheelchairs have a sad life.
2. A police officer trails your car closely for several blocks.	He is going to pull me over.	Whenever a police officer trails people, he is going to pull them over.
3. You see a child crying next to her mother in the grocery store.		
4. You meet a beautiful woman with blond hair.		
5. You notice a man in the library reading a book by Karl Marx.		
6. The teacher asks you to stay after class to tell you that your writing is in great need of improvement.		
7. While in a restaurant, your friend orders a steak cooked very rare.		
8. A friend tells you that she is pregnant and is going to have an abortion.		
9. Your roommate insists on listening to loud music while you are trying to study.		
10. The telephone rings in the middle of the night.		
11. Your significant other does not call you when he promised.		
12. Your significant other says she would rather spend time at the library than at parties.		

Our goal of becoming aware of the inferences we make and the assumptions that underlie our thinking helps us gain command over our thinking. Because all human thinking is inferential in nature, command of our thinking depends on command of the inferences embedded in it and thus of the assumptions that underlie it. Consider the way in which we plan and think our way through everyday events. We think of ourselves as preparing for breakfast, eating our breakfast, getting ready for class, arriving on time, sitting down in the appointed place, participating in class, making plans for lunch, paying bills, engaging in small talk, and so on.

Another way to put this is to say that we are continually interpreting our actions, giving them meaning, making inferences about what is going on in our lives.

This is to say that we must choose among a variety of possible meanings. For example, am I "relaxing" or "wasting time"? Am I being "determined" or "stubborn"? Am I "joining" a conversation or "butting in"? Is someone "laughing *with* me" or "laughing *at* me"? Am I "helping a friend" or "being taken advantage of"? Every time we interpret our actions, every time we give them a meaning, we are making one or more inferences on the basis of one or more assumptions.

We continually make assumptions about ourselves, our jobs, our friends, our instructors; our parents, the world in general. We take some things for granted simply because we can't question everything. Sometimes we take the wrong things for granted. For example, I run off to the store (assuming that I have enough money with me) and arrive to find that I have left my money at home. I assume that I have enough gas in the car only to find that I have run out of gas. I assume that an item marked down in price is a good buy only to find that it was marked up before it was marked down. I assume that it will not, or that it will, rain. I assume that my car will start when I turn the key and press the gas pedal. I assume that I mean well in my dealings with others.

We make hundreds of assumptions without knowing it, without even thinking about it. Many of them are sound and justifiable. Many, however, are not. The question then becomes: "How can we begin to recognize the inferences we are making, the assumptions we are basing those inferences on, and the point of view or the perspective on the world that we are forming?"

There are many ways to foster awareness of our inferences and assumptions. In school, all disciplined subject-matter thinking requires that we learn to make correct assumptions about the content we are studying and that we become practiced in making justifiable inferences. As examples: In math, we make mathematical inferences based on mathematical assumptions. In science, we make scientific inferences based on scientific assumptions. In constructing historical accounts, we make historical inferences based on historical assumptions. In each area, the assumptions we make depend on our understanding of fundamental concepts and principles.

As we become skilled in identifying our inferences and assumptions, we are in a good position to question the extent to which any one of our assumptions is justified. For example, are we justified in assuming that everyone eats lunch at 12:00 noon? Are we justified in assuming that it usually rains when there are black clouds in the sky? Are we justified in assuming that bumps on the head are only caused by blows? The point is that we all make many assumptions as we go about our daily life and we ought to be able to recognize and question them. As you develop these critical intuitions, you should increasingly notice your inferences and those of others. You should increasingly notice what you and others are taking for granted. You should increasingly notice how your point of view shapes your experiences.

2.11 *Think for Yourself*

GETTING MORE PRACTICE IN DIFFERENTIATING INFERENCES AND ASSUMPTIONS

Using the same format as in Think for Yourself 2.10, write down 10 "episodes" of your own that include a situation, a possible inference in the situation, and the assumption that led to the inference.

INFORMATION (SITUATION)	POSSIBLE INFERENCE THAT ONE MIGHT MAKE	ASSUMPTION LEADING TO THE INFERENCE
1.		
2.		
3.		
4.		
5.		
6.		
7.		
8.		
9.		

INFORMATION (SITUATION)	POSSIBLE INFERENCE THAT ONE MIGHT MAKE	ASSUMPTION LEADING TO THE INFERENCE
10.		
11.		
12.		

The Best Thinkers Think Through Implications

Among the most important skills of critical thinking is the ability to distinguish between what a statement or situation actually implies and what people may merely (and wrongly) *infer* from it. An inference, again, is a step of the mind that results in a conclusion. If the sun rises, we can infer that it is morning, for example. Critical thinkers try to monitor their thinking so they infer only what is implied in a situation—no more, no less. If I feel ill and go to the doctor for a diagnosis, I want the doctor to infer exactly what my symptoms imply. For example, I do not want her to infer that I simply have a cold requiring no medication when in fact I have a bacterial infection requiring antibiotics. My symptoms imply that I have a certain illness, which in turn implies a certain course of treatment. I want the doctor to accurately infer what my illness is, then accurately infer the proper treatment for it.

It is often the case that, in thinking, people fail to think successfully through the implications of a situation. They fail to think through the implications of a problem or decision. As a result, negative consequences often follow.

In any situation, three kinds of implications may be involved: possible ones, probable ones, and necessary ones. For example, every time you drive your car, one *possible* implication is that you may have an accident. If you drink heavily and drive very fast on a crowded roadway in the rain, one *probable* implication is that you will have an accident. If while you are driving fast on a major highway all the brake fluid drains out of your brake cylinders and the car immediately in front of you comes to a quick stop, one *necessary* implication is that you will have an accident.

We reserve the word "consequences" for what actually happens in a given case. A consequence is what *in fact* occurs in some situation. If we are good at identifying (making sound inferences about) possible, probable, and necessary implications, we can take steps to maximize positive consequences and minimize negative ones. On the one hand, we do not want possible or probable negative implications to become real consequences. On the other hand, we do want to realize potential positive implications. We want to understand and take advantage of the real possibilities inherent in a situation.

We study the logic of things to become skilled in recognizing implications and acting accordingly. The art of doing this well is the art of making sound inferences about the implications of a situation by understanding exactly the logic of what is going on. As thinkers, then, we want to think through all of the implications (possible, probable, and inevitable) of a potential decision before we make a decision and act on it.

In addition to implications that follow from concrete situations are implications that follow from the words we use. These follow from meanings inherent in natural languages. There are always implications of the words we use in communicating with people. For example, if I tell my daughter that she cannot go to a friend's house because she failed to clean up her room, I am implying that she knew she had a responsibility to clean up her room if she wanted to go to a friend's house. My statement to my daughter and my view that she should have consequences for failing to clean her room are reasonable if:

1. I have previously communicated to her my desire for her to keep her room clean, and

2. I have adequately explained my reasoning and the consequences that will follow if she fails to comply with my request.

As thinkers, then, we want to be aware of what precisely we are implying when we say things. We also want to take into account the reasonability of what we are implying. If we do, we *say what we mean and mean what we say*—an important principle of integrity.

Just as the language we use in communicating has implications, the *way* we say things has implications. For example, the statement "Why didn't you clean the kitchen?" asked calmly has different implications from the same statement shouted aggressively. In the first instance, I am perhaps implying only that I think you should have cleaned the kitchen, and nothing more. In the second, I am implying that your failure to do so is a serious matter, warranting a severe reprimand.

Just as we may fail to notice the implications of a situation or of what we say, we also may fail to notice the implications of what others say to us. People often fail to infer precisely what others are, and are not, implying in their use of language. People often read things into what is being said, inferring more than what is being implied. If, for example, your teacher tells you that you need to work on your paper to improve it and means to imply nothing more, you do not want to infer that he thinks you are not as smart as other students, that you are not capable of learning, or something else.

In sum, as developing thinkers, we want to realize the important role of implications in human life. When we are thinking through a problem, issue, or question, we want to think through all the significant implications of the decisions we might make. We want to infer only what is being implied in specific situations. When we use language, we want to be aware of what we are implying. When others are speaking to us, either verbally or in writing, we want to figure out what they are logically implying. In every case, we want to interpret precisely the logic of what is actually going on and in-fer only what is truly implied, no more, no less.

2.12 *Think for Yourself*

THINKING THROUGH THE IMPLICATIONS OF YOUR POTENTIAL DECISIONS

As we have said, the ability to think through the implications of a decision you are faced with or a problem you are trying to solve is an important critical-thinking skill. For this activity, think of a problem you need to find a solution to or a decision you need to make. Complete these statements:

1. The problem or decision I am facing is . . .

2. Some potential solutions to the problem, or decisions I might make, are . . .

3. For each of these solutions or decisions, some implications that would logically follow from my acting upon the solution or decision are . . .

The Best Thinkers Think Across Points of View

Point of view is one of the most challenging elements to master. On the one hand, most people understand intuitively that when we think, we think within a point of view. On the other hand, when people who are reasoning something through are asked to iden-tify or explain their point of view, they are likely to begin expressing anything and everything they are thinking about. Clearly, most people do not have a clear sense of how to identify someone's point of view, including their own.

Let us begin by recognizing that there are many potential sources for our point of view: time, culture, religion, gender, discipline, profession, peer group, economic in-terests, emotional state, social role, and age group—to name a few. We can look at the world from the perspective of

- a culture (Western, Eastern, South American, Japanese, Turkish, French)
- a religion (Buddhist, Christian, Muslim, Jewish)
- a gender (male, female, homosexual, heterosexual)
- a profession (lawyer, teacher, doctor, social worker, politican, farmer)
- a discipline (biology, chemistry, geology, history, philosophy, anthropology, literature, music, dance)
- a peer group (our circle of friends)
- an economic interest (education funding, rent control, tax cuts, defense spending)
- an emotional state (anger, contentment, depression, frustration)
- an age group (the elderly, young adults)
- a point in time (16th, 17th, 18th, 19th century)
- a club or an organization (the Boy Scouts, the Sierra Club, Amnesty International)

Our dominant point of view as individuals reflects some combination of these dimensions. Unfortunately, most of us are little aware of the extent to which these factors shape our point of view. Typically, people do not say, "This is how I see it from the point of view of . . . ." Instead, they usually say something that implies, "This is the way things are." We tend to believe the way we look at things is the best or only way. We easily lose a sense of our own partiality.

This is not an argument for *intellectual relativity*—the idea that everything is relative and therefore nothing can be proved (which is a self-refuting view). Looking at things from some point of view does not negate our ability to distinguish accurate from inaccurate statements. Doctors look at patients from the point of view of medical health, and that does not make their diagnoses "relative" or arbitrary.

As with all the elements, it is important to be aware of your own point of view, bring it out into the open so that you can understand it. The more clearly you recognize point of view at work in your thinking and in the thinking of others, and the more points of view you learn to think within, the more effective and reasonable your thinking will become.

2.13   *Think for Yourself*

MAKING YOUR POINT OF VIEW EXPLICIT

Below is a list of possible objects of thinking. From this list, choose seven to think about. Then write down how you would look at each, from your own point of view. For example, you might decide, "When I look at people, I see a struggle to find happiness," or "When I look at the future, I see myself as a lawyer taking cases that protect the environment," or "When I look at the health care system, I see a system that does not provide adequately for the poor." Reread each sentence you wrote. How does each one reflect the dimensions listed above? What are the implications of the point of view you've stated?

life	art
men	television
women	computers
human conflict	the news
school	the future of teaching
teaching	my economic future
learning	education in the future
mathematics	my future
the past	the problems we face as a nation
peer groups	the problems we face as a species
politics	mass transportation
power	the environment

our health care system   welfare

people without health insurance   welfare recipients

modern lifestyle   drug use

the modern American city   science

New Age ideas   human values

human sexuality   abortions

marriage   the police

life in America   elections

religion   vegetarians

income tax   liberals

lifelong learning   conservatives

the future   radicals

Complete the following for the seven objects you have chosen to look at:

1. When I look at _____

   I see (from my point of view) _____

   _____

2. When I look at _____

   I see (from my point of view) _____

   _____

3. When I look at _____

   I see (from my point of view) _____

   _____

4. When I look at _____

   I see (from my point of view) _____

5. When I look at _____

   I see (from my point of view) _____

6. When I look at _____

   I see (from my point of view) _____

7. When I look at _____

   I see (from my point of view) _____

The Point of View of the Critical Thinker

Critical thinkers share a common core of purposes in keeping with the values of critical thinking. Most importantly, critical thinkers believe that command of the thinking process is the key to commanding behavior. Applied to the learning process, this entails that they see reading, writing, speaking, and listening as modes of skilled thinking.

When critical thinkers read, they see the text as a verbal representation of the thinking of the author. They strive to enter the writer's point of view. They strive to reconstruct the author's thinking in their own mind. When they write, they think explicitly about the point of view of their intended audience. They use their insight into the thinking of the likely audience to present their ideas in the most accessible way. In speaking, critical thinkers use language to find out the perspectives and concerns of others. They do not try to force their ideas on people. Instead they recognize that people must think their own way to ideas and beliefs. Therefore, they tend to share experiences and information more than final conclusions. They listen attentively to the thinking of others. They ask more questions than they make assertions.

They also recognize that every subject has a distinctive point of view. When studying a subject, they strive to enter that point of view and think within it. When studying math, they strive to develop a mathematical viewpoint, learn how to think like a mathematician. In each subject, they seek fundamental principles, fundamental concepts, and fundamental processes and procedures. They seek to think within the logic of the subject.

Critical thinkers have a distinctive point of view concerning themselves: They see themselves as competent learners. They have a "can do" vision of their own learning. They do not see opposing points of view as a threat to their own beliefs. Instead, they see all beliefs as subject to change in the face of new evidence or better reasoning. They see themselves as lifelong learners.

CONCLUSION

Just as the first step in learning basketball, tennis, soccer, or any sport is to learn the fundamental elements of the sport, the first step to learning critical thinking is to learn the most basic elements of thinking. These are the "bread and butter" of disciplined thinking, for if we cannot analyze someone's thinking accurately, we are in a poor position to assess it. Recognizing the elements of thought is therefore essential to critical thinking.

Analysis of the elements of thought is a *necessary* but not a *sufficient* condition for evaluating thinking. Evaluation requires knowing the intellectual standards that highlight the qualities signaling strengths and weaknesses in thinking. For example, it is a strength in reasoning to be *clear,* a weakness to be *unclear;* a strength to be *accurate,* a weakness to be *inaccurate*. We shall focus on standards such as these in Chapter 3, explaining and illustrating how they apply to the elements of thought.

DISCOVER UNIVERSAL STANDARDS FOR THINKING

One of the fundamental skills of critical thinking is the ability to assess one's own reasoning. To be good at assessment requires that we consistently take apart our thinking and examine the parts (or elements) for quality. We do this using intellectual standards such as clarity, accuracy, precision, relevance, depth, breadth, logic, significance, and fairness. Critical thinkers recognize that, whenever they are reasoning, they reason to some purpose (element of reasoning). Implicit goals are built into their thought processes. But their reasoning is improved when they are clear (intellectual standard) about that purpose or goal. Similarly, to reason well, they need to know that, consciously or unconsciously, they are using information (element of reasoning) in thinking. But their reasoning improves if and when they make sure that the information they are using is accurate (intellectual standard).

Put another way, we assess our reasoning to find out how well we are reasoning. We do not assess the elements of reasoning for the fun of it, or just to satisfy some authority. Rather, we do so because we realize the negative consequences of failing to do so. In assessing reasoning, then, we recommend these intellectual standards as minimal:

- clarity
- accuracy
- precision
- relevance
- depth
- breadth
- logic
- significance
- fairness

These are not the only intellectual standards a person might use. They are simply some of the most fundamental. In this respect, the elements of thought are more basic than the standards, because the eight elements are *universal*—present in *all* reasoning on *all* subjects in *all* cultures for *all* time. On the one hand, one cannot reason with *no* information about *no* question from *no* point of view with *no* assumptions. On the other hand, there is a wide variety of intellectual standards from which to choose in addition to those listed above—such as credibility, predictability, feasibility, and completeness— that we don't use routinely in assessing reasoning but that we sometimes use.

As critical thinkers, then, we think about our thinking with these kinds of questions in mind: Am I being clear? Accurate? Precise? Relevant? Am I thinking logically? Am I dealing with a matter of significance? Is my thinking justifiable in context? Typically, we apply these standards to one or more elements.

3.1   *Think for Yourself*

IDENTIFYING INAPPROPRIATE STANDARDS

Can you identify a class you have taken in which you think your work was graded, at least in part, by one or more inappropriate standards? What was the class? What was the standard? What was the result? Can you see the importance of basing all grades on appropriate intellectual standards? Write out or orally explain your answer.

TAKE A DEEPER LOOK AT UNIVERSAL INTELLECTUAL STANDARDS

Critical thinkers routinely ask questions to assess the quality of reasoning, questions that apply intellectual standards to their thinking. You want to become so familiar with these questions that you ask them automatically. Eventually they will become part of your "inner voice," guiding you to better and better reasoning.

Clarity

Questions you can ask yourself or another person to clarify thinking include:

- Could you elaborate on that point? *or* Do I need to elaborate on that point?
- Could you express that point another way? *or* Can I express that point differently?
- Could you give me an illustration? *or* Should I give an illustration?
- Could you give me an example? *or* Should I provide an example?
- Let me state in my own words what I think you just said. Tell me if I am clear about your meaning. *or* Please tell me in your own words what you think I just said, so I can be sure you understand me.

Clarity means the reader or listener can understand what is being said. Clarity is a "gateway" standard—the first assessment test that has to be passed. If a statement is unclear, we cannot determine whether it is accurate or relevant. In fact, we cannot apply any of the other standards to it, because we don't yet know what it is saying. For example, the question, "What can be done about the education system in America?" is unclear. To adequately address the question, we would need a clearer understanding of what the person asking the question considers the "problem" to be. A clearer question might be, "What can educators do to ensure that students learn the skills and abilities that help them function successfully on the job and in their daily decision making?" Because this question is clearer, it is a better guide to thinking. It lays out more definitively the intellectual task at hand.

3.2 *Think for Yourself*

CONVERTING UNCLEAR THOUGHTS TO CLEAR THOUGHTS

Suppose you are engaged in a discussion about welfare, and someone says, "Let's face it—welfare is corrupt!" What does this mean? What could it mean?

It could mean some very different things. It might mean, "The idea of giving people goods and services they have not personally earned is equivalent to stealing money from those who have earned it" (a moral claim). Or it might mean, "The welfare laws have so many loopholes that people are receiving money and services that were not envisioned when the laws were initially formulated" (a legal claim). Or it might mean, "The people who receive welfare often lie, cheat, and falsify the documents they submit, and they should be thrown in jail" (a claim about the ethical character of the recipients).

For practice in making thoughts clear, take this statement, "She is a good person." This statement is unclear. Because we don't know the *context* within which this statement is being made, we aren't sure in what way "she" is "good." Formulate three possible meanings of this statement.

Now take the statement, "He is a jerk." Again, formulate three different possible meanings of this statement.

When you become skilled in differentiating what is clear from what is unclear, you will find that much of the time we are unclear both about what we are thinking and about what we are saying.

Accuracy

Questions that focus on assessing thinking for accuracy include:

- Is that really true?
- How could we check to see if that is accurate?
- How could we find out if that is true?

A statement may be clear but not accurate, as in "Most dogs weigh more than 300 pounds." To be accurate is to represent something in accordance with the way it actually is. People often present or describe things, events, people, and ideas in a way that differs from the way they actually are. This often happens when people have a "vested interest" in defining things in a certain way. For example, advertisers often do this to keep a buyer from seeing the weaknesses in a product. If an advertisement states, "Our water is 100% pure" when in fact the water contains small amounts of chemicals such as chlorine and lead, it is inaccurate. If an advertisement says, "This bread contains 100% whole wheat" when the whole wheat has been bleached and enriched and the bread contains many additives, the advertisement is inaccurate. Good thinkers listen carefully to statements. When there is reason for skepticism, they question whether what they hear is true and accurate. They also question the extent to which what they read is correct, when asserted as fact. Critical thinking then implies having a healthy skepticism about information presented as fact (when it may well be questionable).

At the same time, because we tend to think from a narrow, self-serving perspective, assessing ideas for accuracy can be difficult. We naturally tend to believe that our thoughts are automatically accurate just because they are ours, and therefore that the thoughts of those who disagree with us are inaccurate. We often fail to question statements that others make that conform to what we already believe, while we tend to question statements that conflict with our views. But as critical thinkers, we force ourselves to accurately assess our own views as well as those of others. We do this even if it means facing deficiencies in our thinking.

3.3   *Think for Yourself*

RECOGNIZING INACCURATE STATEMENTS

Inaccurate statements are common, especially when people are praising or criticizing. People tend to make two kinds of inaccurate statements: false positives (untrue positive statements) about people they personally like and false negatives (untrue negative things) about people they personally dislike. Politically motivated statements tend to follow a similar pattern. Think of examples of inaccurate statements from your recent experience. Write them out or orally explain them.

3.4   *Think for Yourself*

SEARCHING FOR THE FACTS

One of the most important critical thinking skills is that of assessing the accuracy of factual claims. *Factual claims* are statements asserting that something is true. For example, in an ad in the *New York Times* (Nov. 29, 1999, p. A15), a group of 60 nonprofit organizations called the Turning Point Project accused the World Trade Organization (a coalition of 134 nation states) of operating in secret and undermining democratic institutions and the environment. The nonprofit group argued that the working class and the poor have not significantly benefited from the past 20 years of rapid expansion in global trade. They made the following factual claims, among others:

1. "American CEOs are now paid, on average, 419 times more than line workers, and the ratio is increasing."

2. "Median hourly wages for workers are down by 10% in the last 10 years."

3. "The top 20% of the U.S. population owns 84.6% of the country's wealth."

4. "The wealth of the world's 475 billionaires now equals the annual incomes of more than 50% of the world population *combined*."

Discuss the probable accuracy of these claims. Do research to try to confirm or refute them. You might start with the Web site of the Turning Point Project, www.turnpoint.org, and that of the World Trade Organization at www.wto.org. You might find new information and arguments that provide a different perspective than that of the nonprofit coalition.

Precision

Questions that focus on assessing thinking for preciseness include:

- Could you give me more details?
- Could you be more specific?

It is possible for a statement to be both clear and accurate but not precise. An example is "Jack is overweight." We don't know how overweight Jack is—1 pound or 500 pounds. To be *precise* is to give the details needed for someone to understand exactly what is meant. Some situations don't call for precision. If you ask, "Is there any milk in the refrigerator?" and I answer "Yes," both the question and the answer are probably precise enough for the situation (though it might be important to specify how much milk there is). Or imagine that you are ill and you go to the doctor. He wouldn't say, "Take 1.4876946 antibiotic pills every 11.5692 hours." This level of specificity, or precision, would be beyond that which is useful in the situation.

In many situations, however, specifics are essential to good thinking. Let's say that your friend is having financial problems, and she asks you, "What should I do about my situation?" In this case, you want to probe her thinking for details. Without the full specifics, you could not help her. You might ask questions such as, "What *precisely* is the problem? What *exactly* are the variables that bear on the problem? What are some possible solutions to the problem—in detail?"

3.5 *Think for Yourself*

RECOGNIZING IMPRECISE STATEMENTS

Can you think of a recent situation where a lack of precision caused a problem? It might have been a situation where you needed more details to figure something out, or one where you experienced negative consequences because you didn't have enough details. For example, you might have been given directions to someone's house that caused you to get lost because they were not detailed enough.

Think of a situation in which the details were important (for example, in buying a computer, a car, or a stereo system). Then identify the negative consequences that resulted because you didn't get the details you needed to think well in the situation. Write out or orally explain your answer.

Relevance

Questions that focus on assessing thinking for relevance include:

- How is this idea connected to the question we are asking?
- How does this fact bear on the issue?
- How does this idea relate to this other idea?
- How does your question relate to the issue we are dealing with?

It is possible for a statement to be clear, accurate, and precise, but not relevant to the question at issue. For example, students often think the amount of effort they put into a course should contribute to raising their grade in the course. Often, however, effort does not measure the quality of student learning, and therefore it is irrelevant to the grade. Something is *relevant* when it is directly connected with and bears on the issue at hand. Something is relevant when it is pertinent or applicable to a problem we are trying to solve. Relevant thinking stays "on track." In contrast, irrelevant thinking encourages us to consider what we should set aside. People are often irrelevant in their thinking because they lack intellectual discipline. They don't know how to analyze an issue for what truly bears on it. Therefore, they aren't able to think effectively through the problems and issues they face.

3.6 *Think for Yourself*

RECOGNIZING IRRELEVANT STATEMENTS

Though we all sometimes stray from a question or task, we need to be sensitive to when this can have significant negative implications.

First, list some situations in which people tend to bring irrelevant considerations into a discussion (for example, in meetings, in responses to questions in class, in everyday discussions when they have a hidden agenda—or simply want to get control of the conversation for some reason). Then list some specific statements you have heard recently that were irrelevant. How did they affect the thinking process? Write out or orally explain your answer.

Depth

Questions that focus on assessing thinking for depth include:

- How does your answer address the complexities in the question?

- How are you taking into account the problems in the question?
- How are you dealing with the most significant factors in the problem?

We think *deeply* when we get beneath the surface of an issue or problem, identify the complexities in it, and then deal with those complexities in an intellectually responsible way. For some questions, even when we think deeply and deal well with the complexities, a solution or answer may still be difficult to find. Still our thinking will work better for us when we can recognize complicated questions and address each area of complexity in it.

It is possible for a statement to be clear, accurate, precise, and relevant, but superficial—lacking in depth. Suppose you are asked what should be done about the problem of drug abuse in America, and you answer by saying, "Just say no." This slogan, which appeared in anti-drug TV announcements for several years, is clear, accurate, precise, and relevant. Nevertheless, it lacks depth, because it treats a complex issue—the problem of drug abuse among people in our culture—superficially. It does not address the history of the problem, the politics of the problem, the economics of the problem, the psychology of addiction, and so on.

3.7   *Think for Yourself*

RECOGNIZING SUPERFICIAL APPROACHES

Look through a newspaper to find an article that contains a statement that is clear, accurate, precise, and relevant, but superficial with respect to a complex issue. For example, you might find a description of a law that takes a "Band-Aid" approach to a systemic problem such as drugs or crime.

State the problem at issue, then identify how the statement deals with the problem and why this approach is superficial. Think about the issue, trying to go deeply into its roots and complexities. State how the problem might be dealt with more effectively.

Breadth

Questions that focus on assessing thinking for breadth include:

- Do we need to consider another point of view?
- Is there another way to look at this question?
- What would this look like from a conservative or a liberal standpoint?
- What would this look like from the point of view of . . . ?

It is possible for a line of reasoning to be clear, accurate, precise, relevant, and deep, but still to lack breadth. Examples are arguments from either the conservative or the liberal standpoint that go deeply into an issue but show insight into only one side of the question.

Thinking broadly means considering the issue at hand from every relevant viewpoint. When multiple points of view are pertinent to an issue, yet we fail to give due consideration to those perspectives, our thinking is myopic or narrow-minded. We do not try to enter alternative or opposing viewpoints that could help us better address the issue.

Humans are frequently guilty of narrow-mindedness for many reasons: limited education, innate sociocentrism, natural selfishness, self-deception, and intellectual arrogance. Points of view that significantly contradict our own can seem threatening. We may find it easier to ignore perspectives with which we disagree than to consider them, because to consider them, in good faith, might mean reconsidering our own views.

Suppose, for example, that you and I are roommates and that I like to play loud music that annoys you. The question at issue is: "Should I play loud music when you are present?"

Both your viewpoint and mine are relevant to the question at issue. When I recognize your viewpoint as relevant, and then intellectually empathize with it—when I enter your way of thinking so as to actually understand it—I will be forced to see that imposing my loud music on you is unfair and inconsiderate. I will be able to imagine what it would be like to be forced to listen to loud music that I find annoying. But if I don't force myself to enter your viewpoint, I do not have to change my self-serving behavior. One of the primary mechanisms the mind uses to avoid giving up what it wants is unconsciously to refuse to enter viewpoints that differ from its own.

3.8 *Think for Yourself*

THINKING BROADLY ABOUT AN ISSUE

Take the question, "Is abortion ethically justified?" Some people argue that abortion is not ethically justifiable, and others argue that it is. Try to state and elaborate on each of these points of view in detail. Think about each point of view objectively, regardless of your personal views. Present each point of view in such a way that a person who actually takes that position would assess it as accurate. *Each line of reasoning should be clear, accurate, precise, relevant, and deep. Do not take a position on this issue yourself.*

Logic

Questions that focus on assessing thinking to determine whether it is logical include:

- Does all of this fit together logically?
- Does this really make sense?
- Does that conclusion follow from what you said?
- How does that inference follow from the evidence?
- Before, you implied this, and now you are saying that. I don't see how both can be true.

When we think, we bring together a variety of thoughts in some order. When the combined thoughts support each other and make sense together, the thinking is *logical*. When the combination is contradictory in some sense or the ideas do not make sense together, the combination is not logical. Because people often hold conflicting beliefs without being aware that they are doing so, it is not unusual to find inconsistencies in human life and thought.

Let's say we know, by looking at standardized tests of students in schools and the actual work they are able to produce, that for the most part students are deficient in basic academic skills such as reading, writing, speaking, and the core disciplines such as math, science, and history. Despite this evidence, teachers often conclude that there is nothing they can or should do to change their instruction to improve student learning (and in fact that there is nothing fundamentally wrong with the way they teach). Given the evidence, this conclusion seems illogical. The conclusion doesn't seem to follow from the facts.

For another example, suppose you know a person who has had a heart attack, and her doctors have told her she must eat more healthy foods to avoid problems in the future. Yet she concludes that what she eats really doesn't matter. Given the evidence, her conclusion is illogical. It doesn't make sense.

3.9   *Think for Yourself*

RECOGNIZING ILLOGICAL THINKING

Find a newspaper article that contains an example of illogical thinking—thinking that doesn't make sense to you.

1. State the issue that the thinking revolves around.
2. State the thinking that you believe is illogical and why you think it is illogical.
3. State some implications of the illogical thinking. In other words, what are some consequences likely to follow from the illogical thinking?

Significance

Questions that focus on assessing thinking for significance include:

- What is the most significant information we need to gather and use in our thinking if we are to address this issue?
- How is this fact important in context?
- Which of these questions is the most significant?
- Which of these ideas or concepts is the most important?

Thinking is most effective when it concentrates on the most important information and takes into account the most important ideas and concepts. Many ideas may be relevant to an issue, but not all of them are equally important. When we fail to ask important questions, we become mired in superficial questions, questions of little weight. For example, few college students focus on important questions such as, "What does it mean to be an educated person? What do I need to do to become educated?" Instead, they tend to ask questions such as, "What do I need to do to get an A in this course? How many pages does this paper have to be? What do I have to do to satisfy this professor?"

3.10 *Think for Yourself*

FOCUSING ON SIGNIFICANCE IN THINKING

Think about the way you spend your time, How much time do you spend on significant versus trivial things? Answer these questions:

1. What is the most important goal or purpose you should focus on at this point in your life? Why is this purpose important? How much time do you spend focused on it?

2. What are the most trivial or superficial things you spend time focused on (things such as your appearance, impressing your friends, chatting about insignificant things at parties, and the like).

3. What can you do to reduce the amount of time you spend on trivial things and increase the amount of time you spend on significant things?

Fairness

Questions that focus on assessing thinking for fairness include:

- Is my thinking justified given the evidence?
- Am I giving the evidence as much weight as it deserves?
- Are my assumptions justified?
- Is my behavior fair, given its implications?
- Is my selfish interest keeping me from considering the problem from alternative viewpoints?
- Am I using concepts justifiably, or am I using them unfairly in order to manipulate someone (to selfishly get what I want)?

When we think through problems, we want to make sure that our thinking is justified. To be justified is to think fairly in context. In other words, it is to think in accord with reason. If you are careful to meet the other intellectual standards covered thus far in this chapter, you will (by implication) satisfy the standard of fairness or justifiability.

We think it is important to target fairness in its own section because of the powerful nature of self-deception in human thinking. It is easy to deceive ourselves into believing that our ideas are fair and justified, when in fact we are refusing to consider significant relevant information that would cause us to change our view (and therefore not pursue our selfish interest). This is the natural state of the human mind. We often pursue unjustified purposes in order to get what we want even if we have to hurt others to get it. We often use concepts in an unjustified way in order to manipulate people. And we often make unjustified assumptions, unsupported by facts, that then lead to faulty inferences.

Sometimes the problem of unjustified thinking comes from ignoring relevant facts. Suppose that Kristi and Abbey live together. Abbey grew up in Vermont and Kristi is from Arizona. During the winter, Abbey likes to have the windows in the house open, while Kristi likes to keep them closed. But Abbey insists that it is "extremely uncomfortable" with the windows closed. All of the information Abbey is using in her reasoning centers on her own point of view—that *she* is hot, that *she* can't function well if she's hot, and that if Kristi is cold she can wear a sweater. But the fact is that Abbey is not justified in her thinking. She refuses to enter Kristi's point of view and to consider information supporting Kristi's perspective, because to do so would mean that *she would have to give something up.* She would have to adopt a more reasonable or fair point of view.

When we reason to conclusions, we want to check to make sure that the assumptions we are using to come to those conclusions are justifiable given the facts of the situation. For example, all of our prejudices and stereotypes function as assumptions in thinking. And no prejudices and stereotypes are justifiable, given their very nature. For example, we often make generalizations such as these:

- Liberals are soft on crime.
- Elderly people aren't interested in sex.
- Young men are only interested in sex.
- Jocks are cool.
- Blondes are dumb.
- Cheerleaders are airheads.
- Intellectuals are nerds.
- Learning is boring.
- School doesn't have anything to do with life.

The problem with assumptions like these is that they cause us to make basic—and often serious—mistakes in thinking. Because they aren't justifiable, they cause us to prejudge situations and people and to draw faulty inferences—or conclusions—about them. If we believe that all intellectuals are nerds, whenever we meet an intellectual we will infer that he or she is a nerd and act unfairly toward the person.

In sum, justifiability or fairness is an important standard in thinking because it helps us see how we may be distorting our own thinking in order to achieve self-serving ends—or how others are doing so at our expense.

3.11   *Think for Yourself*

ANALYZING ASSUMPTIONS FOR JUSTIFIABILITY (FAIRNESS)

Look back at the assumptions you wrote down for Think for Yourself 2.11. For each one, decide whether it is justifiable given the situation. For each assumption that is *not* justifiable, rewrite it as an assumption that *would* be justified in context.

EXHIBIT 3.1 *Powerful questions are implied by the intellectual standards. Critical thinkers routinely ask them.*

CLARITY	LOGIC
Could you elaborate? Could you illustrate what you mean? Could you give me an example?	Does all of this make sense together? Does your first paragraph fit in with your last? Does what you say follow from the evidence?

ACCURACY	SIGNIFICANCE
How could we check on that? How could we find out if that is true? How could we verify or test that?	Is this the most important problem to consider? Is this the central idea to focus on? Which of these facts are the most important?

PRECISION	BREADTH
Could you be more specific? Could you give me more details? Could you be more exact?	Do we need to look at this from another perspective? Do we need to consider another point of view? Do we need to look at this in other ways?

DEPTH	FAIRNESS
What factors make this a difficult problem? What are some of the complexities of this question? What are some of the difficulties we need to deal with?	Is my thinking justifiable in context? Am I taking into account the thinking of others? Is my purpose fair given the situation? Am I using concepts in keeping with educated usage or am I distorting them to get what I want?

RELEVANCE	
How does that relate to the problem? How does that bear on the question? How does that help us with the issue?	

3.12   *Think for Yourself*

APPLYING THE INTELLECTUAL STANDARDS TO EVERYDAY DISCUSSIONS

Tape-record a discussion between you and a few other people (friends or family) on an important, controversial issue (for example, "What is the best solution to the drug problem in this country?"). Play back the recording two or three remarks at a time. For each remark, note which of the standards are being met and which are being violated. Notice how seldom people tend to use intellectual standards in their thinking and how unclear everyday thinking often is. Notice, also, how people may feel just as confident in their positions as they were before, even after you point out violations of intellectual standards. What does that tell you about those people?

BRING TOGETHER THE ELEMENTS OF REASONING AND THE INTELLECTUAL STANDARDS

We have considered the elements of reasoning and the importance of being able to analyze them so we can recognize flaws in our thinking. We have also introduced intellectual standards as tools for assessment. Now let us look at how intellectual standards are used to assess the elements of reason.

Purpose, Goal, or End in View

Whenever we reason, we reason to some end, to achieve some objective, to satisfy some desire, or fulfill some need. One source of problems in human reasoning is traceable to defects at the level of goal, purpose, or end. If the goal is unrealistic, or if it contradicts other goals, or if it is confused or unclear, the reasoning used to achieve it will suffer. It may *also* be unrealistic, contradictory, confused, or unclear. To avoid this problem, get in the habit of explicitly stating the purposes you are trying to accomplish. You should strive to be clear about your purpose in every situation, so that you can stick to it. If you do not, you will be more likely to fail. Suppose your purpose for being in college is to obtain a degree so you will be more likely to get a good job and make a good income. If you keep that purpose clearly in mind and consistently work to achieve it, you are more likely to be successful. But it is easy to become so involved in the social life at college that you lose sight of your purpose and thus fail to achieve it.

As a student interested in developing your mind, you can begin to ask questions that improve your ability to focus on purpose in your classes. For example: Am I clear as to my purpose in this essay, research project, oral report, discussion? Can I specify my purpose precisely? Is my purpose a significant one? Is it realistic? Achievable? Justifiable? Do I have any contradictory purposes?

3.13   *Think for Yourself*

BRINGING INTELLECTUAL STANDARDS TO BEAR UPON YOUR PURPOSE

Think of an important problem in your life. This might be a problem in a personal relationship, at your place of work, in a class, or in an other situation. State your purpose in the situation *clearly* and *precisely*. What exactly are you trying to accomplish? Is your purpose *fair* and *justifiable?* Is it *realistic?* Explain to a classmate.

EXHIBIT 3.2 *Critical thinkers routinely apply intellectual standards to the elements of reasoning.*

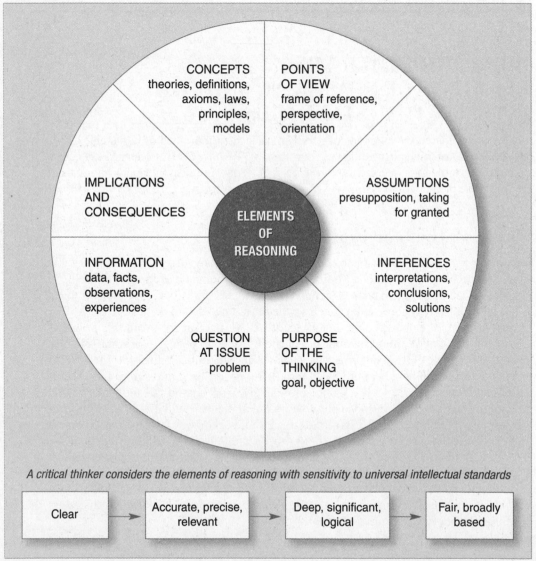

A critical thinker considers the elements of reasoning with sensitivity to universal intellectual standards

| Clear | → | Accurate, precise, relevant | → | Deep, significant, logical | → | Fair, broadly based |

Question at Issue or Problem to Be Solved

Whenever you attempt to reason something through, there is at least one question to answer—the question that emerges from the problem to be solved or issue to resolve. An area of concern in assessing reasoning, therefore, revolves around the question at issue.

To think well, you must be able to state the problem or issue in a clear and relevant way. This involves determining whether the question you are addressing is an important one, whether it is answerable, whether you understand the requirements for settling the question or for solving the problem.

As a student interested in developing your mind, you can begin to ask yourself questions that improve your ability to focus on the important questions in your classes. You can ask questions such as What is the most fundamental question at issue (in this lecture, in this chapter, in this discussion)? What is the question, precisely? Is the question simple or complex? If it is complex, what makes it complex? Am I sticking to the question (in this discussion, in this paper)? Is there more than one important question to be considered here (in this lecture, etc.)?

3.14   *Think for Yourself*

BRINGING INTELLECTUAL STANDARDS TO BEAR UPON THE QUESTION AT ISSUE

Go back to the important problem in Think for Yourself 3.13. Now state the problem you are trying to address. Then state the question that emerges from that problem. State your question *clearly* and *precisely*. What complexities, if any, are inherent in the problem? Is there more than one question you need to address to effectively reason through the problem? Explain to a classmate.

Point of View or Frame of Reference

Whenever we reason, we must reason within some point of view or frame of reference. Any "defect" in that point of view or frame of reference is a possible source of problems in the reasoning.

A point of view may be too narrow, may be based on false or misleading information, may contain contradictions, and may be unfair. Critical thinkers strive to adopt a point of view that is fair to others, even to opposing points of view. They want their point of view to be broad, flexible, and justifiable, to be clearly stated, and to be consistently adhered to. Good thinkers, then, consider alternative points of view as they reason through an issue.

As a person interested in developing your mind, you begin to ask yourself questions that improve your ability to focus on point of view in your classes. These questions might be: From what point of view am I looking at this issue? Am I so locked into my point of view that I am unable to see the issue from other points of view? Must I consider multiple points of view to reason well through the issue at hand? What is the point of view of this author? What is the frame of reference in this discipline? Are different world views implicit in these different perspectives?

3.15   *Think for Yourself*

BRINGING INTELLECTUAL STANDARDS TO BEAR UPON POINTS OF VIEW

Continue with the problem from Think for Yourself 3.14. Now state the point or points of view that are relevant to the issue at hand. State each point of view *clearly* and *precisely*. Make sure you are considering all relevant points of view (that you are thinking *broadly*), and that you are representing each point of view *accurately* (even if it means sympathetically expressing a view that you do not personally hold).

Information, Data, Experiences

Whenever we reason, there is some "stuff," some phenomena about which we are reasoning. Any inaccuracy or inadequacy in the experiences, data, evidence, or other raw material upon which reasoning is based can result in problems in the reasoning process. When you assess reasoning, your own or others', you should evaluate whether the evidence has been gathered and reported clearly, fairly, and accurately.

As a student, you should assess the information you use in coming to conclusions, whether you are working on a paper for class, reasoning through issues within the subjects you take, or reasoning through a problem in your personal life. When you do this, you should consider whether the information is *relevant* to the issue at hand and whether it is *adequate* for achieving your purpose. You should also assess whether you are accurately representing the relevant information or distorting it to fit your own (often self-serving) point of view.

As a student interested in developing your mind, you can begin to ask yourself questions that improve your ability to focus on information in your classes. These questions might be: What is the most important information I need in order to reason well through this issue? Are there alternate information sources I should consider? How can I check to see if the information I am using is accurate? Am I sure that all of the information I am using is relevant to the issue at hand?

3.16   *Think for Yourself*

BRINGING INTELLECTUAL STANDARDS TO BEAR UPON THE INFORMATION YOU ARE USING IN REASONING

Continuing with the same problem you have been working on, state the information you are using in your thinking. This information could be data, facts, or experiences that, in conjunction with your assumptions, lead you to conclusions. The information could come from your own personal experience, word of mouth, research, the media, or other sources. State the information clearly. How could you determine whether the information is *accurate* and *relevant* to the question at issue?

Concepts, Theories, Ideas

All reasoning uses some ideas or concepts and not others. These concepts include the theories, principles, axioms, and rules implicit in our reasoning. Any defect in the concepts or ideas in the reasoning is a possible source of problems in our reasoning.

Begin to think about the concepts you use. When using a concept, think about whether you are clear about its meaning, whether the concept is relevant to the issue at hand, and whether your use of the concepts may be unjustifiably affected by your point of view. Try to notice how you use concepts, what concepts are most important for a given question or issue, and how concepts are intertwined in networks.

As a student interested in developing your mind, begin to ask questions that improve your ability to focus on the importance of concepts in your classes. These questions may include: What is the *most* fundamental concept I need to learn in this class to help me in my life? How does this concept connect with other key concepts in the course? What are the most important theories in this class? Am I clear about the important concepts in the class? What questions do I need to ask to get clear about the concepts the instructor is explaining?

3.17 *Think for Yourself*

BRINGING INTELLECTUAL STANDARDS TO BEAR UPON THE CONCEPTS YOU USE

Continuing with the problem you have been working on, now state the most important concepts you are using to guide your reasoning. For example, if you are concerned with how you can keep in physical shape while also dedicating enough time to classes, work, family, significant others, and so forth, your key concepts might be *physical fitness, quality learning,* and *good relationships.* (You can usually discover the key concepts you are using in your reasoning by looking at your question and purpose.) Elaborate on each of the concepts so you understand exactly how you are using them. State your concepts *clearly* and *precisely.*

Assumptions

All reasoning must begin somewhere. It must take some things for granted. Any defect in the assumptions or presuppositions with which reasoning begins is a possible source of problems in the reasoning.

Critical thinkers are able to recognize and articulate their assumptions. They assess their assumptions for justifiability. Assumptions may be clear or unclear, justifiable or unjustifiable, consistent or contradictory.

As a student interested in developing your mind you should begin to ask questions that target assumptions within subjects, disciplines, lectures, and assignments. These questions could include: What is taken for granted in this academic discipline/this lecture/this discussion/this article/this experiment? Are these assumptions justifiable, or should I question them? What does the author of this textbook assume in Chapter 2? Are these assumptions justified, or should they be questioned?

3.18 *Think for Yourself*

BRINGING INTELLECTUAL STANDARDS TO BEAR UPON YOUR ASSUMPTIONS

Continuing with the problem you have been working on, now state the most important assumptions you are using in your reasoning. What are you taking for granted that might be questioned? For example, if you are trying to decide how to keep in physical shape while also dedicating enough time to other activities and your key relationships, your main assumptions might be:

1. Intellectual work is (is not) more important than relationships.
2. I know enough about fitness to do appropriate exercises.
3. I must spend some time working at a part-time job while in college (rather than getting a student loan).
4. I have enough time to do all of the above well.

State your assumptions *clearly* and *precisely*. Make sure they are *justifiable* in the context of the issue and your situation.

Implications and Consequences

Whenever we reason, implications follow from our reasoning. When we make decisions, consequences result from those decisions. Critical thinkers strive to understand implications whenever and wherever they occur. They try to trace logical consequences in order to see what their actions might lead to and to anticipate possible problems before they arise.

No matter where we stop tracing implications, there always will be further implications. No matter what consequences we do see, there always will be other and further consequences. Any defect in our ability to follow the implications or consequences of our reasoning is a potential source of problems in our thinking. Our ability to reason well, then, is measured in part by our ability to understand and enunciate the implications and consequences of reasoning.

As a student interested in developing your mind, you begin to ask yourself questions that improve your ability to focus on the important implications in your thinking as a student. These questions could include: What are the most significant implications of this biological theory, this phenomenon, this economic policy, this political practice? If we adopt this course of action, what are the likely consequences? What are the implications of failing to act in this context? What are the most significant implications of our tendency to solve this social problem in this way rather than that way? What were the implications (social, political, economic, cultural) of the United States' involvement in World War I?

3.19 *Think for Yourself*

THINKING THROUGH THE IMPLICATIONS OF YOUR REASONING

Continuing with the problem you have been working on, now state the *most* probable implication of the decisions you might make. Fill in the blanks:

If I decide to do _____, then _____ is likely to follow.

If I decide to act differently by doing _____, then _____ is likely to follow.

In this activity, you are emphasizing the *logical* implications or potential consequences of each possible decision. Be sure to emphasize important implications of each decision. For further practice, try listing the most likely implications of the following:

1. Getting married
2. Not staying in college
3. Staying in your hometown for your whole life
4. Doing drugs for the fun of it

Inferences

All reasoning proceeds by steps in which we reason as follows: "Because this is so, that also is so (or is probably so)" or, "Because this, therefore that." The mind perceives a situation or a set of facts and comes to a conclusion based on those facts. When this step of the mind occurs, an inference is made. Any defect in our ability to make logical inferences can cause problems in our reasoning. For example, if you see a person sitting on a street corner wearing tattered clothing, with a worn bedroll beside him and a bottle wrapped in a brown paper bag in his hand, you might infer that he is a bum. This inference is based on the facts you perceive in the situation and on what you assume about those facts. The inference, however, may or may not be justifiable in this situation.

Critical thinkers want to become adept at making sound inferences. First, you want to learn to identify when you or someone else has made an inference. What are the key inferences made in this article? Upon what are the inferences based? Are they justified? What is the key inference (or conclusion) I made in this paper? Was it justified? What is the key inference in this theory, in this way of proceeding, in solving this problem in this way? Is this inference logical? Is this conclusion significant? Is this interpretation justified? These are the kinds of questions you begin to ask.

As a student interested in developing your mind, ask questions that improve your ability to spot important inferences wherever they occur. Given the facts of this case, is there more than one logical inference (conclusion, interpretation) one could come to? What are some other logical conclusions that should be considered? From this point on, develop an inference detector, the skill of recognizing the inferences you are making in order to analyze them.

3.20   *Think for Yourself*

BRINGING INTELLECTUAL STANDARDS TO BEAR UPON YOUR INFERENCES

Continuing with the problem you have been working on, now state the inferences or conclusions you might come to (about the information you have) in solving your problem. You may have already stated these in Think for Yourself 3.19. Once you have thought through the potential conclusions you might come to in reasoning through the question at issue, state a possible final conclusion. Be clear and precise in stating each potential conclusion. Make sure your inferences make good sense, based on the relevant information and concepts.

BRIEF GUIDELINES FOR USING INTELLECTUAL STANDARDS

As we have emphasized, all reasoning contains eight elements, each of which is vulnerable to mistakes. Here we summarize some of the main "checkpoints" that critical thinkers use in their reasoning. You should use these same checkpoints to ensure the soundness of your reasoning.

1. All reasoning has a *purpose*.
   - Take time to state your purpose *clearly*.
   - Choose *significant* and *realistic* purposes.
   - Distinguish your purpose from related purposes.
   - Make sure your purpose is *fair* in context (that it doesn't involve violating the rights of others).
   - Check periodically to be sure you are still focused on your purpose and haven't wandered from it.

2. All reasoning is an attempt to figure something out, to settle some *question,* or to solve some problem.
   - Take time to state the question at issue *clearly* and *precisely*.
   - Express the question in several ways to *clarify* its meaning and scope.
   - Break the question into sub-questions (when you can).
   - Identify the type of question you are dealing with (historical, economic, biological, etc.) and determine whether the question has one right answer, is a matter of opinion, or requires reasoning from more than one point of view.
   - Think through the complexities of the question (think *deeply* through the question).

3. All reasoning is based on *assumptions*.
   - *Clearly* identify your assumptions and determine whether they are *justifiable*.
   - Consider how your assumptions are shaping your point of view.

4. All reasoning is based on *information:* data, facts, and experiences.
    - Restrict your claims to those supported by the relevant data.
    - Search for information that opposes your position as well as information that supports it.
    - Make sure that all information you use is *clear, accurate,* and *relevant* to the question at issue.
    - Make sure you have gathered *sufficient* information.
    - Make sure, especially, that you have considered all *significant* information *relevant* to the issue.

5. All reasoning is expressed through and shaped by *concepts* and ideas.
    - *Clearly* identify key concepts.
    - Consider *alternative* concepts or alternative definitions for concepts.
    - Make sure you are using concepts with care and *precision.*
    - Use concepts *justifiably* (not distorting their established meanings).

6. All reasoning contains *inferences* or interpretations by which we draw *conclusions* and give meaning to data.
    - Infer only what the evidence implies.
    - Check inferences for their *consistency* with each other.
    - Identify the assumptions that lead you to your inferences.
    - Make sure your inferences *logically* follow from the information.

7. All reasoning leads somewhere: it has *implications* and *consequences.*
    - Trace the *logical* implications and consequences that follow from your reasoning.
    - Search for negative as well as positive implications.
    - Consider all possible *significant* consequences.

8. All reasoning is done from some *point of view.*
    - *Clearly* identify your point of view.
    - Seek other *relevant* points of view and identify their strengths as well as weaknesses.
    - Strive to be *fair-minded* in evaluating all points of view.

3.21 *Think for Yourself*

USING CHECKPOINTS IN THINKING

For all of the eight elements, rewrite each checkpoint as a question or a set of questions. What questions does each checkpoint imply? When you have completed your list and you are actively using the questions you formulated, you will have powerful tools for thinking.

For example, under the first category, *All reasoning has a purpose,* the first checkpoint is, *"Take time to state your purpose clearly."* Two questions implied by this checkpoint are: "What exactly is my purpose?" and "Am I clear about my purpose?"

EXHIBIT 3.3 *This chart focuses on* purpose *in thinking. It is useful in seeing how the intellectual standards apply to purpose and in differentiating between the use of purpose by skilled and unskilled reasoners.*

PURPOSE		
All reasoning has a purpose.		

Primary standards: (1) clarity, (2) significance, (3) achievability, (4) consistency, (5) justifiability

Common problems: (1) unclear, (2) trivial, (3) unrealistic, (4) contradictory, (5) unfair

Principle: To reason well, you must clearly understand your purpose, and your purpose must be fair.

Skilled Reasoners	Unskilled Reasoners	Critical Questions
take the time to state their purpose clearly.	are often unclear about their central purpose.	Have I made the purpose of my reasoning clear? What exactly am I trying to achieve? Have I stated the purpose in several ways to clarify it?
distinguish the purpose from related purposes.	oscillate between different, sometimes contradictory, purposes.	What different purposes do I have in mind? How do I see them as related? Am I going off in somewhat different directions? How can I reconcile these contradictory purposes?
periodically remind themselves of their purpose to determine whether they are straying from it.	lose track of their fundamental object or goal.	In writing this proposal, do I seem to be wandering from my purpose? How do my third and fourth paragraphs relate to my central goal?
adopt realistic purposes and goals.	adopt unrealistic purposes and set unrealistic goals.	Am I trying to accomplish too much in this project?
choose significant purposes and goals.	adopt trivial purposes and goals as if they were significant.	What is the significance of pursuing this particular purpose? Is there a more significant purpose I should be focused on?
choose goals and purposes that are consistent with other goals and purposes they have chosen.	inadvertently negate their own purposes and do not monitor their thinking for inconsistent goals.	Does one part of my proposal seem to undermine what I am trying to accomplish in another part?
regularly adjust their thinking to their purpose.	are unable to do the thinking necessary to achieve their purpose.	What thinking do I need to do to achieve my purpose?
choose purposes that are fair-minded, considering the desires and rights of others equally with their own desires and rights.	choose purposes that are self-serving at the expense of others' needs and desires.	Is my purpose self-serving? Does it take into account the rights and needs of other people?

EXHIBIT 3.4 *This chart focuses on* question *in thinking. It is useful in seeing how the intellectual standards apply to questions and in differentiating between the use of questions by skilled and unskilled reasoners.*

QUESTION AT ISSUE OR CENTRAL PROBLEM		

All reasoning is an attempt to figure out something, to settle some question, or to solve some problem.

Primary standards: (1) clarity and precision, (2) significance, (3) answerability, (4) relevance

Common problems: (1) unclear and imprecise, (2) insignificant, (3) not answerable, (4) irrelevant

Principle: To settle a question, it must be answerable, and you must be clear about it and understand what is needed to answer it adequately.

Skilled Reasoners	Unskilled Reasoners	Critical Questions
are clear about the question they are trying to settle.	are often unclear about the question they are asking.	Am I clear about the main question at issue? Am I able to state it precisely?
can express a question in a variety of ways.	express questions vaguely and find questions difficult to reformulate for clarity.	Am I able to reformulate my question in several ways to recognize the complexities in the issue or problem?
can break a question into sub-questions.	are unable to separate the questions they are asking.	Have I broken down the main question into sub-questions? What are the sub-questions embedded in the main question?
routinely distinguish questions of different types.	confuse questions of different types and thus often respond inappropriately to the questions.	Am I confused about the type of question I am asking or being asked? For example: Am I confusing a legal question with an ethical one? Am I confusing a question of preference with a question requiring judgment?
distinguish significant from trivial questions.	confuse trivial questions with significant ones.	Am I focusing on trivial questions while other significant questions need to be addressed?
distinguish relevant questions from irrelevant ones.	confuse irrelevant questions with relevant ones.	Are the questions I'm raising in this discussion relevant to the main question at issue?
are sensitive to the assumptions built into the questions they ask.	often ask loaded questions.	Is the way I'm putting the question loaded? Am I taking for granted from the outset something I should be questioning?
distinguish questions they can answer from questions they can't answer.	try to answer questions they are not in a position to answer.	Am I in a position to answer this question? What information would I need to have before I could answer the question?

EXHIBIT 3.5 *This chart focuses on* point of view *in thinking. It is useful in seeing how the intellectual standards apply to point of view and in differentiating between the use of point of view by skilled and unskilled reasoners.*

POINT OF VIEW		
All reasoning is done from some point of view.		

Primary standards: (1) flexibility, (2) fairness, (3) clarity, (4) breadth, (5) relevance

Common problems: (1) restricted, (2) biased, (3) unclear, (4) narrow, (5) irrelevant

Principle: To reason well, you must identify those points of view relevant to the issue and enter these viewpoints empathetically.

Skilled Reasoners	Unskilled Reasoners	Critical Questions
keep in mind that people have different points of view, especially on controversial issues.	do not credit alternative reasonable viewpoints.	Have I articulated the point of view from which I am approaching this issue? Have I considered opposing points of view regarding this issue?
consistently and accurately articulate other points of view and reason from within those points of view to understand them.	neither value nor practice reasoning within alternative viewpoints; cannot reason with empathy from other points of view.	Let me think aloud within this alternative viewpoint to see if I can accurately articulate it.
seek other viewpoints, especially when the issue is one they believe in passionately.	can sometimes give other points of view when the issue is not emotionally charged but cannot do so for issues they feel strongly about.	Am I presenting X's point of view in an unfair manner? Am I having difficulty appreciating X's viewpoint because I am emotional about this issue?
confine their monological reasoning to problems that are clearly monological.*	confuse multilogical with monological issues; insist that there is only one frame of reference within which a given multilogical question must be decided.	Is the question here monological or multilogical? How can I tell? Am I reasoning as if only one point of view is relevant to this issue when in reality other viewpoints are relevant?
recognize when they are most likely to be prejudiced for or against a viewpoint.	are unaware of their own prejudices.	Is this prejudiced or reasoned judgment? What is causing me to prejudge in this situation?
approach problems and issues with a richness of vision and an appropriately broad point of view.	reason from within inappropriately narrow or superficial points of view.	Is my approach to this question too narrow? Am I thinking broadly enough in order to adequately address the issue?

Monological problems are ones for which there are definite correct and incorrect answers and definite procedures for getting those answers. In *multilogical* problems, there are competing schools of thought to be considered. (See Chapter 5.)

EXHIBIT 3.6 *This chart focuses on* information *in thinking. It is useful in seeing how the intellectual standards apply to information and in differentiating between the use of information by skilled and unskilled reasoners.*

INFORMATION		

All reasoning is based on information: data, evidence, experience, research.

Primary standards: (1) clear, (2) relevant, (3) fairly gathered and reported, (4) accurate, (5) adequate, (6) consistently applied

Common problems: (1) unclear, (2) irrelevant, (3) biased, (4) inaccurate, (5) insufficient, (6) inconsistently applied

Principle: Reasoning can be only as sound as the information it is based on.

Skilled Reasoners	Unskilled Reasoners	Critical Questions
assert a claim only when they have sufficient evidence to support it.	assert claims without considering all relevant information.	Is my assertion supported by evidence? Do I have sufficient evidence to support my position?
can articulate and accurately evaluate the information behind their claims.	don't articulate the information they are using in their reasoning and so do not subject it to rational scrutiny.	Do I have evidence to support my claim that I haven't clearly articulated? Have I evaluated the information I am using for accuracy and relevance?
actively search for information *against* (not just *for*) their own position.	gather information only when it supports their own point of view.	Where is a good place to look for evidence on the opposite side? Have I looked there? Have I honestly considered information that doesn't support my position?
focus on relevant information and disregard what is irrelevant to the question at issue.	do not carefully distinguish between relevant information and irrelevant information.	Are my data relevant to the claim I'm making? Have I failed to consider relevant information?
draw conclusions only to the extent that they are supported by the data and sound reasoning.	make inferences that go beyond what the data support.	Does my claim go beyond the evidence I've cited?
state their evidence clearly and fairly.	distort the information or state it inaccurately.	Is my presentation of the pertinent information clear and coherent? Have I distorted information to support my position?

EXHIBIT 3.7 *This chart focuses on concepts in thinking. It is useful in seeing how the intellectual standards apply to concepts and in differentiating between the use of concepts by skilled and unskilled reasoners.*

CONCEPTS AND IDEAS		
All reasoning is expressed through, and shaped by, concepts and ideas.		
Primary standards: (1) clarity, (2) relevance, (3) depth, (4) accuracy, (5) justifiability		
Common problems: (1) unclear, (2) irrelevant, (3) superficial, (4) inaccurate, (5) not justifiable		
Principle: Reasoning can be only as clear, relevant, realistic, and deep as the concepts that shape it.		
Skilled Reasoners	**Unskilled Reasoners**	**Critical Questions**
are aware of the key concepts and ideas they and others use.	are unaware of the key concepts and ideas they and others use.	What is the main idea I am using in my thinking? What are the main concepts others are using?
are able to explain the basic implications of the key words and phrases they use.	cannot accurately explain basic implications of key words and phrases.	Am I clear about the implications of key concepts? For example: Does the word *cunning* have negative implications that the word *clever* does not?
are able to distinguish special, nonstandard uses of words from standard uses.	are not able to recognize when their use of a word or phrase departs from educated usage.	Where did I get my definition of this central concept? For example: Where did I get my definition of the concept of education, terrorism . . . ? Have I changed the meaning of a concept to fit my own purposes?
are careful to use words in keeping with educated usage.	often use words inappropriately or in ways not justified by the circumstances.	Am I using the concept of *love* appropriately? For example: Do I unknowingly act as if loving a person implies a right to treat him or her discourteously?
think deeply about the concepts they use.	fail to think deeply about the concepts they use.	Am I thinking deeply enough about this concept? For example: The concept of *health care,* as I describe it, does not take into account the patient's rights and privileges. Do I need to consider the idea of health care more deeply?

EXHIBIT 3.8 *This chart focuses on* assumptions *in thinking. It is useful in seeing how the intellectual standards apply to assumptions and in differentiating between the use of assumptions by skilled and unskilled reasoners.*

ASSUMPTIONS		
All reasoning is based on assumptions—beliefs we take for granted.		
Primary standards: (1) clarity, (2) justifiability, (3) consistency		
Common problems: (1) unclear, (2) unjustified, (3) contradictory		
Principle: Reasoning can be only as sound as the assumptions it is based on.		
Skilled Reasoners	**Unskilled Reasoners**	**Critical Questions**
are clear about the assumptions they are making.	are often unclear about the assumptions they make.	Are my assumptions clear to me? Do I clearly understand what my assumptions are based upon?
make assumptions that are reasonable and justifiable given the situation and the evidence.	often make unjustified or unreasonable assumptions.	Do I make assumptions about the future based on just one experience from the past? Can I fully justify what I am taking for granted? Are my assumptions justifiable given the evidence I am using to support them?
make assumptions that are consistent with each other.	often make assumptions that are contradictory.	Do the assumptions I made in the first part of my argument contradict the assumptions I am making now?
consistently seek to figure out their assumptions.	ignore their assumptions.	What assumptions am I making in this situation? Are they justifiable? Where did I get these assumptions?
recognize that assumptions lie at the unconscious level of thought and that those assumptions determine the inferences we make.	don't explicitly realize they make assumptions; don't understand the relationship between inferences and assumptions.	What assumptions in my thinking have I never explained? How might these assumptions lead to illogical inferences?

EXHIBIT 3.9 *This chart focuses on* implications *in thinking. It is useful in seeing how the intellectual standards apply to implications and in differentiating between how skilled and unskilled reasoners think about implications.*

IMPLICATIONS AND CONSEQUENCES		

All reasoning leads somewhere. It has implications and, when acted upon, has consequences.

Primary standards: (1) significance, (2) logic, (3) clarity, (4) precision, (5) completeness

Common problems: (1) unimportant, (2) unrealistic, (3) unclear, (4) imprecise, (5) incomplete

Principle: To reason-well through an issue, you must think-through the implications that follow from your reasoning. You must think-through the consequences likely to follow from the decisions you make.

Skilled Reasoners	Unskilled Reasoners	Critical Questions
trace out a number of significant implications and consequences of their reasoning.	trace out few or none of the implications and consequences of holding a position or making a decision.	Have I spelled out all the significant implications of the action I am advocating? If I were to take this course of action, what other consequences might follow that I haven't considered?
clearly and precisely articulate the implications and possible consequences.	are unclear and imprecise in articulating possible consequences they articulate.	Have I clearly and precisely delineated the consequences likely to follow from my chosen action?
search for negative as well as positive potential consequences.	trace out only the consequences that come immediately to mind, either positive or negative, but usually not both.	I may have done a good job of spelling out some positive implications of the decision I am about to make, but what are some of the negative implications possible?
anticipate the likelihood of unexpected negative and positive implications.	are surprised when their decisions have unexpected consequences.	If I make this decision, what are some unexpected consequences? What are some variables out of my control that might lead to negative consequences?

EXHIBIT 3.10 *This chart focuses on* inferences *in thinking. It is useful in seeing how the intellectual standards apply to inferences and in differentiating between the kinds of inferences made by skilled and unskilled reasoners.*

INFERENCE AND INTERPRETATION		
All reasoning contains inferences from which we draw conclusions and give meaning to data and situations.		
Primary standards: (1) clarity, (2) logic, (3) justifiability, (4) profundity, (5) reasonability, (6) consistency		
Common problems: (1) unclear, (2) illogical, (3) unjustified, (4) superficial, (5) unreasonable, (6) contradictory		
Principle: Reasoning can be only as sound as the inferences it makes (or the conclusions it comes to).		

Skilled Reasoners	Unskilled Reasoners	Critical Questions
are clear about the inferences they are making and articulate their inferences clearly.	are often unclear about the inferences they are making do not clearly articulate their inferences.	Am I clear about the inferences I am making? Have I clearly articulated my conclusions?
usually make inferences that follow from the evidence or reasons that are presented.	often make inferences that do not follow from the evidence or reasons presented.	Do my conclusions logically follow from the evidence and reasons presented?
often make inferences that are deep rather than superficial.	often make inferences that are superficial.	Are my conclusions superficial, given the problem?
often make inferences or come to conclusions that are reasonable.	often make inferences or come to conclusions that are unreasonable.	Are my conclusions reasonable?
make inferences or come to conclusions that are consistent with each other.	often make inferences or come to conclusions that are contradictory.	Do the conclusions I came to in the first part of my analysis seem to contradict the conclusions that I came to at the end?
understand the assumptions that lead to inferences.	do not seek to figure out the assumptions that lead to inferences.	Is my inference based on a faulty assumption? How would my inference be changed if I were to base it on a different, more justifiable assumption?

REDEFINE GRADES AS LEVELS OF THINKING AND LEARNING

The best learners, like the best thinkers, continually assess their learning against standards of excellence. Being passionate about learning, they welcome standards they can use to strive for excellence. The best learners are not dependent on instructors to tell them how well they are doing. They have universal criteria that they apply across all dimensions of learning. To the extent that you need instructors to tell you how well you are doing, and have no independent sense yourself, you are not thinking critically. The best learners avoid being overly dependent on teachers and seek, rather, to develop an independent, disciplined, thinking mind.

Each step in learning, like the process of thinking critically, is tied to a self-reflective step of self-assessment. As a skilled learner, you do not simply have goals in learning; you know what your goals are. Your primary goal is to think within the logic of the subject, to think like a scientist, to think like a psychologist, to think like an artist, and so forth.

The best learners seek to enter the foundation of any subject they study and use that foundation to understand everything else within the subject. They seek to understand the most fundamental questions asked within the subject. They seek to identify the most basic kinds of information used by professionals within the field, the most basic concepts the field employs, the most fundamental assumptions that underlie it, the most basic point of view that defines it.

The best learners do not memorize random bits and pieces of information. Their learning is problem- or question-based. But they do not simply state a problem; they assess that statement for its clarity. They do not simply gather information; they gather it and check it for its relevance and significance. They do not simply form an interpretation; they check their interpretation to see what it is based on and whether that basis is adequate.

DEVELOP STRATEGIES FOR SELF-ASSESSMENT

In the chapter on universal intellectual standards, you were introduced to a host of standards you can use to assess your thinking independent of what you are thinking about. Here we look at more holistic standards for assessing your learning within subjects. Virtually every day of study, for example, you should seek to assess the quality of your work as a learner. You should regularly and explicitly use intellectual standards. But you should go further. You should also regularly examine your learning to determine the extent to which you are constructing in your mind the system that defines the subject or subjects you are studying. In this chapter you will find a set of performance criteria you can use in any course to assess your studying overall, irrespective of the specific subject. You can use these criteria to give yourself grades, independently of the grades given by your instructors. Of course, your instructor may officially adopt these criteria as grade profiles in the class.

USE STUDENT PROFILES TO ASSESS YOUR PERFORMANCE

In every class, you are thinking and learning at some level of quality. You may be thinking and learning at a very high level, absorbing the material very effectively. Or, you may be at the other end of the spectrum: studying ineffectively (or not at all) and finding these habits reflected in your learning. Still yet, you may be somewhere in between. For this chapter we divide performance levels into four categories. We present a profile for each category: a description of how a student working at that level thinks and behaves. These levels are not merely the authors' opinions; they are based on commonly accepted academic values—although many students may be unaware of these profiles. To improve your learning and your grades, get into the habit of reviewing your work with these criteria in mind. If you do so, you will grow as a learner and thinker. If you learn how to perform at the high performing or exemplary level, you can learn effectively in every class you take.

As you read through these profiles, notice that you can take any of the criteria in the profiles, transform the criteria into specific questions you can ask yourself about your own performance, and then answer the questions for any given class you are in. For example, here are the criteria for the "exemplary" student:

> Often raises important questions and issues, analyzes key questions and problems clearly and precisely, recognizes key questionable assumptions, clarifies key concepts effectively, uses language in keeping with educated usage, frequently identifies relevant competing points of view, and demonstrates a commitment to reasoning carefully from clearly stated premises in the subject, as well as marked sensitivity to important implications and consequences.

Based on these criteria, you can ask yourself the following questions:

To what extent do I:

- raise important questions and issues in the class?
- analyze key questions and problems clearly and precisely?
- distinguish relevant from irrelevant, accurate from inaccurate information?
- recognize key assumptions?
- clarify key concepts?
- use language in keeping with educated usage?
- identify competing points of view?
- reason carefully from clearly stated premises?
- note important implications and consequences?

As you read the following four levels of performance, ask yourself which profile describes your level in each of your classes. As you assess yourself using these profiles, figure out how you can use the performance criteria to improve your learning.

Exemplary Students (Grade of A)

Exemplary performance in an academic subject implies excellence in thinking within the subject (e.g. sound historical thinking, sound biological thinking, sound mathematical thinking . . .). Students who function at this level regularly use their intellectual skills to develop a broad range of knowledge. Exemplary work is clear, precise, and well-reasoned, but it is more: it is also insightful and well-informed. Basic terms and distinctions are learned at a level that implies insight into seminal concepts and principles.

The exemplary student has internalized the basic intellectual standards appropriate to assessing his or her own work in a subject and is highly skilled at self-evaluation. Exemplary students regularly:

- raise important questions and issues (formulating them clearly and precisely)
- analyze key questions and problems (logically)
- distinguish accurate from inaccurate, relevant from irrelevant information
- recognize questionable assumptions
- clarify key concepts
- use language in keeping with educated usage
- identify relevant competing points of view
- display sensitivity to important implications and consequences
- reason carefully from clearly stated, well-justified premises in a subject.

Exemplary students display excellent reasoning and problem-solving abilities within a field and work consistently at a high level of intellectual excellence. They typically interrelate ideas within and among fields of study. They regularly apply what they are learning to issues and problems in their lives.

High-Performing Students (Grade of B)

High-performance implies sound thinking within a subject along with the development of a range of knowledge acquired through the exercise of thinking skills and abilities. High-level student thinking is, on the whole, clear, precise, and well-reasoned, but sometimes lacks depth of insight (especially into opposing points of view). Basic terms and distinctions are learned at a level that implies comprehension of important concepts and principles. High-level students perform well because they internalize the intellectual standards relevant to the subject and demonstrate competence in self-evaluation. High-performing students:

- often raise questions and issues (often formulating them clearly and precisely)
- analyze most questions and problems (logically)
- often distinguish accurate from inaccurate, relevant from irrelevant information
- recognize most questionable assumptions
- often clarify key concepts
- typically use language in keeping with educated usage
- commonly identify relevant competing points of view
- display sensitivity to many important implications and consequences
- often reason carefully from clearly stated and well-justified premises in a subject.

High-performing students display sound reasoning and problem-solving skills within a field and work consistently at a commendable level of intellectual performance. They often interrelate ideas within and among fields of study. They often apply what they are learning to issues and problems in their lives.

Mixed-Quality Students (Grade of C)

Students whose thinking is of mixed quality perform inconsistently in a subject, and therefore develop a limited body of knowledge. These students often use memorization as a substitute for understanding. Thinking of mixed quality is sometimes clear, precise, and well-reasoned, but just as often it is unclear, imprecise, and muddled. This type of thinking often lacks depth of insight. Learning at this level demonstrates incomplete comprehension of basic concepts and principles in a subject. Thinkers of mixed quality have internalized a few of the intellectual standards appropriate to the assessment of their own work in a subject, but demonstrate inconsistency in self-evaluation. Mixed-quality students:

- sometimes raise questions and issues (sometimes formulating them clearly and precisely)
- sometimes analyze questions and problems (logically)

- sometimes distinguish accurate from inaccurate, relevant from irrelevant information
- recognize some questionable assumptions
- clarify some concepts
- sometimes use language in keeping with educated usage
- sometimes identify relevant competing points of view
- sometimes reason carefully from clearly stated and well-justified premises in a subject
- are inconsistently sensitive to important implications and consequences.

Mixed-quality students display inconsistent reasoning and problem-solving skills within a field and work, at best, at an inconsistent level of intellectual performance. They sometimes interrelate ideas within and among fields of study. They sometimes apply what they are learning to issues and problems in their lives.

Low-Performing Students (Grade of D or F)

Low-performing students reason poorly within a subject. They frequently try to get through courses by memorizing things rather than by understanding them. Low-performing students generally do not develop the critical-thinking skills or insights they need in order to understand course content. They often produce work that is unclear, imprecise, and poorly reasoned. Low-performing students may achieve competence in reciting information and naming concepts, but they often use terms and concepts incorrectly because their understanding is superficial or mistaken. Low-performing students have not internalized the basic intellectual standards appropriate to the assessment of their own work in a subject and perform poorly in self-evaluation. Low-performing students:

- rarely raise questions and issues
- superficially analyze questions and problems
- rarely distinguish accurate from inaccurate, relevant from irrelevant information
- do not recognize their assumptions
- clarify concepts only partially
- rarely use language in keeping with educated usage
- rarely identify relevant competing points of view
- rarely reason carefully from clearly stated and well-justified premises in a subject
- are insensitive to important implications and consequences.

Low-performing work reflects poor reasoning and problem-solving skills within a subject. Students at this level usually fail to interrelate ideas within and among fields of study. They rarely apply what they are learning to issues and problems in their lives.

4.1   *Think for Yourself*

RATE YOURSELF AS A THINKER

Now that you have read through the student profiles for each competency level, rate yourself as a student overall. Write a brief paper, completing and elaborating the following statements:

1. I see myself at the following skill level as a student (exemplary, high-performing, mixed-quality, or low-performing) . . .

2. I support my position with the following evidence from my work in one or more classes (examples should include excerpts from papers, etc. that directly relate to the skills discussed in the profiles. For example, if you say that you are a mixed-quality student, you might give an equal number of examples of written work that are clear as well as unclear.) . . .

3. To improve as a student, I need to do the following (focus on the skills discussed at the exemplary or high-performing level to formulate a plan) . . .

APPLY STUDENT PROFILES TO ASSESS YOUR PERFORMANCE WITHIN SPECIFIC DISCIPLINES

As a developing thinker, you can apply the skill levels described in this chapter to any subject you study. To provide an example, in this section we apply the competency levels to the study of psychology.

Exemplary Thinking as a Student of Psychology (Grade of A)

A psychology student who shows exemplary thinking demonstrates a true grasp of what psychological thinking is and a broad range of specific psychological thinking skills and knowledge. The student's work at the end of the course is clear, precise, and well-reasoned. In exemplary work, the student uses psychological terms and distinctions effectively. The work demonstrates a mind taking charge of psychological ideas, assumptions, and inferences.

An exemplary student of psychology:

- raises important psychological questions and issues (formulating them clearly and precisely)
- analyzes psychological issues (logically)
- distinguishes relevant from irrelevant information, and accurate from inaccurate information when reasoning through psychological problems
- recognizes questionable psychological assumptions

- regularly clarifies key psychological concepts and checks their use for justifiability
- uses psychological language in keeping with established professional usage, while at the same time questioning inappropriate conceptualizations of human behavior within the field of psychology
- thinks within competing psychological points of view and accurately represents each view
- shows a strong tendency to reason carefully from clearly stated and well-justified premises
- displays sensitivity to important psychological implications and consequences.

Exemplary work displays excellent psychological reasoning and problem-solving skills and is consistently at a high level of intellectual excellence. Students functioning at the exemplary level routinely interrelate ideas within psychology, and between psychology and related fields of study such as history, sociology, anthropology, and philosophy. When relevant, they regularly apply psychological principles and concepts to issues and problems in their lives.

High-Performing Thinking as a Student of Psychology (Grade of B)

Students of psychology who function at the high-performing level demonstrate achievement in grasping what psychological thinking is, and demonstrate a range of specific psychological thinking skills and abilities. At the end of the course, high-performing work is, on the whole, clear, precise, and well-reasoned, though with occasional lapses into weak reasoning. On the whole, the high-performing student of psychology uses psychological terms and distinctions effectively. The student's work demonstrates a mind beginning to take charge of psychological ideas, assumptions, and inferences.

The high-performing student of psychology:

- often raises important questions and issues (often formulating them clearly and precisely)
- usually analyzes psychological questions and problems (logically)
- usually distinguishes accurate from inaccurate, relevant from irrelevant information
- recognizes most questionable psychological assumptions
- often clarifies key psychological concepts and checks their use for justifiability
- typically uses psychological language in keeping with established professional usage, while at the same time often questioning inappropriate conceptualizations of human behavior within the field of psychology
- commonly thinks within competing psychological points of view
- displays sensitivity to many important psychological implications and consequences

■ frequently demonstrates a commitment to reasoning carefully from clearly stated and well-justified psychological premises.

High-performing students of psychology demonstrate sound psychological reasoning and problem-solving skills. They often interrelate ideas within psychology, and between psychology and related fields of study such as history, sociology, anthropology, and philosophy. When relevant, they often apply psychological principles and concepts to issues and problems in their lives.

Mixed-Quality Thinking as a Student of Psychology (Grade of C)

Students of psychology who function at the mixed-quality level illustrate some, but inconsistent, achievement in grasping what psychological thinking is, along with the development of modest psychological thinking skills and abilities. Mixed-quality work at the end of the course shows some emerging psychological thinking skills, but pronounced weaknesses as well. Though some assignments are reasonably well done, others are poorly done, or at best are mediocre. There are more than occasional lapses in reasoning. Though psychological terms and distinctions are sometimes used effectively, they are sometimes used ineffectively. Only on occasion does a thinker of mixed quality display a mind taking charge of psychological ideas, assumptions, and inferences. Only occasionally does mixed-quality thinking display intellectual discipline and clarity. The mixed quality student of psychology *sometimes*:

■ raises psychological questions and issues (sometimes formulating them clearly and precisely)

■ analyzes psychological issues (logically)

■ formulates psychological information accurately

■ distinguishes relevant from irrelevant, accurate from inaccurate information

■ recognizes key questionable psychological assumptions

■ clarifies key psychological concepts, and can identify when psychological concepts are being used justifiably

■ uses psychological language in keeping with established professional usage

■ identifies relevant competing psychological points of view

■ recognizes important psychological implications and consequences

■ reasons carefully from clearly stated psychological premises.

Sometimes psychology students at this level seem to be simply "going through the motions" of assignments, carrying out the work without getting into the spirit of it. On the whole, their work shows only modest (and inconsistent) psychological reasoning and problem-solving skills, and it often displays weak psychological reasoning and problem-solving skills. Students at this level *sometimes* interrelate ideas within psychology and between psychology and related fields of study, and they *sometimes* apply psychological principles and concepts to issues and problems in their lives.

Low-Performing Thinking as a Student of Psychology (Grade of D or F)

Psychology students at the low-performing level show little, if any, understanding of psychological thinking; and any psychological thinking skills and abilities they have developed exist only at a low level. Any psychological thinking they engage in is often uncritical. Most psychological assignments are poorly done, usually because the student is failing to reason through the assignment. Students at this level usually seem to be merely "going through the motions" of assignments, carrying out the work without getting into the spirit of it. Their work rarely shows any effort to understand psychological ideas, assumptions, and inferences. In general, their psychological thinking, however little they demonstrate it, lacks discipline and clarity. In low-level work, the student *rarely,* if ever:

- raises psychological questions and issues
- analyzes psychological issues
- distinguishes accurate from inaccurate, relevant from irrelevant information
- recognizes key questionable assumptions
- clarifies key psychological concepts
- uses psychological language in keeping with established professional usage
- identifies relevant competing psychological points of view
- reasons carefully from clearly stated and well-justified premises or recognizes important implications and consequences.

The work of students at this level displays poor psychological reasoning and problem-solving skills overall. Students at this level almost never interrelate ideas within psychology and between psychology and related fields of study. They rarely, if ever, apply psychological principles and concepts to issues and problems in their lives.

4.2 *Think for Yourself*

EVALUATING YOUR PERFORMANCE IN A SUBJECT YOU ARE STUDYING

Transform the example of thinking with the field of psychology that you have just read into a set of questions you can use to assess the quality of your learning within a subject you are currently studying or have studied. For example, if you are taking a course in biology, you might formulate the following types of questions:

- Am I gaining command over a range of biological thinking skills and abilities that I use to acquire biological knowledge?
- Is my work (papers, exams) clear, precise, and well-reasoned?
- Am I gaining command of the key biological terms and distinctions?

- To what extent have I developed the ability to identify and solve fundamental biological problems?

Then answer each question, stating your answer, then elaborating upon it and giving an example of it.

CONCLUSION

To be a skilled learner, you must be a skilled thinker. To learn most effectively in the context of college, you must take charge of your learning. You must design it—plan it out. You plan learning by becoming clear as to what your goals are, what questions you have to—or want to—answer, what information you need to get, what concepts you need to learn, what you need to focus on and how you need to understand it.

In this chapter we have laid out profiles that you can use throughout your college experience to assess how well you are functioning as a learner in each class you take, within each academic subject you study. With these profiles clearly in mind, you become the master of your own assessment in each class. You realize that your ability to think within a subject is determined by the *skills you develop* in thinking through that subject, not by the grades you are given by instructors. In other words, you take command of your learning. You know how well you are doing in thinking through the content because you can assess your own development. You develop as an independent thinker.

LEARN TO ASK THE QUESTIONS THE BEST THINKERS ASK

From what we have emphasized thus far, it should be clear that to emulate the thinking of the best thinkers, you must:

- Become *interested* in thinking
- Become a *critic* of your own thinking
- Be willing to establish *new habits* of thought
- Develop a *passion* for thinking well
- Study the *interplay* of thoughts, feelings, and desires
- Become interested in the *role* of thinking in your life
- Routinely *analyze* your own and others' thinking into its elements
- Routinely *assess* thinking for its strengths and weaknesses
- Routinely *assess* your study (and learning) habits
- Learn how to think within diverse *systems* of thought

In this chapter we shall explore the role of questions in thinking. We will make explicit the questions the best thinkers ask. By learning to pose and answer them, you will develop important and powerful critical thinking skills.

THE IMPORTANCE OF QUESTIONS IN THINKING

It is not possible to become a good thinker and be a poor questioner. Thinking is not driven by answers but by questions. Those who laid the foundations for new fields—for example, physics or biology—did so by asking questions. If they had not done so the field would never have been developed. Every intellectual field is born out of a cluster of questions to which answers are either needed or highly desirable. Furthermore, every field stays alive only to the extent that fresh questions are generated and taken seriously as the driving force in thinking. When a field of study is no longer pursuing answers to questions, it becomes extinct.

> To learn a subject is to learn to ask the questions the best thinkers in the field routinely ask.

To think through or rethink anything, one must ask questions that stimulate thought. Questions define tasks, express problems, and delineate issues. Answers, on the other hand, often signal a full stop in thought. Only when an answer generates further questions does thought continue. This is why you are really thinking and learning only when you formulate and pursue questions. When you have no questions, you are not pursuing any answers. Moreover, the quality of the questions you ask determines the quality of your thinking.

For example, biologists and biochemists make progress when they ask questions such as, "What are we made of? How do our bodies work? What are the most basic forms of life?" They make even more progress when they take their questioning to the subcellular and molecular level: "What are proteins? What are enzymes? What are enzyme reactions? How do molecular events underlie macroscopic phenomena?" (Jevons, 1964). By focusing on these subcellular questions, they can then move to other important questions, such as, "How do vitamins interact with chemistry in the body to produce healthier functioning? How do cancer cells differ from normal cells? What kinds of foods interact with the body's chemistry to lessen the likelihood of the development of cancerous cells?" The best teachers are those who understand the relationship between learning and asking questions. As Jevons (1964) says of his students, "Those who asked questions helped me most, but even those who merely looked puzzled helped a little, by stimulating me to find more effective ways of making myself understood."

> A field is alive only to the extent that there are live questions in it.

QUESTIONING YOUR QUESTIONS

When you meet people for the first time, what are the questions you would most like to answer about them? In other words, what information do you seek about people when you first meet them? These questions (and the information you seek) reveal a great deal about your values and perspective. They also reveal something about the nature of your personal relationships. The questions we ask can tell us as much about ourselves as they do about the subject, person, or issue we are questioning.

Different types of questions serve different purposes. Consider the following question types, which emerge from one's understanding of the elements of reasoning and intellectual standards.

- Questions about *purpose* force us to define our task.

- Questions about *information* force us to look at our sources of information as well as at the quality of the information.

- Questions about *interpretation* force us to examine how we are organizing or giving meaning to information and to consider alternative ways of giving meaning.

- Questions about *assumption* force us to examine what we are taking for granted.

- Questions about *implication* force us to follow where our thinking is leading us.

- Questions about *point of view* force us to examine our point of view and to consider other *relevant* points of view.

- Questions about *relevance* force us to decide what does and what does not bear on a question.

- Questions about *accuracy* force us to evaluate and test for truth and correctness.

- Questions about *precision* force us to give details and be specific.

- Questions about *consistency* force us to examine our thinking for contradictions.

- Questions about *logic* force us to consider how we are putting the whole of our thought together, to make sure that it all adds up and makes sense within a reasonable system of some kind.

5.1   *Think for Yourself*

QUESTIONING THE DEPTH OF YOUR QUESTIONS

Write out your answers to the following questions:

Are any of the questions you are focused on in your life *deep* questions?

To what extent are you questioning your *purposes* and goals?

To what extent are you questioning your *assumptions*?

To what extent are you questioning the *implications* of your thought and action?

Do you ever question your *point of view?*

Do you ever wonder whether your *point of view* is keeping you from seeing things from an opposing perspective? If so, under what circumstances?

Do you ever question the *consistency* of your thoughts and behavior?

Do you question the *logic* of your thinking?

What do your answers tell you about yourself and about your habits of questioning?

DEAD QUESTIONS REFLECT INERT MINDS

The best thinkers ask live questions that lead to knowledge and further questions that lead to knowledge and yet further questions.

At age 19, Isaac Newton drew up a list of questions under 45 headings. His goal: constantly to question the nature of matter, place, time, and motion.

Most students ask virtually none of the thought-stimulating questions you answered in the last activity. Most tend to stick to "dead" questions, such as, "Is this going to be on the test?" Dead questions usually imply either the desire not to think or a lack of questioning abilities.

We must continually remind ourselves that we are really thinking and learning only when we are asking questions, and that the quality of our questions determines the quality of our thinking. No questions results in no understanding. Superficial questions result in superficial understanding; unclear questions result in unclear understanding. If you sit silently in class, your mind is probably silent as well. When this is the case, either you will ask no questions or your questions will tend to be superficial, ill formed, and self-serving.

You should strive for a state of mind in which, even when you are outwardly quiet, you are inwardly asking questions. Try to formulate deep questions that will lead you to productive learning. The same is true when you study on your own: to learn deeply and independently, strive to stimulate your thinking with questions that lead to further questions.

5.2   *Think for Yourself*

QUESTIONING AS YOU READ

Read a chapter in one of your textbooks with the purpose of generating questions. After reading each section, or every few paragraphs, make a list of all the questions you can think of related to what you are reading. Then see if you can answer these questions—either by looking in the textbook or by raising them in class.

5.3   *Think for Yourself*

QUESTIONING YOUR QUESTIONING ABILITY

At this point in your intellectual development, to what extent would you call yourself a skilled or deep questioner? How would you rate the quality of the questions you ask (both those that you share with others and those you keep to yourself)?

Do you know anyone who you would say is a deep questioner? If so, what makes you believe this person questions deeply?

Write your answers down or discuss them with a partner.

THREE CATEGORIES OF QUESTIONS

Before we go further in our discussion about how to question deeply, we want to introduce a way of categorizing questions. This way of classifying questions provides a sort of "jumpstart" in figuring out the kind of reasoning required in answering a question. These useful three categories of questions might best be labeled *fact, preference,* and *judgment.*

EXHIBIT 5.1   *In approaching a question, it is useful to figure out what type it is. Is it a question with one definitive answer? Is it a question that calls for a subjective choice? Or does the question require you to consider competing answers?*

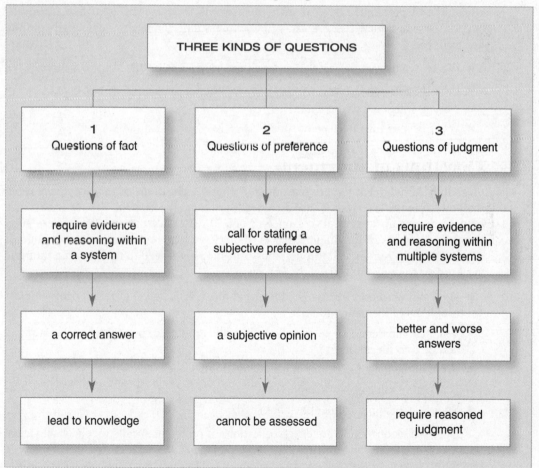

THREE KINDS OF QUESTIONS		
1 Questions of fact	**2** Questions of preference	**3** Questions of judgment
require evidence and reasoning within a system	call for stating a subjective preference	require evidence and reasoning within multiple systems
a correct answer	a subjective opinion	better and worse answers
lead to knowledge	cannot be assessed	require reasoned judgment

Questions of Fact

Questions of fact have one right answer or an established procedure for finding an answer. These questions require evidence and reasoning with one, monological system. For example:

- What is the boiling point of lead?
- What is the size of this room?
- What is the differential of this equation?
- How does the hard drive on a computer operate?

Questions of Preference

Questions of preference have as many answers as there are different human preferences. These are questions that ask you to express a preference or subjective opinion. For example:

- Which would you prefer, a vacation in the mountains or one at the seashore?
- How do you like to wear your hair?
- Do you like to go to the opera?
- What is your favorite type of food?

Questions of Judgment

Questions of judgment require reasoning, but unlike questions of fact they have more than one defensible answer. These are questions that make sense to debate—they have better or worse answers (well-reasoned or poorly reasoned answers). When reasoning through questions of judgment, we seek the *best possible* answer given the range of possibilities. To reason well through these questions, we need to think within multiple systems, or to think multilogically. For example:

- How can we most effectively address the most basic and significant economic problems of the nation today?
- What can be done to significantly reduce the number of people who become addicted to illegal drugs?
- What is the most important thing we can do to "save" the earth?
- Is abortion ethically justifiable?
- Should capital punishment be abolished?

Only the second kind of question (questions of preference) calls for sheer subjective opinion. A question of judgment is a matter of reasoned consideration. We can and should rationally evaluate answers to questions of judgment by applying intellectual standards to the answers—standards such as clarity, depth, consistency, and significance.

Some people mistakenly think of all judgments as either fact or subjective preference and they therefore ask questions that elicit either a factual response or a subjective opinion. Yet, the questions most important to educated people—the questions we most need to be able to competently answer—fall into the third, now almost totally ignored, category: reasoned judgment. For example, a judge in a court of law is expected to engage in reasoned judgment. She is expected not only to render a judgment, but also to base that judgment on sound, relevant evidence and valid legal reasoning. She is under the ethical and legal obligation not to base her judgments on subjective preferences or her personal opinions. Thus, judgment based on sound reasoning goes beyond, and is never to be equated with, fact alone or mere opinion alone. Reasoning depends on facts, but good reasoning does more than just state facts. It determines how it makes the most sense to conceptualize or interpret the facts. Similarly, a position that is well-reasoned is not to be described as simply "opinion." Although we sometimes call the judge's verdict an "opinion," we not only expect, we *demand* that it be based on relevant and sound reasoning.

When questions that require reasoned judgment are treated as matters of preference, counterfeit critical thinking occurs. Some people, then, come to uncritically assume that everyone's "subjective opinion" is of equal value. Their capacity to appreciate the importance of intellectual standards diminishes, and we can expect to hear questions such as these: "What if I don't like these standards? Why shouldn't I use my own standards? Don't I have a right to my own opinion? What if I'm just an emotional person? What if I like to follow my intuition? What if I think spirituality is more important than reason? What if I don't believe in being 'rational'?" When people reject questions that call for reasoned judgment and deep thought, they fail to see the difference between offering legitimate reasons and evidence in support of a view and simply asserting the view as true.

Intellectually responsible persons, in contrast, recognize questions of judgment for what they are: questions that require serious consideration of alternative ways of reasoning. In other words, intellectually responsible persons recognize when a question calls for good reasoning, and they behave in accordance with that responsibility. This means that they recognize when there is more than one reasonable way to answer a question. They also understand the responsibility they have to explore alternative ways of looking at the problem, of entering viewpoints that differ from their own—and enter those viewpoints *in good faith*—before making final judgments.

To summarize, any question calls on us to do one of three things:

1. to express a subjective preference,
2. to establish an objective fact (within a well-defined system), or
3. to come up with the best of competing answers (generated by competing systems).

We do not fully understand the task we are faced with until we know which of these three types of reasoning is called for in our thinking. Is the question calling for a subjective or personal choice? If so, we should answer the question in terms of our personal preferences. If not, is there a way to come up with one correct answer to this question (a definite system in which to find the answer)? Or, finally, are we dealing with a question that could reasonably be answered differently within different points of view? In other words, is it debatable? If the latter, what is the best answer to the question, considering all points of view?

5.4   *Think for Yourself*

DISTINGUISHING TYPES OF QUESTIONS, PART I

Make a random list of questions. State them clearly and precisely. Then decide which questions are questions of fact (with definite right or wrong answers), which questions are matters of subjective preference, and which questions require reasoned judgment (within multiple perspectives). To make these determinations, you might think through each question in the following way:

1. Ask, "Are there any facts that a reasonable person would have to consider to answer this question?" If there are, then the question is not purely a matter of subjective preference. If not, then it is a question of preference.

2. If there are facts relevant to the question, would all reasonable persons interpret those facts in the same way? If so, it is a question of fact. If not, then the facts can be interpreted differently from different competing reasonable perspectives. Therefore, it is a question requiring reasoned judgment that takes into account multiple perspectives.

As you study a subject, distinguish among the three types of questions. Look for the questions that have definitive or correct answers. These will be matters settled by definition or fixed, established, and recognized procedures. Identify those questions that are ultimately a matter of personal choice. And, most important, identify those questions that can be legitimately, or at least arguably, approached from more than one point of view. These questions will arise most often when there are competing traditions, schools, or theories within a discipline. For example, in psychology there are many competing schools: Freudian, Jungian, Adlerian, rational–emotive, gestalt, and so on. Many issues in psychology will be reasoned through differently depending on the academic allegiance of the reasoner. These issues will call for considering argumentation from a variety of perspectives and will result in different reasoned judgments.

5.5   *Think for Yourself*

DISTINGUISHING TYPES OF QUESTIONS, PART 2

Identify at least one subject you have studied in school that involves competing traditions or schools of thought. Then identify some questions that would be answered differently depending on the school of thought used to think through the question. Which of the schools of thought do you best understand or identify most with? How might this school of thought be questioned from the perspective of another competing school of thought?

BECOME A SOCRATIC QUESTIONER

Now that you are beginning to understand how to categorize questions, let us discuss how we can approach questions in general, so that our questions lead us to improved thinking.

As critical thinkers, we want to go beyond questions that are undisciplined, questions that go in multiple directions with neither rhyme nor reason. Therefore, we turn from merely questioning to what might be termed "Socratic questioning." What the word "Socratic" adds to ordinary questioning is systematicity, depth, and a keen interest in assessing the truth or plausibility of things.

One of the primary goals of critical thinking is to establish a disciplined, "executive" component of thinking in our thinking, a powerful inner voice of reason, to monitor, assess, and repair—in a more rational direction—our thinking, feelings, and action. Socratic questioning provides that inner voice. Here are some of the fundamentals of Socratic questioning, followed by examples of questions you might ask in Socratic dialogue to begin to deeply probe the thinking of another person.

- Seek to understand the deepest foundations of a person's statements or beliefs. Use a series of questions to probe the person's thinking, to reach deeper and deeper levels. You might ask, "On what do you base your beliefs? Could you explain your reasoning to me in more detail so I can more fully understand your position?"

EXHIBIT 5.2   *Socratic thinking is an integrated, disciplined approach to thinking.*

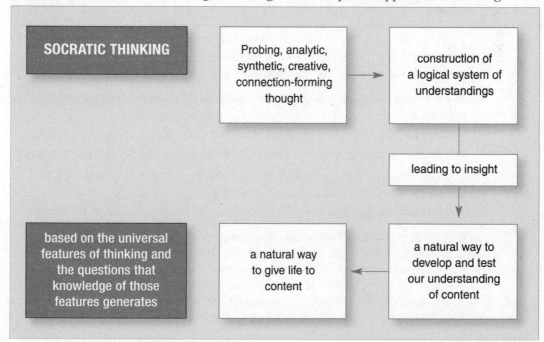

- Recognize that any thought exists in a network of connected thoughts. Therefore, treat all assertions as a connecting point to further thoughts. Pursue those connections. You might ask, "If what you say is true, wouldn't x or y also be so?"

- Treat all thoughts as needing clarification or development. You might ask, "Could you elaborate on what you are saying so I can better understand you?"

- Recognize that all questions presuppose prior questions and all thinking presupposes prior thinking. When raising questions, be open to the questions they presuppose. You might ask, "To answer this complex question, what other questions do we need to answer?"

5.6   *Think for Yourself*

PRACTICING SOCRATIC QUESTIONING

When you become a Socratic questioner, a systematic questioner, you can question practically anyone about practically anything—effectively! Try out your Socratic skills by questioning someone as systematically and as deeply as you can about something he or she deeply believes. Tape-record the discussion. Follow the suggestions we have outlined. When finished, replay the tape and analyze your Socratic questioning abilities. Did you probe beneath the surface of the person's thinking? Did you ask for elaboration when needed? Did you pursue connections? Overall, how you would rate yourself as a Socratic questioner?

To take your thinking to the level of disciplined questioning, to think or question Socratically, you can go in several directions:

1. You can focus your questions on types of questions (fact, preference, or judgment).

2. You can focus your questions on *assessment,* by targeting intellectual standards.

3. You can focus your questions on *analysis,* by targeting the elements of thought.

4. You can "unpack" complex questions by developing questions one would have to answer prior to answering the complex question.

5. You can address the question (if it is complex) through the domains inherent in it.

In this section, we will elaborate these forms of Socratic questioning. Of course, the questions you would ask in a given situation will be determined by the context within which you are thinking. When you become skilled at using these questions, you will begin to see the powerful role they can play in your thinking. And, with practice, they eventually will become intuitive to you. You will begin to naturally ask questions of clarification when you are unclear. You will begin to naturally ask questions focused on *information* when the data seem to be inaccurate or otherwise questionable. You will intuitively recognize when people are mistakenly answering questions of judgment with their subjective preference, and so on. Again, intuitive ability comes only after practice, practice, and then more practice.

EXHIBIT 5.3   *Here are five ways to generate questions systematically.*

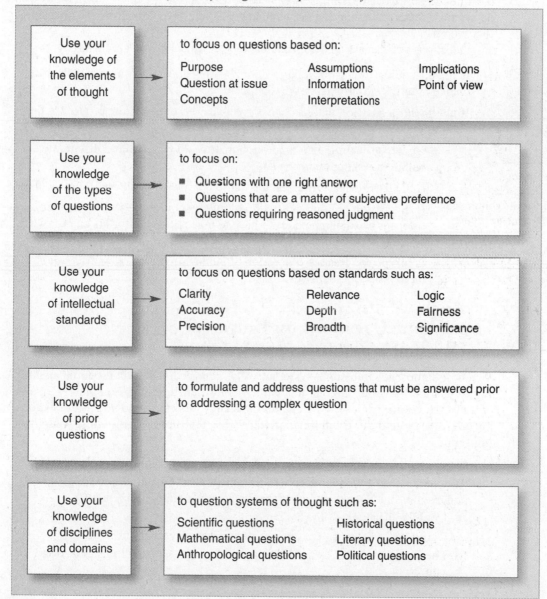

Use your knowledge of the elements of thought	to focus on questions based on:
	Purpose Assumptions Implications
	Question at issue Information Point of view
	Concepts Interpretations

Use your knowledge of the types of questions	to focus on:
	▪ Questions with one right answer
	▪ Questions that are a matter of subjective preference
	▪ Questions requiring reasoned judgment

Use your knowledge of intellectual standards	to focus on questions based on standards such as:
	Clarity Relevance Logic
	Accuracy Depth Fairness
	Precision Broadth Significance

Use your knowledge of prior questions	to formulate and address questions that must be answered prior to addressing a complex question

Use your knowledge of disciplines and domains	to question systems of thought such as:
	Scientific questions Historical questions
	Mathematical questions Literary questions
	Anthropological questions Political questions

Focus Your Thinking on the Type of Question Being Asked

As discussed earlier in this chapter, when you approach questions systematically, you are able to recognize that all thought has three possible functions: to express a subjective preference, to establish an objective fact (within a well-defined system), or to determine the best of competing answers (using reasoned judgment). Assume that you do not fully understand thinking until you know which type of thinking the question is focused on.

Questions you can ask to determine the type of question you are dealing with:

- Is the question calling for a subjective or personal choice? If so, let's make that choice in terms of our personal preferences.

- If not, is this a question that has one correct answer, or a definite procedure for finding the correct answer?

  - Or are we dealing with a question that would be answered differently within different points of view?

  - If the latter, what is the best answer to the question, all things considered?

  - Is this person treating a question of judgment as a question of preference (perhaps by saying he doesn't have to give reasoning for his answer when actually he does)?

  - Is this person treating a question of judgment as a question for which there is one right answer?

> In pursuing questions, Charles Darwin relied on perseverance and continual reflection. He wrote, "I have never been able to remember for more than a few days a single date or line of poetry."

Focus Your Questions on Universal Intellectual Standards for Thought

When you approach questions systematically, you recognize when people are failing to use the universal intellectual standards in their thinking. You also recognize when you are failing to use these standards in your thinking. And you ask questions, specifically targeting the intellectual standards, that upgrade thinking. Use these guidelines:

1. Recognize that thinking is always more or less *clear.* Assume that you do not fully understand a thought except to the extent that you can elaborate, illustrate, and exemplify it. Questions that focus on *clarity* in thinking include:

   - Could you elaborate on what you are saying?
   - Could you give me an example or illustration of your point?
   - I hear you saying "x." Am I hearing you correctly, or have I misunderstood you?

2. Recognize that thinking is always more or less *precise*. Assume that you do not fully understand a thought until you can specify it in detail. Questions that focus on *precision* in thinking include:
   - Could you give me more details about that?
   - Could you be more specific?
   - Could you specify your allegations more fully?

3. Recognize that thinking is always more or less *accurate*. Assume that you have not fully assessed an idea until you have verified that it represents things as they really are. Questions that focus on *accuracy* in thinking include:
   - How could we check that to see if it is true?
   - How could we verify these alleged facts?
   - Can we trust the accuracy of these data given the questionable source from which they come?

4. Recognize that thinking is always capable of straying from the task, question, problem, or issue under consideration. Assume that you have not fully assessed thinking until you have ensured that all considerations used in addressing it are *relevant* to it. Questions that focus on *relevance* in thinking include:
   - I don't see how what you said bears on the question. Could you show me how it is relevant?
   - Could you explain what you think the connection is between your question and the question we have focused on?

5. Recognize that thinking can either remain at the surface of things or probe beneath the surface to deeper issues. Assume that you have not fully assessed a line of thinking until you have determined the *depth* required for the task at hand (and compared that with the depth that actually has been achieved). Questions that focus on *depth* in thinking include:
   - Is this question simple or complex? Is it easy or difficult to answer?
   - What makes this a complex question?
   - How are we dealing with the complexities inherent in the question?

6. Recognize that thinking can be more or less broad-minded (or narrow-minded) and that *breadth* of thinking requires the thinker to reason insightfully within *more than one point of view or frame of reference*. Assume that you have not fully assessed a line of thinking except to the extent that you have determined how much *breadth* of thinking is required (and how much has in fact been exercised). Questions that focus on *breadth* in thinking include:
   - What points of view are relevant to this issue?
   - What relevant points of view have I ignored thus far?
   - Am I failing to consider this issue from an opposing viewpoint because I don't want to change my view?

- Have I entered the opposing views in good faith, or only enough to find flaws in them?
- I have looked at the question from an economic point of view. What is the ethical point of view?
- I have considered a liberal position on the issue. What would conservatives say?

5.7   *Think for Yourself*

FOCUSING YOUR QUESTIONS ON INTELLECTUAL STANDARDS

For each of the intellectual standards listed above, think of a situation where you did *not* apply the standard and suffered negative consequences as a result. For example, name a situation in which you should have asked a question of clarification and didn't, or should have asked a question focusing on precision and didn't, and so on. State what happened as a result of each failure. For example, you might recall a time when you asked for directions to someone's house but got lost because you failed to ask questions focused on important details (in other words, the directions were not as precise as they needed to be).

Focus Your Questions on the Elements of Thought

Another powerful way to discipline your questions is to focus on the elements or parts of thinking. As you formulate your questions, use the following guidelines:

1. All thought reflects an agenda or *purpose*. Assume that you do not fully understand someone's thought (including your own) until you understand the agenda behind it. Questions that focus on *purpose* in thinking include:

> The best questions are those that keep us focused on achieving our most significant goals and purposes.

- What are you trying to accomplish in saying this?
- What is your central aim in this line of thought?
- What is the purpose of this meeting?
- What is the purpose of this chapter?
- What is the purpose of our relationship?
- What is my purpose for being in college?

2. All thoughts presuppose an *information* base. Assume that you do not fully understand a thought until you understand the background information (facts, data, experiences) that supports or informs it. Questions that focus on *information* in thinking include:
   - On what information are you basing that comment?
   - What experience convinced you of this? Could your experience be distorted?
   - How do we know this information is accurate?
   - Have we left out any important information that we need to consider?

3. All thought requires the making of *inferences,* the drawing of conclusions, the creation of meaning. Assume that you do not fully understand a thought until you

understand the inferences that have shaped it. Questions that focus on *inferences* in thinking include:
- How did you reach that conclusion?
- Could you explain your reasoning?
- Is there an alternative plausible conclusion?
- Given all the facts what is the best possible conclusion?

4. All thought involves the application of *concepts*. Assume that you do not fully understand a thought until you understand the concepts that define and shape it. Questions that focus on *concepts* in thinking include:
- What is the main idea you are using in your reasoning?
- Could you explain that idea?
- Are we using our concepts justifiably?

5. All thought rests upon other thoughts, which are taken for granted or *assumed*. Assume that you do not fully understand a thought until you understand what it takes for granted. Questions that focus on *assumptions* in thinking include:
- What exactly are you taking for granted here?
- Why are you assuming that?
- Should I question the assumptions I am making about my roommate, my friends, my intimate other, my parents, my instructors, my country?

6. All thought is headed in a direction. It not only rests on something (assumptions), but it is also going somewhere: toward *implications* and consequences. Assume that you do not fully understand a thought unless you know the implications and consequences that follow from it. Questions that focus on *implications* in thinking include:
- What are you implying when you say that?
- What is likely to happen if we do this versus that?
- Are you implying that . . . ?

7. All thought takes place within a *point of view* or frame of reference. Assume that you do not fully understand a thought until you understand the point of view or frame of reference that places it on an intellectual map. Questions that focus on *point of view* in thinking include:
- From what point of view are you looking at this?
- Is there another point of view we should consider?
- Which of these possible viewpoints makes the most sense given the situation?

8. All thought is responsive to a *question*. Assume that you do not fully understand a thought until you understand the question that gave rise to it. Questions that focus on the *question* in thinking include:
- I am not sure exactly what question you are raising. Could you explain it?
- Is this question the best one to focus on at this point, or is there a more pressing question we need to address?
- The question in my mind is this: How do you see the question?
- How is your question related to the question we have been reasoning through?

5.8 *Think for Yourself*

FOCUSING YOUR QUESTIONS ON THE ELEMENTS OF REASONING

From each of the eight categories we just outlined, ask yourself at least one question about your view of marriage (or family). For example, you might begin with the question, "In my view, what is the basic purpose or goal of marriage?" (Answer each question after you ask it.) Afterward, question a friend about his or her views, using the same questions (you should feel free to ask additional questions as they occur to you). Write out an analysis of your questioning process. Do you notice yourself beginning to think at a deeper level—given the questions you are now asking? Focus on all eight elements when formulating your questions.

Focus Your Questions on Prior Questions

Learning to reason well through complex questions can be difficult precisely because they are complex. They may seem "too big" or you may have trouble knowing where to start. Sometimes it works best to think backward, by asking questions you need to answer before you can answer the more complex question. We call these questions "prior questions."

For example, to answer the question "What is multiculturalism?" we should be able to first settle the question, "What is culture?" And to settle that question, we should be able to settle the question, "What are the aspects of a person that determine what culture he or she belongs to?" When you learn to formulate and pursue prior questions, you have another important strategy for learning.

To construct a list of prior questions, simply write down the complex question you are trying to answer and then formulate as many questions as you can think of that you would have to answer before you could answer the first. Then take this list and determine what questions you would have to answer before answering these questions. Continue, following the same procedure for every new set of questions on your list.

As you proceed to construct your list, keep your attention focused on the first question on the list as well as on the last. If you do this well, you should end up with a list of questions that probe the logic of the first question.

For example, suppose you were trying to answer the question, "What is history?" Here is a list of questions you would need to answer first:

■ What do historians write about?

■ What is "the past"?

■ Is it possible to include all of the past in a history book?

■ How many of the events during a given time period are left out in a history of that time period?

■ Is more left out than is included?

- How does a historian know what to emphasize?
- Do historians make value judgments in deciding what to include and what to leave out?
- Is it possible to simply list facts in a history book, or does all history writing involve interpretations as well as facts?
- Is it possible to decide what to include and exclude and how to interpret facts without adopting a historical point of view?
- How can we begin to judge a historical interpretation?
- How can we begin to judge a historical point of view?

5.9 *Think for Yourself*

CONSTRUCTING A LIST OF PRIOR QUESTIONS

Formulate a complex question you would like to answer. Then use the procedure for constructing prior questions described above until you have a list of at least 10 questions. Afterward, see if you have gained insight into how the first question has to be thought-through in light of the prior questions you formulated. What complexities have to be considered?

Formulating prior questions for a complex question is a valuable Socratic questioning tool that you can use whenever you face a complicated question. With practice, you will notice that you automatically think of questions that are prior to other questions. You will also learn to recognize when others are failing to consider the complexities in a question.

Focus Your Questions on Domains of Thinking

Complex questions often cover more than one *domain* of thought—more than one discipline or area of knowledge. In this case, you can target your prior questions by exploring the domains of thinking inherent in the question. A complex question might have an economic dimension, or it might have a biological, sociological, cultural, political, ethical, psychological, religious, historical, or some other dimension. For each dimension of thinking inherent in the question, you can formulate questions that force you to consider complexities you otherwise may miss. Consider the following question, some of the domains imbedded in the question, and some of the questions imbedded in those domains.

Complex question: What can be done about the number of people who abuse illegal drugs?

Domains and prior questions:

1. Economic
   - What economic forces support drug use?
   - What can be done to minimize the influence of money involved in drug sales?

2. Political
   - What possible solutions to drug abuse are politically unacceptable?
   - Are there any realistic solutions that the power structure would accept?
   - To what extent does the political structure exacerbate the problem?

3. Social/Sociological
   - What social structures and practices support drug abuse?
   - How does gang membership contribute to drug abuse?
   - How does membership in any group either contribute to the problem or insulate group members from abusing drugs?

4. Psychological
   - How do factors such as stress, individual personality differences, and childhood traumas support drug abuse?
   - What role, if any, does human irrationality play in drug abuse?

5. Biological
   - How do genetics play a role in drug abuse?
   - What biological changes in the body resulting from drug abuse contribute to the problem?

6. Educational
   - What roles are schools and teachers now playing to support or diminish the problem?

7. Religious
   - What can religious institutions do to reduce the incidence of drug abuse?
   - What role are they now playing in regard to the problem?

8. Cultural
   - What cultural beliefs support the drug-abuse problem?
   - What can we learn from cultures that have a low incidence of drug abuse?

5.10 *Think for Yourself*

FORMULATING QUESTIONS WITHIN DOMAINS OF THINKING

Focus on the question: What can be done to significantly improve the health of the ecosystems on Earth? Using the domains listed above, figure out as many domains within the question that you would have to think within to address the complexities in the question. Then formulate as many questions as you can within each domain. (The question you are originally addressing determines the domains within which you need to think.)

When we approach questions by targeting the domains inherent in them, we are able to ask questions such as:

- What are the domains of questions inherent in this complex question?
- Is this person dealing with all the relevant domains within the question?
- Am I leaving out some important domains when reasoning through this issue?

THE QUESTIONING MIND: NEWTON, DARWIN & EINSTEIN

Most people think that genius is the primary determinant of intellectual achievement. Yet three of the all-time greatest thinkers had in common not genius, but a questioning mind. Their intellectual skills and inquisitive drive embodied the essence of critical thinking. Through skilled deep questioning they redesigned our view of the physical universe.

Consider Newton. Uninterested in the set curriculum at Cambridge, at age 19 Newton drew up a list of questions under 45 headings. His title, "*Quaestiones,*" signaled his goal: to question constantly the nature of matter, place, time, and motion.

Newton's style was to slog his way to knowledge. For example, he "bought Descartes's Geometry and read it by himself. When he got over 2 or 3 pages he could understand no farther, then he began again and advanced farther and continued so doing till he made himself master of the whole . . . "

When asked how he had discovered the law of universal gravitation, Newton said, "By thinking on it continually I keep the subject constantly before me and wait till the first dawnings open slowly, by little and little, into a full and clear light."

Darwin's experience and approach were similar. First, he found traditional instruction discouraging. "During my second year at Edinburgh I attended lectures on Geology and Zoology, but they were incredibly dull. The sole effect they produced in me was the determination never as long as I lived to read a book on Geology, or in any way to study the science." He continues: "During the three years which I spent at Cambridge my time was wasted . . . The work was repugnant to me, chiefly from my not being able to see any meaning in [it] . . . "

Like Newton and Einstein, Darwin had a careful mind rather than a quick one: "I have as much difficulty as ever in expressing myself clearly and concisely; and this difficulty has caused me a very great loss of time, but it has had the compensating advantage of forcing me to think long and intently about every sentence, and thus I have been led to see errors in reasoning and in my own observations or those of others."

> "I have no particular talent. I am merely extremely inquisitive."
> Einstein

In pursuing intellectual questions, Darwin relied upon perseverance and continual reflection, rather than memory and quick reflexes. "I have never been able to remember for more than a few days a single date or line of poetry." Instead, he had "the patience to reflect or ponder for any number of years over any unexplained problem." "At no time am I a quick thinker or writer: whatever I have done in science has solely been by long pondering, patience, and industry."

Einstein, for his part, did so poorly in school that when his father asked his son's headmaster what profession his son should adopt, the answer was simply, "It doesn't matter; he'll never make a success of anything." In high school, the regimentation "created in him a deep suspicion of authority. This feeling lasted all his life, without qualification."

Einstein commented that his schooling required "the obedience of a corpse." The effect of the regimented school was a clear-cut reaction by Einstein; he learned "to question and doubt." He concluded: ". . . youth is intentionally being deceived by the state through lies."

> "One of [Einstein's] greatest intellectual gifts, in small matters as well as great, was to strip off the irrelevant frills from a problem."

He showed no signs of being a genius, and as an adult denied that his mind was extraordinary: "I have no particular talent. I am merely extremely inquisitive."

Einstein failed his entrance examination to the Zurich Polytechnic. When he finally passed, "the examinations so constrained his mind that, when he had graduated, he did not want to think about scientific problems for a year." His final exam was so non-distinguished that afterward he was refused a post as an assistant (the lowest grade of postgraduate job).

Exam-taking, then, was not Einstein's forte. Questioning deeply and thinking critically were.

Sources: Quotes about Newton from Westfall (1993); quotes about Darwin from Darwin (1958); quotes about Einstein from Clark (1984) and Snow (1967).

CONCLUSION

Questions play a crucial role in thought. Because there is a sense in which "you think only as well as the questions you ask," you want to force yourself as a developing thinker to focus on the role that questions are playing in your thinking. To what extent are you asking significant questions? To what extent are you able to figure out whether a question is asking for a factual answer, preference, or reasoned judgment? To what extent are you asking questions that follow a disciplined path, leading to rationally defensible answers? To what extent are you able to take apart complex questions, to figure out questions you would have to answer prior to answering those questions? When you are practicing the fundamental questioning steps we have explored in this chapter, you will find yourself progressing as a questioner—and as a thinker.

CHAPTER 6

DISCOVER HOW THE BEST THINKERS LEARN

A man may hear a thousand lectures, and read a thousand volumes, and be at the end of the process very much where he was, as regards knowledge. Something more than merely admitting it in a negative way into the mind is necessary, if it is to remain there. It must not be passively received, but actually and actively entered into, embraced, mastered. The mind must go half-way to meet what comes to it from without.

John Henry Newman, *The Idea of a University* (1852)

The best thinkers are skilled learners. They take charge of their learning. They design it—plan it out. You plan learning by becoming clear as to what your goals are, what questions you have to—or want to—answer, what information you need to get, what concepts you need to learn, and what point of view or perspective you need to adopt. Skilled learners figure out the *logic* of what they are trying to understand. They have strategies for studying well. This chapter covers a number of these strategies—probably more than you can learn all at once. The goal is for you to begin to practice a range of strategies that will take you out of the mainstream of most students—strategies that are effective and powerful.

We begin with 18 ideas expressed simply. The rest of the chapter will give explanations and examples for most of these ideas. The chapter will close with a test you can take to determine your level of proficiency in using powerful learning strategies. The strategies of close reading and substantive writing (two of the most important tools for learning) will be covered in a separate chapter.

18 IDEAS FOR IMPROVING YOUR LEARNING

Idea #1.   Make sure you thoroughly understand the requirements of each class, how it will be taught, and what will be expected of you. Ask questions about the grading policies and ask for advice on how best to prepare for class.

Idea #2.   Become an active learner. Be prepared to work ideas into your thinking by active reading, writing, speaking, and listening.

Idea #3.   Think of each subject you study as a form of thinking. If you are in a history class, your goal should be to think historically; in a chemistry class, to think chemically; and so forth.

Idea #4.   Become a questioner. Engage in lectures and discussions by asking questions. If you don't ask questions, you will probably not discover what you do and do not know.

Idea #5.   Look for interconnections. The content in every class is always a *system* of interconnected ideas, never a random list of things to memorize. Don't memorize like a parrot. Study like a detective, always relating new learning to previous learning.

Idea #6.   Think of your instructor as your coach. Think of yourself as a team member trying to practice the thinking exemplified by your instructor. For example, in an algebra class, think of yourself as going out for the algebra team and your teacher as demonstrating how to prepare for the games (tests).

Idea #7.   Think of the textbook as the thinking of the author. Your job is to think the thinking of the author. The best way to do this is to frequently role-play the author. Explain the main points of the text to another student, as if you were the author.

Idea #8.   Consider class time as a time in which you *practice* thinking within the subject, using the fundamental concepts and principles of the course. Don't sit back passively, waiting for knowledge to fall into your head like rain into a rain barrel. It won't.

Idea #9.   Relate content whenever possible to issues, problems, and practical situations in your life. If you can't connect it to your life, you don't know it.

Idea #10.   Figure out what study and learning skills you need to develop. Practice those skills whenever possible. Recognizing and correcting your weaknesses is a strength.

Idea #11.   Frequently ask yourself: "Can I explain this to someone who is not in this class?" If not, you haven't learned it well enough.

Idea #12.   Identify and elaborate for yourself the key concept of the course during the first two or three class meetings. For example, in a biology course, try explaining what biology is in your own words. Then relate that definition to each segment of what you learn afterward. Fundamental ideas are the basis for all others.

Idea #13.   Routinely ask questions to fill in the missing pieces in your learning. Ask them of yourself and your teacher. Can you elaborate further on idea x? Can you give an example of idea y? If you are not creating everyday examples for ideas, you are not connecting what you are learning to your life.

Idea #14.   Test yourself before you come to class by trying to summarize, orally or in writing, the main points of the previous class meeting. If you cannot summarize the main points, you haven't learned them.

Idea #15.   Learn to test your thinking by using intellectual standards. Ask yourself: Am I being clear? Accurate? Precise? Relevant? Logical? Am I looking for what is most significant?

Idea #16.   Use writing as a way to learn. Write summaries in your own words of important points from the textbook or other reading material. Make up test questions and write out answers to your own questions.

Idea #17.   Frequently evaluate your listening. Are you actively listening for main points? Can you summarize what your instructor is saying in your own words? Can you explain what is meant by key terms?

Idea #18.   Frequently evaluate your reading. Are you reading the textbook actively? Are you asking questions as you read? Can you distinguish what you understand from what you don't?

6.1   *Think for Yourself*

WHERE DO YOU STAND?

To what extent have you "designed" any part of your learning (in high school or college)? Have you ever developed any strategies for learning? Can you name any strategies you use for learning? If you can, how well did it work? If you can't think of any strategies you use to learn, why not? On a scale of 1 to 10, how skilled a learner would you say you are?

EXHIBIT 6.1   *Critical thinkers have confidence in their ability to figure out the logic of anything they choose.*

The spirit of critical thinking

There is a logic to this, and I can figure it out!

THE LOGIC OF X

THE LOGIC OF A COLLEGE AS IT IS

Because you are learning through the medium of college classes, it is helpful to understand the logic of college classes. To understand the logic of college classes, consider college in the light of its history and traditions.

College today is a product of college yesterday. Traditions in college instruction go back hundreds of years. For example, the most common way for professors to try to get students to learn a body of knowledge is to state that body of knowledge in a sequence of lectures, and then to ask students to internalize that knowledge outside of class, largely on their own. Quizzes and examinations are interspersed among the lectures as means of assessing the extent to which students have learned what the lectures covered. Often a quiz or exam is not given for six weeks or more. In this typical class structure, students often use one or both of the following strategies, neither of which is conducive to deep learning:

1. Taking random notes during the lecture (writing down points that might be on the test)

2. Intensive cramming one or two nights before the quiz or test (striving to store a large amount of information in short-term memory).

Under these conditions, students often go from being passive learners to being *desperate* learners, and from being largely inactive learners to being frantic ones.

6.2 *Think for Yourself*

ARE YOU A PASSIVE LEARNER?

To what extent would you say that you follow the traditional college student survival pattern described above (largely passive and periodically frantic)? To what extent do you think this pattern is effective for deep learning? Why have you fallen into this pattern (if you have)? Or, why haven't you fallen into this pattern (if you have not)?

HOW THE BEST STUDENTS LEARN

The ideal way to learn in college has been described in various ways. Almost all of them agree on some important skills and dispositions. Practicing them will enable you to learn as the best students do. They include:

1. proficiency in reading, writing, speaking, and listening

2. acquiring and effectively use significant information, reasoning well, communicating effectively, solving problems, and exercising sound personal and professional judgment

3. proficiency in formulating, using, and assessing goals and purposes, questions and problems, information and data, conclusions and interpretations, concepts and theoretical constructs, assumptions and presuppositions, implications and consequences, and points of view and frames of reference

4. thinking more clearly, accurately, precisely, relevantly, deeply, broadly, logically, and fairly

5. being more intellectually perseverant, intellectually responsible, intellectually disciplined, intellectually humble, intellectually empathic, and intellectually productive

6. acting more reasonably, ethically, and effectively in reasoning through personal and professional issues

7. a lifelong commitment to learning in order to deal effectively with a world of accelerating change, intensifying complexity, and increasing interdependence.

These characteristics and skills will not emerge simply as the result of taking notes in lecture and cramming for quizzes and exams. Therefore, if you value the goals expressed in the above ideals, you will have to conduct yourself differently from the typical student. You will have to establish for yourself personal imperatives that set you apart from your fellow students. You must rise above peer-group expectations (and possibly peer group scorn), and learn for reasons of your own at higher and higher levels.

You must recognize that to gain knowledge, you must construct it in your mind. You must translate it from the thoughts of someone else into your own thoughts. To think it into your mind, you must be able to state it, elaborate it, give examples of it, and illustrate it. You must become proficient in the process of taking ownership of ideas. Ideas may come from lectures, from textbooks, or from other sources. Do not be fooled by the ability to restate ideas in the same words that they were originally expressed by the instructor or text. A parrot, a tape recorder, or a rote memorizer is not a knower. Until you can express an idea in your own words, and give examples of it from your own experience, it is not yours—you do not *know* it.

6.3   *Think for Yourself*

DO YOU OWN THE IDEAL?

Which of the goals stated above do you most identify with? Which the least? Why? Note that goals 3, 4, and 5 presuppose some knowledge of critical thinking. Can you see how these are more specific than the others? Take one of these goals—for example, learning to be more proficient in using concepts and theoretical constructs. How could you begin to incorporate this goal more thoroughly into your strategies for learning?

THE DESIGN OF A COLLEGE CLASS

Though all college students take college classes, few master the logic of any academic discipline they study. Few students understand how college classes are designed or what challenges they will face in the learning process. Here are some important background facts:

1. Every field of study is subject to continual and (in most cases) enormous expansion.

2. Textbooks, which are the basis for most college classes, are getting larger and larger, and lectures are, in turn, tending to "cover" more and more content.

3. Most students do not know how to internalize large bodies of content independently.

4. Most students use periodic cramming to pass their exams.

5. Most students read, write, and listen at a superficial level.

6. Most students lack intellectual standards by which to assess their own thinking and learning.

7. Many colleges assess faculty through what amounts to popularity contests, with student evaluations of faculty heavily influenced by the grade they expect to get.

6.4 *Think for Yourself*

How would you rate yourself on items 3, 4, 5, and 6 above? Comment on each separately. Then comment on the implications of your answers. For example, for number 5, if you read at a superficial level, what is a consequence of your limited reading ability?

The facts outlined above have a number of important implications:

1. Most college exams are constructed so that the majority of students in class can cram well enough to pass them. (If a significant number of students were to fail the exams, the instructor would get low evaluations from the students.)

2. Grade inflation—the practice of giving higher and higher grades for the same level of work—is rampant.

3. Most students probably could not pass the final exam for a course six months after the course ends.

4. Most students do not learn to think in the broader context of the course (for example, they take history but do not learn to think historically; they take science but do not learn to think scientifically).

An important implication of these facts is that college generates a great deal of self-deception: Instructors who certify students as understanding subjects that they do not in fact understand; students who forget most of what they temporarily cram into their head but who think they are learning; accrediting teams and accrediting departments that show no real evidence that students are learning what these teams and departments claim they are learning.

This book is written for students who want to do more than survive in college. It is for those who want their college education to help them become effective lifelong learners and thinkers.

6.5 *Think for Yourself*

To develop as a critical thinker, you must be willing to face the fact that humans engage in a great deal of self-deception. Self-deception in college is part of the broader problem of self-deception in human life. Do you see any ways in which you have deceived yourself in terms of your learning? In your personal relationships? Do you see any ways in which your high school teachers deceived themselves? Do you see any ways in which your friends are deceiving themselves?

Your first goal in any course should be to understand how the course you are taking is designed. This includes figuring out the logic of the course through an analysis of the course syllabus, the textbook, and how the instructor has introduced the course. First, what are the official requirements of the class? What is the assigned reading, writing, and testing or assessment? When will papers, if any, be due? When will quizzes and tests occur? These are some obvious requirements to clarify for yourself.

However you study, you want to meet the formal requirements at a high level. But there is something far more important than getting good grades. It is learning to think within the disciplines you study, internalizing core concepts, and gaining the most basic insights that underlie the disciplines. Your goal should be to make the mode of thinking in the discipline a permanent part of your thinking. To aim at these high goals, you should routinely ask and pursue three interconnected key questions:

1. What is the central underlying concept of the course or subject?

2. What form(s) of thinking is (are) essential to this course or subject?

3. How can I begin to think within the logic of the subject?

Let us consider these questions in order.

FIGURE OUT THE UNDERLYING CONCEPT OF YOUR COURSES

At first it may appear that the sequence of items a course covers are random bits and pieces of information. The course may seem to lack unity. But virtually all courses do have some inherent unity that, when understood, ties everything in the course together like a tapestry. You can usually discover this unity in foundational concepts that define the subject and its goals.

For example, if you understand history, you understand that historical accounts are determined by individual historians who are looking at a specific time period in the past, at a specific set of events, from a specific point of view. You understand that the historical thinking covered in the textbook and lectures are products of a particular historian's historical thought. You will then read the textbook and listen to the lectures in a special way, seeking components of a particular historical perspective. You will recognize that, to understand any written history, you must understand the point of view, the perspective of the historian.

You should be able to identify the:

1. historical *goals* or purposes

2. historical *questions* or problems

3. specific selection of historical *events* the historian considers relevant to the historical questions he is addressing

4. specific *interpretations* of those events (and their significance)

5. theoretical *concepts* that play a central role in the historian's interpretations of events

6. underlying *assumptions* that define the historian's perspective

7. *implications* of the historical events for the future

8. *point of view* that shapes the historical reasoning throughout.

If, in addition, we recognize that we all do historical thinking every day of our lives, history takes on a new meaning. Each and every day of our lives, we use in our thinking a story that entails our personal history (a story created by our own mind). That story, or the way we view our past, determines the decisions we make today and the plans we make for the future. In developing our own personal history, we formulate our own historical assumptions, concepts, and point of view. Because of the way we define history, we ask certain questions with certain purposes in mind. We make certain inferences based on information we see as important in our past. And there are implications that follow from our historical perspective—from the way we define and describe our "history."

When you see history in this richly interconnected way, you look for the historical goals and questions that define the construction of a given historical account. You notice what events are included but also look for what is left out of the history. You look at the key historical conclusions the historian comes to, the key assumptions made, the underlying historical point of view. Most students, however, never learn what it means to think historically. They never learn to take command of their **historical thinking**. They lack the organizing idea behind the discipline of history. They lack insight into the logic of historical thinking. As a result, they never learn to critique the historical thinking they do about their own lives, nor the historical thinking that underlies historical texts.

Consider another subject: economics. If we understand *scarcity* as the underlying concept in economics, we study economics in a special way. We see that all the other concepts that economists use are related to this central point behind economics: that it is not possible for any one of us to have everything we want (the fact of scarcity) and, as a result, all of us have to give up some things to get others. What people are willing to give up to get something else forms the basis for their economic decision-making. *Power* enters economics when some people control what is scarce and highly desired. They thereby cause others to make sacrifices in order to gain access to what is scarce.

Behind every discipline are organizing ideas. Here are the most basic organizing ideas behind a few other disciplines:

- *Mathematics* is the development of a language for quantification.
- *Algebra* is arithmetic with unknowns.
- *Sociology* is the study of how the thinking and behavior of humans is shaped by the groups in which they are members.
- *Physics* is the study of mass and energy and the interrelations between the two.
- *Philosophy* is the study of ultimate questions and their possible answers.
- *Biochemistry* is the study of the chemistry of life at the molecular level.

6.6 *Think for Yourself*

GETTING THE KEY IDEA

For practice, choose a discipline and consider its most basic idea (e.g., economics, anthropology, astronomy, etc.). Explain that idea to a friend. Encourage him or her to ask you questions. See if you can explain the importance of understanding the underlying idea behind a subject as a way to begin to integrate all that you learn about it.

FIGURE OUT THE FORM OF THINKING ESSENTIAL TO A COURSE OR SUBJECT

The organizing concept behind a course is typically the same as the organizing concept behind a subject or discipline. If you have worked it into your own thinking, then you have command of one of the eight central structures that define a *form of thought*. Each form of thought answers these questions about the eight elements of thought in a slightly different way.

1. What are the *goals* or objectives of the course or discipline?
2. What *questions* or problems will be central?
3. What *concepts* will be fundamental?
4. What *information* will I need to reason well within the subject?
5. What *point of view* or frame of reference do I need to learn to reason within?
6. What *assumptions* define the course or discipline?
7. What kinds of *conclusions* will I need to learn how to reason to?
8. What are the payoffs (*implications*) of reasoning well within this discipline?

Since each subject has a corresponding form of thought, each of your classes offers an invitation to you to think within one or more of those forms. By understanding the form of thought that defines the subject you actually think within the discipline, in a way that is similar to experts in the field. Consider the following thinking on the part of a student taking a course in history.

> To do well in this course, I must begin to think *historically*. I must read the textbook not as a bunch of disconnected stuff to remember but instead as the thinking of a historian. I must begin to think like a historian myself. I must begin to be clear about historical purposes. (What are historians trying to accomplish?) I must begin to ask historical questions (and recognize the historical questions being asked in the lectures and textbook). I must begin to sift through historical information, drawing some historical conclusions. I must begin to question where historical information comes from.
>
> I must notice the historical interpretations historians form to give meaning to historical information. I must question those interpretations (at least sufficiently to understand them). I must begin to question the implications of various historical interpretations and begin to see how historians reason to their conclusions. I must begin to look at the world as historians do, to develop a historical viewpoint.
>
> I will read each chapter in the textbook looking explicitly for the elements of thought in that chapter. I will actively ask historical questions in class from the critical-thinking perspective. I will begin to pay attention to my own historical thinking in my everyday life. In short, I will try to make historical thinking a more explicit and prominent part of my thinking.

Students who approach history classes as historical thinking begin to understand the historical dimension of other subjects as well. For example, they begin to recognize that every subject itself has a history and that the present state of the subject is a product of its historical evolution. What is more, historically thinking students notice the overlap between history as a study of the relatively recent past of humans (the last 30,000 years), and the much longer history of humans (canvassed in anthropology). They are able to place these last 30,000 years (which seem like such a long time when we first think about it) into the larger historical perspective of anthropology, which begins its study of humans some 4.4 million years ago, when our ancestors were small, hairy, apelike creatures who used tools such as digging sticks and clubs, walked upright, carried their tools, and lived on plant food.

What is more, they see this longer history as breaking down into stages: from hunting and gathering civilizations to agricultural civilizations to industrial civilizations to post-industrial civilizations. And that is not all. They then are able to place this historical perspective into a still larger historical view by shifting from anthropological thinking to geographical thinking. They realize that human history is itself a small part of a much older history, that of mammals, and that the age of mammals was preceded by an age of reptiles, and that age by the age of coal plants, and that by the age of fish, and that by the age of mollusks. They then can take the next step and grasp that geological history, even though it reaches back thousands of millions of years, is comparatively short when compared to that of the solar system, and that of the solar system is comparatively short when compared to the galaxy, and that of the galaxy is comparatively short when compared to the universe itself.

The capacity to think historically in larger and larger time spans continues to develop as the study of all subjects is transformed by a developing sense of the drama of time itself. Historical thinkers then are able to shift from history to prehistory, from prehistory to anthropological history, from anthropological history to geological history, and from geological history to astronomical history. In this ever-expanding perspective, the history of human knowledge is pitifully short: a millisecond geologically, a milli-millisecond astronomically. Only a second ago—astronomically speaking—did a species emerge: *Homo sapiens*, which adapts the world to itself and creates the conditions to which it itself must adapt, in new and unpredictable ways. Only a millisecond ago did a species emerge that has the capacity, but not the propensity, to think critically.

6.7   *Think for Yourself*

DEVELOPING YOUR THINKING

Examine in detail the "quote" on the previous page from a student thinking about history. Write out some thinking of your own about any subject you are studying. If you wish, simply adapt the example to your subject, but try to begin to see how each of the parts fits together and contributes to an organized way to begin to understand not only a body of content but also the learning process itself.

Next, read and explain to a classmate or a friend what you wrote. Encourage him or her to ask you questions whenever what you say is not clear. Only when you can accurately explain the logic of a course in your own words and elaborate on that logic can you begin to use it in your thinking. Finally, think about how your thinking within this discipline can help you gain insights into other disciplines as well.

THINK WITHIN THE LOGIC OF THE SUBJECT

Once you have some sense of the big picture in a course, begin to plan your learning in parts, in light of the order or sequence in which content is being presented in the class and in the textbook. Then go to class armed with questions you generate by reading your class notes and the textbook. You also might read encyclopedia entries for help with the basic logic of a subject. Some possible starting questions are:

What is the main goal of studying this subject?

What are people in this field trying to accomplish?

What kinds of questions do they ask? What kinds of problems do they try to solve?

What sort of information or data do they gather?

How do they go about gathering information in ways that are distinctive to this field?

What is the most basic idea, concept, or theory in this field?

How should studying this field affect my view of the world?

How are the products of this field used in everyday life?

These questions can be contextualized for any given class day, chapter in the textbook, and dimension of study. For example, on any given day you might ask one or more of the following questions:

What is our main goal today?

What are we trying to accomplish?

What kinds of questions are we asking? What kinds of problems are we trying to solve?

What sort of information or data do we need?

How can we get that information?

What is the most basic idea, concept, or theory we need to understand to solve the problem we are considering?

How should we look at this problem?

How does this problem relate to everyday life?

6.8 *Think for Yourself*

ASKING GOOD QUESTIONS

Write out a series of questions that reflect the spirit of the questions immediately above for a class you are taking. Compare your questions with the questions of another student.

A CASE: THE LOGIC OF BIOCHEMISTRY

Let us now take one discipline and examine its logic by analyzing some key passages from the kind of text you might find in a book on the subject.

[In biochemistry] attention is directed to the problems of finding out how molecular events underlie macroscopic phenomena, with special reference to the modes of action of vitamins, drugs, and genetic factors. One kind of job that biochemists undertake is, of course, to isolate compounds from living things and determine their structures. In this they share the preoccupation of other kinds of biologists with spatial form.

Biochemistry includes a sort of submicroscopic anatomy that elucidates structure on the minute scale of molecules. The classical anatomists cut up bodies to describe the parts of which they are made insofar as they are visible to the naked eye. Microscopy revealed a whole new world of structure and organization smaller than this, and . . . cells became the focus of interest. With the advance of chemistry, it gradually became possible to tackle biological architecture even on the molecular scale.

The grand strategy remains the same—a better understanding of living things in terms of their constituent parts. The tactics, however, . . . depend on the order of size of the parts being examined. For gross anatomy, the scalpel is appropriate; for cellular structure the microscope; for parts as small as molecules, the relevant techniques are those we call chemical. . . . Seen in this light, biochemistry is the logical extrapolation of dissection. The idea is epitomized in the expression "molecular biology" . . . .

Merely to determine structure, however, is far from the summit of the ambitions of biochemists. They are interested not only in what the constituents of living things are like, but also in what they do—in the way that chemical processes underlie the more obvious vital manifestations. The continuous change that is one of the most striking characteristics of life rests on unceasing chemical activity inside living organisms. Biochemistry thus continues another classical tradition of biology in linking form with function. Like anatomy divorced from physiology, static divorced from dynamic biochemistry . . . fails to . . . increase man's power over nature. Life, after all, is a matter of keeping events going, not only of maintaining structures; and biochemists seek to elucidate events as well as structures by isolation.

By and large, then, while the techniques of biochemistry are chemical, its problems are the basic ones of biology. Chemistry is its means, biology its end. It is the extreme extension of that approach to the phenomena of life that seeks to explain them in terms of the sub-units of which living organisms are composed. Of this kind of biological analysis, it represents the ultimate state—ultimate because pushing the analysis a stage further, from the molecular level down to the atomic, leaves no characteristically biological kind of organization, the atoms being the same in the inorganic realm. . . . Biochemistry concentrates on the farthest removal from immediate biological reality; insofar as it concerns itself with molecules, it remains remote from intact organisms. Data on the molecular level have to be related to observations made on more highly organized, less disrupted systems. (Jevons, 1964)

Biochemical Goals

It is clear from this passage that the goals of biochemistry are to determine the biochemical foundations of life. It aims to understand biology, and to answer biological questions, through the chemistry that exists and interacts in living things.

Biochemical Questions

From this passage we can see that biochemistry is concerned with fundamental questions of biology: What are we made of? How do our bodies work? What is life? More particularly, for biochemists the questions are: How do molecular events underlie macroscopic phenomena of life? What compounds underlie living things? What is their structure? And what do they do? We can assume that biochemists ask specific questions like these: How do vitamins work in the body? How do drugs? How do genetic factors influence both? We can go on to consider questions such as: What molecular parts of living organisms are the special concern of biochemistry? (What are proteins, carbohydrates, and fats? What do they do? What are nucleic acids? What do they do?) How do enzymes catalyze virtually every reaction in living organisms? What is the role of enzymes in biological thought? How can we understand the biochemical unity of living matter? What is the similarity of yeast and muscle? What do proteins do inside living organisms? How can we correlate observations made at different levels of organization? How can we use drugs and other chemicals in medicine?

Biochemical Information

From the questions above, we can begin to see the kinds of information that biochemists seek: information about proteins and enzymes as the kind of chemical units out of which life is constructed, about the process of catalysis as the means by which key chemical reactions essential to the construction of life take place, information about artificial lifelike reactions (such as the study of a single enzyme reaction in a test tube), information about the variety of enzymes in living cells, about the molecular structures within cells, about multi-enzyme systems and how they operate, and so on.

Biochemical Judgments

The passage we read suggests that biochemists seek to make judgments about the important processes and structures in biology that exist at the chemical level: properties of enzymes, their protein nature, the agents that make things happen in living organisms, metabolism, and in general the complex process of maintenance and growth of which life basically consists.

Biochemical Concepts

Our thinking thus far indicates we have to understand some essential concepts to understand the logic of biochemistry: the concept of life processes being organized in levels (the molecular level, the subcellular particle level, the cellular level, the organ level, and the level of the total organism); the concept of life structures and life processes; the concept of the dynamics of life; the concepts of proteins, enzymes, catalysis; the concept of metabolism as reducible to a consecutive series of enzyme-catalyzed reactions; the concept of the unity of life processes amid a diversity of life forms; and so on.

Biochemical Assumptions

From reading this text, we can see that some key assumptions behind biochemical thinking are: that there are biochemical foundations to life, that these foundations are found at the molecular level, that the techniques of chemistry are most fitting for the study of life at the molecular level, that it is possible to use chemical concepts to explain life, that it is possible to analyze and discover the structure and dynamics of isolated molecules and events on the molecular scale, that proteins and enzymes are key agents in fundamental life processes, that enzyme reactions are crucial to understanding life, that it is possible to use chemicals in medicine and everyday life planning.

Biochemical Implications

The present logic of biochemistry has specific and general implications. The specific implications have to do with the kind of questioning, the kind of information-gathering and information-interpreting processes that biochemists are using today. (For example, the state of the field implies the importance of focusing questions and analysis on the concepts above, of seeking key answers at the molecular level, involving proteins, enzymes, and catalyzed chemical reactions.) The general implications are that, if modern biochemical theory is on the right track, we will be increasingly able to enhance human and other forms of life and diminish disease, through treatment with chemicals.

Biochemical Point of View

The biochemical viewpoint is directed at the molecular level of life and sees that level as providing the most fundamental disclosures about the nature, function, and foundations of life. It sees the essential methods of study to be chemical. It sees the essential problems to be biological. It sees life processes at the molecular level to be highly unified and consistent and life process at the whole-animal level to be highly diversified. It considers processes at the molecular level to be key, along with genetics, to the explanation of diversity at the macro level.

When you understand the basic logic of biochemistry, you will bring questions to class that are "biochemical" versions of the following generic questions:

What is our main goal today?

What are we trying to accomplish?

What kinds of questions are we asking? What kinds of problems are we trying to solve?

What sort of information or data do we need?

How can we get that information?

What is the most basic idea, concept, or theory that we need to understand to solve the problem we are trying to answer right now?

How should we look at this problem?

How does this problem relate to everyday life?

Sometimes courses seem to jump randomly from one topic to another: on one day the class may be focusing on catalysis, on another day on big molecules, on another day on subcellular particles, on another coenzymes, on another energy transactions, on another DNA. Understanding the overall logic of biochemistry will help you make sense of where you are, why it is significant, and how to relate it to what came before and what will come after.

MAKE THE DESIGN OF THE COURSE WORK FOR YOU

At the beginning of any course you take, ask yourself: How am I going to learn so as to make the design of the class work for me? How am I going to get actively involved? How am I going to develop essential insights, understandings, knowledge, and abilities? How am I going to learn to reason my way to the answers to questions in the field?

You should know from the beginning what in general is going to be happening in the course, how you are going to be assessed, and what you should be striving to achieve. To put it another way, you should know from the start what will be happening in class most of the time and what exactly is expected of you daily.

You should study the syllabus, looking for an explanation of the concept of the course, the organization and plan for the course, the requirements, and any other important characteristics. As you proceed through the course, you should try to integrate all the features of the course into a comprehensive understanding, in order to see the course, and the subject, as a comprehensive whole.

6.9   *Think for Yourself*

WRITING OUT THE LOGIC OF A COURSE

Look again at the example of biochemistry and at the summary of an America History course on pages 119–120. Using these as a guide, write out the logic of a course you are now taking. Use textbooks, encyclopedias, and other resources as references. You also might refer to Exhibits 6.2 through 6.7, which give the basic logic of several subjects.

EXHIBIT 6.2   *The logic of science.*

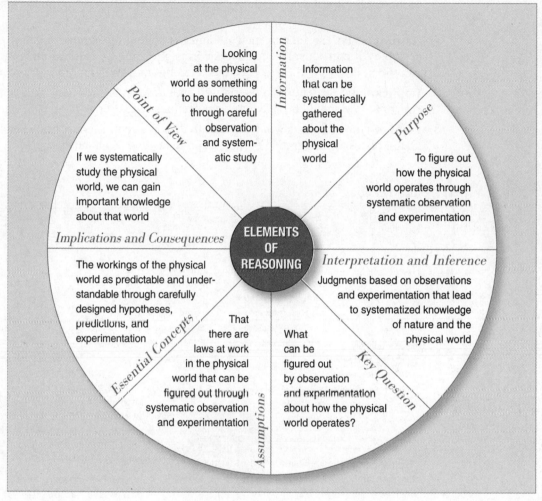

Sample Course: American History, 1600–1800

1. **Purpose:** The purpose of the course is to think historically about the major trends and patterns in American history, 1600 to 1800.

2. **Key question:** What are the major patterns and trends in American history from 1600 to 1800?

3. **Information:** The students will work with a variety of primary and secondary sources of information: records, diaries, letters, biographies, newspapers, and historical accounts from textbooks and articles.

4. **Skills of interpretation:** The students will learn how to gather and interpret data from a variety of historical sources.

5. **Essential concepts:** The students will need to learn how to use basic historical, economic, political, and religious concepts, as well as those from social life and values.

6. **Assumptions:** The fundamental assumption behind this course is that it is possible for entry-level students to gain insights into the patterns and events in American life from 1600 to 1800 that shed light on contemporary problems.

7. **Implications:** Students who reason well about events in 17th- and 18th-century American life should be able to see connections with events in the 20th century.

8. **Point of view:** Students will learn how to reason as both a conservative and a liberal historian, integrating economic, political, and social analyses.

EXHIBIT 6.3 *The logic of history.*

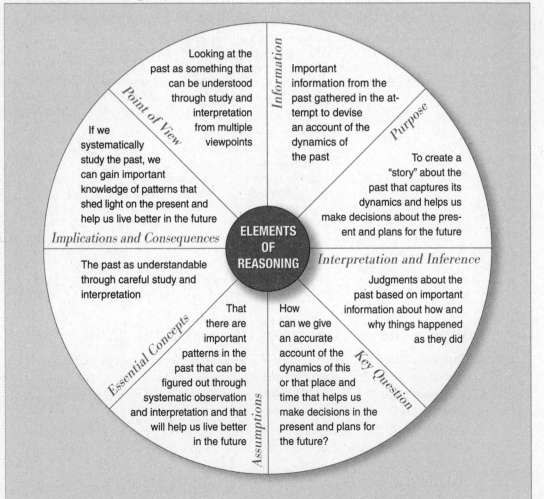

6.10   *Think for Yourself*

EVALUATING THE LOGIC OF A COURSE

Examine the course description below for a course in Critical Thinking. To what extent do you think it is based on the conception of critical thinking in this book? Support your conclusions with reasons.

CLASS SYLLABUS: CRITICAL THINKING

Key Concept of the Course

This course is entirely and exclusively concerned with the development of potential capacities that all of you have, even though you have not developed them—capacities in that part of your mind known as your "intellect." Most people don't develop their intellect. They use it ineffectively and often mainly to rationalize or justify their infantile or egocentric drives. Most people are not in charge of their ideas and thinking. Most of their ideas have come into their mind without their having thought about them. They unconsciously pick up what the people around them think and what is on television or in the movies. They unconsciously absorb ideas from the family in which they were reared. They are the products, through and through, of forces they did not choose. They reflect those forces without understanding them. They are like puppets that don't know their strings are being pulled.

To become a critical thinker is to reverse that process—by learning skills that enable one to take charge of the ideas that run one's life. It is to think consciously, deliberately, and skillfully in ways that transform oneself. It is to begin to remake one's own mind. It is to run one's inner workings and to understand the "system" one is running. It is to develop a mind that is analogous to the body of a person who is physically fit. It is like becoming an excellent dancer who can perform any dance that can be choreographed. It is like being a puppet that discovers the strings and figures out how to gain control of the way each is pulled.

Whenever you are doing a task in or for the class, ask yourself: Would an independent observer, watching you closely, conclude that you are engaged in taking charge of your mind, your ideas, and your thinking, or would such a person conclude that you are merely going through the motions of formally doing an assignment, trying to get by with some memorized formula or procedure?

General Plan

The class will focus on practice, not on lecture. It will emphasize your figuring out things by using your own mind, not memorizing what is in a textbook. On a typical class day, you will be in small groups practicing "disciplined" thinking. For every class day you will have a written assignment that involves disciplined thinking. Outside of class, you will enter disciplined reflections into a journal, using a special format. You will be responsible for regularly assessing your own work with criteria and standards discussed in class. If at any time in the semester you feel unsure about your grade, you should request an assessment from the professor.

EXHIBIT 6.4   *The logic of business.*

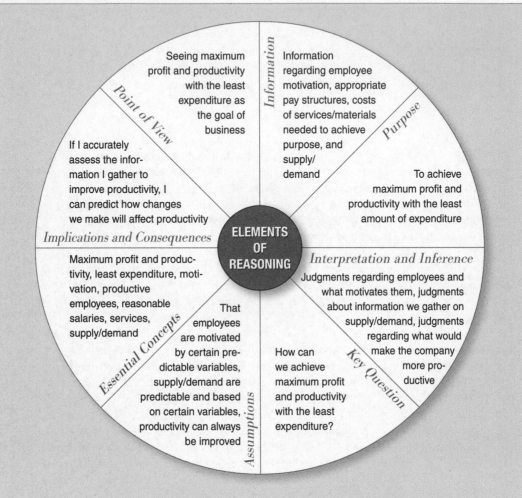

The diagram shows a wheel divided into six segments around a central hub labeled "ELEMENTS OF REASONING."

Point of View: Seeing maximum profit and productivity with the least expenditure as the goal of business

Information: Information regarding employee motivation, appropriate pay structures, costs of services/materials needed to achieve purpose, and supply/demand

Purpose: To achieve maximum profit and productivity with the least amount of expenditure

Implications and Consequences: If I accurately assess the information I gather to improve productivity, I can predict how changes we make will affect productivity

Interpretation and Inference: Judgments regarding employees and what motivates them, judgments about information we gather on supply/demand, judgments regarding what would make the company more productive

Essential Concepts: Maximum profit and productivity, least expenditure, motivation, productive employees, reasonable salaries, services, supply/demand

Assumptions: That employees are motivated by certain predictable variables, supply/demand are predictable and based on certain variables, productivity can always be improved

Key Question: How can we achieve maximum profit and productivity with the least expenditure?

READING, WRITING, SPEAKING, LISTENING, AND THINKING

Let us turn now to reading, writing, speaking, and listening. Clearly, these activities are important to your success as a student.

If you are a skilled *reader*, you are able to master a subject from a textbook alone, without benefit of lectures or class discussion. Many excellent readers have become educated through reading alone.

Or consider *writing*. The art of writing well forces us to make explicit the ideas we understand and how we understand those ideas in relation to each other. Often, we have

EXHIBIT 6.5   *The logic of abnormal psychology.*

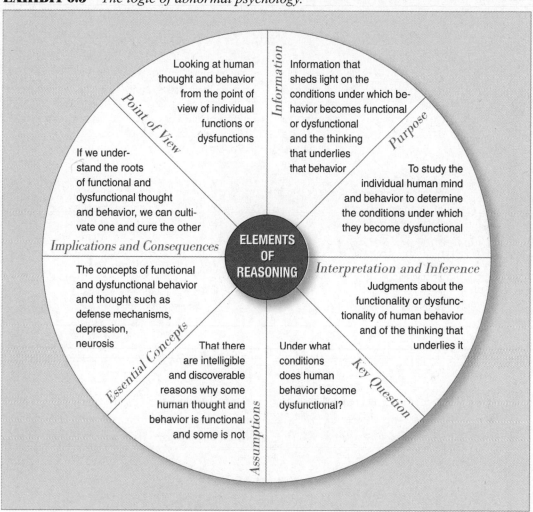

the illusion that we understand an idea, until we try to place our understanding into written words. Suddenly we see problems. We discover that we cannot state what we think we understand clearly, or we have trouble elaborating, or we find it difficult to give apt examples or illustrations. Writing to learn is a powerful tool for learning deeply and well. Those who cannot write out what they are learning are often poor learners. Chapter 7 will focus on reading and writing in depth.

Speaking is another powerful tool in learning. By explaining to another person what we are learning, we can often take our learning to a deeper level. This is the meaning of the saying, "In teaching you will learn." Discussing your understanding of ideas with other learners is a powerful tool in developing your understanding of those ideas, but only when the dialog is disciplined. Poorly discussed ideas may result in "activated

EXHIBIT 6.6   *The logic of philosophy.*

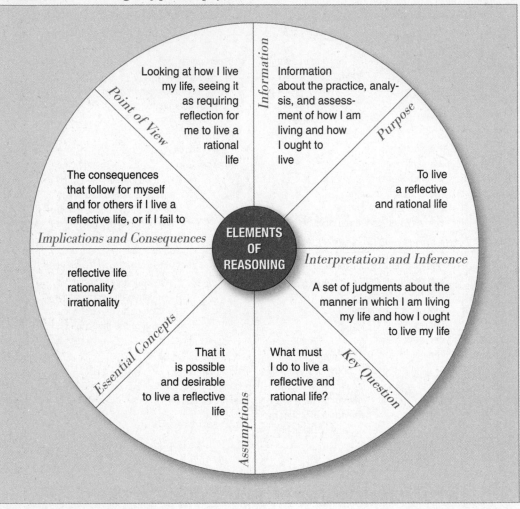

ignorance," the illusion that we understand when we do not. Then speaking solidifies misunderstanding rather than furthers understanding. For this reason, we must discipline our thinking, so that we express ourselves clearly and precisely, so that we use concepts justifiably, so that we ask relevant and significant questions, so that we assess our learning as we "teach."

Listening well is probably the least understood of the four modalities of communication we are considering. Much student listening is unskilled—passive, associational, unquestioned, and superficial. Poor listening leads not only to incomplete internalization but also to blatant misunderstanding.

Reading, writing, speaking, and listening are all modes of *thinking*. Your primary goals as a student should be to learn how to think like a good reader (while

EXHIBIT 6.7 *The logic of sociology.*

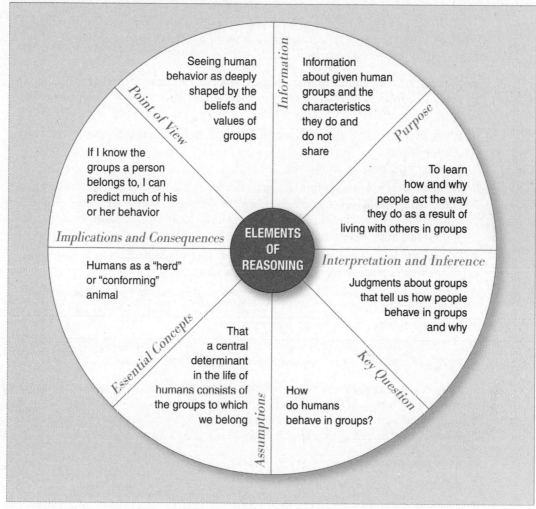

reading), like a good writer (while writing), like an effective speaker (while speaking), and like an insightful listener (while listening). These four different modes of thinking are highly interrelated, and learning how to take charge of one of them will help you take charge of the other three. This is true because each is a form of thinking, and all forms of thinking share characteristics—as we emphasize throughout this book.

Whenever you are reading, writing, speaking, or listening, you want your thinking to be clear, precise, accurate, relevant, responsive to complexity, as broad as the issue requires, and focused on the appropriate point(s) of view. Good readers, writers, speakers, listeners, and thinkers have agendas, deal with questions and problems, make assumptions, utilize information and concepts, make inferences and draw conclusions, consider implications and consequences, and reason within a point of view.

Consider writing as an example. Good writing reflects command of the elements of reasoning and intellectual standards; poor writing reflects poor understanding of the elements of thought and poor application of the standards. Consider:

- When you write sentences that can be interpreted in many different ways, and you do not make clear which meaning you intend, your writing and thinking are vague or confused.

- When you do not give examples and illustrations to make your point clear, your writing shows that you do not know how to clarify your thought (or you do not see the importance of doing so).

- When you do not use appropriate transitional words and critical vocabulary to make clear the logical relations between the sentences you write, you make evident that you are not thinking in terms of the logic of your thought, and that you do not fully understand the structure of your own reasoning.

- When you do not analyze key concepts and show readers their logic, your writing shows that you are weak at conceptual analysis.

- When you do not make it clear what question or issue you are dealing with, or when you drift from one issue to another, your writing reveals that you lack intellectual focus and a sense of relevance.

- When you make sweeping judgments about a point of view that you have not analyzed empathetically, you demonstrate intellectual arrogance.

Take reading as another example. When you have difficulty comprehending what you are reading it is clear that you lack understanding of the elements of reasoning and the intellectual standards—or of how to apply them to what you read. Or it shows deficiencies on the part of the writer. You should be able to identify:

- the *agenda* (underlying purpose) of a text
- the *key questions* the author is addressing
- the *key assumptions* that the author makes
- the *key information* the author uses in reasoning through the issues
- the *key concepts* that guide the author's thinking
- the *main conclusions* that the writer arrives at
- the *key implications* of those conclusions
- the *point of view* of the author.

If you cannot identify all of these elements, consider carefully whether the deficiency lies in the writing or in your analysis.

Speaking and listening can be analyzed in a similar way. Let us now apply these principles to reading an article or essay.

FIGURE OUT THE LOGIC
OF AN ARTICLE OR ESSAY

To understand an essay or article, you must be able to identify the elements of the author's reasoning. Once you have done this, you can evaluate that reasoning by using intellectual standards.

6.11   *Think for Yourself*

ANALYZING THE LOGIC OF AN ARTICLE

Select an article (chapter or essay) that you have been assigned to read for class. Using the template below, identify its logic. When you become practiced in using this approach, you will have a powerful intellectual tool for understanding the reasoning of any author.

THE LOGIC OF "(NAME OF THE ARTICLE)"

1. The main *purpose* of this article is _____. *(Here you are trying to state as accurately as possible the author's purpose for writing the article. What was the author trying to accomplish?)*

2. The key *question* that the author is addressing is _____. *(Your goal is to figure out the key question that was in the author's mind when he or she wrote the article. What was the key question the article addressed?)*

3. The most important *information* in this article is _____. *(Identify the key information the author used, or presupposed, in the article to support his or her main arguments. Here you are looking for facts, experiences, and data the author is using to support his or her conclusions.)*

4. The main *inferences/conclusions* in this article are _____. *(Identify the most important conclusions the author comes to and presents in the article.)*

5. The key *concept(s)* we need to understand in this article is (are) _____. By these concepts, the author means _____. *(To identify these concepts, ask yourself: What are the most important ideas that you would have to understand to understand the author's line of reasoning? Then elaborate briefly on what the author means by these concepts.)*

6. The main *assumption(s)* underlying the author's thinking is (are) _____. *(What is the author taking for granted that might be questioned? The assumptions are generalizations that the author does not think he or she has to defend, and they are usually unstated. This is where the author's thinking logically begins.)*

7. a. If we take this line of reasoning seriously, the *implications* are _____. *(What consequences are likely to follow if people take the author's reasoning seriously? Follow*

the logical implications of the author's position. You should include implications that the author states, if you believe them to be logical, but you should also do your best thinking to determine on your own what you think the implications are.)

b. If we fail to take this line of reasoning seriously, the *implications* are _____. *(What consequences are likely to follow if people ignore or reject the author's reasoning?)*

8. The main *point(s) of view* presented in this article is (are) _____. *(The main question you are trying to answer here is: What is the author looking at, and how is he or she seeing it? For example, in this book we are looking at education and seeing it as involving the development of intellectual skills. We are also looking at learning as the responsibility of students.)*

FIGURE OUT THE LOGIC OF A TEXTBOOK

Just as you can understand an essay or article by analyzing the parts of the author's reasoning, you can also figure out the logic of a textbook by focusing on the parts of the author's reasoning within the textbook. To understand the elements of a textbook author's reasoning, use the template given in Think for Yourself 6.12.

6.12 *Think for Yourself*

FIGURING OUT THE LOGIC OF A TEXTBOOK

Choose a textbook from a class you are taking. Using the template below, analyze its logic. Imagine you are doing this for a person who is new to the field of study, and be as detailed as you need to be to help that person understand the logic of the textbook.

1. The main *purpose* of this textbook is _____. *(Here you are trying to determine the author's purpose for writing the textbook. What was the author trying to accomplish?)*

2. The key *question(s)* that the author is addressing in the textbook is (are) _____. *(You are trying to figure out the key question(s) that were in the author's mind when he or she wrote the textbook. What key question does the textbook answer? Here, you might identify the broadest question the textbook answers, along with the most important sub-questions it focuses on.)*

3. The most important kinds of *information* in this textbook are _____. *(Identify the types of information the author uses in the textbook to support his or her main arguments. These might include research results, observations, examples, or experience.)*

4. The main *inferences/conclusions* in this textbook are _____. *(Identify the most important conclusions the author comes to and presents in the textbook. What are the*

most important conclusions the author presents—conclusions that, if you understand them, shed light on key beliefs in the field?)

5. The key *concept(s)* we need to understand in this textbook is (are) _____. By these concepts, the author means _____. *(To identify these concepts, ask yourself: What are the most important ideas you would have to understand to understand the textbook? Then elaborate on what the author means by these basic concepts. Begin with the most fundamental concept presented, such as "science," "biology," or "psychology." These usually can be found in the first chapter. Then identify other significant concepts that are tied to the most fundamental one.)*

6. The main *assumption(s)* underlying the author's thinking is (are) _____. *(What is the author taking for granted that might be questioned? The assumptions are usually generalizations that the author does not think he or she has to defend. They are sometimes stated explicitly in the first chapter.)*

7. a. If people take the textbook seriously, the *implications* are _____. *(What consequences are likely to follow if readers take the textbook seriously? Follow the logical implications of the information/ideas in the textbook. You should include implications that the author argues for, if you believe them to be well-founded, but you should also do your best thinking to determine on your own what you think the implications are.)*

   b. If people fail to take the textbook seriously, the *implications* are _____. *(What consequences are likely to follow if the author's thinking is ignored in a situation when it is relevant?)*

8. The main *point(s) of view* presented in this textbook is (are) _____. *(The main question you are trying to answer here is: What is the author looking at, and how is he or she seeing it? For example, the author might be looking at science and seeing it as "our main tool in helping us better understand the physical world and how it operates.")*

CRITERIA FOR EVALUATING AN AUTHOR'S REASONING

Now that you have analyzed the logic of an article and a textbook, you are ready to assess the author's reasoning. To do this, you will focus on how well the author uses each of the elements of reasoning. Use your analysis from Think for Yourself 6.11 or 6.12. Review each of the elements of the author's reasoning and evaluate them using the intellectual standards outlined here:

1. Focusing on the author's *purpose:* Is the purpose well stated? Is it clear and justifiable?

2. Focusing on the key *question* that the written piece answers: Is the question at issue well stated (or clearly implied)? Is it clear and unbiased? Does the way the

question is stated do justice to the complexity of the matter at issue? Are the question and purpose directly relevant to each other?

3. Focusing on the most important *information* the author presents: Does the writer cite relevant evidence, experiences, and other information essential to the issue? Is the information accurate and directly relevant to the question at issue? Does the writer address the complexities of the issue?

4. Focusing on the most fundamental *concepts* that are at the heart of the author's reasoning: Does the writer clarify key concepts when necessary? Are the concepts used justifiably?

5. Focusing on the author's *assumptions:* Does the writer show a sensitivity to what he or she is taking for granted or assuming (insofar as those assumptions might reasonably be questioned)? Or does the writer use questionable assumptions without addressing problems that might be inherent in those assumptions?

6. Focusing on the most important *inferences* or conclusions in the written piece: Do the inferences and conclusions the author makes follow from the information relevant to the issue, or does the author jump to unjustifiable conclusions? Does the author consider alternative conclusions where the issue is complex? Does the author use a sound line of reasoning to come to logical conclusions, or can you identify flaws in the reasoning somewhere?

7. Focusing on the author's *point of view:* Does the author show a sensitivity to alternative relevant points of view or lines of reasoning? Does he or she consider and respond to objections framed from other relevant points of view?

8. Focusing on *implications*: Does the writer show a sensitivity to the implications and consequences of the position her or she is taking?

WHAT HAVE YOU LEARNED?
TEST YOURSELF IN EVERY SUBJECT

We have shown how every academic field has its own logic, or system of meanings. To learn the field is to learn its logic. This is true whether one is talking of poems or essays, paintings or dances, histories or anthropological reports, experiments or scientific theories, philosophies or psychologies, particular events or general theories. Whether we are designing a new screwdriver or working out a perspective on religion, we must create a logic—a system of meanings—that makes sense to us. To learn the system underlying a discipline is to create it in your mind. This requires that your thinking be permanently reshaped and modified. As you study a subject, periodically ask yourself,

"Can I explain the underlying system of ideas that defines this subject?" (Imagine you are writing the encyclopedia entry for it.)

"Can I explain the most basic ideas in it to someone who doesn't understand it?" (What questions would this person have? Can you answer them?)

"Could I write a glossary of this subject's most basic vocabulary?" (Define the concepts, without using technical terms.)

"Do I understand the extent to which experts in the subject disagree on important aspects?" (A great deal of disagreement among experts means that this is a competing system field. Little disagreement means it is probably a one-system field.)

"Have I written out the basic logic of the subject?" (Using the eight elements of thought.)

"Can I compare and contrast the logic of the subject I am learning with that of other subjects I have learned?" (Seeing how they are both similar and different will help you understand them better.)

"To what extent can I relate this subject to significant problems in the world?" (See if you can list important problems that studying this subject would help us address.)

"To what extent has studying this subject helped me develop intellectual traits or habits of mind (like intellectual empathy, intellectual integrity, fair-mindedness, intellectual autonomy, and intellectual perserverance)?"

THE BEST THINKERS READ CLOSELY AND WRITE SUBSTANTIVELY

Close reading and substantive writing are abilities essential to the educated mind. The best thinkers read closely and write substantively. To read closely is to engage in a disciplined process by which you accurately reconstruct the thinking of an author in your own mind. The goal is to understand the author's meaning so that if the author could hear your summary, he or she would say, "Excellent, you understand exactly what I was saying!"

The best thinkers realize that many of the most important ideas and insights are to be found only in books and printed matter. They also realize that there is a significant difference between reading closely—in a way that enables you to summarize accurately and precisely what is being said in a text—and reading superficially—in a way that allows you to make only a vague, and often erroneous, summary of the text.

To write substantively is to say something worth saying about something worth saying something about. To do this, you must be able to identify important ideas and express significant implications of those ideas in clear and precise writing.

The best thinkers realize that there is a very important difference between writing that is merely fluent (but says nothing really worth saying) and writing that is substantial (that says something important). They realize, in other words, the difference between "style" and "substance." For example, think of the difference between a politician's speech that flatters the audience with intellectually empty talk about God and country:

"Fellow citizens: It is a noble land that God has given us. . . . It is a mighty people that He has planted on this soil; a people sprung from the most masterful blood of history. . . . It is a glorious history our God has bestowed on His chosen people. . . . "

and one that appeals to the intellect by saying something of undeniable importance:

"We hold these truths to be self-evident, that all men are created equal, that they are endowed by their Creator with certain unalienable Rights, that among these are Life, Liberty, and the pursuit of happiness."

In this chapter we focus on both *close reading* and *substantive writing.* First we develop the two concepts theoretically. Then we provide activities for you to work through to develop skills of close reading and substantive writing. If you prefer a hands-on (practice before theory) approach, go straight to the exercises in Part III of this chapter. After you practice the skills, it is important to return to the theory so that you make conceptual connections. By doing so you will make these two key concepts—*close reading* and *substantive writing*—intuitive in your thinking.

THE INTERRELATIONSHIP BETWEEN REApING AND WRITING

There is an intimate relationship between reading well and writing well. Any significant deficiency in reading will entail a parallel deficiency in writing. Any significant deficiency in writing will entail a parallel deficiency in reading.

For example, if you cannot distinguish writing that is clear from writing that is unclear, you will not be able to read closely. You will probably mistake vague ideas for clear ones and think you understand when you really don't. For example, suppose you read the sentence, "Democracy is a form of government in which the people rule." As a close reader, you should recognize that you don't really know what that sentence means until you find answers to the following questions: "Who exactly are *the people?*" and "What exactly is meant by the word *rule?*" It is extremely important to pin down the meaning of these two concepts.

Similarly, if you cannot detect significant vagueness and ambiguity in texts that you read, you will have difficulty formulating significant concepts as you write. In fact, to write substantively, you must be able to read the works of important authors critically, bringing ideas from these texts into your thinking and arranging them logically in clear prose style.

Close reading and substantive writing are symbiotic skills of disciplined thought—they support and reinforce one another. Both require that we think from multiple perspectives, and both require that we use the elements of reasoning well. In other words, both require the intellectual ability to:

1. **Clarify purposes**—an author's purpose(s) when we read and our own purpose(s) when we write

2. **Formulate clear questions**—those that an author is asking (as we read) and those we are pursuing (as we write)

3. **Distinguish accurate and relevant information**—as opposed to inaccurate and irrelevant information—in texts that we read and in preparation for our own writing

4. **Distinguish justifiable from unjustifiable assumptions**—those that an author is using or those that we are using in our own thinking as we write

5. **Identify significant and deep concepts**—those of an author and those that we want to guide our own thinking while we write

6. **Trace logical implications**—those of an author's thinking and those that may follow from our own written work

7. **Identify and think within multiple viewpoints**—those that an author presents (or fails to present) and those relevant to the issues in our written work

8. **Reach logical inferences or conclusions**—based on what we read, and in preparation for writing

These are just a few examples that shed light on the intimate relationship between close reading and substantive writing and the important connection between disciplined thought and high-quality reading and writing. As you develop your abilities to read closely and write substantively, you come to see more ways in which the two processes are related.

To integrate the idea of close reading with that of substantive writing, keep the following question at the forefront of your thinking as you work through this chapter: How do close reading and substantive writing interrelate? How do the same abilities and standards apply to both? How can learning one help me learn the other?

PART I: DISCOVER CLOSE READING

When you read, you translate words into meanings. The author has previously translated his or her ideas and experiences into words. You must take those same words and re-translate them back into the author's original meaning, using your own ideas and experiences as aids. Accurately translating words into their author's intended meanings requires analysis, evaluation, and creativity.

> The best thinkers are able to step outside their own point of view and think within the points of view of others.

Unfortunately, few people are skilled at translation. Few are able to accurately mirror the meaning the author intended. Readers often project their own meanings into a text and unintentionally distort or violate the author's original meaning. As Horace Mann put it in 1838:

> I have devoted especial pains to learn, with some degree of numerical accuracy, how far the reading, in our schools, is an exercise of the mind in thinking and feeling and how far it is a barren action of the organs of speech upon the atmosphere. My information is derived principally from the written statements of the school committees of the respective towns—gentlemen who are certainly exempt from all temptation to disparage the schools they superintend. The result is that more than 11/12ths of all the children in the reading classes do not understand the meanings of the words they read; and that the ideas and feelings intended by the author to be conveyed to and excited in the reader's mind still rest in the author's intention, never having yet reached the place of their destination. (Second Report to the Massachusetts Board of Education)

In general, we read to figure out what authors mean. Our reading is further influenced by our purpose for reading and by the nature of the text itself. For example, if we are reading for pure pleasure and personal amusement, it may not matter if we do not fully understand the text. We may simply enjoy the ideas or images that the text stimulates. This is fine as long as we know that we do not deeply understand the text. The various purposes for reading include:

1. Sheer pleasure. This requires no particular skill level.
2. To locate a simple idea in the text. This may require skimming it.
3. To gain specific technical information. Skimming skills are required.
4. To enter, understand, and appreciate a new world view. This requires close reading skills in working through a challenging series of tasks that stretch our minds.
5. To learn a new subject. This requires close reading skills for internalizing and taking ownership of an organized system of meanings.

Reading is also influenced by the nature of the text. In other words, how you read should be determined in part by what you are reading. Reflective readers read a textbook, for example, with a different mind-set than they have when they read an article in a newspaper. Reflective readers also read a textbook in biology, for example, differently from the way they read a textbook in history.

Yet there are core reading tools and skills for reading any substantive text. These are the tools and skills we are concerned with in this text.

Consider the Author's Purpose

In addition to being clear about your own purpose in reading, you must be clear about the author's purpose in writing. Both are relevant. Consider the following agendas. Think about what adjustments you would make in your reading given the differing purposes of these writers.

- Politicians and their media advisors developing political campaign literature
- Newspaper editors deciding which stories their readers would be most interested in and how to tell the story to maintain that interest
- Advertisers working with media consultants while writing copy for advertisements (to sell a product or service)
- A chemist writing a laboratory report
- A novelist writing a novel
- A poet writing a poem
- A student writing a research report

To read productively, you must take into account the author's purpose in writing as well as your own in reading. For example, if you read a historical novel to learn history, you should consider whether the author's purpose is to give an accurate account of events—or something else. After considering this, you might conclude that you would do well to read further in history books and primary sources to confirm the accuracy of what you read in the historical novel. Novelists blend fact and imagination to achieve their purpose, but readers in pursuit of historical fact must separate them.

Avoid Impressionistic Reading

The impressionistic mind follows associations, wandering from paragraph to paragraph, drawing no clear distinction between its own thinking and the author's thinking. Being fragmented, it fragments what it reads. Being uncritical, it judges an author's view to be correct only if that view concurs with its own beliefs. Being self-deceived, it fails to see itself as undisciplined. Being rigid, it does not learn from what it reads.

Whatever knowledge the impressionistic mind absorbs is uncritically intermixed with prejudices, biases, myths, and stereotypes. It lacks insight into how minds create meaning and how reflective minds monitor and evaluate as they read.

Read Reflectively

The reflective mind seeks meaning, monitors what is being said from paragraph to paragraph, draws a clear distinction between the thinking of an author and its own thinking. The reflective mind, being purposeful, adjusts reading to specific goals.

> The best readers and thinkers have well-developed reflective minds.

Being integrated, it interrelates ideas in the text with ideas it already commands. Being critical, it assesses what it reads for clarity, accuracy, precision, relevance, depth, breadth, logic, significance, and fairness. Being open to new ways of thinking, it values new ideas and learns from what it reads.

Think About Reading While Reading

The reflective mind improves its thinking by reflectively thinking about it. Likewise, it improves its reading by reflectively thinking about how it is reading. It moves back and forth between the cognitive (thinking) and the meta-cognitive (thinking about thinking). It moves forward a bit, then loops back upon itself to check on its own operations. It checks its tracks. It makes good its ground. It rises above itself and exercises oversight on itself.

One of the most important abilities that a thinker can have is the ability to monitor and assess his or her own thinking while processing the thinking of others. In reading, the reflective mind monitors how it is reading while it is reading. The foundation for this ability is knowledge of how the mind functions when reading well. For example, if I know that what I am reading is difficult for me to understand, I intentionally slow down and paraphrase each sentence. I put the meaning of each sentence that I read into my own words.

If I realize that I am unsympathetic to an author's viewpoint, I suspend judgment about the text's meaning until I have verified that I truly understand what the author is saying. I strive not to commit a common mistake that some readers make in reading:

"I don't really know what this means, but it is wrong, wrong, wrong!" Instead I try to accurately understand the author's viewpoint while reading. I attempt to enter that viewpoint, to be open to it as much as possible. And even if I don't agree fully with the author's view, I appropriate important ideas whenever possible. I take command of the ideas that I think are worthwhile rather than dismissing all the ideas simply because I don't completely agree with the author's view.

Engage the Text While Reading

The reflective mind interacts with the author's thinking. In this interaction, the reader's mind reconstructs the author's thinking. It does this through a process of inner dialogue with the sentences of the text, assessing each sentence for its intelligibility and questioning in a disciplined way:

- Can I summarize the meaning of this text in my own words?
- Can I give examples from my own experience of what the text is saying?
- Can I generate metaphors and diagrams to illustrate what the text is saying?
- What is clear to me and what do I need clarified?
- Can I connect the core ideas in this text to other core ideas I understand?

Think of Books as Teachers

Every book we read is a potential teacher. Reading is a systematic process for learning the essential meanings of that teacher. When we become good readers, we can learn the essential meanings of an unlimited number of teachers whose teachings live on, ever available, in the books they have written. When we take the core ideas of those teachings into our minds through careful reading, we can productively use them in our lives.

Reading Minds

You have a mind. But do you know how your mind operates? Are you aware of your prejudices and preconceptions? Are you aware of the extent to which your thinking mirrors the thinking of those around you? Are you aware of the extent to which your thinking has been influenced by the thinking of the culture in which you have been raised and conditioned? To what extent can you step outside your day-to-day mindset and into the mindset of those who think differently from you? Are you able to imagine being "wrong" in some of your beliefs? What criteria would you use to evaluate your personal beliefs? Are you aware of how to improve the quality of your own beliefs?

When you read the work of others, you enter their minds. By coming to terms with the mind of another, you can come to better discover your own mind—both its strengths and its weaknesses. When you can effectively move back and forth between what you are reading and what you are thinking, you bring what you think to bear upon what you read and what you read to bear upon what you think. You are able to change your thinking when the logic of what you read is an improvement on what you think. You are also able to withhold accepting new ideas when you cannot reconcile them with your own. Perhaps one of the most important functions of reading is to help you recognize that you may be wrong in some of your beliefs.

The Work of Reading

Reading is a form of intellectual work. And intellectual work requires willingness to persevere through difficulties. But to do this kind of intellectual work, you must understand what it entails. This is where most students fall short.

> The best readers view reading as a form of intellectual work.

Compare the challenge of analyzing, evaluating, and reconstructing an author's reasoning with the challenge of analyzing, evaluating, and repairing an automobile engine. The biggest challenge is in knowing how to do what needs to be done: how to use the tools of auto mechanics in taking the engine apart, how to run tests on specific systems in it, how to make needed repairs or improvements, and how to put it all together again. To do all this, you must know how an automobile engine functions.

No one would expect to know how to repair an automobile engine without training, involving both theory and practice. Similarly, if you learn to read without understanding what good reading involves, you learn to read poorly. That is why reading is a fundamentally passive activity for many students. It is as if their theory of reading is something like this: "You let your eyes move from left to right, scanning one line at a time, until somehow, in some inexplicable way, meaning automatically and effortlessly enters the mind." Just like repairing a car, reading requires training in specific skills and then applying those skills on a regular basis.

Structural Reading

Structural reading is a form of close reading applied to the overall structure of an extended text (usually a book). In structural reading, you focus on what you can learn about a book from its title, preface, introduction, and table of contents. Structural reading has two main uses. First, it enables you to evaluate a book to determine whether you want to spend the time to read it carefully. Second, it provides an overview you can use as scaffolding when you read the text.

> The best readers can extract the essential meaning from a text by carefully thinking through its structure.

If you can get a basic idea of what a book is driving at before you read it in detail, you will be much better able to make sense of the parts of it. Knowledge of a whole helps us understand all of its parts. Knowledge of a part helps us better understand the whole.

To read structurally, ask these questions:

- What does the title tell me about this book?
- What is the main idea in the book? (You should be able to figure this out from skimming the introduction, preface, and first chapter.)

- What are the parts of the whole, and how does the book deal with those parts? (Again, you may find this in an overview in the introduction or by reading the preface, first chapter, or table of contents.)
- In the light of my structural reading, what questions would I pursue during close reading?

How to Read a Sentence

Reading a sentence consists, first of all, in finding a way to state what the sentence says so we can think the thought the sentence expresses. You may have to analyze or reword the sentence in order to do that. Further ways to make the meaning of a sentence clear are: elaborating the sentence, finding an example of the idea expressed in the sentence, and illustrating its meaning.

Finding key sentences means finding the sentences that are the driving force within a book. Structural reading is one way by which we locate key paragraphs and boil them down to key sentences, and then to key ideas and key questions.

An important part of reading with discipline is to connect sentences to their broader context, to see how they fit within the written piece. For every sentence you read, you might ask:

- How does this sentence connect with the other sentences in the text?
- How does this sentence relate to the organizing idea of this text as a whole?

The best readers read a sentence in relation to other sentences.

Always read sentences in relationship to other sentences, connecting each sentence with the purpose of the written piece. Taking a sentence out of context can pose problems because sentences read in isolation from those that precede or follow them often overstate a point. The sentences that precede or follow usually clarify the author's true meaning or bring it in line with supporting facts. Read a text charitably and generously. Look for qualifications of points that otherwise might seem false or overstated.

How to Read a Paragraph

The best readers read a paragraph in relation to other paragraphs.

Carefully reading a paragraph involves one or more of the tools discussed in Part III of this chapter. These tools (especially paraphrasing and explicating the thesis) help us find the idea or question that is the driving force within the paragraph. Finding key paragraphs consists of finding the ideas or questions that are the driving force within the book. Structural reading, you will remember, is an important means by which we locate key paragraphs.

All paragraphs within a written piece should connect to every other paragraph so that we can see logical connections between ideas. All ideas should form a system of meanings—a logic. As you move from paragraph to paragraph, ask:

- What is the most important idea in this paragraph?
- How do the ideas in this paragraph relate to the ideas in previous paragraphs?
- How are the important ideas in the text connected?

Look for paragraphs that focus on significant ideas or questions. To understand their significance, connect those ideas, when possible, to situations and experiences that are meaningful in your life. To connect ideas to life situations, ask:

- How can I relate this idea to something I already understand?
- Is there an important idea here that I can use in my thinking?
- Have I ever experienced a situation that sheds light on this idea?

> The best readers construct a system of meanings when reading a text.

How to Read a Textbook

The first and most important insight necessary for successfully reading a textbook is that all textbooks focus on "systems" which, when internalized, can help us reason through a specific set of problems. Each textbook, with its system, focuses on a special way of thinking about a special set of things. History textbooks teach a special way of thinking about events in the past. Biology textbooks teach a special way of thinking about living things. Mathematics textbooks teach a special way of thinking about numbers and shapes. Physics textbooks teach a special way of thinking about mass, energy, and their interrelations.

Thus, there is no way to learn mathematics from a math textbook without learning how to figure out correct answers to mathematical questions and problems. There is no way to learn history from a history textbook without learning how to figure out correct or reasonable answers to historical questions and problems. There is no way to learn biology from a biology textbook without learning how to figure out answers to biological questions and problems. Any subject can therefore be understood as a system of figuring out correct or reasonable answers to a certain set of questions. We study chemistry to understand chemicals and how they interact (to answer questions about chemicals). We study psychology to figure out human behavior (to answer questions about certain human problems). All subjects can be understood in this way, and all textbooks can be read in this way.

Most textbooks begin with an introductory chapter or preface that introduces readers to the field of study: What is biology? What is physics? What is history? It is important to read this material closely, because it can provide insight into the most basic and fundamental concepts in the field. The rest of the textbook will build on it.

Once you have a basic idea of a subject from the preface or introductory chapter, you should be able to do some thinking within the system represented in the textbook. Thus, with a basic idea of biology, you should be able to do some simple biological thinking—to ask some basic biological questions and identify some relevant biological information. Having this basic idea is crucial to success in reading the remainder of the textbook, because if you do not have a clear concept of the subject as a whole, you will not be able to relate the parts (the individual chapters) to that whole.

Your reading strategy should not be *whole, part, part, part, part, part. . .* but, rather, *whole, part, whole, part, whole, part.* First, ground yourself in a basic (though introductory) idea of the whole. Then, relate each part (each subsequent chapter) to that whole. Try to understand the whole through integrating the parts into it. Use the "whole"—your understanding of the subject—as a

> The best readers first seek to discover the basic idea behind the whole text and then relate each part to that whole.

tool to relate the parts. The whole helps you with synthesis. Use your knowledge of the parts as a tool of analysis—to break down the subject as a whole into parts you can digest and use.

How to Read an Editorial

To become adept at reading editorials, you must first understand their purpose. The goal of the editorial writer is to make a brief case for *one side* of a controversial issue. His or her goal is not to consider all sides or to do what a writer of a research paper or report is expected to do. Most people read editorials in the following way: If the writer is defending what they believe, they praise the editorial. If the writer is criticizing what they believe, they criticize the editorial. With this approach, they are unable to gain insights from people with whom they disagree. The fact is that most people are rigid in their thinking and largely closed-minded. There are many points of view into which they cannot enter. There are many ways to look at the world that they never examine or appreciate.

By contrast, critical readers recognize that they have been wrong at times in the past and may be wrong now. They recognize what they would like to believe, while at the same time realizing that they may be prejudiced by that very desire. It is in this spirit of open-mindedness that we should learn to read editorials—especially the ones to which we are least sympathetic. We must learn how to step outside of our own point of view and enter points of view with which we are unfamiliar.

Of course, we should not assume that the editorials in our own culture's newspapers provide us with a full range of points of view. What we can expect is merely that these newspapers provide us with the range of views held by the mainstream readers within the society. The goal of a newspaper is not to educate readers concerning international and dissenting points of view but rather to make money. And a newspaper makes money only when it caters to the beliefs and preconceptions of its readers. Thus, newspapers rarely present radically dissenting perspectives, and when they do, they emphasize that these are "merely opinions."

Critical readers read all editorials with equal sympathy. They read to discover and digest a wide range of points of view, especially points of view that tend to be ignored in the mainstream of the culture. To enhance their breadth of vision and overcome ethnocentrism and sociocentrism, critical readers search out dissenting media sources.

Take Ownership of What You Read: Mark It Up

When you were a student in elementary school, you probably were taught never to write in your books. No doubt this was necessary, as other students would be using the book after you. This situation is different when you own a book and are reading a challenging work of substance. Close reading requires that you interact with the text by making specific decisions about its meanings, that you write down the ideas as you read, and that you connect important ideas to ideas you already understand and use.

One of the best ways to do this is by marking in books as you read them—highlighting key ideas, questions, assumptions, and facts, and noting implications, points of view, doubts, and wonderings. You can do this in many ways; the best ways are those you develop for yourself.

Here are some ideas you might find useful in developing your own system of marking. Start with just a couple of these marks and add more when you are ready.

1. Circle important concepts and underline their definitions. Circle the foundational ideas, and underline the definitions the author gives. Then draw a line between the two to show they are connected. (The foundational ideas are those that explain most or many of the other ideas. Use a good dictionary if a word is not clear.)

2. Write exclamation marks (in the margins) beside important conclusions. You might use one exclamation mark for an important conclusion, two for a more important one, and three for a crucial one (!, !!, !!!).

3. Put a question mark in the margin whenever you don't understand something. As you read, routinely ask yourself: Do I understand what the author is saying? Whenever you don't, write your question in the margin, or just put a question mark there (?). Later, come back to your questions and see if you can answer them, having read further.

4. Note important problems or issues. Usually each chapter in a book has an underlying key problem or issue. Mark these with an abbreviation such as *prob.*

5. Note important information, data, or evidence. When you come across information the author is using to support conclusions, circle it and note it in the margin as *info, data,* or *evidence.*

6. Record in the margin the author's point of view when you notice it. Use the abbreviation *POV.*

7. Record in the margin the author's most questionable assumptions when you notice them. Use the abbreviation *assump.*

8. Record in the margin the most important implications of the thinking in the text when you notice them. Use the abbreviation *implic.*

9. Formulate ideas of your own as they occur to you. You may write these ideas in the margin, on the extra pages at the back of the book, or at the end of chapters. The more often you write down ideas as they occur to you, the clearer you will be about your own thinking in relation to that of the author. Of course, be careful not to decide you disagree with an author until you are sure that you thoroughly understand his or her views.

10. Diagram important concepts and how they are connected. As you read, strive to develop a sense of the whole. One good way to do this is by drawing diagrams that show interrelationships between concepts. Use the pages at the front or back of the book, or write in a notebook if your drawings become elaborate and you need more space.

EXHIBIT 7.1   *Markings and abbreviations.*

Circle around (word) or phrase	foundational or other important concept
def	an important definition
!, !!, or !!!	important conclusion
?	something reader doesn't understand
prob or *issue*	a key problem or issue the author is addressing
info, data, or *evidence*	key information
POV	key point of view
assump	a questionable assumption being made
implic	key implications or consequences
notes in margin or on extra pages	reader's thoughts
diagrams	sketched by the reader to show interrelationships between important ideas

The Best Readers Read to Learn

To learn well, you must read well. It is far more important to read a few things well than to read many things badly. Among the things we should read well are substantive texts—texts containing important ideas, texts that ground our thinking in powerful ideas. As we have said, it is quite possible to educate yourself entirely through reading, if you have the intellectual skills to work through complex written material, enter conflicting viewpoints, internalize important ideas, and apply those ideas to your own life.

Conversely, you cannot be an educated person without consistently learning through reading. Why? Because education is a lifelong process that only *begins* in school. Unless you continually integrate new ideas with the ones you have already established in your thinking, your ideas will become stagnant and rigid.

PART II: DISCOVER SUBSTANTIVE WRITING

Reading is essential to learning, and so is writing. You cannot be educated without being able to "test" and communicate your ideas by putting them in written form. As with reading, learning to write occurs only through a process of cultivation requiring intellectual discipline. As with any set of complex skills, there are fundamentals of writing that must be internalized and then applied using one's thinking. In this section we focus on the most important of those fundamentals.

Write for a Purpose

Skilled writers do not write randomly. They always have a purpose, agenda, goal, or objective. Their purpose, together with the nature of what they are writing (and their situation), determines how they write. They write in different ways in different situations or for different purposes. A specific piece of writing may have any of a variety of purposes, but all writing shares one underlying, universal purpose: to say something worth saying about something worth saying something about.

> The best writers write with a clear purpose in view.

In general, when we write, we translate inner meanings into public words. We put our ideas and experiences into written form. Accurately translating an intended meaning into written words requires analysis, evaluation, and creativity (just like translating words into meaning during reading). Unfortunately, few people are skilled in this work of translation. Few are able to select and combine words that so combined, convey an intended meaning to an audience of readers.

> The best writers write analytically and creatively.

People may write in pursuit of many specific and varied agendas. Consider how the purposes would vary for the following writers:

- a media advisor writing political campaign literature
- a newspaper editor deciding how to edit a story to maintain reader interest
- a media consultant writing copy for an advertisement
- a chemist writing a laboratory report
- a novelist writing a novel
- a poet writing a poem
- a student writing a research report

Clearly, one's purpose in writing influences the kinds of writing skills one needs and uses. Nevertheless, there are some fundamental writing skills we all need if we are to develop the art of saying something worth saying about something worth saying something about. Learning the art of substantive writing has many important implications for our development as thinkers. It is important in learning how to learn and in coming to understand ourselves. It can lead us to self-insight, as well as to insight into the many dimensions of our lives.

Substantive Writing

To write something worth reading, keep two questions in mind: "Do I have a subject or idea worth writing about?" and "Do I have something of significance to say about it?" Once you are clear about the topic you will be writing about, you will need to use core writing tools and skills in developing your written piece. These tools and skills are the focus of this section.

The Problem of Impressionistic Writing

The impressionistic mind follows associations, wandering from paragraph to paragraph, drawing no clear distinctions within its thinking and its writing from moment to moment. Being fragmented, it fragments what it writes. Being uncritical, it assumes its own point of view to be insightful and justified, and therefore not in need of justification in comparison to competing points of view. Being self-deceived, it fails to see itself as undisciplined. Being rigid, it does not learn from what it reads, writes, or experiences. Whatever knowledge the impressionistic mind absorbs is uncritically intermixed with prejudices, biases, myths, and stereotypes. It lacks insight into the importance of understanding how minds create meaning and how reflective minds monitor and evaluate as they write. To discipline our writing, we must go beyond impressionistic thinking.

> The best writers do not write impressionistically.

Write Reflectively

Unlike the impressionistic mind, the reflective mind seeks meaning, monitors what it writes, draws a clear distinction between its thinking and the thinking of its audience. The reflective mind, being purposeful, adjusts writing to specific goals. Being integrated, it interrelates ideas it is writing with ideas it already commands. Being critical, it assesses what it writes for clarity, accuracy, precision, relevance, depth, breadth, logic, significance, and fairness. Being open to new ways of thinking, it values new ideas and learns from what it writes.

The reflective mind improves its thinking by thinking (reflectively) about it. Likewise, it improves its writing by thinking (reflectively) about its writing. It moves back and forth between writing and thinking about how it is writing. It moves forward a bit, and then loops back upon itself to check on its own operations. It checks its tracks. It makes good its ground. It rises above itself and exercises oversight. This applies to the reflective mind while writing—or reading or listening or making decisions.

> Reflective writers think about their writing while they are writing, continually improving what they write as they write.

The foundation for this ability is knowledge of how the mind functions when writing well. For example, if I know (or discover) that what I am writing is or might be difficult for others to understand, I carefully explain each key sentence more thoroughly and give more examples and illustrations. I look at what I am writing from the readers' point of view.

If I realize that my readers are likely to be unsympathetic to my viewpoint, I try to help them connect the primary beliefs they already hold to primary beliefs in my viewpoint. I try to put myself into their circumstances with their beliefs and outlook. I show them that I understand their perspective.

Reflective writers create an inner dialogue with themselves, assessing what they are writing while they are writing. They ask:

1. Have I stated my point clearly?
2. Have I explained my main point adequately?

3. Have I given my readers examples from my own experience that connect important ideas to their experience?

4. Have I included metaphors or analogies that illustrate for the reader what I am saying?

How to Write a Sentence

Within a piece of written work, every sentence should stand in a clear relationship to other sentences. Each sentence, and indeed every word of every sentence, should support the purpose of the written piece.

An important part of substantive writing is connecting sentences to their broader context, and making it clear to the reader how they fit within the whole. For every sentence you write, ask:

- How does this sentence connect with the other sentences in the paragraph?
- How does this sentence relate to the organizing idea of this text as a whole?

Write to Learn

Everything we write is a potential learning experience. Writing is, among other things, a systematic process for learning essential meanings. When we write to become good writers, we teach ourselves as we explain things to others. In fact, teaching through writing is one of the most powerful strategies for learning. When we take core ideas, ideas of substance, and work them into our minds by developing them on paper, they become ideas we can use productively in our lives.

> The best thinkers use writing as an effective tool in learning.

At the same time, to learn well, one must write well. One learns to write well not by writing many things badly, but by writing a few things well.

The few things we should write well are substantive pieces, paragraphs and papers containing important ideas, elaborations that ground our thinking in powerful ideas. It is quite possible to educate oneself entirely through writing, if one has the intellectual skills to work through important texts, enter conflicting viewpoints, internalize important ideas learned, and apply those ideas to one's life. Alternatively, one cannot be an educated person without consistently learning through writing. Why? Because education is a lifelong process that at best only begins in school. Without continually integrating new ideas into the ones already established in our thinking, our ideas become stagnant and rigid.

> The best thinkers view education as a lifelong process.

Substantive Writing in Content Areas

To gain knowledge, you must construct it in your mind. Writing what you are trying to internalize helps you achieve that purpose. When you are able to make connections in writing, you begin to take ownership of these connections. To do this, you must learn

EXHIBIT 7.2   *Essential Idea: Closely reading about primary and secondary ideas in a discipline is a key to understanding the discipline.*

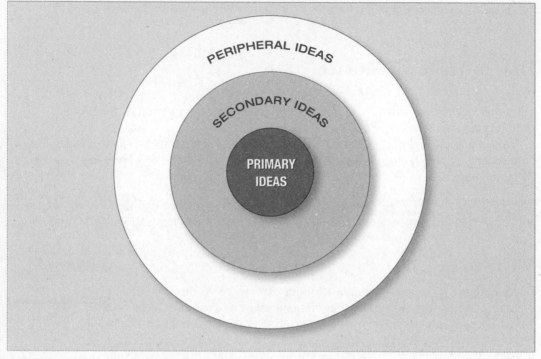

how to identify core ideas in the books you read, and then explain those ideas in writing, along with the role they play within the subjects you are studying.

All knowledge exists in systems of meanings. These systems have primary, secondary, and peripheral ideas, all of which are interrelated. Imagine a series of circles. In the center is a small core circle of primary ideas. It is surrounded by a concentric circle of secondary ideas, which is surrounded by an outer circle of peripheral ideas. The primary ideas, at the core, explain the secondary and peripheral ideas. Whenever you read to acquire knowledge, you must also write in order to take ownership of the primary ideas. They are key to understanding all the other ideas.

> The best thinkers recognize that all knowledge is systematic, not fragmented.

Furthermore, just as you must write to gain an understanding of the primary ideas, you must also write in order to understand the system as a whole and make interconnections between ideas. The sooner you begin to think, and therefore write, within a system, the sooner the system will become meaningful to you. When you take command of a core of historical ideas, you begin to think and write historically. When you take command of a core of scientific ideas, you begin to think and write scientifically. Core or primary ideas are the key to every system of knowledge. They are the key to learning any subject. They are

> The best thinkers see knowledge and understanding as tools of learning, not as objects to memorize.

the key to retaining what you learn and applying what you learn to life's problems. If you do not write about these ideas, they will never fully take root in your mind. But by seeking out core ideas and digesting them through writing, you multiply the important subjects you can write about, as well as the important things you can say about them.

Relate Core Ideas to Other Core Ideas

Writing can help you relate core ideas you learn within one discipline or domain to core ideas in other systems of knowledge. Knowledge exists not only within a system but also in relation to all other systems of knowledge. Writing can help you integrate insights from multiple disciplines or domains.

Mastering any set of foundational ideas makes it easier to learn other foundational ideas, as well as derivative ones. Learning to think within one system of knowledge helps you learn within other systems. Writing is crucial to this process.

> The best thinkers recognize that by learning foundational ideas they can more easily learn all the ideas that derive from them.

For example, if in studying botany you learn that all plants have cells, you should connect this idea to the fact that all animals have cells (which you learned in biology). You then can begin to consider the similarities and differences between the types of animal and plant cells. A cell is a foundational concept that applies to both botany and biology and helps you understand both. Or consider the relationship between psychology and sociology. Psychology focuses on individual behavior, while sociology focuses on group behavior. But people's individual psychology influences how they relate to group norms, and social groups shape how individuals deal with their perceived life problems and opportunities. By putting core ideas within these two disciplines into words, you can better understand both fields and apply your knowledge about them to the real world more effectively—because, in the real world, the psychological and sociological are deeply intertwined.

Writing Within Disciplines

To write within a discipline, you must recognize that it is a system of thought. Indeed, often a discipline is a system of systems. Scientific thinking, for example, forms a large-scale system of thought. Science also contains subsystems (physics, chemistry, biology, physiology, and so forth). Science, therefore, is a system of systems.

But, unlike science in which there is agreement on the most basic principles guiding scientific thinking, some systems of systems lack agreement even on their most basic assumptions. For example, the disciplines of philosophy, psychology, and economics are systems of conflicting systems. In contrast to science (wherein all systems work together), philosophical, psychological, and economic systems vie with one another for dominance. Each of these disciplines contains competing schools of thought that contradict each other in important ways.

To be an effective writer within a discipline, you must learn to identify whether the discipline is best understood as a system of supporting systems (such as math and science) or a system of conflicting systems (such as philosophy, psychology,

The best thinkers understand the basic nature of the disciplines they study and understand the systems within them.

and economics). If you are thinking within a system-harmonious discipline like science or math, your task is to understand how the systems within it support one another. If you are thinking within a system-conflicting field, your task is to master how and why the systems within it conflict. Of course, in seeing how conflicting systems diverge, you also discover how they overlap. Conflict between systems of thought is rarely, if ever, total and absolute.

To test your knowledge of any given system of thought, you should be able to state, elaborate, exemplify, and illustrate the most fundamental concept within that system. For example, if you are studying science, you should be able to write your understanding of what science is in a way that would satisfy scientists. If you are studying history, or indeed any other field of study, you should be able to do the same. You should be able, as well, to explain in writing how fundamental concepts overlap or conflict between and among disciplines.

The Work of Writing

Writing, then, is a form of intellectual work. And intellectual work requires a willingness to persevere through difficulties. But perhaps even more important, good writing requires understanding what intellectual work *is* and how it relates to writing. This is where most students fall short. Here is an illustration: Creating a paragraph well is like building a house. You need a foundation, and everything else must be built upon that foundation. The house must have at least one entrance, and it must be apparent to people where that entrance is. The first floor must fit the foundation, and the second floor must match up with the first, with some stairway that enables us to get from the first floor to the second. Building a house involves the work of both design and construction. Each is essential. No one would expect students to know how to design and construct houses without being taught. But sometimes we approach writing as if the knowledge of how to design and write a paragraph or a paper were apparent to all students.

The best thinkers recognize writing to be a form of intellectual work.

If a person tries to write without understanding what writing involves, the writing will likely be poor. For example, many students see writing as a fundamentally passive activity. Their theory of writing seems to be something like this: "You write whatever comes to your mind, sentence by sentence, until you have written the assigned length." By contrast, substantive writing requires first choosing (constructing) a subject worth writing about and then thinking through (constructing) something worth saying about that subject. It is a highly selective activity. There are at least five intellectual acts required for developing substance in your writing:

- Choosing a subject or idea of importance.
- Deciding on something important to say about it.
- Explaining or elaborating on your basic meaning.

- Constructing examples that will help readers connect what you are saying to events and experiences in their lives.
- Constructing one or more analogies or metaphors that will help readers connect what you are writing about with something similar in their lives.

QUESTIONING AS WE WRITE

Skilled writers approach writing as an active dialogue involving questioning. They question as they write. They question to understand. They question to evaluate what they are writing. They question to bring important ideas into their thinking. Here are some of the questions good writers ask while writing:

- Why am I writing this? What is my purpose? What do I want the reader to come away with?
- Is there some part of what I have written that I don't really understand? Perhaps I am repeating what I have heard people say without ever having thought through exactly what it means.
- If something I have written is vague, how can I make it clearer or more precise?
- Do I understand the meaning of the key words I have used, or do I need to look them up in a dictionary?
- Am I using any words in special or unusual ways? Have I explained special meanings to the reader?
- Am I sure that what I have said is accurate? Do I need to qualify anything?
- Am I clear about my main point and why I think it is important?
- Do I know what question my paragraph answers?
- Do I need to spend more time investigating my topic or issue? Do I need more information?

Nonsubstantive Writing

It is possible to learn to write with an emphasis on style, variety of sentence structure, and rhetorical principles without learning to write in a substantive manner. Rhetorically powerful writing may be, and in our culture often is, intellectually bankrupt. Many intellectually impoverished thinkers write well in the purely rhetorical sense. Propaganda is often expressed in a rhetorically effective way; and political speeches that are empty of significant content are often rhetorically well-designed. Sophistry and self-delusion often thrive in rhetorically proficient prose.

> The best thinkers distinguish rhetorically smooth from intellectually deep writing.

A *New York Times* special supplement on education (Aug. 4, 2002) included a description of a new section in the Scholastic Aptitude Test that consists of a "20-minute writing exercise." Students were asked to write on the subject: "There is always a however."

One might as justifiably ask a person to write on the theme, "There is always an always!" or "There is never a never!" Such writing prompts are the equivalent of an intellectual Rorschach inkblot. They do not define a clear intellectual task; there is no issue to be reasoned through. Thus, the writer is encouraged to pontificate using rhetorical and stylistic devices rather than to reason using intellectual good sense—to talk about nothing as if it were something.

Substantive writing requires that the writer begin with a significant, intellectually well-defined task. Writing with this kind of basis can be assessed for clarity, accuracy, relevance, depth, breadth, logic, significance, and fairness (rather than rhetorical style and flourish). Substantive writing enables the author to take ownership of ideas worth understanding. There are numerous ways to design a substantive writing task. The next section gives some examples.

PART III: PRACTICE CLOSE READING AND SUBSTANTIVE WRITING

You now know something about the theory of close reading and substantive writing. In the exercises that follow, you will be given strategies for practicing these processes. In some of these activities you will be asked to read and then discuss what you have read. In others you will be asked to write out your ideas or given a choice. In all of these activities, you should be able to see the connection between close reading and substantive writing.

Close reading and substantive writing are based on foundational critical-thinking principles and concepts—the elements and standards of thought. The elements of thought enable us to break down a product of thought into its constituent parts (purpose, question, information, inference, concept, assumption, implication, point of view). Standards of thought enable us to evaluate thought for clarity, accuracy, precision, relevance, depth, breadth, logic, significance, and fairness. Knowing how to analyze and evaluate thinking is essential to high-quality reading and writing. You will apply your understanding of how to analyze and assess thinking in several of the activities in this section.

> The best thinkers recognize that practice in learning to read and write well is indispensable.

To introduce examples of substantive thought, we have identified and include in this section some classic texts and quotations. They serve as a springboard to close reading and substantive writing. If you can study a substantive text and then capture its essential meaning in writing (using your own words and thoughts), you have begun to grasp the process of close reading and substantive writing.

Most of the exercises in this section will require you to use the most prominent critical-thinking strategy for taking initial ownership of an idea: to state, elaborate, exemplify, and illustrate it. Paraphrasing—putting what a sentence or text is saying into your own words—is also at the heart of these exercises. When you can say what great minds have thought, you can think what great minds have said. Analysis and evaluation are a logical follow-up to paraphrasing.

Some of these exercises are easier than others. If you decide that a particular exercise is too challenging, pass it by and work on others, then come back to the difficult ones later. Our goal is to help you proceed from the simple to the complex, but what is simple for one person is sometimes complex to another.

> If you cannot express a thought in your own words, you do not understand it.

Finally, we do not have the space to give examples of all possible patterns of close reading and substantive writing. But the patterns we do provide are basic and, when routinely practiced, lead to a progressively deeper understanding of how to read and how to write, critically and insightfully.

FIVE LEVELS OF CLOSE READING (THAT OVERLAP WITH SUBSTANTIVE WRITING)

There are at least five levels of close reading. Insightful writing at the first four levels exemplifies substantive writing. You will practice one or more of the first four levels during many of the activities in this section.

FIRST LEVEL

Paraphrasing the Text Sentence by Sentence

State in your own words, either orally or in writing, the meaning of each sentence as you read.

SECOND LEVEL

Explicating the Thesis of a Paragraph

1. State the main point of the paragraph in one or two sentences.
2. Then elaborate on what you have paraphrased. ("In other words, . . . ")
3. Give examples of the meaning by tying it to concrete situations in the real world. ("For example, . . . ")
4. Generate metaphors, analogies, pictures, or diagrams of the basic thesis to connect it to other meanings you already understand.

THIRD LEVEL: ANALYSIS

Analyzing the Logic of a Text

Anytime you read, you are reading the product of an author's reasoning. You can use your understanding of the elements of reasoning, therefore, to bring your reading to a higher level. You can do this by writing your answers to the following questions (you may ask these questions in any order you want):

(Continued)

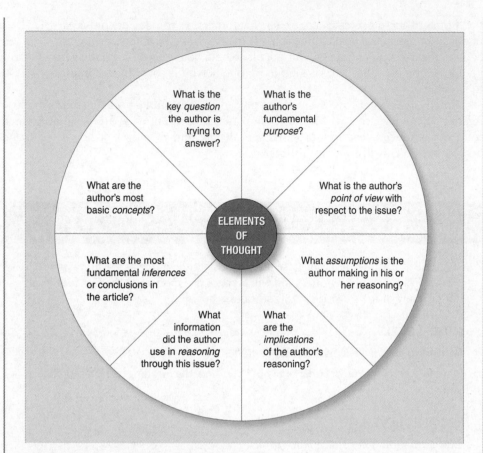

Use the template provided in Think for Yourself 6.11 on page 127, to clarify the logic of the author's reasoning.

FOURTH LEVEL: EVALUATION

Assessing the Logic of a Text

Every written piece is not of the same quality. We assess what we read by applying intellectual standards to it, standards such as clarity, precision, accuracy, relevance, significance, depth, breadth, logic, and fairness. Authors often adhere to some standards while violating others. For example, an author might be clear in stating a position but use information that is not accurate. An author might use relevant information but fail to think through the complexities of the issue (fail to achieve depth). An author's argument might be logical but not significant. As readers we need to become adept at assessing the quality of an author's reasoning. Part of this task is to accurately state in our own words the author's meaning.

To assess an author's work, answer the following questions:

■ Does the author clearly state his or her meaning, or is the text vague, confused, or muddled in some way?

- Are the author's claims accurate?
- Is the author sufficiently precise in providing details and specifics when specifics are relevant?
- Does the author introduce irrelevant material, thereby wandering from the purpose?
- Does the author take us into the important complexities in the subject, or is the writing superficial?
- Does the author consider other relevant points of view, or is the writing overly narrow in its perspective?
- Is the text internally consistent, or does the text contain unexplained contradictions?
- Is the text significant, or is the subject dealt with in a trivial manner?
- Does the author display fairness, or does the author take a one-sided, narrow approach?

FIFTH LEVEL: ROLE-PLAYING

Speaking in the Voice of an Author

Role-playing an author is, in one way, the ultimate test of understanding. When we role-play, in essence we say: "Look, I will enter the mind of the author and speak as if I were the author. I will discuss any questions you may have about the text, and I will answer your questions as I think the author would. I will speak in the first person singular. I will be like an actor playing a part. I will try to be the author fully and truly for the purpose of this exercise."

To role-play an author, you need a partner who has read the text and is willing to ask you important questions about it. Responding to questions forces you to think within the author's logic. Practicing talking in the voice of an author is a good way to get a personal sense of whether you have really absorbed the core meanings of a text. If you do not have a partner, write out a dialogue between the author and a questioner who is attempting to understand the logic of the author's reasoning.

Paraphrasing

In the practice exercises that follow, you will begin with paraphrasing (level one). According to the *Oxford English Dictionary,* to "paraphrase" is to express the meaning of a word, phrase, passage, or work in other words, usually with the object of providing a fuller and clearer exposition. Unless we can state in our own words the meaning of a word, sentence, or passage, we lack an understanding of that word, sentence, or passage. We make ideas our own by "thinking them into our thinking." One of the best ways to do this is to practice paraphrasing—stating or writing in your own words your understanding of an idea, sentence, or passage.

> Test your understanding of others by expressing, in your own words, what you have understood them to say—then see if they concur.

This is easier said than done. To paraphrase a substantive passage effectively, you must come to think and appreciate the substantive thought behind the passage. Without this appreciation—without deeply understanding the thought expressed in the original—you cannot render that thought adequately in different words.

It is possible to understand a deep thought at varying levels of depth. Many will say, for example, that they understand the thought, "A little learning is a dangerous thing." But subsequent discussion often proves that they do not fully appreciate it—for example, they fail to see how it applies to their life. The fact is that few people have had practice in paraphrasing substantive passages. Few have thought about the significance of the art of paraphrasing and understand its essential connection to substantive learning.

An insightful paraphrase of an important text suggests one way to think the thought in that text, for a paraphrase re-creates an original thought in new words. To select the words that do the job, you must struggle with the thought and with possible words to express it.

To rephrase a powerful thought adequately, it is usually necessary to express it in a more extended form. That is why paraphrasing a thought is sometimes called *unpacking* it. The original is compact. The paraphrase takes it apart, lays out the elements, and therefore expresses it in more, rather than fewer, words.

It should be clear that there is no exact form of paraphrase. Most substantial thoughts can be captured by a variety of formulations, each giving a different angle of vision. Practice in paraphrasing is, therefore, practice in taking ownership of thinking that stretches the mind, thinking that will bring you to deeper and deeper levels of understanding. In a world of glorified superficiality, disciplined practice in paraphrasing significant thought is rare.

CLARIFICATION STRATEGIES

- The ability to state a thesis clearly in a sentence. If we cannot accurately state our key idea in a sentence using our own words, we don't really know what we want to say.
- The ability to explain a thesis sentence in greater detail. If we cannot elaborate our key idea, then we have not yet connected its meaning to other concepts that we understand.
- The ability to give examples of what we are saying. If we cannot connect what we have elaborated with concrete situations in the real world, our knowledge of the meanings is still abstract, and, to some extent, vague.
- The ability to illustrate what we are saying with a metaphor, analogy, picture, diagram, or drawing. If we cannot generate metaphors, analogies, pictures, or diagrams of the meanings we are constructing, we have not yet connected what we understand with other domains of knowledge and experience.

Now consider the four questions that can be used to clarify what someone is saying:

1. Could you state your basic point in one simple sentence?
2. Could you elaborate your basic point more fully (in other words)?
3. Could you give me an example of your point from your experience?
4. Could you give me an analogy or metaphor to help me see what you mean?

Each of these clarification strategies requires intellectual discipline on the part of the speaker or writer.

Sample Paraphrases

Consider the following sample paraphrases before we move on to more detailed paraphrasing:

"He who passively accepts evil is as much involved in it as he who helps to perpetuate it."   —*Martin Luther King, Jr.*

People who see unethical things being done to others but who fail to intervene (when they are able to intervene) are as unethical as those who are causing harm in the first place.

"Every effort to confine Americanism to a single pattern, to constrain it to a single formula, is disloyalty to everything that is valid in Americanism."
                                                    —*Henry Steele Commager*

There is no one "right way" to be an American. When everyone in America is expected to think within one belief system, when people are ostracized or persecuted for thinking autonomously, when people are labeled "un-American" for independent thinking, the only legitimate definition of "American" is annulled.

"In a free society, standards of public morality can be measured only by whether physical coercion—violence against persons or property—occurs. There is no right to be offended by words, actions, or symbols."   —*Richard E. Sincere, Jr.*

Ethics in a free society is determined by whether violence has occurred against a person or property. People do not have the right to be protected against being shocked by the lifestyles of others.

"Liberty is the only thing you cannot have unless you are willing to give it to others."   —*William Allen White*

If you want to be free, you have to allow others their freedom.

"I can't understand why people are frightened of new ideas. I'm frightened of the old ones."   —*John Cage*

Many of the ideas that have permeated human thinking throughout the years are harmful or dangerous. An old idea is not necessarily a good idea, nor is a new idea necessarily a bad one.

"The legitimate powers of government extend to such acts only as are injurious to others."   —*Thomas Jefferson*

The only authority government should have is to stop people from harming one another.

"The propagandist's purpose is to make one set of people forget that certain other sets of people are human."   —*Aldous Huxley*

The goal of propaganda is to convince people that other groups of people are inhuman, and therefore not worthy of respect and just treatment.

"The shepherd always tries to persuade the sheep that their interests and his own are the same."   —*Stendhal*

People in control always try to manipulate people into believing that what is good for those in control is good for the other people as well.

Paraphrasing Short Quotes

One way to paraphrase quotes is to begin by writing out your initial thoughts. Explain the significance of what is being talked about and what is being said. If there is an important concept at the heart of the quote—a concept such as *democracy* or *power,* as in the two example quotes below—think through that concept. Then paraphrase the quote in the light of what you have written.

FIRST EXERCISE

Directions: This section presents short quotes based on significant insights. Try to paraphrase each one. But first write out your initial thoughts. When paraphrasing, try to use more rather than less elaboration to unpack the ideas in the quote. We provide two examples, but without showing the initial thoughts.

Example One

"Democracy is rule by the people."

Possible paraphrase: Democracy exists only to the extent that there is a broad basis of equality of political power among the people at large. This means that all people within the state should have relatively equal power and equal input in determining what the laws will be. By implication, a state fails to be democratic to the extent that a few people—whether they be wealthy or otherwise influential—have more power than others.

Example Two

"Power corrupts, and absolute power corrupts absolutely."

Possible paraphrase: The more control people gain over the lives of others, the greater is their propensity to exploit those people, and their consequent loss of personal integrity and honesty.

Now it is your turn to practice, using the quotes that follow. In this exercise, you may either orally state your paraphrase or write it out:

"If a man empties his purse into his head, no man can take it away from him. An investment in knowledge always pays the best interest."   —*Benjamin Franklin*

Possible paraphrase:

"Universal suffrage, without universal education, would be a curse."
                                                                    —*H. L. Wayland*
Possible paraphrase:

"The school should always have as its aim that the young leave it as a harmonious personality, not as a specialist. . . . The development of general ability for independent thinking and judgment should always be placed foremost, not the acquisition of special knowledge."   —*Albert Einstein*

Possible paraphrase:

"Do not ask if a man has been through college; ask if a college has been through him—if he is a walking university."   —*E. H. Chapin*

Possible paraphrase:

In this activity, you have interpreted important quotes by paraphrasing them. In the next activity you will practice another way of approaching deep understanding of important texts.

SECOND EXERCISE

Directions: Use the following template to guide you in explicating the following quotes.

1. The essence of this quote is . . .
2. In other words . . .
3. For example . . .
4. To give you a metaphor (or analogy) so you can better understand what I am saying . . .

For this exercise we suggest you write out your elaborations.

Example

"All truly wise thoughts have been thought already thousands of times; but to make them truly ours, we must think them over again honestly, till they take root in our personal experience."   —*Goethe*

1. The essence of this quote is that the most important ideas are not new, but what is new is using them in our thinking. We have to think them through for ourselves, again and again, until we can use them in our lives.

2. In other words, we don't have to be brilliant to use significant ideas in our lives. All of the most important ideas have already been figured out and thought through numerous times throughout history. But if we want to take possession of these ideas, we have to be committed to working them into our thinking, connecting them to personal experience, and then using them to guide our behavior. If we want to live better lives, we don't have to come up with novel or original ideas. Rather, we need to learn how to live the ones already available to us.

3. For example, consider what Socrates proposed (around 600 B.C.): The unexamined life is not worth living. Throughout history, many people have said that if you want to improve your life, you have to look at the way you live; you have to think about your behavior and what causes you to behave irrationally. Yet, few people take this idea seriously and think about what it would mean to examine their life. Few have any tools for doing this. Few have related this idea to their personal experience and really faced themselves straight on.

4. To give you a metaphor (or analogy) so you can better understand what I am saying, consider this: Every city has libraries containing thousands of books that express important ideas and experiences. Yet, most of these books are ignored, not read. Few think of the library as a place to gain ideas that can change their lives for the better. Few realize that rather than to seek out a flashy (and probably superficial) new idea from the mass media, they should master some of the many old, time-tested, deep, and important ideas (from a library or good bookstore).

NOW IT'S YOUR TURN

Use the structure outlined above to write substantively about the following quotes.

"No man is free who is not master of himself."   —*Epictetus*

"All our freedoms are a single bundle; all must be secure if any is to be preserved."
—*Dwight D. Eisenhower*

"None are more hopelessly enslaved than those who falsely believe they are free."
—*Goethe*

"Security is never an absolute. . . . The government of a free people must take certain chances for the sake of maintaining freedom which the government of a police state avoids."   —*Bartholini*

"The first step to knowledge is to know that we are ignorant."   —*Cecil*

"The more you practice what you know, the more shall you know what to practice."   —*W. Jenkin*

"What is not fully understood is not possessed."   —*Goethe*

"If you would thoroughly know anything, teach it to others."   —*Tyron Edwards*

"The mind is but a barren soil . . . unless it be continually fertilized and enriched with foreign matter."   —*Sir J. Reynolds*

"What stubbing, plowing, digging, and harrowing is to land, that thinking, reflecting, examining is to the mind."   —*Berkeley*

"Don't despair of a student if he has one clear idea."   —*Nathaniel Emmons*

"Narrow minds think nothing right that is beyond their own capacity."
—*Rochefoucauld*

"There is no more independence in politics than there is in jail."
—*Will Rogers*

"If you wish the sympathy of broad masses then you must tell them the crudest and most stupid things."   —*Adolf Hitler*

"Two kinds of men generally best succeed in political life: men of no principle, but of great talent; and men of no talent, but of one principle—that of obedience to their superiors."   —*Wendell Phillips*

"Justice without power is inefficient; power without justice is tyranny."

—*Pascal*

"Power is ever stealing from the many to the few."   —*Wendell Phillips*

"Power, like the diamond, dazzles the beholder, and also the wearer; it dignifies meanness; it magnifies littleness; to what is contemptible, it gives authority; to what is low, exaltation."   —*Charles Caleb Colton*

"Even legal punishments lose all appearance of justice, when too strictly inflicted on men compelled by the last extremity of distress to incur them."

—*Junius*

"Thinking is the hardest work there is, which is the probable reason why so few engage in it."   —*Henry Ford*

"Thought engenders thought. Place one idea upon paper, another will follow it, and still another, until you have written a page. . . . Learn to think, and you will learn to write; the more you think, the better you will express your ideas."   —*G. A. Sala*

"Our thoughts are ours, their ends none of our own."   —*William Shakespeare*

"The key to every man is his thought."   —*Ralph Waldo Emerson*

Exercises in the Five Levels of Close Reading and Substantive Writing

In the next few sections, you will get practice in the five levels of close reading and substantive writing introduced on pages 153–155.

We begin with extended paraphrases, focusing on several substantive passages that have influenced the thinking of many reflective persons. Your job is to recapture the thinking within the passage by expressing it in your own words. In the excerpts that follow, each text is presented twice, first without our interpretation, second, with our interpretation. After you paraphrase the passages sentence by sentence, read our sample interpretations. (We suggest that you complete your paraphrase before you look at our paraphrase.) View our interpretations not as the right answers but as reasonable interpretations of the passages. Keep in mind that there is always more than one way to accurately paraphrase a sentence. We then provide examples of how one might explicate the thesis of the passage using the clarification format previously introduced. Construct your own explication before reading our example.

We recommend that you look up any words in a dictionary or thesaurus when you are unsure how to express a given phrase or sentence in your own words. Do not rush through these interpretations. Rather, work at every phrase until you are satisfied that you have captured the essential meaning of it as precisely as you can. The art of paraphrase is a cornerstone in close reading.

Reading One

For this reading and for subsequent readings, we begin with some background information and the text to be paraphrased.

THE DECLARATION OF INDEPENDENCE

Background information: To make sense of these paragraphs from the Declaration of Independence, July 4, 1776, one must understand that they are part of a political manifesto adopted by the Continental Congress proclaiming the independence of the 13 British colonies in America from Great Britain.

When in the course of human events, it becomes necessary for one people to dissolve the political bands which have connected them with another, and to assume among the powers of the earth, the separate and equal station to which the laws of nature and of nature's god entitle them, a decent respect to the opinions of mankind requires that they should declare the causes which impel them to the separation.

We hold these truths to be self-evident, that all men are created equal, that they are endowed by their Creator with certain unalienable Rights, that among these are Life, Liberty, and the pursuit of happiness. That to secure these rights, Governments are instituted among Men, deriving their just powers from the consent of the governed. That whenever any Form of Government becomes destructive of these ends, it is the Right of the People to alter or abolish it, and to institute new Government, having its foundation on such principles and organizing its powers in such form, as to them shall seem most likely to effect their Safety and Happiness. Prudence, indeed, will dictate that Governments long established should not be changed for light and transient causes; and accordingly all experience hath shown that mankind are more disposed to suffer, while evils are sufferable, than to right themselves by abolishing the forms to which they are accustomed. But when a long train of abuses and usurpations pursuing invariably the same Object evinces a design to reduce them under absolute Despotism, it is their right, it is their duty, to throw off such Government, and to provide new Guards for their Future security.

FIRST-LEVEL READING: PARAPHRASING

Directions: For the above reading and each one that follows, test your grasp of the passages by paraphrasing them—putting them into your own words. This can be done either in verbal or written form. Compare your reading with the sample interpretation that follows. Before paraphrasing, read the excerpt through one time.

When in the course of human events it becomes necessary for one people to dissolve the political bands which have connected them with another

Paraphrase:

and to assume among the powers of the earth, the separate and equal station to which the laws of nature and of nature's god entitle them,

Paraphrase:

a decent respect to the opinions of mankind requires that they should declare the causes which impel them to the separation.

Paraphrase:

We hold these truths to be self-evident, that all men are created equal, that they are endowed by their Creator with certain unalienable Rights, that among these are Life, Liberty, and the pursuit of happiness.

Paraphrase:

That to secure these rights, Governments are instituted among Men, deriving their just powers from the consent of the governed.

Paraphrase:

That whenever any Form of Government becomes destructive of these ends, it is the Right of the People to alter or abolish it,

Paraphrase:

and to institute new Government, having its foundation on such principles and organizing its powers in such form, as to them shall seem most likely to effect their Safety and Happiness.

Paraphrase:

Prudence, indeed, will dictate that Governments long established should not be changed for light and transient causes;

Paraphrase:

and accordingly all experience hath shown that mankind are more disposed to suffer, while evils are sufferable, than to right themselves by abolishing the forms to which they are accustomed.

Paraphrase:

But when a long train of abuses and usurpations pursuing invariably the same Object evinces a design to reduce them under absolute Despotism, it is their right, it is their duty, to throw off such Government, and to provide new Guards for their Future security.

Paraphrase:

FIRST-LEVEL READING: SAMPLE INTERPRETATION

When in the course of human events, it becomes necessary for one people to dissolve the political bands which have connected them with another

Paraphrase: "Political" arrangements (forms of government) are not necessarily permanent. It is important sometimes to abolish them and set up new arrangements. When this is true, one group of people have to separate themselves from the group to which they were formerly joined.

and to assume among the powers of the earth, the separate and equal station to which the laws of nature and of nature's god entitle them,

Paraphrase: No government should dominate any other government, but all should have the same status (be "separate and equal"). The act of a people declaring themselves independent of other peoples (with whom they were formerly connected) is a perfectly natural act based on "the laws of nature." Therefore the 13 states are "entitled" by natural law to revolt and declare themselves "separate [from] and equal" to all other countries of the world.

a decent respect to the opinions of mankind requires that they should declare the causes which impel them to the separation.

Paraphrase: But when a people decide to break away from another people and establish their own nation, they should—out of respect for the views of other peoples in the world—lay out the reasons that have led them to make their revolutionary decision.

We hold these truths to be self-evident, that all men are created equal, that they are endowed by their Creator with certain unalienable Rights, that among these are Life, Liberty, and the pursuit of happiness.

Paraphrase: There are some truths so obvious that everyone should recognize their truths simply by thinking them through. This includes the truth that every person is as good as any other, and the truth that every person should be accorded the same basic rights. These rights include the right to not be hurt, harmed, or killed; the right to as much freedom (of thought, of movement, of choice of associates, of belief) as is possible; and the right to live their lives as they please.

That to secure these rights, Governments are instituted among Men, deriving their just powers from the consent of the governed.

Paraphrase: The main reason for having a government is to protect our rights to equality, life, liberty, and our own preferred way of living. Governments should have only the power we freely give it to protect our rights. Governments should not rule us; we should rule the government.

That whenever any Form of Government becomes destructive of these ends, it is the Right of the People to alter or abolish it,

Paraphrase: Whenever any government stops protecting our rights (to equality, life, liberty, and our own preferred way of living), we have a right to change that government or end it altogether; for people have an inherent right to revolt against and overthrow any government that fails to enhance our quality of life, our equality, our freedom, and our preferred ways of living. If government is really doing its job, we should all of us experience maximum freedom in our lives and a minimum of restrictions. In a well-governed country, laws should be kept to an absolute minimum.

and to institute new Government, having its foundation on such principles and organizing its powers in such form, as to them shall seem most likely to effect their Safety and Happiness.

Paraphrase: If we do overthrow a government that is failing to provide us with our natural rights, we should start a new government that does.

Prudence, indeed, will dictate that Governments long established should not be changed for light and transient causes;

Paraphrase: If we are practical and discreet and have good judgment, we will not overthrow a government except for important and enduring reasons.

and accordingly all experience hath shown that mankind are more disposed to suffer, while evils are sufferable, than to right themselves by abolishing the forms to which they are accustomed.

Paraphrase: And, in fact, the whole of human history shows us that people are much more apt to suffer their rights being abused than to revolt against such abuse.

But when a long train of abuses and usurpations pursuing invariably the same Object evinces a design to reduce them under absolute Despotism, it is their right, it is their duty, to throw off such Government, and to provide new Guards for their Future security.

Paraphrase: When a government displays a long-standing disregard for the human rights of its own citizens, it is not only the right of such citizens but also the obligation of such citizens to revolt against the government and set up a new one that upholds their natural rights.

SECOND-LEVEL READING: THESIS OF THE DECLARATION

Directions: Complete the following four tasks:

1. State the thesis of the passage in your own words.
2. Elaborate the thesis.
3. Give one or more examples of the thesis.
4. Illustrate the thesis with a metaphor or analogy.

This exercise can be done either in oral or written form.

Statement of thesis. All peoples in the world have a right to revolt against their government and establish a new government—if and when their human rights are systematically violated.

Elaboration of thesis. People are sometimes governed in such a way as to oppress or exploit them and violate their rights as humans. When that occurs, the oppressed people have a revolutionary right to set up their own country and government.

Exemplification of thesis. This situation occurred in France, leading to the French revolution; in America, leading to the American revolution; and in Russia, leading to the Russian revolution.

Illustration of thesis. A political revolution is like a divorce within a family, in which part of the family separates itself from another part and they go their separate ways. Each part becomes a family of its own, with a separate life. Divorces, like revolutions, usually occur when one or more persons have a long-standing grievance that they believe will never be redressed in the present family structure. Like political revolutions, divorces in the family sometimes involve violence.

THIRD-LEVEL READING: LOGIC OF THE DECLARATION

Directions: Analyze the Declaration of Independence. Identify the authors' purpose, and then state:

- the most important question, problem, or issue in the text
- the most significant information or data
- the most basic conclusion
- the most basic concepts, theories, or ideas
- the most fundamental assumptions
- the most significant implications
- the point of view

See pages 127–128 for the template to follow (logic of an article).

After you have completed your third-level reading of the Declaration of Independence, read through the following sample third-level reading.

1. The authors' *purpose:* to enunciate human rights, and their violation, as a justification for the 1776 political revolt of American colonists against Great Britain.

2. The most important *questions,* problems, or issues in the text: Are there universal human rights? Under what conditions are people justified in attempting to overthrow a government? Were the colonists justified in their revolt against Great Britain?

3. The most significant *information* or data in the text: information supporting the view that American colonists were being denied basic rights, that they were suffering at the hands of the government.

4. The most basic *conclusions* of the authors: that the proper function of governments is to protect the universal human rights of citizens so they can live the freest life possible; and that if a government fails to protect the human rights of its citizens, the people have the right to overthrow the government.

5. The most basic *concepts,* theories, or ideas used by the authors: human rights, revolution, and the role and duty of government.

6. The most fundamental *assumptions* of the authors: that all people have the same basic rights, that all governments have the same basic duties to the people, that governments should serve people rather than people serving governments.

7. The most significant *implications* of the text: that of setting an example to the world of people enunciating universal human rights, including, and most important, the right of revolution.

8. The authors' *point of view:* seeing all humans as equal in worth and in human rights; at the same time, seeing all governments as having the obligation to be subservient to people, rather than to dominate them.

FOURTH-LEVEL READING: EVALUATION OF THE DECLARATION THROUGH INTELLECTUAL STANDARDS

Directions: Assess the Declaration of Independence from the point of view of nine basic intellectual standards: clarity, accuracy, precision, depth, breadth, relevance, significance, logic, and fairness.

After you have completed your fourth-level reading of the Declaration of Independence, read through the following sample fourth-level reading:

1. **Clarity:** Do the authors say clearly what they mean, or is the text vague, confused, or muddled in some way? The text is eminently clear, though written in the archaic language of the time.

2. **Accuracy:** Are the authors accurate in what they claim? The standard of accuracy applies most readily to the list of specific grievances that follows but is not incorporated into the text here. The section of the Declaration we read enunciates ideals, not facts. Many people in government would theoretically accept those ideals while violating them in practice. The U.N. Declaration of Human Rights is a modern amplification of basic human rights. It has been signed by all of the nations in the world, yet the violation of human rights is a reality in virtually every country.

3. **Precision:** Are the authors sufficiently precise in providing details and specifics (when relevant)? Like the standard of accuracy, the standard of precision applies most readily to the list of specific grievances that follows the text we read here.

4. **Relevance:** All of the text seems highly relevant to the central purpose of detailing human rights, and their violation, as a justification for the political revolt of American colonists against Great Britain.

5. **Depth:** Do the authors take us into the important complexities inherent in the subject, or is the writing superficial? In a very short text, the Declaration introduces concepts and ideals that are profoundly important in human life and history. Of course, there are many complexities inherent in the subject that are not discussed.

6. **Breadth:** Do the authors consider other relevant points of view, or is the writing overly narrow in its perspective? As a political manifesto, it defends universal human rights and hence is broad in its sweep. At the same time, it excludes a "power rules in a hard, cruel, world" orientation, which seems to motivate many, if not most, politicians and seems to underlie most political reality.

7. **Logic:** Is the text internally consistent, or does it have unexplained contradictions? The text is highly consistent internally. At the same time it is inconsistent with a view that would privilege vested interest over the rights of the common people.

8. **Significance:** Is what the text says significant, or is the subject dealt with in a trivial manner? This manifesto is one of the most significant documents in human history.

9. **Fairness:** Do the authors display fairness, or is the subject dealt with in an unfair manner? Because the Declaration of Independence defends the basic rights of all humans, it is, by implication, fair.

FIFTH-LEVEL READING: ROLE-PLAYING

Directions: You may now deepen your insight even more by role-playing the principal author of the Declaration, namely, Thomas Jefferson. In role playing Jefferson, find someone to question you about the Declaration. Then respond to the questions as if you were Jefferson. Encourage the person to ask whatever questions occur to him or her. Answer by trying to reconstruct what you think Jefferson might say. Make sure that what you "attribute" to him is implied in some way in the text.

Reading Two

"ON CIVIL DISOBEDIENCE"

Background information: This is the opening paragraph of the essay "On Civil Disobedience," originally written in 1849 by Henry David Thoreau, a well-known figure in 19th-century American cultural and literary thought. For this passage we provide first- and second-level readings.

> I heartily accept the motto,—"That government is best which governs least;" and I should like to see it acted up to more rapidly and systematically. Carried out, it finally amounts to this, which also I believe, "That government is best which governs not at all," and when men are prepared for it, that will be the kind of government which they will have. Government is at best but an expedient; but most governments are usually, and all governments are sometimes, inexpedient. The objections which have been brought against a standing army, and they are many and weighty, and deserve to prevail, may also at last be brought against a standing government. The standing army is only an army of the standing government. The government itself, which is only the mode which the people have chosen to execute their will, is equally liable to be abused and perverted before the people can act through it.

FIRST-LEVEL READING: PARAPHRASING

I heartily accept the motto,—"That government is best which governs least;" and I should like to see it acted up to more rapidly and systematically.

Paraphrase:

Carried out, it finally amounts to this, which also I believe,—"That government is best which governs not at all,"

Paraphrase:

and when men are prepared for it, that will be the kind of government which they will have.

Paraphrase:

Government is at best, but an expedient; but most governments are usually, and all governments are sometimes, inexpedient.

Paraphrase:

The objections which have been brought against a standing army, and they are many and weighty, and deserve to prevail, may also at last be brought against a standing government. The standing army is only an army of the standing government. The government itself, which is only the mode which the people have chosen to execute their will, is equally liable to be abused and perverted before the people can act through it.

Paraphrase:

FIRST-LEVEL READING: SAMPLE INTERPRETATION

I heartily accept the motto,—"That government is best which governs least;" and I should like to see it acted up to more rapidly and systematically.

Paraphrase: The most effective form of government is one that establishes the least number of rules, regulations, and laws, so that people are as free as possible to make their own decisions and live in the ways they see fit. The U.S. government is not yet living up to this ideal and Thoreau would like to see the government moving toward that ideal more quickly and more methodically.

Carried out, it finally amounts to this, which also I believe,—"That government is best which governs not at all,"

Paraphrase: The ideal form of government is one that places no rules and regulations on people whatsoever.

and when men are prepared for it, that will be the kind of government which they will have.

Paraphrase: When people can live rationally, respecting the rights and needs of others as a matter of course, making reasonable decisions in thinking through issues and problems, when they rise above needing to be restrained, they will then demand a government that doesn't interfere with their ability to live life as they so choose.

Government is at best, but an expedient; but most governments are usually, and all governments are sometimes, inexpedient.

Paraphrase: Government, at best, is a necessary evil, a contrivance that is useful in the short run. But most governments typically are not useful and beneficial to people, and all governments sometimes fail to serve the people usefully.

The objections which have been brought against a standing army, and they are many and weighty, and deserve to prevail, may also at last be brought against a standing government. The standing army is only an army of the standing government. The government itself, which is only the mode which the people have chosen to execute their will, is equally liable to be abused and perverted before the people can act through it.

Paraphrase: The problems inherent in established governments are similar to the problems that typically emerge where you have established armies within a country. And the two sets of problems are interrelated, because fixed armies are controlled by fixed governments. When governments are established, they presumably are established to carry out the desires of the people they represent. But they often become dysfunctional, failing to achieve their original purposes and intentions, and are used by the "powers that be" to serve the interests of those who are governing rather than those they should be representing. This often happens before the people even have the opportunity to take advantage of the expressed purposes and goals of the government. In other words, this problem seems to be almost a natural implication of an established government (given historical examples).

SECOND-LEVEL READING: THE THESIS OF "ON CIVIL DISOBEDIENCE"

Statement of thesis. All governments tend to abuse power, to generate laws and to make decisions that unduly restrict people's freedom. Therefore, people are best served by governments that govern as little as possible. When people are able to live without being governed, they will demand to live without government.

Elaboration of thesis. Though a democratic government is chosen by the people to carry out the will of the people, it is far too easy and common for governmental power to be used for purposes of vested interests rather than for the best interest of the people. When this happens, the rights of the people are subverted. Therefore a minimalist type of government is the best. But people can have such a government only when they think well enough to demand it and can live rationally without unnecessary governance.

Exemplification of thesis. We can see this thesis illustrated in the U.S.–Mexican War. Though the voters never approved of that war, it was forced on the citizenry by politicians and business people who were greedy for more land, more power, and more profits.

Illustration of thesis. Governments abusing power and doing what is in their interest rather than the interest of the people is similar to bureaucrats designing regulations to fit their own desires or the desires of pressure groups rather than the needs of the people the bureaucracy is supposed to serve.

Reading Three

"ON CIVIL DISOBEDIENCE" (SECOND EXCERPT)

Background information: Here is another paragraph from "On Civil Disobedience," written in 1849 by Henry David Thoreau. For this passage we provide first- and second-level readings.

Can there not be a government in which majorities do not virtually decide what is right and wrong, but conscience? . . . Must the citizen ever for a moment, or in the least degree, resign his conscience, to the legislator? Why has every man a conscience then? I think that we should be men first, and subjects afterward. It is not desirable to cultivate a respect for the law, so much as for the right. The only obligation which I have a right to assume is to do at any time what I think right. . . If the injustice is part of the necessary friction of the machine of government, let it go, let it go. . . . If the injustice has a spring, or a pulley, or a rope, or a crank, exclusively for itself, then perhaps you can consider whether the remedy will not be worse than the evil; but if it is of such a nature that it requires you to be the agent of injustice to another, then I say, break the law. Let your life be a counter friction to stop the machine.

FIRST-LEVEL READING: PARAPHRASING

Can there not be a government in which majorities do not virtually decide what is right and wrong, but conscience?

Paraphrase:

Must the citizen ever for a moment, or in the least degree, resign his conscience, to the legislator? Why has every man a conscience then? I think that we should be men first, and subjects afterward.

Paraphrase:

It is not desirable to cultivate a respect for the law, so much as for the right. The only obligation which I have a right to assume is to do at any time what I think right.

Paraphrase:

If the injustice is part of the necessary friction of the machine of government, let it go, let it go. . . . If the injustice has a spring, or a pulley, or a rope, or a crank, exclusively for itself, then perhaps you can consider whether the remedy will not be worse than the evil;

Paraphrase:

but if it is of such a nature that it requires you to be the agent of injustice to another, then I say, break the law. Let your life be a counter friction to stop the machine.

Paraphrase:

FIRST-LEVEL READING: SAMPLE INTERPRETATION

Can there not be a government in which majorities do not virtually decide what is right and wrong, but conscience?

Paraphrase: Is it possible to be governed in such a way that one can decide for oneself what is right or wrong, based on one's own ethical sense of right and wrong, rather than having a government dictate what is right or wrong based on what most people think?

Must the citizen ever for a moment, or in the least degree, resign his conscience to the legislator? Why has every man a conscience then? I think that we should be men first, and subjects afterward.

Paraphrase: Individual citizens should never, under any circumstances or at any time, give up what they know to be ethically right and instead allow legislators to decide what is right. Why do people have the intellectual ability to figure out what is right and wrong if they are not willing to live in accordance with their sense of what is right? Doing what one deeply judges to be right takes precedence over doing what governments say we should or must do.

It is not desirable to cultivate a respect for the law, so much as for the right. The only obligation which I have a right to assume is to do at any time what I think right.

Paraphrase: It is much more important for people to develop a respect for and understanding of what is right than uncritically to adhere to laws (which may be unjust). The only thing that people are really obligated to do is what they think is right, not what the law says is right. (Of course, this assumes that people understand ethics, and can distinguish it from cultural norms and values.)

If the injustice is part of the necessary friction of the machine of government, let it go, let it go. . . . If the injustice has a spring, or a pulley, or a rope, or a crank, exclusively for itself, then perhaps you can consider whether the remedy will not be worse than the evil;

Paraphrase: Some situations and circumstances are inherently unjust to some people no matter what is done to reduce injustice within systems. It may be the case, for example, that reducing injustice leads to even greater injustice. If this is likely to happen, don't try to change the system. Let it keep functioning as it is.

but if it is of such a nature that it requires you to be the agent of injustice to another, then I say, break the law. Let your life be a counter friction to stop the machine.

Paraphrase: But if the problems within the government are so great that by adhering to laws, you deny someone a fundamental human right, you are ethically obligated to break the law. In that case, stand up against the government. Do whatever you can to stop the government from unjust actions.

SECOND-LEVEL READING: THE THESIS OF "ON CIVIL DISOBEDIENCE"

Statement of thesis. People need to behave more in accordance with their conscience than in accordance with the law. If a law requires you to behave in an unjust way toward another, you are ethically obligated to break the law.

Elaboration of thesis. Some laws might be considered necessary evils, because to change such laws would lead only to greater injustices than the original law. But if the only way to change a truly unjust law is to refuse to abide by the law, a person of conscience will refuse. People should be willing to sacrifice themselves to reduce injustice caused by unfair laws.

Exemplification of thesis. For example, in the U.S. during the 1800s, after slaves in the north were freed, many people helped slaves in the south escape to the north. Though they risked imprisonment for helping free slaves on southern plantations, many people were willing to do this rather than abide by an unjust law.

Illustration of thesis. Think of how we teach children to behave with respect to their peer group. Often a peer group will expect everyone in the group to accept an unjust act. For example, it is common for bullying to be practiced toward outsiders of children's peer groups. Bullying, then, becomes the accepted practice. Those in the group who object to bullying are usually subjected to penalties from the group—for example, they may be ridiculed. Nevertheless, we have taught children well only when they are ready to rebel against the authority of the peer group. So too should adults rebel when dealing with unjust laws passed by their government.

For more practice in paraphrasing and explicating theses of excerpts, see Appendix A.

Exploring Conflicting Ideas

People hold conflicting ideas on many topics that are significant in human life. By reading about the ideas and working out the relationships between them, you will find yourself engaged in substantive writing.

EXERCISE

Directions: In the following exercises the focus is on identifying and writing in a disciplined way about ideas that conflict with one another. Use the following structure:

1. Find two important potentially conflicting ideas. These ideas may be embedded in a text or not. The text may be literary, political, economic, ethical, scientific, personal, sociological, historical, and so forth: freedom vs. law; democracy vs. wealth; power vs. justice; passion vs. objectivity; love vs. control; loyalty vs. prejudice; fact vs. ideology; freedom vs. tradition; new vs. old; nationalism vs. internationalism; politician vs. statesman; ideal vs. real.

2. Express an important problem that exists because of one conflict between the ideas you have selected.

3. Decide on an important point to make about that problem. This is your thesis.

4. Elaborate your thesis.

5. Exemplify your thesis.

6. Illustrate your thesis.

7. Formulate at least one reasonable objection to your position.

8. Respond to that objection (crediting any point in it that is worthy of concession).

Consider the following example. Note that we use a reference to support our thesis.

1. Find two important conflicting ideas. The two ideas I will focus on for this example are the ideas of freedom versus law.

2. Express an important problem that exists because of one conflict between the ideas you have selected. There is often a conflict between the freedoms people should be allowed and the laws that are passed to protect people who might misuse their freedoms.

3. Decide on an important point you want to make about that idea. This is your thesis. It is my belief that the laws and the administration of those laws should allow for the maximum possible individual freedoms, and that all laws that deny people their basic rights should be revoked.

4. Elaborate your thesis. In the United States, at present, there seems to be a growing number of laws that deny people some fundamental human right or other. More and more behavior is being criminalized. More and more people are going to prison for acts that don't harm other people. In many cases the laws—penalizing acts that are merely socially disapproved of—are themselves unethical.

5. Exemplify your thesis. Consider, for example, the many laws governing consensual adult behaviors. In his book entitled *Ain't Nobody's Business If You Do,* Peter McWilliams (1996) says: "More than 750,000 people are in jail right now because of something they did that did not physically harm the person or property of another. In addition, more than 3,000,000 people are on parole or probation for consensual crimes. Further, more than 4,000,000 people are arrested each year for doing something that hurts no one but, potentially, themselves." Among McWilliams' list of the most popular consensual crimes are: "gambling, recreational drug use, religious and psychological therapeutic drug use, prostitution, pornography and obscenity, violations of marriage (adultery, fornication, cohabitation, sodomy, bigamy, polygamy), homosexuality, regenerative drug use, unorthodox medical practices ('Quacks!'), unconventional religious practices ('Cults!'), unpopular political views ('Commies!'), suicide and assisted suicide, transvestism, not using safety devices (such as motorcycle helmets and seat belts), public drunkenness, jaywalking, and loitering and vagrancy (as long as they don't become trespassing or disturbing the peace)." In short, I agree with McWilliams when he says, "You should be allowed to do whatever you want with your own person and property, as long as you don't physically harm the person or property of a non-consenting other."

6. Illustrate your thesis. To illustrate, consider public nudity, which is against the law. For most people it is upsetting to imagine humans walking around in public without clothes on. Such behavior is considered unethical, and has been made illegal. But imagine what the animal kingdom would look like if all animals, not just humans, were forced to clothe themselves, to keep their private parts covered. Imagine horses and dogs and cats wearing shorts and shirts. Consider making it illegal for animals to go about living an animal life without clothes. The very idea is absurd. The fact is that we get upset if people are publicly nude but not if animals are nude. Yet, we too are animals. Human nudity is no more innately disgusting than any other animal nudity.

7. Formulate at least one problem that a reasonable person (who thinks differently from you) might have with your position. A reasonable person opposed to my viewpoint might argue that though many laws violate people's basic rights, legislators who make the laws in a democratic society are carrying out the views of the majority of the people. The person might argue that the only way to change this in a democratic society is to educate people about the implications of unethical laws and hope that they will fight for more reasonable ones.

8. Respond to that problem (crediting any point in the objection that is worthy of concession). I agree that the only way a democracy can work well is when people are educated and therefore able to think through complex issues. I agree that the people are allowing legislators to speak for them, rather than speaking up for themselves, and that people need to become involved in important issues and refuse to support overzealous law-making. Nevertheless, I also think that the majority often is prone to think in a narrow sociocentric manner and therefore inadvertently to support the violation of human rights. I think that the U.S. Bill of Rights should be expanded to encompass the whole of the U.N. Declaration of Human Rights, and that through education we should move toward living in accordance with both of these documents.

Exploring Key Ideas Within Disciplines

This section includes two exercises that focus on key ideas in a number of disciplines. The ideas are significant both academically and in human life. In some cases we ask you to focus on the very idea of the discipline itself. By stating, elaborating, exemplifying, and illustrating the ideas, you will find yourself engaged in substantive writing about each of the disciplines you consider.

For example, consider answering the following questions, as part of the process of learning to think biologically:

- Could you state what photosynthesis is in one simple sentence?
- Could you elaborate more fully what is involved in photosynthesis?
- Could you give me an example of photosynthesis?
- Could you give me an analogy or metaphor to help me see what photosynthesis is like?

The same types of questions can be formulated for explaining a democracy, an equation, mass, energy, a chemical reaction, the key problem facing the main character in a story, the main point in a story, or any other important concept. Every subject area has a network or system of concepts that a person must internalize to think successfully within the subject. When you can answer these four questions for fundamental concepts within a discipline, you begin to take command of both the concepts and the discipline.

We now can suggest a practice pattern for any concept, say "X."

- X is best defined as _____
- In other words, _____
- For example, _____
- To illustrate my explanation with an analogy, X is like _____

Directions: Practice writing your understanding of key concepts within disciplines, using the format above. Here are some disciplines you might consider: Science, Chemistry, Biology, Botany, Geology, Ecology, Anthropology, Sociology, History, Economics, Politics, Psychology, Ethics, Theology, Literature, Philosophy, Painting, Sculpture, Music, Engineering, Logic, Mathematics, Physics. We suggest that you use relevant encyclopedias or other reference materials (e.g., textbooks) to figure out the meanings of these key concepts. But always write the meanings in your own words.

   Once you have written your understanding of each concept, assess your writing by re-reading the explanation of the concept (from the relevant section in a textbook or other resource). By carefully comparing what you said (and didn't say) with the explanation in the textbook, you can identify strengths and weaknesses in your initial understanding of the concept.

Because every discipline contains key concepts or organizing ideas that guide everything else within the discipline, it is important to learn how to write in ways that help you internalize those concepts. Key concepts enable you to grasp the big picture of a discipline. You should master these concepts before learning subordinate concepts. The next exercise provides examples of writing exercises that will enable you to "open up" key concepts in a discipline. This exercise builds on the previous one.

EXERCISE 2

Use the following guides to capture the essence of key concepts:

1. State the meaning of the concept in one simple sentence.
2. State the significance of the idea to the discipline (in other words).
3. Give an example of the concept (as it applies to real life).
4. Give an analogy or metaphor of the concept to link the concept to similar ideas in other domains.
5. Connect the idea to other important ideas within the same domain of thought.
6. Give examples for item 5.

Here is a pattern for practicing the guidelines above:

1. [This concept] is . . .
2. In other words . . .
3. For example . . .
4. To illustrate my explanation with an analogy, X is like . . .
5. This idea is connected to the following ideas within the discipline . . .
6. Some examples that show the relationship between this idea and other important ideas are . . .

Example 1: The Concept "History"

1. State the meaning of the concept in one simple sentence. History is the development of "stories" or accounts of the past with the purpose of understanding how and why things happened, and how we can use that understanding to live better in the present and future.

2. State the significance of the idea to the discipline. Understanding the concept of history is vital to one's ability to think historically, to think like a historian. When we think about the nature of historical thinking, we discover that it is highly selective. For example, during any given historical period, even one as short as a day, millions of events take place, forcing those who would give an account that day to leave out most of what actually happened. No written history contains anything more than a tiny percentage of the total events that took place within the studied historical period. Historians therefore must regularly make value judgments to decide what to include and exclude from their accounts. The result is that there are different possible stories and accounts that highlight different patterns in the events. One historian focuses on great and influential politicians and military figures, another on great ideas and artists, another on technology and its development, another on the role of economics, and another tries to say a little about each of these historical points of view. Because history is always told from some perspective, and every perspective is not equally sound, historical accounts are not necessarily of the same quality. Some historical accounts more accurately represent past events and provide more reasonable interpretations of those events.

3. Give an example of the concept (as it applies to real life). To think historically is to begin to connect history to everyday life. For example, all humans create their own story in the privacy of their minds. This is a form of historical thinking. By recognizing this, we can begin to analyze how we tell the story of our life. We can seek to determine the extent to which we accurately portray events in our past by listening to the historical accounts of our lives given by others. We might find that we are avoiding the truth about some part of our behavior. We might learn from the perspectives of others.

4. Give an analogy or metaphor of the concept to link the concept to similar ideas in other domains. We might compare history to novels. Just as history focuses on giving an account of the past, all novels are set in some time and place and give some account of what it was like to live at that time in that place. Mark Twain's *Huckleberry Finn* gives an account of life along the Mississippi River in the 19th century. Charles Dickens' *A Christmas Carol* gives an account of what life was like for the rich and poor in London in the mid-nineteenth century. John Steinbeck's *The Grapes of Wrath* gives an account of the social dislocation of poor farmers (and of the indifference of large industry to private suffering) in the American states suffering from drought in the 1930s. Both history and novels usually include the character, decisions, and actions of people. Implications of decisions and events are usually highlighted in both.

5. Connect the idea to other important ideas within the same domain of thought. The idea of history is related to the ideas of time, change, growth, progress, conflict, revolution, evolution, permanence, sociocentrism, social conventions, vested interest, and power. To understand history, one must understand how it is connected to the human search to find meaning in life. The past is the key to the present and the future. In it we can find success and failure, waste and war, triumph and suffering, the beginnings of things, their growth and transformations, and their endings.

6. Give examples. History reveals short-term and long-term patterns. In history we find civilizations that last hundreds or thousands of years. We see the omnipresence of war and suffering. We see powerful nations dominating weak nations. We see some groups of people (the technologically advanced) virtually eliminating other groups— as in the domination of European peoples who conquered the Americas.

Example 2: The Concept "Biology"

1. State the meaning of the concept in one simple sentence. Biology is the scientific study of all life forms. Its basic goal is to understand how life forms work, including the fundamental processes and ingredients of all life forms.

2. State the significance of the idea to the discipline. Once one understands the basic idea of a life form, one is ready to understand the common denominators between the 10 million species of living things that exist in the world today. For example, all life forms, no matter how diverse, have the following common characteristics: (1) they are made up of cells, enclosed by a membrane that maintains internal conditions different from their surroundings; (2) they contain DNA or RNA as the material that carries their master plan; and (3) they carry out a process, called metabolism, that involves the conversion of different forms of energy through predictable chemical reactions.

3. Give an example of the concept (as it applies to real life). To think biologically is to see the world as divided into living and non-living matter. It is to see all living things as part of complicated ecosystems. Thinking biologically, you also see living things in terms of the concepts of structure and function. Wherever there is life, you look for it to be structured in specific ways, and you look for all structures to have a function in that living thing.

4. Give an analogy or metaphor of the concept to link the concept to similar ideas in other domains. The notion of living things existing in systems, both internal and external, is similar to the way in which non-living matter exists in physical systems. Looking for "systems" is a hallmark of all science, not just of biology. For example, all chemists see the world as made up of atoms that can cluster together in structural patterns. Furthermore, they see these patterns as making possible transformations of substances from one state to another. If you take one kind of chemical substance and mix it with or expose it to another kind of chemical substance, you may get a chemical reaction resulting in one or more new chemical substances.

5. Connect the idea to other important ideas within the same domain of thought. The idea of life forms is connected with the ideas of the structures that exist at different levels of life (from the smallest to the largest). For example, life at the level of chemical molecules, at the level of organelles, and at the levels of cell, tissue, organ, organism, population, ecological community, and biosphere.

6. Give examples. Biologists can study the role of specific molecules in the structure of organelles, or the role of organelles in the structure of cells, or the role of cells in the structure of tissues, or the role of tissues in the structure of organs, or the role of organs in the structure of organisms, and so forth. Each level of life has a specific relationship to all the others. This multi-system nature makes possible the linking of all sciences together into a massive system of systems.

NOW YOU SHOULD PRACTICE

Focus on key concepts within a discipline (see page 177 for ideas) and use the pattern just modeled to write substantively about them. Use good dictionaries, encyclopedias, and textbooks as references. Remember, there is no one correct answer for what you are doing. The question is: Does writing about this key concept help you gain insight into important dimensions of the powerful ways of thinking that all disciplines and subjects make possible?

Analyzing Reasoning

Substantive writing can be used to understand an author's reasoning—to enter into the author's thinking. To think through the logic of an author's reasoning, complete the following statements in writing (see pp. 127–128 for a fuller template):

■ The author's purpose is . . .

■ The main question the author addresses in the article is . . .

- The most important information the author uses in reasoning through the question is . . .
- The most important inferences or conclusions the author comes to are . . .
- The key concepts the author uses in his or her thinking in writing the article are . . .
- The assumptions underlying the author's reasoning are . . .
- The implications of the author's views (if people take them seriously) are . . .
- The main point of view presented in the article is . . .

We now provide two brief excerpts. Read each one, then, using the template on pages 127–128, write out the logic of the author's reasoning. After doing so, compare your written work to the sample analysis that follows each excerpt.

Writing Substantively to Analyze Reasoning: An Example

A sample analysis follows this brief article.*

IS IT POSSIBLE FOR THE NEWS MEDIA TO REFORM?

To provide their publics with non-biased writing, journalists around the world would have to, first, enter empathically into world views to which they are not at present sympathetic. They would have to imagine writing for audiences that hold views antithetical to the ones they hold. They would have to develop insights into their own sociocentrism. They would have to do the things done by critical consumers of the news. The most significant problem is that, were they to do so, their readers would perceive their articles as "biased" and "slanted," as "propaganda." These reporters would be seen as irresponsible, as allowing their personal point of view to bias their journalistic writings. Imagine Israeli journalists writing articles that present the Palestinian point of view sympathetically. Imagine Pakistani journalists writing articles that present the Indian point of view sympathetically.

The most basic point is this: journalists do not determine the nature and demands of their job. They do not determine what their readers want or think or hate or fear. The nature and demands of their job are determined by the broader nature of societies themselves and the beliefs, values and world views of its members. It is human nature to see the world, in the first instance, in egocentric and sociocentric terms. Most people are not interested in having their minds broadened. They want their present beliefs and values extolled and confirmed. Like football fans, they want the home team to win, and when it wins to triumph gloriously. If they lose, they want to be told that the game wasn't important, or that the other side cheated, or that the officials were biased against them.

---

*Paul, R. and Elder, L. (2003). *The Miniature Guide for Conscientious Citizens on How to Detect Media Bias and Propaganda.* Dillon Beach, CA: Foundation for Critical Thinking.

As long as the overwhelming mass of persons in the broader society are drawn to news articles that reinforce, and do not question, their fundamental views or passions, the economic imperatives will remain the same. The logic is parallel to that of reforming a nation's eating habits. As long as the mass of people want high fat processed foods, the market will sell high fat and processed foods to them. And as long as the mass of people want simplistic news articles that reinforce egocentric and sociocentric thinking, that present the world in sweeping terms of good and evil (with the reader's views and passions treated as good and those of the reader's conceived enemies as evil), the news media will generate such articles for them. The profit and ratings of news sources that routinely reinforce the passions and prejudices of their readers will continue to soar.

Sample Analysis

The main purpose of this article is: To show why the news media are not likely to alter their traditional practices of slanting the news in keeping with their audience's preconceptions.

The key question that the authors are addressing is: "Why is it not possible for the news media to reform?"

The most important information in this article is:

1. Information about how and why the news media currently operates:
   a. That the news media slant stories to fit the viewpoint of their audience. "Most people are not interested in having their views broadened. . . . Like football fans they want the home team to win. . . . The overwhelming mass of persons in the broader society are drawn to news articles that reinforce, and do not question, their fundamental views or passions."
   b. That the fundamental purpose of the mainstream news media is to make money. "As long as the mass of people want simplistic news articles . . . the news media will generate such articles for them. The profit and ratings of news sources that routinely reinforce the passions and prejudices of their readers will continue to soar."

2. Information about how the news media would have to change to be more intellectually responsible:
   a. That the news media would actively have to enter differing world views. "Imagine Israeli journalists writing articles that present the Palestinian point of view sympathetically. Imagine Pakistani journalists writing articles that present the Indian point of view sympathetically."
   b. That the news media would have to "develop insights into their own sociocentrism."

The main assumptions underlying the authors' thinking are: The driving force behind the news media is vested interest—i.e., making money; that the news media therefore pander to their readers' views so as to sell more papers; but that, at the same time, the news media must appear to function objectively and fairly.

The key concepts that guide the authors' reasoning in this article are: biased and unbiased journalism, egocentrism and sociocentrism, propaganda. (Each of these concepts should be elaborated.)

The main inferences in this article are: "As long as the overwhelming mass of persons in the broader society are drawn to news articles that reinforce, and do not question, their fundamental views or passions," the news will be presented in a biased way. Because the fundamental purpose of the media is to make money, and the only way people will buy papers is if their sociocentric views are reinforced and not questioned, the media will continue distort events in accordance with audience views.

If this line of reasoning is justified, the implications are: Citizens need to think critically about the news media and how they systematically distort stories in accordance with reader bias. People need to notice how their own sociocentric views are intensified by what they read.

The main point of view presented in this article is: The world news media function as profit-making enterprises that structure the news to pander to reader and society prejudices.

THE PROBLEM OF PSEUDO-ETHICS: THE SOCIOCENTRIC COUNTERFEITS OF ETHICAL REASONING*

Skilled ethical thinkers routinely distinguish ethics from other domains of thinking such as those of social conventions (conventional thinking), religion (theological thinking), politics (ideological thinking), and the law (legal thinking). Too often, ethics is confused with these very different modes of thinking. It is not uncommon, for example, for highly variant and conflicting social values and taboos to be treated as if they were universal ethical principles.

Thus, religious ideologies, social "rules," and laws are often mistakenly taken to be inherently ethical in nature. If we were to accept this amalgamation of domains, by implication every practice within any religious system would necessarily be ethical, every social rule ethically obligatory, and every law ethically justified.

If religion were to define ethics, we could not then judge any religious practices— e.g., torturing unbelievers or burning them alive—as unethical. In the same way, if ethical and conventional thinking were one and the same, every social practice within any culture would necessarily be ethically obligatory—including social conventions in

---

*Elder, L. and Paul, R. (2003). *The Miniature Guide to the Foundations of Analytic Thinking*. Dillon Beach, CA: Foundation for Critical Thinking.

Nazi Germany. We could not, then, condemn any social traditions, norms, mores, and taboos from an ethical standpoint—however ethically bankrupt they were. What's more, if the law were to define ethics, by implication politicians and lawyers would be considered experts on ethics and every law they finagled to get on the books would take on the status of a moral truth.

It is essential, then, to differentiate ethics from other modes of thinking commonly confused with ethics. We must remain free to critique commonly accepted social conventions, religious practices, political ideas, and laws, using ethical concepts not defined by them. No one lacking this ability can become proficient in ethical reasoning.

Examples of confusing ethical principles with theological beliefs:

- Members of majority religious groups sometimes enforce their beliefs on minorities.

- Members of religious groups sometimes act as if their theological beliefs are self-evidently true, scorning those who hold other views.

- Members of religious groups sometimes fail to recognize that "sin" is a theological concept, not an ethical one. ("Sin" is theologically defined.)

- Divergent religions do not agree on what is sinful (but often expect their views to be enforced on all others as if a matter of universal ethics).

Examples of confusion between ethics and social conventions:

- Many societies have created taboos against showing various parts of the body and have severely punished those who violated the taboos.

- Many societies have created taboos against giving women the same rights as men.

- Many societies have socially legitimized religious persecution.

- Many societies have socially stigmatized interracial marriages.

Examples of confusing ethics and the law:

- Many sexual practices (such as homosexuality) have been unjustly punished with life imprisonment or death (under the laws of one society or another).

- Many societies have enforced unjust laws based on racist views.

- Many societies have enforced laws that discriminated against women.

- Many societies have enforced laws that discriminated against children.

- Many societies have made torture and/or slavery legal.

- Many societies have enforced laws arbitrarily punishing people for using some drugs but not others.

Sample Analysis

The main purpose of this article is: To convince the reader that ethics should not be confused with other modes of thinking—specifically religion, social conventions, and the law.

The key question that the authors are addressing is: How does ethics differ from other ways of thinking?

The most important information in this article consists of:

1. Examples of confusing ethical principles with theological beliefs: Members of majority religious groups often enforce their beliefs on minorities.
2. Examples of confusion between ethics and social conventions: Many societies have created taboos against showing various parts of the body and have severely punished those who violated the taboos.
3. Examples of confusing ethics and the law: Many sexual practices (such as homosexuality) have been unjustly punished with life imprisonment or death.

The key concepts that guide the authors' reasoning in this article are: ethical reasoning, social conventions (conventional thinking), religion (theological thinking), politics (ideological thinking), and the law (legal thinking).

The main assumptions underlying the authors' thinking are: That it is important for people to understand that ethics cannot be confused with or subordinated to other modes of thinking, that many people do not understand ethics as separate from other modes of reasoning, and that it is dangerous for people to consider ethics as something that can be defined by theology, society, or laws.

The main inferences/conclusions in this article are: "It is essential to differentiate ethics from other modes of thinking commonly confused with ethics," and that only when we can differentiate ethics from other modes of thinking can we critique practices within other modes of thinking from an ethical perspective.

If this line of reasoning is justified, the implications are: People need to understand ethics and to separate clearly in their own minds ethics from other modes of thinking often confused with ethics. Moreover, people need to call into question the common practice of confusing ethics with other domains of thought. If they fail to do so, religious practices, social conventions, and the law will determine what is to be considered ethical within a society.

The main point of view presented in this article is: People largely fail to differentiate ethics from other modes of thinking, and, therefore, they often use the wrong standards for determining what is ethically right and wrong in human conduct.

Evaluating Reasoning

Every written piece is not of the same quality. You can assess your own writing by applying intellectual standards to it—standards such as clarity, accuracy, precision, depth, breadth, relevance, significance, logic, and fairness. You might be clear in stating your position, while using information that is not accurate. You might use relevant information in a written piece but fail to think through the complexities of the issue (e.g., fail to achieve depth). Your argument might be logical but not significant. As a writer, then, you need to become adept at assessing the quality of your reasoning.

To assess our writing, we should ask the following questions:

1. Is our meaning **clearly** stated (or is our writing vague, confused, or muddled in some way)?

2. Have we been **accurate** in what we have claimed?

3. Have we been sufficiently **precise** in providing details and specifics (when specifics are relevant)?

4. Do we stray from our purpose (thereby straying away from **relevant** material)?

5. Do we take the reader into the important **complexities** inherent in the subject (or is our writing superficial)?

6. Is our writing overly **narrow** in its perspective?

7. Is our writing internally **consistent** (or are there unexplained contradictions in the text)?

8. Have we said something **significant** (or have we dealt with the subject in a trivial manner)?

9. Have we been **fair** (or have we taken a one-sided, narrow approach)?

YOUR TURN TO PRACTICE

Use the questions about the intellectual standards to assess the logic of the authors' reasoning in the texts given on page 182–185.

BECOME A FAIR-MINDED THINKER

I t is possible to develop as a thinker and yet not to develop as a *fair-minded* thinker. In other words, it is possible to learn to use your thinking skills in a narrow, self-serving way. In fact, many highly skilled thinkers do just that. Many politicians, for example, manipulate people through smooth talk, promise what they have no intention of delivering, and say whatever they need to say to maintain their positions of power and prestige. In a sense, these people are skilled thinkers, because their thinking enables them to *get what they want*. But the best thinkers do not pursue selfish goals, and they do not manipulate others. They strive to be fair-minded, even when it means they have to give something up. They recognize that the mind is not naturally fair-minded, but selfish. And they understand that to be fair-minded, they must also develop particular traits of mind, traits such as intellectual humility, intellectual integrity, intellectual courage, intellectual autonomy, intellectual empathy, intellectual perseverance, and confidence in reason.

This chapter focuses on what it means to be fair-minded. We will also discuss other traits of mind that accompany fair-mindedness. If you are to develop as a fair-minded thinker, you will need to practice being fair-minded. You will need to catch yourself in acts of selfishness and begin to correct your behavior. You will need to become committed to living a rational, compassionate, contributory life, to looking outside yourself and seeing how your behavior affects other people. You will need to decide, again and again, that being fair-minded is important to you.

EXHIBIT 8.1 *Critical thinkers strive to develop essential traits or characteristics of mind. These are interrelated intellectual habits that enable one to discipline and improve mental functioning.*

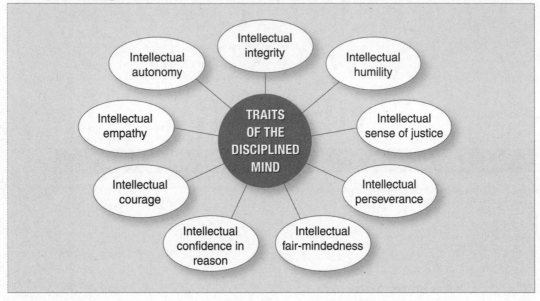

EXHIBIT 8.2 *These are the opposites of the intellectual virtues. Our natural tendency to develop them is an important reason why we need to develop countervailing traits.*

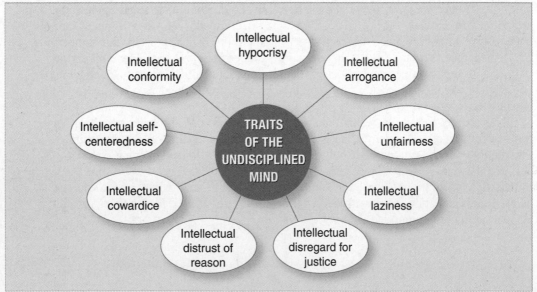

WEAK VERSUS STRONG CRITICAL THINKING

Critical thinking can be used to serve two incompatible ends: self-centeredness or fair-mindedness. As you learn the basic intellectual skills that critical thinking entails, you can begin to use those skills either in a selfish or in a fair-minded way. For example, when students are taught how to recognize mistakes in reasoning (commonly called fallacies), most students readily see those mistakes in the reasoning of others but do not see them so readily in their own reasoning. Often they enjoy pointing out others' errors and develop some proficiency in making their opponents' thinking look bad, but they don't generally use their understanding of fallacies to analyze and assess their own reasoning.

Liberals see mistakes in the arguments of conservatives; conservatives see mistakes in the arguments of liberals. Believers see mistakes in the thinking of nonbelievers; nonbelievers see mistakes in the thinking of believers. Those who oppose abortion see mistakes in the arguments for choice; those who favor choice readily see mistakes in the arguments against it.

We call these thinkers *weak-sense* critical thinkers. We call their thinking "weak" because, though it is working well for the thinker in some respects, it is missing certain important higher-level skills and values of critical thinking. Most significantly, these thinkers fail to consider, in good faith, viewpoints that contradict their own viewpoint. They lack fair-mindedness.

Another traditional name for the weak-sense thinker is *sophist.* Sophistry is the art of winning arguments regardless of whether there are problems in the thinking being used, regardless of whether relevant viewpoints are being ignored. The objective in sophistic thinking is to win—period. Sophistic thinkers generally use lower-level skills of rhetoric, or argumentation, by which they make unreasonable thinking look reasonable and reasonable thinking look unreasonable. This form of thinking can be easily seen in unethical lawyers, prosecutors, and politicians who are more concerned with winning than with being fair. They use emotionalism and trickery in an intellectually skilled way. Consider the case of Delma Banks, a man convicted of murder in 1980. According to the *New York Times* (Feb. 25, 2004),

> The Supreme Court overturned a Texas inmate's death sentence on Tuesday on the ground that the prosecution deliberately withheld evidence that would have made jurors less likely to impose the death penalty had they been aware of it. . . . In her majority opinion, Justice Ruth Bader Ginsburg directly rebuked the Texas prosecutors for concealing facts they had a legal obligation to disclose and for permitting the state's witnesses to testify untruthfully. . . . Mr. Banks, who was convicted in 1980 of killing a 16-year-old co-worker at a Texarkana steak house to steal his car, came within 10 minutes of execution last March before the Supreme Court granted a stay and agreed to hear his appeal.

Or consider the case of Martin Tankleff, a man convicted of murdering his parents when he was 17 years old. According to the *New York Times* (April 4, 2004),

> K. James McCready, a veteran Suffolk County [New York] homicide detective, was off duty the morning of Sept. 7, 1988, when his beeper summoned him to a murder scene at a luxury waterfront home in Belle Terre. Inside was a gruesome sight. Arlen Tankleff

had been stabbed and bludgeoned to death. Her brutally wounded husband, Seymour, was unconscious and died weeks later in a hospital. Within hours of surveying the scene, Detective McCready declared the case solved. He singled out the couple's son, Martin, 17, as the prime suspect. In a long interrogation that day, the detective later boasted, he used deception to trick him into confessing. But Mr. Tankleff promptly disavowed the confession, refused to sign it, and the physical evidence did not implicate him. Yet he was convicted in 1990, based on the statement extracted by Detective McCready and his testimony as the star prosecution witness. . . . The Suffolk County system that prosecuted Mr. Tankleff [at that time] was under attack from many quarters as inept and even corrupt. . . . A State Investigation Commission report in 1989 found that the authorities had botched major cases. . . by coercing false confessions, brutalizing suspects, illegally tapping phones, lying on the witness stand, engaging in cover-ups and ignoring, losing or faking crucial evidence.

In both of these we see examples of intellectual sophistry at work—in particular, skillfully hiding or distorting evidence in pursuit of a particular goal.

8.1   *Think for Yourself*

FINDING EVIDENCE OF INTELLECTUAL SOPHISTRY

In the next week, read articles in newspapers, news magazines, and so forth; looking for intellectual sophistry at work. Look for situations where someone deliberately hides or distorts information in pursuing a goal. Note whether the person gets away with the sophistry.

Sophistic thinkers succeed only if they do not come up against what we call *strong-sense* critical thinkers. Strong-sense critical thinkers are not easily tricked by slick argumentation, sophistry, or intellectual trickery. The striking characteristic of strong-sense critical thinkers is a consistent pursuit of the fair and just. These thinkers strive always to be ethical—to behave in ways that do not exploit or otherwise harm others. They work to empathize with the viewpoints of others. They are willing to listen to arguments they do not necessarily hold. They change their views when faced with better reasoning. Rather than using their thinking to manipulate others and to hide from the truth (in a weak-sense way), they use thinking in an ethical, reasonable manner. William Graham Sumner (1906) depicted strong-sense critical thinkers almost a century ago. He said they:

> cannot be stampeded . . . are slow to believe . . . can hold things as possible or probable in all degrees, without certainty and without pain . . . can wait for evidence and weigh evidence . . . can resist appeals to their dearest prejudices. . . .

We believe that the world already has too many skilled selfish thinkers, too many sophists and intellectual con artists, too many unscrupulous lawyers and politicians who specialize in twisting information and evidence to support their selfish interests and the vested interests of those who pay them. We hope that you will develop as a highly skilled, fair-minded thinker, someone capable of exposing those who are masters at playing intellectual games at the expense of the well-being of innocent people.

We hope as well that you develop the intellectual courage to argue publicly against what is unethical in human thinking. We write this book hoping that you will pursue critical thinking skills, but will use those skills fair-mindedly.

To think critically in the strong sense, you must develop fair-mindedness at the same time that you learn basic critical thinking skills, and begin to "practice" fair-mindedness in your thinking right away. Avoid using your skills to gain advantage over others. Treat all thinking according to the same high standards, whether it is your own or someone else's. Expect good reasoning from those who support you as well as those who oppose you. Subject your own reasoning to the same criteria you apply to reasoning to which you are unsympathetic. Question your own purposes, evidence, conclusions, implications, and point of view with the same vigor as you question those of others.

Fair-minded thinkers try to see the actual strengths and weaknesses of any reasoning they assess. This is the kind of thinker we hope this book will help you become. As you learn the concepts in this book, we hope you apply them in the strongest, most fair-minded way. As you have worked through the book to this point, we hope you have noticed how we have attempted to foster strong-sense critical thinking. In fact, our concept of critical thinking, and the definition of critical thinking we find most defensible, is critical thinking in the *strong sense*.

In the remainder of this chapter, we explore the various intellectual "virtues" that fair-minded thinking requires. There is much more to fair-mindedness than most people realize. Fair-mindedness requires a family of interrelated and interdependent states of mind. It implies commitment to fair thinking, as well as higher order, highly skilled thinking. As you develop your reasoning abilities and internalize the traits of mind in this chapter, you will develop a variety of skills and insights that weak-sense critical thinkers do not have.

As we examine the various traits of mind that are conducive to fair-mindedness, we will also look at the ways these same traits contribute to quality of thought in general. In addition to fairness, strong-sense critical thinking implies depth of thinking and high-quality thinking. Weak-sense critical thinkers do develop a range of intellectual skills (for example, skills of argumentation) and may achieve some success in getting what they want, but they do not develop the traits highlighted in this chapter.

Some students are able to use their intelligence and thinking skills to get high grades without taking seriously the subjects they are studying. They become masters, if you will, of "beating the system." They develop test-taking and note-taking skills. They develop short-term memory skills. They learn to appeal to the prejudices of their teachers. They become academic sophists, skilled at getting by and getting what they want. They may even transfer these abilities to other domains of their lives. But they do not develop as fair-minded critical thinkers.

Let us turn to the traits of the strong-sense critical thinker. In each section we will:

1. introduce an intellectual trait or virtue
2. discuss the opposite form of the trait
3. point out how the trait relates to the development of critical thinking
4. relate the trait to fair-mindedness.

But first, let us understand the basic concept of fair-mindedness.

WHAT DOES FAIR-MINDEDNESS REQUIRE?

To be fair-minded is to strive to treat every viewpoint relevant to a situation in an unbiased, unprejudiced way. It entails a consciousness of the fact that we, by nature, tend to prejudge the views of others, placing them into "favorable" (agrees with us) and "unfavorable" (disagrees with us) categories. We tend to give less weight to contrary views than to our own. This is especially true when we have selfish reasons for disregarding opposing views. If, for example, we can ignore the viewpoint of the millions of people in the world who live in extreme poverty, we can avoid having to give up something to help them. Thus fair-mindedness is especially important when a situation calls on us to consider views that we don't want to consider.

> Fair-mindedness entails the predisposition to equally consider all relevant viewpoints, without reference to one's own feelings or selfish interests, or the feelings or selfish interests of one's friends, community, or nation. It implies adherence to intellectual standards (such as accuracy, sound logic, and breadth of vision), uninfluenced by one's own advantage or the advantage of one's group.

The opposite of fair-mindedness is *intellectual unfairness*. To be intellectually unfair is to lack any sense of responsibility to represent accurately and fairly viewpoints with which one disagrees. When we are intellectually unfair we almost always see ourselves as being fair. There is almost always an element of self-deception in our unfair thoughts and actions. We justify ourselves, rationalize our behavior, and convince ourselves that we are "right."

Because we are naturally egocentric, each of us falls prey at times to unfair thinking. Indeed, egocentrism (and therefore unfair thinking) is the natural state of the human mind—we will discuss this further in the chapter on human irrationality (Chapter 9). We simply want to stress here that the traits in this chapter can *never* be fully achieved. No one is always fair-minded. The mind is naturally too egocentric and too self-interested. Maintaining fair-mindedness is a constant inner struggle that we must face each and every day. But the reward is a mind that is self-disciplined, that cannot be easily manipulated, that is able to see the truth, and that strives at all times to deal fairmindedly.

Achieving a truly fair-minded state of mind, then, is challenging. Fair-mindedness requires us to be, simultaneously, intellectually humble, intellectually courageous, intellectually empathetic, intellectually honest, intellectually perseverant, confident in reason (willing to be persuaded by good reasoning), and intellectually autonomous. Without this family of traits functioning together, there is no true fair-mindedness.

But these traits are not commonly valued. They are virtually never discussed in everyday life, and they are rarely taught. They are not discussed on television, nor are they part of the school curriculum. They are not assessed in standardized testing. Yet each of them is essential to fair-mindedness and inherent in strong-sense critical thinking. Let us see how and why this is so.

Intellectual Humility: The Best Thinkers Strive to Discover the Extent of Their Ignorance

We will begin with the fair-minded trait of *intellectual humility*.

> To have intellectual humility is to be aware of the limits of one's knowledge and to understand the natural inclination of the mind to overestimate what it knows. Thus intellectual humility includes an acute awareness of the fact that our egocentrism is likely to deceive us (to tell the mind, in other words, that it knows more than it does). Intellectual humility means being aware of one's biases and prejudices as well as the limitations of one's viewpoint. It involves being keenly aware of the extent of one's ignorance when thinking through any particular issue or thinking within any content area. Intellectual humility depends on recognizing that one should not claim more than one actually knows. It does not imply spinelessness or submissiveness. It implies the lack of intellectual arrogance, pretentiousness, boastfulness, or conceit. It requires identifying and assessing the foundations of one's beliefs, looking especially for those that cannot be justified through good reasons.

The opposite of intellectual humility is *intellectual arrogance,* a natural tendency to think one knows more than one does know. Intellectual arrogance involves having little or no insight into self-deception or into the limitations of one's point of view. Intellectually arrogant people often fall prey to their own biases and prejudices, and frequently claim to know more than they actually know.

Intellectual arrogance does not necessarily imply that a person is outwardly smug, haughty, insolent, or pompous. Outwardly, the person may appear humble. For example, people who uncritically follow a cult leader may be outwardly self-deprecating ("I am nothing. You are everything"), but intellectually they believe things that do not make sense to believe while at the same time being fully confident in their beliefs.

Unfortunately, people of all personality types are capable of believing they know what they don't know. Our own false beliefs, misconceptions, prejudices, illusions, myths, propaganda, and ignorance often appear to us as the plain truth. What is more, when challenged, we often resist admitting that our thinking is "defective." Rather than recognizing the limits of our knowledge, we ignore and obscure those limits. From such arrogance, much suffering and waste result.

For example, when Columbus "discovered" North America, he believed that enslaving the Indians was compatible with God's will. He did not inwardly—as far as we know—recognize that it was only through intellectual arrogance that he could believe he was privy to "God's will." Consider the following excerpt from Howard Zinn's *A People's History of the United States* (1995):

> The Indians, Columbus reported, "are so naïve and so free with their possessions that no one who has not witnessed them would believe it. When you ask for something they

have, they never say no. To the contrary, they offer to share with anyone. . . . " He concluded his report by asking for a little help from their Majesties, and in return he would bring them from his next voyage "as much gold as they need . . . and as many slaves as they ask." He was full of religious talk: "Thus the eternal God, our Lord, gives victory to those who follow His way over apparent impossibilities. . . . " Columbus later wrote, "Let us in the name of the Holy Trinity go on sending all the slaves that can be sold." (pp. 3–4)

Intellectual arrogance is incompatible with fair-mindedness because we cannot judge fairly when we are in a state of ignorance about that which we are judging. If we are ignorant about a religion (say, Buddhism), we cannot be fair in judging it. And if we have misconceptions, prejudices, or illusions about it, we will unfairly distort it. We will misrepresent it in order to discount it. Our false knowledge, misconceptions, prejudices, and illusions will keep us from being fair. We will be inclined to judge too quickly and be overly confident in our judgment. These tendencies are all too common in human thinking.

Why is intellectual humility essential to higher-level thinking? In addition to helping you become a fair-minded thinker, knowledge of your own ignorance can improve your thinking in a variety of ways. It can enable you to recognize the prejudices, false beliefs, and habits of mind that lead to flawed learning. Consider, for example, the tendency to learn superficially. We learn a little and (by nature) think we know a lot. We get limited information and hastily generalize from it. We confuse memorized definitions with deep learning. We uncritically accept much that we hear and read—especially when what we hear or read agrees with our intensely held beliefs or the beliefs of groups to which we belong.

To develop at all as a thinker requires some intellectual humility. The more intellectual humility you have, or develop, the more you can learn and grow, the more open you are to new ideas. Starting now, make the commitment to continually seek the limitations of your knowledge. Work on detecting your intellectual arrogance in action (which you should be able to see on a daily basis). When you do detect it, celebrate that awareness. Reward yourself for finding weaknesses in your thinking. Consider *recognition* of weakness an important strength, not a weakness. As a start, answer the following questions:

- Can you construct a list of your most significant prejudices? (Think of what you believe about your country, your religion, your friends, and your family, simply because others—parents, friends, peer group, media—have conveyed these beliefs to you.)
- To what extent do you argue for or against views when you have little evidence upon which to base your judgment?
- To what extent do you assume that your group (your family, your religion, your nation, or your friends) is correct (when it is in conflict with others), even when you don't have enough information to determine that it actually is correct?

8.2   *Think for Yourself*

INTELLECTUAL HUMILITY

Name a person you think you know fairly well. Make two lists. In the first list include everything you know for sure about the person. In the second list include everything you know you *don't know* about him or her. For example: "I know for sure that my grandmother liked to cook, but I'm also sure that I never knew her views on intimate relationships or politics. I knew many superficial things about her, but about her inner self I knew little." Be prepared to back up what you claim with an explanation of your thinking.

8.3   *Think for Yourself*

RECOGNIZING SUPERFICIAL LEARNING

Intellectual humility involves the ability to distinguish between learning that is deep and learning that is superficial. In this activity we ask you to test your ability to do this. Think of a course you completed in which you received a high or fairly high final grade. On a blank sheet of paper write and elaborate on, without consulting any sources, answers to the following questions:

What is the subject (for example, history or biology)?

What is the main goal of studying this subject?

What are people in this field trying to accomplish?

What kinds of questions do they ask?

What kinds of problems do they solve?

What sorts of information or data do they gather?

How do they go about gathering information in ways that are distinctive to this field?

What is the most basic idea, concept, or theory in this field?

How did studying this field change your view of the world?

If you find it difficult to answer these questions, consider the possibility that you might have received your high grade by cramming for tests or by some other means of superficial learning. Are you able to identify the difference between what you have learned superficially and what you have learned deeply?

Intellectual Courage: The Best Thinkers Have the Courage to Challenge Popular Beliefs

Now let's consider *intellectual courage.*

Having intellectual courage means facing and fairly addressing ideas, beliefs, or viewpoints even when it is painful to do so. It means closely examining beliefs toward which one has strong negative emotions and to which one has not given a serious hearing. An important part of intellectual courage is recognizing that ideas society considers dangerous or absurd are sometimes rationally justified (in whole or in part) or simply matters of subjective taste. Conclusions and beliefs inculcated in people by society are sometimes false or misleading. To determine what makes sense to believe, one must not passively and uncritically accept what one has learned. Having intellectual courage is especially important because there may be some truth in ideas considered dangerous or absurd, as well as distortion or falsity in ideas strongly held by social groups to which we belong. To be fair-minded thinkers in these circumstances, we must develop intellectual courage. We must be willing not only to examine beliefs we hold dear, but also to stand alone, when necessary, against the crowd. We must have the *courage* to do so. Realize that the penalties placed on us by society for nonconformity can be severe.

The opposite of intellectual courage, *intellectual cowardice,* is the fear of ideas that do not conform to one's own. If we lack intellectual courage, we are afraid of giving serious consideration to ideas, beliefs, or viewpoints that we perceive as dangerous. We feel personally threatened by ideas that seem to conflict with our personal identity. The unwillingness to examine one's beliefs implies that there may be some problem with the justifiability of those beliefs.

All of the following ideas are "sacred" in the minds of some people: being a conservative, being a liberal; believing in God, disbelieving in God; believing in capitalism, believing in socialism; believing in abortion, disbelieving in abortion; believing in capital punishment, disbelieving in capital punishment. We often say of ourselves: "I am a(an)_____ (insert sacred belief here; for example, I am a *Christian.* I am a *conservative.* I am a *socialist.* I am an *atheist).*"

Once we define who we are through an emotional commitment to our beliefs, we are likely to experience inner fear when those beliefs are questioned. This is the first form of intellectual cowardice. Questioning our beliefs can seem to mean questioning who we are as persons. The intensely personal fear that we feel keeps us from being fair to opposing beliefs. When we "consider" opposing ideas, we may subconsciously undermine them, presenting them in their weakest forms, so that we can reject them. We need intellectual courage to overcome self-created inner fear—the fear we ourselves have created by linking our identity to a specific set of beliefs.

Another important reason for developing intellectual courage is to overcome the fear of being rejected by others when we challenge their beliefs, or merely differ with them. When we fear rejection of our beliefs, we often allow others to intimidate us. Many people judge themselves according to the views of others, and cannot approve of themselves unless they are approved of by others. Fear of rejection often lurks in the back of their minds. Few people challenge the ideologies or belief systems of the groups to which they belong. This is the

The best thinkers do not connect their identities to their beliefs.

second form of intellectual cowardice. Both forms make it impossible to consider ideas fairly, either our own or others.

Instead of forming your identity according to your personal beliefs, it is far better to define yourself according to the *processes* by which you formulate beliefs. This is what it means to be a critical thinker. Consider the following resolution:

> I will not *identify* with the content of any belief. I will identify only with the *way* I come to my beliefs. I am a critical thinker and, as such, am willing to examine my beliefs and abandon any beliefs that cannot be supported by evidence and rational considerations. I am ready to follow evidence and reason wherever they lead. My true identity is that of being a critical thinker, a lifelong learner, a person always looking to improve my thinking by becoming more reasonable in my beliefs.

When we refuse to connect our identity with our beliefs, we become more intellectually courageous and more fair-minded. We are no longer afraid to consider beliefs that are contrary to our present beliefs. We are not afraid of being proven wrong. We freely admit to having made mistakes in the past. We are happy to correct any mistakes we are still making. "Tell me what you believe and why you believe it, and maybe I can learn from your thinking. I have cast off many early beliefs. I am ready to abandon any of my present beliefs that are not consistent with the truth." Given this definition, how many people do you know who have intellectual courage?

> The best thinkers follow evidence and reason wherever they lead.

8.4   *Think for Yourself*

INTELLECTUAL COURAGE I

Think of the groups to which you belong, and select one. Complete the following statements:

1. One main belief common to members of this group that might be questioned is . . . (identify at least one belief that may lead group members to behave irrationally).
2. This belief might be questioned because . . .
3. I would or would not be able to stand up to my group, pointing out the problems with this belief, because . . .

8.5   *Think for Yourself*

INTELLECTUAL COURAGE II

Try to think of a time when either you or someone you know defended a view that was unpopular in a group to which you belonged. Describe the circumstances and especially how the group responded. If you can't think of an example, what does that fact tell you?

Intellectual Empathy: The Best Thinkers Empathically Enter Opposing Views

Next let's consider *intellectual empathy,* another trait of mind necessary to fair-mindedness.

> To have intellectual empathy is to imaginatively put oneself in the place of others on a routine basis, so as to genuinely understand them. It requires one to accurately reconstruct the viewpoints and reasoning of others and to reason from premises, assumptions, and ideas other than one's own. This trait requires the motivation to recall occasions when one was wrong in the past despite an intense conviction of being right, and the ability to imagine that the same might be true now.

The opposite of intellectual empathy is *intellectual self-centeredness.* It is thinking centered on self. When we think from a self-centered perspective, we are unable to understand others' thoughts, feelings, and emotions. This, unfortunately, is the natural state of the human mind. From this perspective, most of our attention is focused on ourselves. Our own pain, desires, and hopes are most pressing. The needs of others pale in significance to our own. We are unable to consider issues, problems, and questions from a viewpoint that might force us to change our perspective.

How can we be fair to the thinking of others if we haven't genuinely tried to understand that thinking? Fair-minded judgment requires a good-faith effort to put oneself into the mind-set of another. It requires an appreciation of the different contexts and situations within which varying perspectives emerge. Human thinking comes out of the conditions of human life, from very different contexts and situations. If we do not learn how to take on the perspectives of others and to accurately think as they think, we will not be able to fairly judge their ideas and beliefs. Trying to think within the viewpoint of others can be quite difficult—especially when we disagree with a viewpoint.

To develop your ability to intellectually empathize with others, practice using the following strategies:

1. During a disagreement with someone, switch roles. Tell the person, "I will speak from your viewpoint for 10 minutes if you will speak from mine. This way perhaps we can better understand one another." Make sure you are accurately representing one another's viewpoint.

2. During a discussion, summarize what another person is saying, using this structure: "What I understand you to be saying is _____. Is this correct?"

3. When reading, say to yourself what you think the author is saying. This enables you to bring ideas concretely into your mind so that you can accurately think within the viewpoint of the author. Only then are you in a position to critique the author's viewpoint.

8.6   *Think for Yourself*

INTELLECTUAL EMPATHY I

Try to reconstruct in your mind the last argument you had with someone (a friend, parent, intimate other, or supervisor). Reconstruct the argument from both your perspective and that of the other person. Complete the statements below. As you do, be sure that you do not distort the other person's viewpoint. Try to enter it in good faith, even if it means you have to admit you were wrong. (Remember that critical thinkers want to see the truth in the situation even when the truth is painful.) After you have completed this assignment, show it to the person you argued with to see if you have accurately represented that person's view.

1. My perspective was as follows (state and elaborate your view in detail):
2. The other person's view was as follows (state and elaborate the other person's view in detail):

8.7   *Think for Yourself*

INTELLECTUAL EMPATHY II

Just as a self-centered perspective can impede our ability to think within another's viewpoint, so can a group-centered perspective. In this activity, we ask you to think beyond a group, in this case national, perspective; to intellectually empathize with an "enemy" of one's country. Think of an international political leader who is represented negatively in the news (for example, Castro in Cuba or Gadhafi in Libya). Gather enough information about that person to be able to explain how he or she might defend himself or herself against the representation. Then ask yourself: Have you ever seriously considered the possibility that any of the "enemies" of the United States might be more justified in opposing us than we are in opposing them? If you have never heard the defense of a national "enemy" from that person's point of view, how might that affect your ability to empathize with that person?

Intellectual Integrity: The Best Thinkers Hold Themselves to the Same Standards to Which They Hold Others

Let us now consider *intellectual integrity.*

Intellectual integrity means striving to be true to one's own disciplined thinking and holding oneself to the same standards one expects others to meet. For example, it involves holding oneself to the same rigorous standards of evidence and proof to which one holds one's antagonists. It means practicing on a daily basis what one advocates for others. It requires honestly admitting discrepancies and inconsistencies in one's own thought and action, and identifying inconsistencies within one's thinking.

The opposite of intellectual integrity is *intellectual hypocrisy,* a state of mind unconcerned with true honesty. It is often marked by unconscious contradictions and inconsistencies. Because the mind is naturally egocentric, it is also naturally hypocritical. Yet, at the same time, it is skillfully able to rationalize whatever it thinks and however it leads us to act. In other words, due to its innate need to project a positive image, the *appearance* of integrity is important to the egocentric mind. Therefore, we actively hide our hypocrisy from ourselves. And though we expect others to adhere to much more rigid standards than the standards we impose on ourselves, we see ourselves as fair. Though we profess certain beliefs, we often fail to behave in accordance with those beliefs.

Suppose I were to say to you that our friendship is really important to me, but you find out that I have lied to you about something important to you. My behavior lacks integrity. I have acted hypocritically. Yet in my own egocentric, self-serving mind, I have rationalized my lying by telling myself things like, "It is better that he or she not know. It will only upset him or her, and it won't help our friendship. The issue isn't that important anyway. It's really no big deal. He or she is better off not knowing." When I rationalize in this way, I can hide my hypocrisy from myself, which is vitally important (to me). Though I have acted dishonestly, I can tell myself that everything I have done is the best thing to do in the situation. In short, I can appear *right* in my own mind.

To the extent that our beliefs and actions are consistent, we have intellectual integrity. We practice what we preach, so to speak. We don't say one thing and do another.

Clearly, we cannot be fair to others if we think we are justified in thinking and acting in contradictory ways. Hypocrisy by its very nature is a form of injustice. If we are not sensitive to contradictions and inconsistencies in our own thinking and behavior, we cannot reason well through ethical questions. We will distort other viewpoints in order to come out ahead.

Consider this political example. From time to time the media discloses highly questionable practices by the Central Intelligence Agency. These practices run from documentation of attempted assassinations of foreign political leaders (for example, attempts to assassinate President Castro of Cuba) to the practice of teaching police and military representatives in other countries (such as Central America or South America) how to torture prisoners. To appreciate how such disclosures reveal intellectual hypocrisy, we only have to imagine how we would respond if another nation were to attempt to assassinate our president or train American police or military in methods of torture. Once we imagine this, we recognize a basic inconsistency in our behavior and a lack of intellectual integrity on the part of those who plan, engage in, or approve of this kind of behavior.

Every human sometimes fails to act with intellectual integrity. When we do, we reveal a lack of fair-mindedness on our part, and a failure to think well enough to detect internal contradictions in our thought or actions.

8.8 *Think for Yourself*

INTELLECTUAL INTEGRITY

Discuss an aspect of your life that you suspect holds some inconsistencies or contradictions—areas where you probably are not holding yourself to the same standard to which you would hold someone else. Think of a situation where your behavior contradicts what you say you believe. This might be in an intimate relationship, for example. Complete the following statements:

1. The context within which I fail to have intellectual integrity is . . .
2. In this context, I would (or do) expect others to behave as follows (though I am not willing to behave in the same way myself):
3. The reason I fail to have intellectual integrity in this situation is . . .
4. To change this situation, I need to . . .

Intellectual Perseverance: The Best Thinkers Do Not Give Up Easily, But Work Their Way Through Complexities and Frustration

Let us now consider *intellectual perseverance.*

Intellectual perseverance is the disposition to work one's way through intellectual complexities despite frustrations. Some problems are complicated and cannot be easily solved. One has intellectual perseverance when one does not give up in the face of complexity or frustration. The intellectually perseverant person understands that carefully and methodically reasoning through complex issues and problems takes precedence over quickly coming to conclusions. Intellectual perseverance involves firmly adhering to rational principles despite the natural tendency to go with first impressions and simplistic answers. It also entails a realistic sense of the need to struggle with confusion and unsettled questions over time in order to achieve understanding or insight.

The opposite of intellectual perseverance is *intellectual laziness,* the tendency to give up quickly when faced with an intellectually challenging task. The intellectually indolent or lazy person has a low tolerance for intellectual pain or frustration.

Intellectual perseverance is essential to almost all areas of higher-level thinking, because virtually all higher-level thinking involves some intellectual challenges. Without intellectual perseverance, those challenges cannot be overcome. Intellectual perseverance is required for high-quality reasoning in math, chemistry, physics, literature, art, and indeed any domain. Many students give up during the early stages of learning a subject. Lacking intellectual perseverance, they cut themselves off from the many insights that would be available to them if they were willing to think through a subject. They avoid intellectual frustration, but they end up with the everyday frustrations of not being able to solve the complex problems they face.

There are at least two important reasons why students often lack intellectual perseverance. First, the mind is naturally averse to intellectual difficulties. It much prefers things to be easy, and it will take the simplest route to an answer when it can. This is the natural egocentric state of the mind. Second, intellectual perseverance is rarely fostered in school. Instead, students are often encouraged to complete tasks quickly. Those who finish first are seen as the smartest and brightest. Slowly and carefully working through tasks is not usually valued. Consequently, students conclude that quickness is what matters most in learning. And those who are not able to finish tasks quickly come to view themselves as inadequate or inferior. Yet the most important questions we will reason through in our lives will most likely be complex and will therefore require diligence and intellectual discipline, not speed. The thoroughness and attentiveness we bring to the process will determine whether, and to what extent, we can answer them.

It is also important to realize that students who are intellectually quick are often the same students who give up when the intellectual task becomes difficult. They see themselves as capable of getting the "right" answer quickly and without intellectual pain. When the answer does not come immediately and painlessly, they often blame the teacher for giving a "dumb assignment." Indeed, these students often fail to recognize that not every question has a "right" answer; many have only better and worse answers. And there is no effective way to work through these complex questions simply and easily.

How does a lack of intellectual perseverance impede fair-mindedness? Understanding the views of others requires intellectual work. It requires intellectual perseverance—insofar as those views are complex or are different from our own. If we are unable or unwilling to work through the views of others, to consider the information they use and how they interpret that information, to look closely at their beliefs and analyze those beliefs for ourselves, to understand what they are trying to accomplish and how they see the world, we will not be able to think fairly within their viewpoint. For example, suppose I am a Christian and I want to be fair to the views of atheists. Unless I read and understand the reasoning of intelligent and insightful atheists, I cannot be fair to their views. Some intelligent and insightful atheists have written books to explain how and why they think as they do. Some of their reasoning is complicated or deals with issues of some complexity. It follows that only those Christians who have the intellectual perseverance to read and understand atheists can be fair to atheist views. Of course, a parallel case could be made for atheists' understanding of the views of intelligent and insightful Christians.

8.9   *Think for Yourself*

INTELLECTUAL PERSEVERANCE

Many people have much more physical perseverance than intellectual perseverance. They will say, "No pain, no gain!" when talking about the body, but they give up quickly, when faced with a frustrating intellectual problem. Consider your own responses to intellectual challenges. How would you evaluate your intellectual perseverance (on a scale of 0 to 10)? Explain to a classmate how you would support your score. On what do you base your conclusion?

Confidence in Reason: The Best Thinkers Respect Evidence and Reasoning and Value Them as Tools for Discovering the Truth

Let us now consider the trait of *confidence in reason.*

Confidence in reason is based on the belief that one's own higher interests and those of humankind at large are best served by giving the freest play to reason and by encouraging people to come to their own conclusions through the use of their own rational faculties. It is based on the belief that, with proper encouragement and cultivation, people can learn to think for themselves; form insightful viewpoints; draw reasonable conclusions; think clearly, accurately, relevantly, and logically; persuade each other by appeal to good reason and sound evidence; and become reasonable persons, despite deep-seated obstacles in human nature and social life. When one has confidence in reason, one is moved by reason in appropriate ways. The very idea of reasonability becomes one of the most important values and a focal point in one's life. In short, to have confidence in reason is to use good reasoning as the fundamental criterion by which to judge whether to accept or reject any belief or position.

The opposite of confidence in reason is *intellectual distrust of reason,* which results from the threat that reasoning and rational analysis pose to the undisciplined thinker. People are not, by nature, adept at analyzing their views. Yet they tend to have complete confidence in their views. The more we analyze our views, the more we see problems in them, and the less we want to hold on to views we have not analyzed. But without confidence in reason, people will naturally have confidence in the truth of their own beliefs, however flawed those beliefs might be. It is as if the mind unconsciously engages in something like the following inner dialog:

"I have formulated many beliefs throughout my life that I have not analyzed. If I examined the beliefs I am often driven by, I would be appalled at my thinking and behavior. Yet I cling to my beliefs because it would be too time consuming and painful to analyze them closely. So I will just hang on to all of my beliefs and everything will work out all right in the end."

In many ways we live in an irrational world, surrounded by curious forms of irrational beliefs and behaviors. For example, despite the success of science in providing plausible explanations based on careful study of evidence gathered through methodical and disciplined observations, many people still believe in unsubstantiated systems such as astrology. Many people, when faced with a problem, follow their natural impulses. For example, many follow leaders whose only claim to credibility is skill in manipulating a crowd and whipping up enthusiasm. Few people seem to recognize the power of sound thinking in helping us solve our problems and live a fulfilling life. Few people, in short, have genuine confidence in reason. Instead, people tend to have uncritical or blind faith in one or more of the following—faith often resulting from irrational drives and emotions:

1. Faith in charismatic national leaders (think of leaders able to excite millions of people and manipulate them into supporting unjust wars or even genocide of an entire religious group, such as Hitler)
2. Faith in charismatic cult leaders
3. Faith in the father as the traditional head of the family (as defined by religious or social tradition)
4. Faith in institutional authorities (police, social workers, judges, priests, evangelical preachers, and so forth)
5. Faith in spiritual powers (such as a "holy spirit," as defined by various religious belief systems)
6. Faith in some social group, official or unofficial (faith in a gang, in the business community, in a church, in a political party, and so on)
7. Faith in a political ideology (such as right-wing fundamentalism, left-wing fundamentalism, communism, capitalism, Fascism)
8. Faith in intuition
9. Faith in one's unanalyzed emotions
10. Faith in one's gut impulses
11. Faith in fate (some unnamed force that supposedly guides our destiny)
12. Faith in social or legal institutions (the courts, schools, business community, government)
13. Faith in the folkways, conventions, and taboos of a social group or culture
14. Faith in one's own unanalyzed experience (faith in the idea that one's interpretations about past experiences are the only *right* and *true* way to interpret those experiences)
15. Faith in people who have social status or position (the rich, the famous, the powerful)

Under certain conditions, confidence in reason may be compatible with some of the above. The key factor is the extent to which the form of faith is based on sound reasoning and evidence. The acid test, then, is: Are there good grounds for having that faith? For example, it makes sense to have faith in a friend if that friend has consistently acted as a friend over an extended period of time. On the other hand, it does not make sense to have faith in a new acquaintance, even if you are emotionally attracted to that individual and that person professes friendship with you.

As you consider your own thinking about different kinds of faith, and the extent to which you have appropriate confidence in reason and evidence, ask yourself to what extent you can be moved by well-reasoned appeals. Suppose you meet someone who shows so much interest in your boyfriend or girlfriend that you feel intensely jealous and negative toward that person. Would you shift your view if you learned that the person you are negative about is actually exceptionally kind, thoughtful, and generous? Could you shift your view even when you really want your boyfriend or girlfriend to reject this person in favor of you? Would you be moved by reason if you thought that your boyfriend or girlfriend would be *happier* with another person than with you? Have you ever given up a belief you held dear because, through your reading, experience, and reflection, you became persuaded that it was not reasonable to believe as you did? Are you ready and willing to admit that some of your most passionate beliefs (for example, your religious or political beliefs) may not in fact be reasonable?

A close relationship exists between confidence in reason and fair-mindedness. One cannot be fair-minded and yet be blind to the importance of reason. If I profess to be fair-minded, yet I am unwilling to consider good reasons with which I disagree, this shows that I lack confidence in reason and cannot be fair-minded. Fair-mindedness often requires one to consider reasoning not yet before considered, to consider that reasoning in good faith, and to change one's reasoning when faced with more reasonable reasoning—reasoning that is more logical, accurate, justifiable. All of this presupposes confidence in reason—confidence that when we place good reasons at the heart of our thinking, we will do a better job of thinking.

8.10   *Think for Yourself*

CONFIDENCE IN REASON

Think of a recent situation in which you felt yourself being defensive and unable to listen to an argument that you did not agree with, though the argument had merit. In this situation, you apparently could not be moved by good reasons. Briefly write what happened in the situation. Then write the reasonable arguments against your position that you were not willing to listen to. Why weren't you able to give credit to the other person's argument? In answering this question, review the list of sources of faith that people often rely on. Were you relying on some form of blind faith when you originally reasoned through the issue?

Intellectual Autonomy: The Best Thinkers Value Their Independence in Thought

The final intellectual trait we will consider here is *intellectual autonomy*.

Intellectual autonomy is thinking for oneself while adhering to standards of rationality. It means thinking through issues using one's own thinking rather than uncritically accepting the viewpoints of others. In other words, intellectually autonomous thinkers do not depend on others when deciding what to believe and what to reject. They are influenced by others' views only to the extent that those views are reasonable given the evidence.

In forming beliefs, critical thinkers do not passively accept the beliefs of others. Rather, they think through situations and issues for themselves. They reject unjustified claims made by authorities while recognizing the contributions of reasonable authorities. They carefully form principles of thought and action and do not mindlessly accept those presented to them. They are not limited by accepted ways of doing things. They evaluate the traditions and practices that others often unquestioningly accept. Independent thinkers strive to incorporate insightful ideas into their thinking, regardless of whether those ideas are considered acceptable or appropriate by the society within which they live. Independent thinkers are not willful, stubborn, or unresponsive to the reasonable suggestions of others. They are self-monitoring thinkers who are sensitive to mistakes they make and problems in their thinking. They freely choose the values by which they live.

Of course, intellectual autonomy should not be understood as a thing-in-itself. Instead, we must recognize it as a dimension of our minds that works in conjunction with and is tempered by the other intellectual virtues.

The opposite of intellectual autonomy is *intellectual conformity* or intellectual dependence. Intellectual autonomy is difficult to develop because social institutions, as they now stand, depend heavily on passive acceptance of the status quo, whether intellectual, political, or economic. Thinking for oneself almost certainly leads to unpopular conclusions not sanctioned by the powers that be. On the other hand, for those who simply conform in thought and action to social expectations, there are many rewards.

Consequently, the large masses of people are unknowing conformists in thought and deed. They are like mirrors reflecting the belief systems and values of those who surround them. They lack the intellectual skills and the incentive to think for themselves. They are intellectually conforming thinkers. Because they uncritically accept cultural values, because they conform to beliefs they have not analyzed for themselves, they are not intellectually free.

Even those who spend years earning advanced degrees may be intellectually dependent, both academically and personally. They may uncritically accept faulty practices within their disciplines and even uncritically defend these practices against legitimate critics. Despite all their years of school, they may yet be persons enslaved by social conventions and rules. They may have little or no insight into the human harm and suffering caused by social rules and taboos.

One cannot be fair-minded and lack intellectual autonomy, for independent thinking is a prerequisite to thinking within multiple perspectives. When we intellectually conform, we are able to think only within "accepted" viewpoints. But to be fair-minded is to refuse to accept beliefs without thinking through the merits (and demerits) of those beliefs for oneself. Without the virtue of intellectual autonomy, when we attempt to think within other viewpoints, we are either too easily swayed by those viewpoints (because we are unable to see through manipulation and propaganda) or we distort the viewpoints (because they do not conform with the belief system we have uncritically formulated).

8.11   *Think for Yourself*

INTELLECTUAL AUTONOMY I

Briefly review some of the many influences to which you have been exposed in your life (your culture, family, religion, peer groups, teachers, media, personal relationships). Then consider various dimensions of your thought and behavior, and try to identify where you have done the *least* thinking for yourself and where you have done the *most*. What makes this activity difficult is that we often perceive ourselves as thinking for ourselves when we are actually conforming to others. What you should look for, therefore, are instances when you actively questioned beliefs, values, or practices to which others in your "group" were conforming.

By the way, don't assume that teenage rebellion against parents and school authorities (if you engaged in it) was necessarily evidence of independent thought. Rebellious teens are often simply trading one form of conformity (e.g., to parents) for another (peer group).

Be prepared to explain how you arrived at your conclusions.

8.12   *Think for Yourself*

INTELLECTUAL AUTONOMY II

To begin analyzing some of the beliefs you have come to accept, complete the following statements:

1. One belief I have been taught by my culture about the way people should behave in groups is . . . . The person or people who taught me this were . . . . In analyzing this belief, I do/do not think it is rational because . . . .

2. One belief I have been taught within or about religion is . . . . The person or people who taught me this were . . . . In analyzing this belief, I do/do not think it is rational because . . . .

3. One belief I have been taught by my parents is . . . . In analyzing this belief, I do/do not think it is rational because . . . .

4. One belief I have learned from my peer group is . . . . In analyzing this belief, I do/do not think it is rational because . . . .

5. One belief I have been taught by teachers is . . . . In analyzing this belief, I do/do not think it is rational because . . . .

The Best Thinkers Recognize the Interdependence of Intellectual Virtues

The traits of mind essential for critical thinking are interdependent. Consider intellectual humility. To become aware of the limits of our knowledge, we need the intellectual courage to face our own prejudices and ignorance. To discover our own prejudices, in turn, we often must intellectually empathize with and reason within points of view with which we fundamentally disagree. To achieve this end, we typically must engage in intellectual perseverance, as learning to empathically enter a point of view against which we are biased takes time and significant effort. That effort will not seem justified unless we have the necessary confidence in reason to believe we will not be tainted or "taken in" by whatever is false or misleading in the opposing viewpoint.

Furthermore, merely believing we won't be harmed by considering "alien" viewpoints is not enough to motivate most of us to consider them seriously. We also must be motivated by an intellectual sense of justice. We must also recognize an intellectual responsibility to be fair to views we oppose. We must feel obliged to hear them in their strongest form to ensure that we are not condemning them out of ignorance or bias. At this point, we come full circle to where we began: the need for intellectual humility.

To begin at another point, consider intellectual integrity or good faith. Intellectual integrity is clearly a difficult trait to develop. We are often motivated—generally without admitting to or being aware of this motivation—to set up inconsistent standards for thinking. Our egocentric or sociocentric tendencies, for example, make us ready to believe positive information about those viewpoints we like and negative information about those we dislike. We likewise are strongly inclined to believe information that serves to justify our selfish interests or validate our strongest desires. Hence, all humans have some innate mental tendencies to operate with double standards, which is typical of intellectual bad faith. These modes of thinking often facilitate getting ahead in the world, maximizing our power or advantage, and getting more of what we want.

To take a negative example, consider those who choose to indulge their innate egocentricity and operate with double standards. It is difficult to operate explicitly or overtly with a double standard. These people therefore need to avoid looking at the evidence too closely. They need to avoid scrutinizing their inferences and interpretations too carefully. At this point, a certain amount of intellectual arrogance is quite useful. For example, if I were one of these people, I may assume that I know just what you're going to say before you say it, precisely what you are really after before the evidence demonstrates it, and what actually is going on before I have studied the situation carefully. My intellectual arrogance makes it easier for me to avoid noticing the discrepancy between the standards I apply to you and the standards I apply to myself. Not having to empathize with you makes it easier to avoid seeing my self-deception. I can also more easily maintain my viewpoint if I don't feel a need to be fair to your point of view. A little background fear of what I might discover if I seriously consider the consistency of my own judgments can

EXHIBIT 8.3   *Natural versus critical thinking.*

- As humans we think; as critical thinkers we analyze our thinking.

- As humans we think egocentrically; as critical thinkers we expose the egocentric roots of our thinking to close scrutiny.

- As humans we are drawn to standards of thinking unworthy of belief; as critical thinkers we expose inappropriate standards and replace them with sound ones.

- As humans we live in systems of meanings that typically entrap us; as critical thinkers we learn how to raise our thinking to conscious examination, enabling us to free ourselves from many of the traps of undisciplined, instinctive thought.

- As humans we use logical systems whose root structures are not apparent to us; as critical thinkers we develop tools for explicating and assessing the logical systems in which we live.

- As humans we live with the illusion of intellectual and emotion freedom; as critical thinkers we take explicit intellectual and emotional command of who we are, what we are, and the ends to which our lives are tending.

- As human thinkers we are governed by our thoughts; as critical thinkers we learn how to govern the thoughts that govern us.

be quite useful as well. In this case, my lack of intellectual integrity is supported by my lack of intellectual humility, empathy, and fair-mindedness.

Going in the other direction, it will be difficult to use a double standard if I feel a responsibility to be fair to your point of view and if I see that this responsibility requires me to view things from your perspective empathically, with humility, recognizing that I could be wrong and you could be right. The more I dislike you personally or feel wronged in the past by you or by others who share your way of thinking, the more intellectual integrity and good faith I will need in order to be fair.

8.13   *Think for Yourself*

A COMMITMENT TO SELF-TRANSFORMATION

To what extent would you like to possess the intellectual traits explained in this chapter? How important is that goal to you? Discuss your commitment, or lack thereof, with a classmate. In this activity, honesty is the key.

CONCLUSION

True excellence in thinking does not result simply from the use of isolated intellectual skills. There are inevitable problems in the thinking of persons who, without knowing it, lack intellectual virtues. These people frequently display the traits of the undisciplined mind. To the extent that they are unconsciously motivated to believe what they want to believe, what is most comfortable to believe, what puts them in a good light, and what serves their selfish interest, they are unable to function as rational persons. As you continue to develop your thinking, we hope you find yourself internalizing the essential traits. We hope you will resist the influence of both the conformist thinkers around you and the egocentric thinker within you.

DEAL WITH YOUR IRRATIONAL MIND

Humans often engage in irrational behavior. We fight. We start wars. We kill. We are self-destructive. We are petty and vindictive. We act out when we don't get our way. We abuse our spouses. We neglect our children. We rationalize, project, and stereotype. We act inconsistently, ignore relevant evidence, jump to conclusions, and say and believe things that don't make good sense. We deceive ourselves in many ways. We are our own worst enemy.

There are two overlapping and interrelated motivating impulses behind human irrationality. These impulses are the focus of this chapter. They are:

1. *Human egocentrism,* the natural human tendency "to view everything within the world in relationship to oneself, to be self-centered" *(Webster's New World Dictionary)*

2. *Human sociocentrism,* most simply conceptualized as *group egocentricity.* To define sociocentricity, we might take Webster's definition of egocentricity and substitute *group* for *self.* Sociocentric thinking is the natural human tendency to view everything within the world in relationship to one's group—to be group-centered.

Human egocentricity has two basic tendencies. One is to see the world in **self-serving** terms, constantly to seek that which makes one feel good or that which one selfishly wants, at the expense of the rights and needs of others. The second primary tendency of egocentricity is the desire to maintain its beliefs. It manifests itself in **rigidity of thought.** It views its irrational beliefs as rational. The problem of egocentricity in human life will be elaborated in Part I of this chapter.

Sociocentric thinking is an extension of egocentric thinking. Humans are herd animals, largely influenced by and functioning within groups. And because most people are largely egocentric, or centered in themselves, they end up forming groups that are also largely centered in themselves. As a result of egocentrism and sociocentrism, most people are self-serving and rigid, they conform to group thinking, and they assume the correctness of their own beliefs and that of their groups.

Sociocentric thought, then, is a direct extension of egocentric thought in that it operates from the two primary tendencies of egocentric thought:

1. Seeking to get what it (or its group) wants without regard to the rights and needs of others

2. Rationalizing the beliefs and behavior of the group, regardless of whether those beliefs and behaviors are irrational

Sociocentric thought, then, presupposes the egocentric tendencies of the human mind. The selfish mind finds its natural home in the self-centered group. And virtually all groups operate with in-group advantages denied to those in the out-groups. The result is many forms of social conflict, punishment, and vengeance. Sociocentrism is also close to the root of most wars and war crimes. It enables some (advantaged) people to be comfortable in the face of the wretched suffering of masses of (disadvantaged) others. It enables some in a group (the elite) to manipulate others in the group (the non-elite).

Consider the similarity between street gangs and nations. Gangs collectively pursue irrational purposes and engage in violence against other gangs—behavior that can appear justified only in one-sided, group-serving thought. In a similar way, countries often attack other countries using equally one-sided, group-serving thought. The difference is often merely one of sophistication, not of kind. Gang violence is censured by society, international acts of war validated (at least by the attacking country).

In short, people are either born into or join groups. They then egocentrically identify with those groups. They rarely dissent. They rarely think for themselves. They rarely notice their own conformity and irrationality. Humans seek what is in their selfish interests and see the world from the perspectives of the (sociocentric) groups to which they belong. Both egocentric and sociocentric thought represent enormous barriers to the development of rational thought. This is true, in part, because these two tendencies in the mind *appear to the mind as perfectly rational*. Unless we fully understand these overlapping tendencies and fight to combat them, we can never fully develop as rational, autonomous, fair-minded thinkers. We shall elaborate further on these points in Part II of this chapter.

PART I: THE BEST THINKERS TAKE CHARGE OF THEIR EGOCENTRIC NATURE

Egocentric thinking results from the fact that humans do not naturally consider the rights and needs of others, nor do we naturally appreciate the point of view of others or the limitations in our own point of view. As humans, we become explicitly aware of our egocentric thinking only if specially trained to do so. We do not naturally recognize our egocentric assumptions, the egocentric way we use information, the egocentric way we interpret data, the sources of our egocentric

The best thinkers realize they are largely egocentric.

concepts and ideas, the implications of our egocentric thought. We do not naturally recognize our self-serving perspective.

Humans live with the unrealistic but confident sense that we have fundamentally figured out *the way things actually are,* and that we have done this objectively. We naturally believe in our immediate perceptions—however inaccurate they may be. Instead of using intellectual standards in thinking, humans often use self-centered psychological standards to determine what to believe and what to reject. Here are the most commonly used psychological standards in human thinking:

- **"It's true because *I* believe it."** This is innate egocentrism: I assume that what I believe is true even though I have never questioned the basis for my beliefs.

- **"It's true because *we* believe it."** This is innate sociocentrism: I assume that the dominant beliefs within the groups to which I belong are true even though I have never questioned the basis for these beliefs.

- **"It's true because I *want* to believe it."** This is innate wish fulfillment: I believe in, for example, accounts of my own or my group's behavior that put me or "us" in a positive rather than a negative light, even though I have not seriously considered the evidence for the more negative account. I believe what "feels good," what supports my other beliefs, what does not require me to change my thinking in any significant way, what does not require me to admit I have been wrong.

- **"It's true because I *have always believed it.*"** This is innate self-validation: I have a strong desire to maintain beliefs that I have long held, even though I have not seriously considered the extent to which those beliefs are justified, given the evidence.

- **"It's true because it is *in my selfish interest* to believe it."** This is innate selfishness: I hold fast to beliefs that justify my getting more power, money, or personal advantage, even though these beliefs are not grounded in sound reasoning or evidence.

9.1   *Think for Yourself*

IDENTIFYING SOME OF YOUR IRRATIONAL BELIEFS

For the five categories of irrational beliefs given above, identify at least one belief you hold in each of the categories.

It's true because *I* believe it.

It's true because *my group* believes it.

It's true because I *want* to believe it.

It's true because I *have always believed it.*

It's true because it is *in my selfish interest* to believe it.

On a scale of 1 to 10 (10 being "highly irrational" and 1 being "highly rational"), how would you rate yourself? Why?

Given that humans are naturally prone to assess thinking in keeping with the above criteria, it is not surprising that we (as humans) have not developed a significant interest in establishing and teaching legitimate intellectual standards. There are too many domains of our thinking that we do not want to have questioned. We have too many prejudices that we do not want to be challenged. We are committed to having our selfish interests served. We are not typically concerned with protecting the rights of others. We are not typically willing to sacrifice our desires to meet someone else's basic needs. We do not want to discover that beliefs we have taken to be obvious and sacred might be neither. We will ignore any number of basic principles if doing so enables us to maintain our power or to gain more power and advantage.

Fortunately, humans are not always guided by egocentric thinking. Within each person are, metaphorically speaking, two potential minds: one that characterizes innate egocentric, self-serving tendencies, and the other, cultivated rational, higher-order capacities. In this section we focus on the problem of egocentric tendencies in human life. We then contrast this defective mode of thinking with its opposite: rational or reasonable thinking. We explore what it means to use our minds to create rational beliefs, emotions, and values—in contrast to egocentric ones. We then focus on two distinct manifestations of egocentric thinking: dominating behavior and submissive behavior.

> Humans naturally see themselves as right even in the face of clear evidence to the contrary.

Understand Egocentric Thinking

Egocentric thinking emerges from our innate human tendency to see the world from a narrow self-serving perspective. We naturally think of the world in terms of how *it* can serve *us*. Our instinct is to operate within the world by manipulating situations and people in accordance with our selfish interests.

At the same time, we naturally assume that our thinking is rational. No matter how irrational our thinking is, no matter how destructive, when we are operating from an egocentric perspective, we see our thinking as reasonable. Our thinking seems to us to be right, true, good, and justifiable. Our egocentric nature, therefore, creates perhaps the most formidable barrier to critical thinking. We inherit from our childhood the sense that we have basically figured out the truth about the world. We naturally *believe* in our sense of who and what we are and what we are engaged in. Therefore, if we behave or think irrationally, it is because we are, in a sense, trapped in the beliefs and thought processes we have developed through life. Our native egocentric thinking is commanding us.

> We naturally think of the world in terms of how *it* can serve *us*.

As we age, our rational capacities develop to some extent. We come to think more reasonably in some areas of our lives. This development can come from explicit instruction or experience. If we are in an environment where reasonable behavior is modeled, we become more reasonable. Yet it is hard to imagine making significant inroads into egocentric thinking unless we become explicitly aware of it and learn

EXHIBIT 9.1 *The logic of egocentrism.*

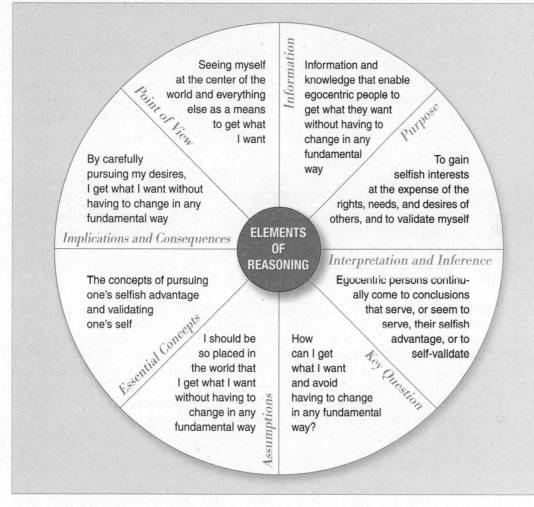

how to undermine or short-circuit it in some way. The human mind can think irrationally in too many ways while masking itself with a façade of reasonability.

The mere *appearance* of rationality, of course, is not the same as true rationality. And, unfortunately, much seemingly rational adult behavior is at its root egocentric or sociocentric. This irrationality stems, in part, from the fact that people generally do not have a clear understanding of how the human mind functions. Most important, they fail to realize that thinking, if left to itself, is inherently flawed with prejudices, half-truths, biases, vagueness, arrogance, and the like.

9.2 *Think for Yourself*

BEGINNING TO UNDERSTAND EGOCENTRIC THINKING

Try to think of a disagreement you were in recently in which you now realize you were not fair-mindedly listening to the views of the other person (and remember, everyone does this at times). Perhaps you were defensive during the conversation or were trying to dominate the other person. You were not trying to see the situation from the other perspective. At the time, you believed that you were being reasonable. Now you realize that you were closed-minded. Complete these statements:

1. The situation was as follows:
2. My behavior/thinking in the situation was as follows:
3. I now realize that I was closed-minded because:

If you cannot think of an example, think of a situation in which someone else was closed-minded. Also, ask yourself why you cannot think of any examples of closed-mindedness on your part.

Understand Egocentrism as a Mind Within the Mind

Egocentric thinking functions subconsciously, like a mind within us that we deny we have. No one says, "I think I will think egocentrically for a while." The ultimate goals of egocentricity are gratification and self-validation. It does not respect the rights and needs of others—though it may be protective of those with whom it ego-identifies. When we are thinking egocentrically, we see ourselves as right and just. We see those who disagree with us as wrong and unjustified.

EXHIBIT 9.2 *The two fundamental motives behind egocentric thinking.*

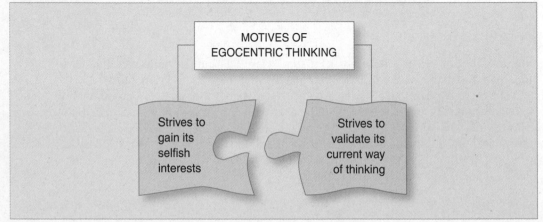

MOTIVES OF EGOCENTRIC THINKING

Strives to gain its selfish interests

Strives to validate its current way of thinking

Our family, our children, our country, our religion, our beliefs, our feelings, our values—all are specially privileged in our egocentric mind. Our own validation is crucial to us, and we seek it even if we have been unfair to others or irresponsibly harmed them in a flagrant way. Egocentrically, we are interested only in facts we can twist to support us. We dislike or fear people who point out our inconsistencies. If we criticize ourselves, we typically do not do so to change our behavior but, rather, to avoid changing it. For example, if I think, "I know I have a short fuse, but I can't help it. I lose my temper just like my father did!" my self-criticism justifies my continuing to lose my temper.

> Egocentric thinking functions subconsciously, like a mind within us that we deny we have.

One of the ways we use egocentric thinking, then, is to validate our current belief system. When we feel internally validated, we live comfortably with ourselves even if what we are doing is actually unethical. For example, if I am brought up to believe that people of a certain race are inferior, my egocentric thinking enables me to maintain all of the following beliefs: (1) I am not prejudiced (they simply are inferior), (2) I judge each person I meet on his or her own merits, and (3) I am an open-minded person.

With these beliefs operating in my thinking, I do not see myself as jumping to conclusions about members of this race. I do not think of myself as wronging them in any way. I see myself as simply recognizing them for what they are. I ignore the evidence that demonstrates the falsity of what I believe, but I do not see myself as ignoring the evidence. I do not think of myself as a racist, for being a racist is bad, and I am not bad.

Only when we explicitly develop the ability to rationally analyze ourselves can we begin to see these tendencies in ourselves. When we do, it almost never happens at the precise moments when our egocentric mind is in control. Once egocentric thinking begins to take control, it spontaneously rationalizes and deceives itself into believing that its position is the *only* justifiable position. It sees itself as experiencing the truth, no matter how inaccurate a picture of things it is painting. This skilled self-deception blocks reasonable thoughts from correcting distorted ones. And the more highly self-deceived we are, the less likely we are to recognize our irrationality, the less likely we are to consider relevant information indicating that our egocentricity is blocking from our view, and the less motivated we are to develop truly rational beliefs and views.

Successful Egocentric Thinking

Egocentric thinking is irrational by nature, but it can be "functional," within a dysfunctional logic. For example, it often enables us to get what we want without having to concern ourselves with the rights of the people we violate in getting what we want. This type of thinking—though defective as to evidence, sound reasoning, objectivity, and fair play—is often "successful" from the point of view of self-gratification. Hence, though egocentric thinking is inherently flawed, it can be successful in achieving what it is motivated to achieve.

We see examples of this in many persons of power and status in the world—successful politicians, lawyers, businesspeople, and others. They are often skilled in getting what they want and are able to rationalize unethical behavior with great sophistication. The rationalization can be as simple as, "This is a hard, cruel world. One

9.3 *Think for Yourself*

DISCOVERING PREJUDICES IN YOUR BELIEFS

As egocentric thinkers, we see ourselves as possessing the truth. At the same time, we form many beliefs without evidence to justify them, and we form many prejudices (judgments before the evidence). If this is true, we should be able to unearth some of our prejudices by using our rational capacity. In an attempt to begin this process, complete the following statements:

1. One of the prejudices I have is . . . (Think of generalizations you tend to make even though you don't have the evidence to justify them. They can be about anything: a religion, atheists, men, women, homosexuals, heterosexuals, and so on. Put your prejudices in this form: All X are Y, as in, "All *women* are _____ " or "All *men* are _____ ".)

2. A more rational belief with which I should replace this faulty belief is . . .

3. If I use this new belief in my thinking, my behavior would change in the following ways:

has to be realistic. We have to realize we don't live in a perfect world. I wish we did. And, after all, we are doing things the way they have always been done." Conversely, rationalization can be very complex, such as in a highly developed philosophy, ideology, or party platform.

Hence, though egocentric thinkers may use ethical concepts in their rationalizations, they are not responsive to ethical considerations. They do not in fact respect ethical principles. They think of ethical principles only when those principles seem to justify their getting what they want for selfish reasons.

> Though egocentric thinking is inherently flawed, it can successfully achieve what it wants.

Egocentric thinking, then, is inherently indifferent to ethical principles and genuine conscience. We cannot be focused on getting what we selfishly want and at the same time genuinely take into account the rights and needs of others. The only time egocentric thinking takes others into account is when it is forced to do so to get what it wants. Hence, an egocentric politician may take into account the views of a public-interest group, but only when her reelection depends on their support. She is not focused on the justice of their cause but, rather, on the fact that if she fails to publicly validate those views, that group will refuse to support her reelection. She cares only about what is in her selfish interest. As long as the concern is selfish, by definition, the rights and needs of others are not perceived as relevant.

Corporate executives who cause the expected earnings of the company to be significantly overstated (to enable them to sell out their stocks at a high price) cause innocent people to lose money by investing in a company that appears to be, but is not, on the upswing. Most CEOs who manipulate data in this way do not worry about the well-being of potential investors. Their justification must be, "Let the buyer beware!" With this type of justification, they don't have to face the unethical nature of their behavior.

Highly skilled egocentric thought can take place in every type of human situation, from simple, everyday interactions between two people to situations involving the rights and needs of thousands of people. Imagine that a couple, Max and Maxine, routinely go to the video store to rent movies. Max always wants to rent an action-filled movie, while Maxine wants to rent a love story. Though Maxine is often willing to set aside her choices to go along with Max's desires, Max is never willing to go along with Maxine's choices. Max rationalizes his position to Maxine, telling her that his movie choices are better because they are filled with thrilling action, because love stories are always slow-moving and boring, because his movies are always award winners, because "no one likes to watch movies that make you cry," because, because, because. . . . Max gives many reasons. Yet all of them camouflage the real reasons for his behavior: that he simply wants to get the types of movies he likes, that he thinks he shouldn't have to watch movies that he does not want to watch. In his mind, he should get to do it because he wants to. Period.

Max's egocentrism hides the truth even from himself. He is unable to grasp Maxine's viewpoint. He cannot see how his self-centered thinking adversely affects Maxine. Insofar as his thinking works to achieve his desires, and he is therefore unable to detect any flaws in his reasoning, he is egocentrically successful.

9.4   *Think for Yourself*

RECOGNIZING EGOCENTRIC THINKING IN ACTION

Think of a situation in which someone you know was selfishly trying to manipulate you into doing something incompatible with your interest. Complete the following statements:

1. The situation was as follows:
2. This person was trying to manipulate me in the following way (by giving me these reasons for going along with him or her):
3. At the time, these reasons (did/did not) seem rational because . . . .
4. I now believe this person was trying to manipulate me because . . . .
5. I think the real (irrational) reason why he or she wanted me to go along with his or her reasoning was . . . .

Unsuccessful Egocentric Thinking

When egocentric thought is unsuccessful, it creates problems not only for those influenced by the thinker but also for the thinker himself or herself. Let's return to Max and Maxine and the movies. Imagine that for many months Max and Maxine go through this video-store routine in which, through self-serving argumentation, Max is able to manipulate Maxine into going along with his choices. But one day Maxine decides that

EXHIBIT 9.3 *These are some of the many feelings that might accompany egocentric thinking. They often occur when egocentric thinking is "unsuccessful."*

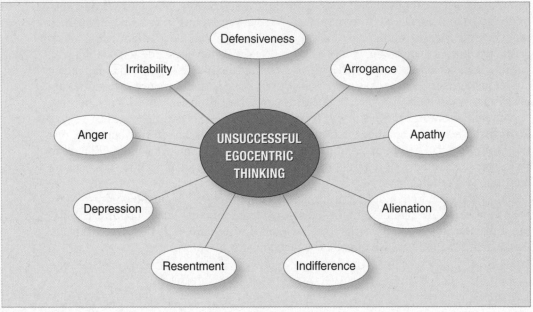

she simply isn't going along with Max's selfish behavior. She begins to feel resentment toward Max. She begins to think that perhaps Max isn't truly concerned about her. The more she thinks about it, the more she begins to see that Max is selfish in the relationship in a number of ways. Not only is he unwilling to go along with her movie choices, but he also tries to control where they go to lunch every day, when they eat lunch, when they visit with friends, and so on.

Maxine begins to feel manipulated and used by Max, and out of her resentment emerges a defensive attitude toward Max. She rebels. She no longer simply goes along with Max's unilateral decisions. She begins to tell him when she doesn't agree with his choices.

At this point, the table is turned. Max's egocentric thinking is no longer working for him. He feels anger when he doesn't get his way. Because Maxine's resentment is now leading to acts of retaliation on her part, Max's life is less successful than it was. Maxine may end up deciding that she is not going to agree to Max's movie choices in the future. Her resentment may lead her to seek subtle ways to punish Max for his unfair treatment of her. If she does go along with his movie choices, she might sulk while they are watching the movie. They may both become unhappy as a result of Maxine's rebellion and begin to interrelate in a perpetual state of war, as it were. However, because Max lacks insight into his dysfunctional thinking, he doesn't realize that he has been abusing Maxine and treating her unfairly.

This is merely one of a myriad of possible patterns of egocentric thinking leading to personal or social failure. Egocentric thinking and its social equivalent, sociocentric thinking, can lead to social prejudice, social conflict, warfare, genocide, and a variety of forms of dehumanization. Though on occasion some person or group might be "successful" as a result of the ability to wield superior power, quite often the consequences will be highly negative for themselves as well as their victims. Consider a gang that randomly chooses a person to harass for wearing a certain color. The members might begin with verbal assaults, which quickly lead to physical attacks, which in turn result in serious injury to the victim. Consequently, the gang members responsible for the attack are arrested on suspicion, then found guilty of a serious crime, which leads to their imprisonment.

> When we are egocentrically unsuccessful we create problems for ourselves and others.

Even if it does not cause direct harm to others, egocentric thinking may lead to chronic self-pity or depression. When problems emerge, the egocentric thinker may revert to this type of thinking: "I don't know why I should always get the short end of the stick. Just when I think things are going well for me, I have to face another problem. Is there no end? Life seems to be nothing but one problem after another. My instructors expect too much of me. My parents won't lend me the money I need to get by. My boss doesn't think I'm doing a good enough job. My wife is always complaining about something I do, and now I've got to figure out how to deal with this car. Life is just a pain in the neck. I don't know why things don't ever go my way."

Egocentric, self-pitying persons fail to recognize the positives in life. They screen these out in favor of self-pity and inflict unnecessary suffering on themselves. They say to themselves, "I have a right to feel all the self-pity I want, given the conditions of my life." In situations such as this, because the mind is unable to correct itself, it is its own victim. It chooses to focus on the negative and engage in self-punitive behavior.

EXHIBIT 9.4 *Problems in thinking can be either egocentrically or non-egocentrically based.*

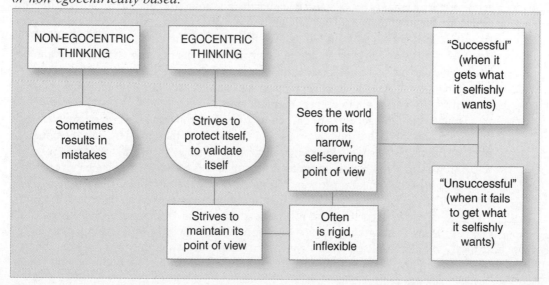

That is not all. Important moral implications follow from sociocentrism. Thinking that ignores the rights and needs of others will necessarily violate those rights and needs. Hence, for example, when people are under the sway of highly sociocentric thinking, that thinking gives the desires and aspirations of the group a privileged position over other groups. One consequence of such thinking is that the needs and desires of other groups are systematically ignored for the in-group to justify getting its way. The double standards of the in-group are camouflaged. History is full of examples of social groups imposing on other groups pain, suffering, and deprivation that they would object to if these were inflicted on them. These inconsistencies, characteristic of hypocrisy, easily avoid our notice when we are under the sway of sociocentrism.

9.5   *Think for Yourself*

UNEARTHING DYSFUNCTIONAL EGOCENTRIC THINKING

Try to think of a time when your selfish desire to get what you wanted failed because of your egocentric behavior. Complete these statements:

1. The situation was as follows:
2. When I didn't get what I wanted, I thought and behaved as follows:
3. A more rational way to think would have been . . . .
4. A more rational way to act would have been . . . .

Rational Thinking

Although irrationality plays a significant role in human life, human beings are in principle capable of thinking and behaving rationally. We can learn to respect evidence even though it does not support our views. We can learn to enter empathically into the viewpoint of others. We can learn to attend to the implications of our own reasoning and behavior. We can become compassionate. We can make sacrifices for others. We can work with others to solve important problems. We can discover our own tendency to think egocentrically and begin to correct that tendency.

Hence, though egocentrism causes us to suffer from illusions of perspective, we can transcend these illusions by practicing the thinking that takes us into the perspectives of others. We can egocentrically assimilate what we hear into our own perspective, but we can also learn to role-play the perspectives of others. Egocentrism can keep us unaware of the thinking process that guides our behavior, but critical thinking can help us learn to explicitly recognize that thinking process. We can take our own point of view to be absolute, but we also can learn to recognize that our point of view is always incomplete and sometimes blatantly self-serving. We can remain completely confident in our ideas even when they are illogical, but we can also learn to look for lapses of logic in our thinking and recognize those lapses as problematic.

Though humans are naturally egocentric, they can learn to be rational.

EXHIBIT 9.5 *The logic of the non-egocentric or rational mind.*

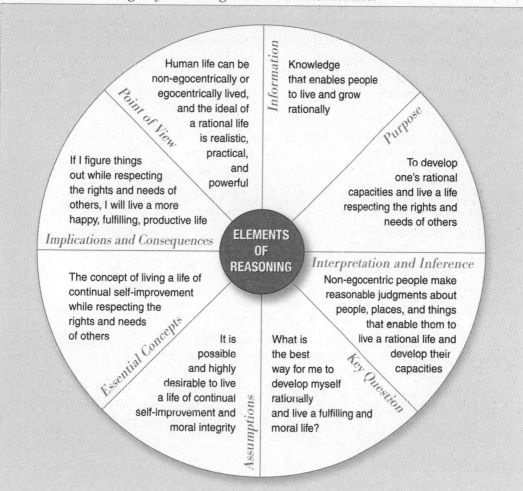

Human life can be non-egocentrically or egocentrically lived, and the ideal of a rational life is realistic, practical, and powerful

Point of View

If I figure things out while respecting the rights and needs of others, I will live a more happy, fulfilling, productive life

Implications and Consequences

The concept of living a life of continual self-improvement while respecting the rights and needs of others

Essential Concepts

It is possible and highly desirable to live a life of continual self-improvement and moral integrity

Assumptions

Information

Knowledge that enables people to live and grow rationally

Purpose

To develop one's rational capacities and live a life respecting the rights and needs of others

ELEMENTS OF REASONING

Interpretation and Inference

Non-egocentric people make reasonable judgments about people, places, and things that enable them to live a rational life and develop their capacities

Key Question

What is the best way for me to develop myself rationally and live a fulfilling and moral life?

We need not continually confuse the actual world with our own perspective of the world. We can learn to consider and understand others' points of view and to see situations from more than one point of view. We can learn to assess our thinking for soundness. We can strive to become conscious of our egocentrism as we develop our "second nature."

Each of us has the potential for developing a rational mind and using that development to resist or correct for egocentric thought patterns. This requires a certain level of command over the mind that few people have. It involves disciplined thinking. It means holding oneself accountable. It means developing an inner voice that guides thinking so as to improve it. It means thinking through the implications of thinking, before acting. It involves identifying and scrutinizing our purposes and agendas, explicitly checking for egocentric tendencies. It involves identifying irrational thinking and transforming it into reasonable thinking.

EXHIBIT 9.6 *Comparing the tendencies of inherent egocentric thinking with those of cultivated non-egocentric thinking.*

THE EGOCENTRIC MIND	THE NON-EGOCENTRIC MIND
Pursues selfish interests at the expense of the rights, needs, and desires of others while stunting development of the rational mind	Respects the needs and desires of others while pursuing its own needs and desires and is motivated to develop itself, to learn, and to grow intellectually
Seeks self-validation	
Can be inflexible (unless it can achieve its selfish interests through flexibility)	Is flexible, adaptable
	Strives to be fair-minded
Is selfish	Strives to interpret information accurately
Makes global, sweeping positive or negative generalizations	Strives to gather and consider all relevant information
Distorts information and ignores significant information	Reacts rationally to situations by taking charge of emotions and using emotional energy productively
Reacts with negative, counterproductive emotions when it fails to have its desires met	

For example, imagine Todd and Teresa, who are dating. Todd finds himself feeling jealous when Teresa talks with another man. Then Todd recognizes the feeling of jealousy as irrational. Now he can intervene to prevent his egocentric nature from asserting itself. He can ask himself questions that enable him to begin to distance himself from his "ego": "Why shouldn't she talk to other men? Do I really have any good reason for distrusting her? If not, why is her behavior bothering me?"

EXHIBIT 9.7 *At any given moment, depending on the situation, the three functions of the mind are controlled by either egocentric or non-egocentric thinking.*

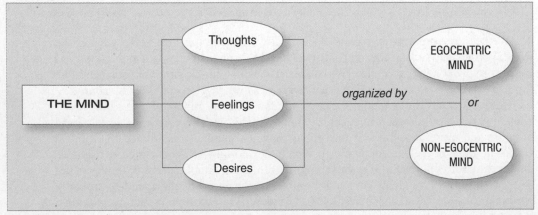

Through this sort of self-scrutinizing, reasonable persons seek to understand what lies behind their motivations. They come to terms with their own egocentrism. They establish relationships characterized by reasonability and mutual respect.

Rational thinking, then, is flexible, disciplined, and fair-minded in its approach. It is able to chart its own course while adhering to ethical demands. It guides itself deliberately away from irrational tendencies. Thus—just as unconscious, self-deceptive thinking is the vehicle for accomplishing irrational ends—conscious, self-perceptive thinking is the vehicle for achieving rational ends. An important part of rational thinking, therefore, is raising to the conscious level all instinctive irrational thought. We cannot improve by ignoring our bad habits, only by breaking them down. This requires that we admit we have bad habits, and it requires an active self-analytic orientation.

Following this line of reasoning, a rational act is one that can withstand reasonable criticism when brought entirely into the open. Any thought that we cannot entirely own up to should be considered suspect. Like a contract with many pages of fine print that the contract writer hopes the reader will not understand, the egocentric mind operates to hide the truth about what it is actually doing. It hides the truth both from itself and from others, all the while representing itself as reasonable and fair.

Rational thinking, in contrast, is justified by good reasons. It is not self-deceptive. It is not a cover for a hidden agenda. It is not trapped within one point of view when other points of view are relevant. It strives to gather all important relevant information and is committed to self-consistency and integrity. Reasonable people seek to see things as they are, to understand and experience the world richly and fully; they are actively engaged in life. They are willing to admit when they are wrong, and to learn from their mistakes. Indeed, they *want* to see themselves as wrong when they are wrong.

To develop your rational capacities, then, you must recognize that at any given moment, your thoughts, feelings, and desires can be controlled either by egocentric or by rational thinking. When your rational mind prevails over your egocentric tendencies, you function in a way analogous to that of an orchestra leader. The leader controls the process of musical production, maintains discipline within the orchestra, assesses the quality of the music, listens for flaws in delivery and points out those flaws for correction, and, through routine scrutiny and continual practice, is finally able to elicit music of high quality.

To reach more of your rational potential, you must become a student of the interplay between rational and irrational thought and motivation in your life. You must come to see that, ultimately, your thinking is what is controlling who and what you are, determining the essential quality of your life, and impacting those with whom you come into contact and form relationships.

Two Egocentric Functions

We have introduced you to the contrast between rationality and irrationality. Now we will discuss two distinctly different patterns of egocentric thinking. Both represent general strategies the egocentric mind uses to get what it wants; both represent ways of irrationally acquiring and using power.

9.6   *Think for Yourself*

TO WHAT EXTENT ARE YOU RATIONAL?

Now that you have read an introduction to rationality and irrationality (egocentrism), think about the extent to which you think you are either rational or irrational. Answer these questions:

1. If you were to divide yourself into two parts, one being egocentric and the other rational, to what extent would you say you are either? Would you say you are 100% rational, 50% rational and 50% egocentric, or some other ratio?

2. What reasoning would you give to support your answer to question 1? Give examples from your life.

3. To the extent that you are egocentric, what problems does your egocentrism cause?

4. Does your egocentric thinking tend to cause more problems for yourself or for others? Explain.

First let's focus on the role that power plays in everyday life. All of us need to feel that we have some power. If we are powerless, we are unable to satisfy our needs. Without power, we are at the mercy of others. Virtually all that we do requires the exercise of some kind of power. Hence, the acquisition of power is essential for human life. But we can pursue power through either rational or irrational means, and we can use the power we get to serve rational or irrational ends.

Two irrational ways to gain and use power correspond to two distinct forms of egocentric strategy:

1. The art of dominating others (as a *direct* means to getting what one wants)

2. The art of submitting to others (as an *indirect* means to getting what one wants)

To get what we want egocentrically, we try either to dominate others or submit to them.

Insofar as we are thinking egocentrically, we seek to satisfy our egocentric desires either directly, by exercising overt power and control over others, or indirectly, by submitting to those who can act to serve our interest. To put it crudely, the ego either bullies or grovels. It either threatens those weaker or subordinates itself to those more powerful, or both.

Both of these methods for pursuing our interests are irrational, and both are fundamentally flawed, because both are grounded in unjustified thinking. Both result from the assumption that egocentric persons' needs and rights are more important than those of the people they exploit for their advantage. We will briefly explore these two patterns of irrational thinking, laying out the basic logic of each.

Before we discuss these patterns, one caveat is in order. As we have mentioned, many situations in life involve using power. Using power need not imply an inappropriate use, however. For example, in a business setting, managers may make decisions with which their employees may not agree. The responsibility inherent in the managers' position calls for them to use their power to make decisions. They are responsible for

EXHIBIT 9.8 *Whenever we think egocentrically to serve our interests, we attempt either to dominate or to submit to others.*

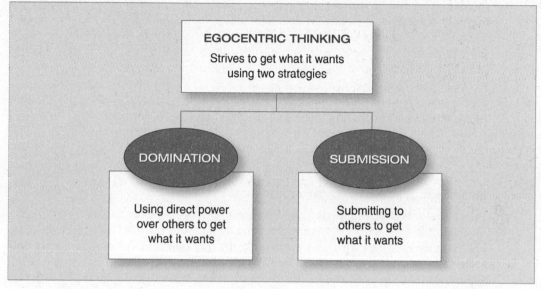

ensuring that certain tasks are completed. Therefore, they must use their power to see those tasks to completion. Indeed, managers who are unable to use the authority vested in their positions are usually ineffective. Of course, that does not justify managers' using power unjustifiably to serve selfish ends.

The use of power, then, is and must be part of human life. But power can be used either rationally or irrationally, depending on the motivation and manner of the person wielding it. Thus, if power is used to serve rational ends in a reasonable manner, it is justified. In contrast, if power is used to control and manipulate others for irrational, self-serving ends, that is another matter entirely.

Let us now turn to the two patterns of irrational thinking that all of us use to the extent that we are egocentric. The first we refer to as the *dominating ego function.* "I can get what I want by fighting my way to the top." The second we term the *submissive ego function.* "I can get what I want by pleasing others." The egocentric mind chooses one over the other either through habit or through an assessment of the situation. For example, an egocentric person seeking to fulfill a desire can either forcefully displace those at the top or please those on top. Of course, these choices and the thinking that accompanies them take place subconsciously.

Egocentric Domination

Of the two functions of egocentric thinking, perhaps the one more easily understood is the dominating function—or the *dominating ego,* as we usually will refer to it for the purposes of this chapter. A person who is operating within this mode of thinking is concerned, first and foremost, to get others to do precisely what he or she wants by means of power over them. Thus, the dominating ego uses physical force, verbal intimidation, coercion, violence, aggression, "authority," and any other form of overt power to achieve its agenda. It is driven by the fundamental belief that to get what we want, we must control others in such a way that if they were to resist us, we could force them to do what we want. At times, of course, domination may be quite subtle and indirect, with a quiet voice and what appears to be a mild manner.

For examples of the dominating ego at work, we need only to consider the many people who are verbally or physically abused by their spouses, or the many children similarly abused by their parents. The basic unspoken pattern is, "If others don't do what I want, I force them to do it." Or consider the man in a bar who gets into a fight to force another man away from his girlfriend. His purpose, on the surface, is to protect her. In reality, his purpose may be to ensure that she won't be tempted into a romantic relationship with someone else, or embarrass him in front of his peers.

> The dominating ego uses force and control over others to get what it wants.

Domination over others typically generates feelings of power and self-importance. Through self-deception, it also commonly entails a high sense of self-righteousness. The dominator is typically arrogant and thinks that control over others is right and proper. The dominator often uses force and control "for the good" of the person being dominated. The key is that there is self-confirmation and self-gain in using power and forcing others to submit. As a result, others must undergo undeserved inconvenience, pain, suffering, or deprivation.

Given these mutually supporting mental structures, it is difficult for those who successfully dominate others to recognize any problems in their own behavior or reasoning. Why change when, in your mind, you are doing what ought to be done? Hence, as long as the dominating ego is "successful," it experiences positive emotions. To the extent that it is "unsuccessful"—unable to control, dominate, or manipulate others—it experiences negative emotions.

The failure to achieve control can result in strong negative emotions, including anger, rage, wrath, rancor, hostility, antagonism, depression, and sadness. Consider the abusive husband who, for many years, is successfully able to control his wife. When she decides to leave him, he may go into a fit of rage and kill her, and perhaps even himself. As long as he thinks he is in control of her, he feels satisfied. But when he no longer can dominate her, his irrational anger may well lead him to the extreme of physical violence.

Examples of the kinds of thinking that dominating persons use in justifying their irrational controlling behavior are:

- "I know more than you do."
- "Since I know more than you, I have an obligation to take charge."
- "If I have to use force to make things right, I should do so because I understand better what needs to be done."
- "If I have more power than you do, it is because I am superior to you in skill and understanding."

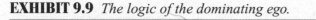

EXHIBIT 9.9 *The logic of the dominating ego.*

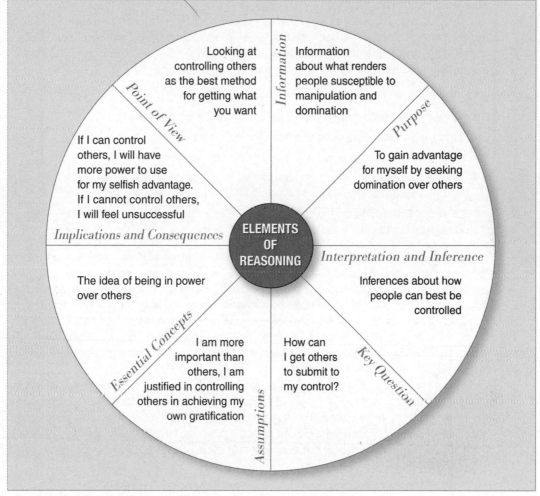

- "I have a right to take the lead. I understand the situation best."
- "You are behaving stupidly. I cannot let you hurt yourself."

Given these subconscious beliefs and thoughts, it follows that people who operate primarily from the dominating ego would likely have difficulties in interpersonal relationships, especially when they come up against another dominating ego or against a strong rational person.

Just as the unconscious tendency to dominate impedes healthy personal relationships, so it often impedes the learning process. Students who have been able to avoid disciplined learning by using the strategy and tactics of a dominating ego may find genuine learning to be a frustrating challenge.

Intellectual arrogance is a common byproduct of the tendency to dominate. All of the following thoughts—often unconscious—lead to or derive from intellectual arrogance. They are common to students who have successfully avoided significant learning through the exercise of power over teachers and parents:

- "Why should I have to learn this? It's useless to me."
- "This is just theory and abstraction. I want practical knowledge."
- "I know as much as I need to know about this subject."
- "This is not in my major. I will never have any use for it."
- "I'm intelligent. If I don't understand what is being taught to me, there is obviously something wrong with the way the instructor is presenting it."
- "I've always made good grades before. So, if I don't make a good grade in this class, it's the teacher's fault."

Another tendency of the dominating ego is to impose higher standards on others than it imposes on itself. For example, a dominating person may require something near perfection in others while ignoring blatant flaws in herself. For a simple, everyday example, consider what often happens in traffic jams. People often drive as if their "rights" were sacred ("No one should ever cut me off") while they themselves frequently cut off others ("I have to get into this lane—too bad if others have to wait"). In short, the dominating ego expects others to adhere to rules and regulations it has the "right" to thrust aside at will.

From an ethical point of view, those who seek control over others frequently violate the rights and ignore the needs of others. Selfishness and cruelty are common in these people. It is, of course, difficult to gain any ground by reasoning with people who are under the sway of their dominating ego, for they will use any number of intellectual dodges to avoid taking moral responsibility for their behavior.

9.7 *Think for Yourself*

TO WHAT EXTENT ARE YOU EGOCENTRICALLY DOMINATING?

Think about your typical patterns of interaction with friends, family members, co-workers, and others. Complete the following statements:

1. I tend to be the most (egocentrically) dominating in the following types of situations:
2. Some examples of my dominating behavior are . . . .
3. I usually am successful/unsuccessful in dominating others. My strategy is . . . .
4. My controlling behavior creates problems because . . . .

In the next section we lay out the logic of egocentric submissive thinking—thinking that seeks power and security through attachment to those who dominate and wield power. Bear in mind as we continue that not everyone who has power has achieved it through irrational means or for irrational ends. A given person who has power may well have achieved it through rational means. With this caveat in mind, let us begin with an outline of the submissive ego.

Egocentric Submission

If the hallmark of the dominating ego is control over others, the hallmark of the submissive ego is *strategic subservience*. In this mode of thinking, people gain power not through the direct struggle for power but, instead, through subservience to others who

EXHIBIT 9.10 *The logic of the submissive ego.*

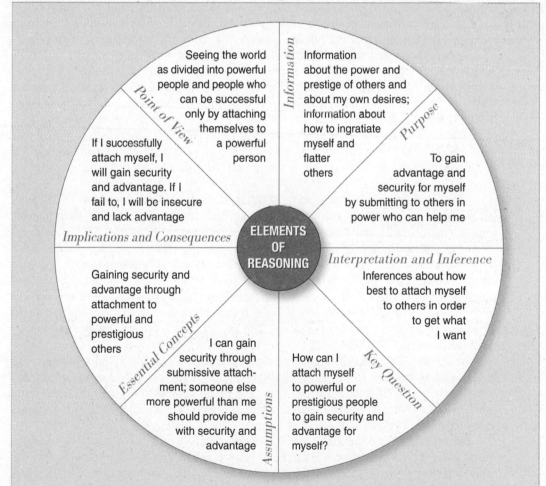

have power. They submit to the will of others to get those others to act in their selfish interest. In this way, people with submissive egos gain indirect power. To be successful, they learn the arts of flattery and personal manipulation. They become skilled actors and actresses, appearing to be genuinely interested in the well-being and interests of the person with power while in reality pursuing their own interest. At the same time, they must hide this mode of functioning from themselves, as they have to maintain self-respect. If they had to consciously admit to themselves that they were submitting to others to gain indirect power, they would have trouble feeling justified.

There are countless examples of this mode of functioning in everyday life. A teenage girl who pretends to enjoy fishing, while being inwardly bored by it, so that her boyfriend will like her better is engaging in this type of thinking. She submits to his desires and his will only because she wants to gain specific ends (for example, having a prestigious boyfriend, gaining attention from him, feeling secure in the relationship, and so on). Though she readily agrees to go fishing with him, she probably will end up resenting having done so in the long run—especially once she secures his commitment to her. Because of the bad faith implicit in the strategies of the submissive ego, it is common for the person who functions consistently in this mind-set to develop resentment.

> The submissive ego submits to those in power to get what it wants.

If the pattern of thinking of the submissive ego takes root in this young woman, she eventually may marry a financially secure man so she can be taken care of, will not have to work, and can enjoy the luxuries of a life without personal sacrifice. Consciously she may deceive herself into believing she loves the man. Yet, because she does not relate to him rationally, the relationship is likely to be dysfunctional.

A similar pattern often occurs in social groups. Within most groups there will be a structure of power, with some members playing a dominant and others a submissive role.

Most people will play both roles at times, depending on the situation. Nazi Germany and the ideology of Fascism provide an excellent example of a system that simultaneously cultivated both dominating and submissive behavior. In this system, nearly everyone had to learn to function within both egocentric types, depending on the context. A hierarchy was established in which everyone was required to give absolute obedience to those above them and to have absolute authority over everyone below them. Only Hitler did not have to use the strategy of submission, as there was no one for him to submit to. Theoretically, no one in such a system has to rationally persuade anyone below him or her in the system. The expectation is clear: Anyone below submits; anyone above dominates.

In the ideology of most human cultures, a greater place is officially given to the use of reason than it was in Fascist Germany. Much of the official ideology of any society, however, is more window dressing than reality. Because all societies are stratified and all stratified societies have a hierarchical structure of power, all societies encourage the thinking of the dominating and submissive egos.

Stratification is commonly found in work-related contexts. In many work situations, men and women alike feel forced to behave submissively with their supervisors, allowing themselves to be dominated and manipulated by their superiors so they can stay in favor, keep their jobs, or get promotions.

Thus, the submissive ego operates through artifice and skillful self-delusion to ensure its security, advantage, and gratification. Submissive people engage in behavior that is compliant, servile, cowering, and acquiescent to achieve their objectives—though all of these characteristics may be highly disguised. They continually capitulate, defer, cave in, succumb, and yield to the will of others to gain advantage and maintain their artificial self-esteem.

To avoid the feeling of caving in to superiors, submissive people adopt various image-saving devices. One of the most effective is to adopt the point of view of the superior. In this case, the submission appears to be merely agreement: "He didn't pressure me; I agree with him."

As long as the submissive ego achieves "success," it experiences positive emotions—satisfaction, happiness, fulfillment, pleasure, and the like. To the extent that it is not achieving its goals and is failing to gain its ends through submission, however, it feels any of a number of negative emotions including bitterness, resentment, animosity, ill will, spite, vindictiveness, enmity, antipathy, and loathing. What is more, depending on the situation, a sense of having failed may lead to insecurity, fear, helplessness, depression, and anxiety.

When unsuccessful, the person with a submissive ego tends to punish himself inwardly—much more than the person with a dominating ego, who tends to respond to pain by inflicting pain on others. Egocentric feelings mirror egocentric thought. Hence, when inflicting pain on himself, the person of submissive ego sees himself as justified in feeling bad. He experiences a form of sick pleasure in reminding himself that he has every reason to feel negative emotions.

Consider, for example, a woman who believes that her husband should deal with all the unpleasant decisions that have to be made. If he asks her to handle some of those decisions, she goes along with him but is resentful as a result. She may think thoughts such as: "Why should I have to deal with these unpleasant decisions? They are his responsibility. I always have to do the things he doesn't want to do. He doesn't really care about me because if he did, he wouldn't ask me to do this." She feels justified in thinking these negative thoughts, and in a way she enjoys the feelings of resentment that accompany such thoughts.

The person predominantly operating from the submissive ego often has a "successful" relationship with a person who functions within the dominating-ego mind-set. The paradigm case of this phenomenon can be found in marriages in which the male dominates and the female submits. She submits to his will. He may require that she do all the household chores. In return, either implicitly or explicitly, he agrees to take care of her (serve as the primary bread-winner). Although she may at times resent his domination, she understands and, at some level, accepts the bargain. Through rationalization she convinces herself that she probably couldn't do better with any other man, that this one provides the comforts she requires, and that in essence she can put up with his domineering behavior because the payoffs are worth it.

Thus, the submissive ego can experience a form of dysfunctional "success" as long as it feels that its desires are being met. Take the employee who behaves in a subservient manner to a verbally abusive manager in order to get promotions. As long as the manager takes care of the employee—by looking after his interests, and giving him the promotions he is striving toward—the employee has positive feelings. When the manager ceases doing this, however, and therefore no longer seems to be concerned with the employee's needs and desires, the employee may feel degraded and resentful of the manager and the subservient role he is forced to play. If given an opportunity, he may turn on his supervisor.

As the submissive ego relates to others, its feelings, behaviors, and thoughts are controlled by beliefs deriving from its own subconscious sense of inferiority. To justify its need to submit to the desires and will of another person, it must perceive itself as inferior to that person. Otherwise it would be unable to rationalize its subservience. It would be forced to recognize its dysfunctional thinking and behavior. Consider the following unconscious beliefs that drive the thinking of the submissive ego:

- "I must go along with this (decision, situation) even though I don't agree with it. Otherwise I won't be accepted."
- "For me to get what I want, I must submit to those who are more powerful than I am."
- "Since I'm not very smart, I must rely on others to think for me."
- "Since I'm not a powerful person, I must use manipulative strategies to get others to provide what I want."

As is true for all manifestations of egocentric thinking, none of these beliefs exists in a fully conscious form. They require self-deception; otherwise, the mind would immediately recognize them as irrational, dysfunctional, and absurd. Consequently, what the mind consciously tells itself is very different from the beliefs that are actually operating in egocentric functioning. Consider the first belief, "I must go along with this even though I don't agree with it. Otherwise I won't be accepted." The conscious thought parallel to this unconscious one is something like: "I don't know enough about the situation to decide for myself. Even though I'm not sure this is the right decision, I'm sure the others are in a better position than I to decide." This is the thought the mind believes it is acting upon, when in reality it is basing its reasoning on the unconscious belief. Thinking within this logic, the person is "dishonestly" going along with the decision, in a sense pretending to agree, but doing so only to forward an agenda of acceptance.

In addition to serving as a major barrier to the pursuit of rational relationships, the submissive ego stunts the development of the rational mind, limiting its capacity for insight into self. The submissive ego does this through a number of self-protecting beliefs, including:

- "I'm too stupid to learn this."
- "If I have a question, others might think I'm ignorant."
- "I'm not as smart as others."
- "No matter how hard I try, I can't do any better than I'm already doing."
- "I'll never be able to figure this out."
- "Since I know I'm too dumb to learn this, there's no point in really trying."

Thus, the submissive ego, like the dominating ego, creates significant barriers to development. It routinely turns to others for help when it is capable of performing without that help. The submissive ego experiences frustration, anxiety, and even depression when it fails, or when it anticipates failure, in learning situations. Whereas the dominating ego believes it already knows what it needs to know, the submissive ego often believes it is incapable of learning.

9.8   *Think for Yourself*

TO WHAT EXTENT ARE YOU EGOCENTRICALLY SUBMISSIVE?

Think about your typical patterns of interaction with friends, family members, co-workers, and others. Complete the following statements:

1. I tend to be the most (egocentrically) submissive in the following types of situations:
2. Some examples of my submissive egocentric behavior are . . .
3. I am usually successful/unsuccessful when I try to manipulate others through submissiveness. My strategy is . . .
4. My submissive behavior creates problems because . . .

9.9   *Think for Yourself*

TO WHAT EXTENT ARE YOU EGOCENTRICALLY DOMINATING VERSUS SUBMISSIVE?

Think about your typical patterns of interaction with friends, family members, co-workers, and others. Do you tend to be more dominating or submissive in most situations in which you are egocentric? What about your friends, family members, co-workers—do they tend to be more dominating or submissive? In your experience, what problems emerge from people behaving in dominating or submissive ways?

Pathological Tendencies of the Human Mind

We can now describe an array of interrelated natural dispositions of the human mind that follow as consequences of egocentricity. To significantly develop your thinking, you must identify these tendencies as they operate in your life and correct them through critical-thinking processes. As you read them, ask yourself whether you recognize these as processes that take place regularly in your own mind (if you conclude, "not me!" think again):

- **Egocentric memory:** the natural tendency to "forget" evidence and information that do not support our thinking and to "remember" evidence and information that do

- **Egocentric myopia:** the natural tendency to think in an absolutist way within an overly narrow point of view

- **Egocentric righteousness:** the natural tendency to feel superior in the light of our confidence that we possess the "Truth" when we do not

- **Egocentric hypocrisy:** the natural tendency to ignore flagrant inconsistencies—for example, between what we profess to believe and the actual beliefs our behavior implies, or between the standards to which we hold ourselves and those to which we expect others to adhere

- **Egocentric oversimplification:** the natural tendency to ignore real and important complexities in the world in favor of simplistic notions when considering those complexities would require us to modify our beliefs or values

- **Egocentric blindness:** the natural tendency not to notice facts and evidence that contradict our favored beliefs or values

- **Egocentric immediacy:** the natural tendency to overgeneralize immediate feelings and experiences, so that when one or a few events in our life are highly favorable or unfavorable, all of life seems favorable or unfavorable

- **Egocentric absurdity:** the natural tendency to fail to notice thinking that has "absurd" consequences

The Best Thinkers Challenge the Pathological Tendencies of Their Minds

It is not enough to recognize abstractly that the human mind has a tendency to egocentricity. As critical thinkers, we must take concrete steps to correct it. This requires us to develop the habit of identifying these tendencies in action. This is a long-term project that is never complete. To some extent, it is like stripping off onion skins. After we remove one, we find another beneath it. We have to remove the outer layer to be able to recognize the one underneath. Each of the following admonitions, therefore, should not be taken as a simple suggestion that any person could immediately put into action, but rather as a strategic formulation of a long-range goal. We all can reach these goals, but only over time and only with considerable practice.

Correcting egocentric memory.   We can correct our natural tendency to "forget" evidence and information that do not support our thinking and to "remember" evidence and information that do, by carefully seeking evidence and information that do not support our thinking and directing attention to them. If you try and cannot find such evidence, you should assume you have not conducted your search properly.

Correcting egocentric myopia.   We can correct our natural tendency to think in an absolutistic way within an overly narrow point of view by routinely thinking within points of view that conflict with our own. For example, if a person is liberal, she can take the time to read books by insightful conservatives. If a person is conservative, she can take the time to read books by insightful liberals. If a person is North American, he can study a contrasting South American point of view or a European or Far-Eastern or Middle-Eastern or African point of view. If you don't discover significant personal prejudices through this process, you should question whether you are truly, in good faith, trying to identify your prejudices.

Correcting egocentric righteousness.   We can correct our natural tendency to feel superior in light of our confidence that we possess the "Truth" by regularly reminding ourselves how little we actually know. One way to do this is to state explicitly the unanswered questions that surround whatever knowledge we may have. If you don't discover that there is much more that you do not know than you do know, you should question the manner in which you are seeking questions to which you do not have answers.

Correcting egocentric hypocrisy.   We can correct our natural tendency to ignore flagrant inconsistencies between what we profess to believe and the actual beliefs our behavior implies, and between the standards to which we hold ourselves and those to which we expect others to adhere. We can do this by regularly comparing the criteria and standards by which we are judging others with those by which we are judging ourselves. If you don't find many flagrant inconsistencies in your own thinking and behavior, you should doubt whether you have dug deeply enough.

Correcting egocentric oversimplification.   We can correct our natural tendency to ignore real and important complexities in the world by regularly focusing on those complexities, formulating them explicitly in words, and targeting them. If you don't discover over time that you have oversimplified many important issues, you should question whether you have really confronted the complexities inherent in the issues.

Correcting egocentric blindness.   We can correct our natural tendency to ignore facts or evidence that contradicts our favored beliefs or values by explicitly seeking out those facts and evidence. If you don't find yourself experiencing significant discomfort as you pursue these facts, you should question whether you are taking them seriously. If you discover that your traditional beliefs have all been confirmed, you have probably moved to a new and more sophisticated level of self-deception.

Correcting egocentric immediacy.   We can correct our natural tendency to overgeneralize immediate feelings and experiences by getting into the habit of putting positive and negative events into a much larger perspective. We can temper the negative events by reminding ourselves of how much we have that many others lack. We can temper the positive events by reminding ourselves of how much is yet to be done, of how many problems remain. You know you are keeping an even keel if you find that you have the energy to act effectively in either negative or positive circumstances. You know that you are falling victim to your emotions if and when you are immobilized by them.

Correcting egocentric absurdity.   We can correct our natural tendency to ignore thinking that has absurd consequences by making the consequences of our thinking explicit. This requires that we frequently trace the implications of our beliefs and their consequences for our behavior. For example, we should frequently ask ourselves: "If I really believed this, how would I act? Do I really act that way?" Personal ethics is a fruitful area for discovering egocentric absurdity. We frequently act in ways that are "absurd," given what we insist we believe in. If, after what you consider to be a serious search, you find no egocentric absurdity in your life, think again. You are probably just developing your ability to deceive yourself.

The Challenge of Rationality

If the human mind has a natural tendency toward irrationality in the form of dominating and submissive ego functions, it also has a capacity for rationality, in the form of a capacity for self-knowledge and reasonability. We all have a tendency toward hypocrisy and inconsistency, but we nevertheless can move toward greater and greater integrity and consistency. We can counteract our natural tendency toward intellectual arrogance by developing our capacity for intellectual humility. Put another way, we can learn to question what we "know" to ensure that we are not uncritically accepting beliefs that have no foundation in fact.

Moreover, we can counteract our tendency to be trapped in our own point of view by learning how to enter empathically into the points of view of others. We can counteract our tendency to jump to conclusions by learning how to test our conclusions for their validity and soundness. We can counteract our tendency to play roles of domination or submission by learning how to recognize when we are doing so. We can begin to see clearly why submission and domination are inherently problematic. We can learn to search out options for avoiding these modes of functioning. And we can practice self-analysis and self-critique in order to learn and grow in directions that render us less and less egocentric.

PART II: THE BEST THINKERS TAKE CHARGE OF THEIR SOCIOCENTRIC TENDENCIES

> Sociocentric thinking is egocentric thinking raised to the level of the group.

Just as all humans are egocentric by nature, we are sociocentric as well. *Sociocentric thinking,* as you may remember, is egocentric thinking raised to the level of the group. And it can be even more destructive than egocentric thinking, since it carries with it the sanction of a social group (which clearly wields more power than does the typical individual).* Both egocentric and sociocentric thought are implicitly or explicitly self-serving, and/or rigid. Like egocentric thinking, sociocentric thinking is absurd—if it were made explicit in the mind of the thinker, its unreasonableness would be obvious. Thus our objective, as critical

---

*Consider, for example, the fact that close to 500 million people died in the 20th century due to violent group conflicts (war, that is).

thinkers, is to make explicit in our own minds the sociocentric thinking that influences our behavior.

Note the following parallels between egocentric and sociocentric patterns of thought:

- **Egocentric standard:** "It's true because I believe it."
  Related sociocentric standard: "It's true because we believe it."
- **Egocentric standard:** "It's true because I want to believe it."
  Related sociocentric standard: "It's true because we want to believe it."
- **Egocentric standard:** "It's true because it's in my vested interest to believe it."
  Related sociocentric standard: "It's true because it's in our vested interest to believe it."
- **Egocentric standard:** "It's true because I have always believed it."
  Related sociocentric standard: "It's true because we have always believed it."

Just as individuals deceive themselves through egocentric thinking, groups deceive themselves through sociocentric thinking. Just as egocentric thinking functions to serve one's selfish interest, sociocentric thinking functions to serve the selfish interests of the group. And just as egocentric thinking operates to validate the uncritical thinking of the individual, sociocentric thinking operates to validate the uncritical thinking of the group.

The Nature of Sociocentrism

Living a human life entails membership in a variety of human groups—groups such as nation, culture, profession, religion, family, and peer group. We find ourselves participating in groups even before we are aware of ourselves as living beings. We find ourselves in groups in virtually every setting in which we function as persons. What is more, every group to which we belong has some social definition of itself and some usually unspoken "rules" that guide the behavior of all members. Each group to which we belong imposes some level of conformity on us as a condition of acceptance—a set of rules, conventions, and taboos.

All of us, to varying degrees, uncritically accept as right and correct whatever ways of acting and believing are fostered in the social groups to which we belong. This becomes clear to us if we reflect on what happens when, for example, adolescents join an urban street gang. When joining the group, members are expected to identify themselves with:

- a name that defines who and what they are
- a way of talking
- a set of friends and enemies
- gang rituals in which they must participate
- expected behaviors involving fellow gang members
- expected behaviors when around the enemies of the gang
- a hierarchy of power within the gang
- a way of dressing and speaking

- social requirements to which every gang member must conform
- a set of taboos—forbidden acts that every gang member must studiously avoid under threat of (sometimes severe) punishment

Group membership is in various ways "required" for ordinary acts of living. Suppose, for example, you wanted to belong to no nation, to be a citizen not of a country but of the world. You would not be allowed that freedom. You would find that you were allowed no place to live, nor any way to travel from place to place. Every place in the world is claimed by some nation (as their "sovereign" possession) and every nation requires that all visitors to it come as a citizen of some other country (with a "passport"). In addition, everywhere a nation imposes its "sovereignty," it requires the obedience of all persons to literally thousands (if not hundreds of thousands) of laws. Of course, since

EXHIBIT 9.11 *The logic of sociology.*

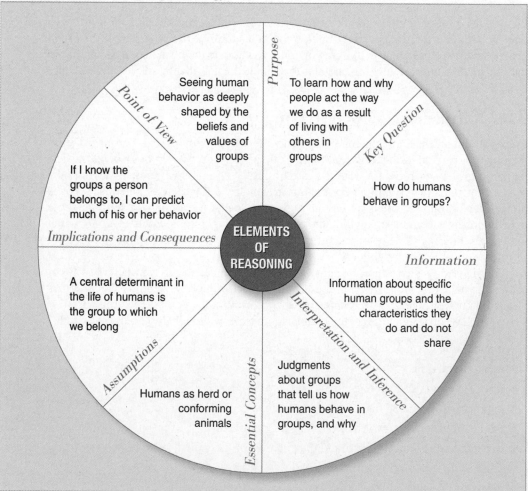

no one can memorize thousands of laws, it is virtually impossible to live in any society without breaking (unknowingly) many of its laws. Because there is a hierarchy of power within every country, the most powerful subgroups within the country can usually find ways to "punish" weak members of the group, or get more advantages for themselves.

Group membership clearly offers some "advantages." But those advantages come with a price. Groups impose their rules (conventions, folkways, taboos) on individuals. For most people, blind conformity to group restrictions is automatic and unreflective. Most effortlessly conform without recognizing that they are doing so. They internalize group norms and beliefs, take on the group identity, and act as they are expected to act—without the least sense that what they are doing might reasonably be questioned. Most people function in social groups as unreflective participants in a range of beliefs, attitudes, and behaviors, just as do members of urban street gangs.

> For most people, blind conformity to group restrictions is automatic and unreflective.

9.10 *Think for Yourself*

THINKING ABOUT THE GROUPS YOU BELONG TO

Make a list of the groups you belong to. Then choose the group you think has influenced you the most in your beliefs, values, and behavior. If you can't think of any groups you belong to, focus on your country—which you belong to whether you want to or not. Complete the following statements:

1. The group that has influenced me the most is probably . . . .
2. This group's main function or agenda is . . . .
3. One of the key "requirements" of this group is . . .
4. One of the key "taboos" (what I am forbidden to do) is . . . .
5. A group that my group would look down upon is . . . . We think of this group as beneath us because . . . .

Next, focusing on the same group, comment on as many of the following variables as you can: To what extent does your membership in this group involve the following? As you comment on each of these variables, be as detailed as possible.

- a name that defines who and what the members are
- a way of talking
- a set of friends and enemies
- group rituals in which you must participate
- expected behaviors involving fellow members
- expected behaviors when around the "enemies" of the group
- a hierarchy of power within the group
- a way of dressing and speaking
- social requirements to which you must conform
- a set of taboos—forbidden acts, whose violation is punished

This conformity of thought, emotion, and action is not restricted to the masses, or the lowly, or the poor. It is characteristic of people in general, regardless of their role in society, regardless of status and prestige, regardless of years of schooling. It is in all likelihood as true of college professors and presidents as it is of students and custodians, as true of senators and chief executives as it is of construction and assembly-line workers. Conformity of thought and behavior is the rule in humans; independence the rare exception.

The idea of sociocentric thinking is not new. Under one label or another, many books have been written on the subject. And it has been the focus of important sociological studies. Almost a hundred years ago, in his seminal book *Folkways,* originally published in 1902, William Graham Sumner wrote extensively about social expectations and taboos. One of the founders of sociology, Sumner documented the manner in which *group think* penetrates virtually every dimension of human life. He introduced the concept of ethnocentrism in this way:

> Ethnocentrism is the technical name for this view of thinking in which one's own group is the center of everything, and all others are scaled and rated with reference to it. . . . Each group nourishes its own pride and vanity, boasts itself superior, exacts its own divines, and looks with contempt on outsiders. Each group thinks its own folkways the only right ones, and if it observes that other groups have other folkways, these excite its scorn. (p. 13)

Sumner describes folkways as the socially perceived "right" ways to think and behave according to group norms and standards. He says that in every society:

> There is a right way to catch game, to win a wife, to make one's self appear . . . to treat comrades or strangers, to behave when a child is born. . . . The "right" way is the way which ancestors used and which has been handed down. The tradition is its own warrant. It is not held subject to verification by experience. . . . In the folkways, whatever is, is right. (p. 28)

In regard to expectations of group members, Sumner states:

> Every group of any kind whatsoever demands that each of its members shall help defend group interests. The group force is also employed to enforce the obligations of devotion to group interests. It follows that judgments are precluded and criticism silenced. . . . The patriotic bias is a recognized perversion of thought and judgment against which our education should guard us. (p. 15)

Even young children exhibit sociocentric thinking and behavior. Consider this passage from Jean Piaget's study for UNESCO (Campbell, 1976), which is a dialogue between an interviewer and three children (italic type) regarding the causes of war:

> **Michael M. (9 years, 6 months old):** Have you heard of such people as foreigners? *Yes, the French, the Americans, the Russians, the English* . . . Quite right. Are there differences between all these people? *Oh, yes, they don't speak the same language.* And what else? *I don't know.* What do you think of the French, for instance? *The French are very serious, they don't worry about anything, an' it's dirty there.* And what do you think of the Russians? *They're bad, they're always wanting to make war.* And what's your

opinion of the English? *I don't know . . . they're nice . . .* Now look, how did you come to know all you've told me? *I don't know . . . I've heard it . . . that's what people say.*

Maurice D. (8 years, 3 months old): If you didn't have any nationality and you were given a free choice of nationality, which would you choose? *Swiss nationality.* Why? *Because I was born in Switzerland.* Now look, do you think the French and Swiss are equally nice, or the one nicer or less nice than the other? *The Swiss are nicer.* Why? *The French are always nasty.* Who is more intelligent, the Swiss or the French, or do you think they're just the same? *The Swiss are more intelligent.* Why? *Because they learn French quickly.* If I asked a French boy to choose any nationality he liked, what country do you think he'd choose? *He'd choose France.* Why? *Because he was born in France.* And what would he say about who's the nicer? Would he think the Swiss and French equally nice, or one better than the other? *He'd say the French are nicer.* Why? *Because he was born in France.* And who would he think more intelligent? *The French.* Why? *He'd say the French want to learn quicker than the Swiss.* Now you and the French boy don't really give the same answer. Who do you think answered best? *I did.* Why? *Because Switzerland is always better.*

Marina T. (7 years, 9 months old): If you were born without any nationality and you were given a free choice, what nationality would you choose? *Italian.* Why? *Because it's my country. I like it better than Argentina where my father works, because Argentina isn't my country.* Are Italians just the same, or more, or less intelligent than the Argentineans? What do you think? *The Italians are more intelligent.* Why? *I can see people I live with, they're Italians.* If I were to give a child from Argentina a free choice of nationality, what do you think he would choose? *He'd want to stay an Argentinean.* Why? *Because that's his country.* And if I were to ask him who is more intelligent, the Argentineans or the Italians, what do you think he would answer? *He'd say Argentineans.* Why? *Because there wasn't any war.* Now who was really right in the choice he made and what he said, the Argentinean child, you, or both? *I was right.* Why? *Because I chose Italy.*

It is clear that these children are thinking sociocentrically. They have been indoctrinated into the belief systems, with accompanying ideologies, of their nation and culture. They cannot articulate why they think their country is better than others, but they have no doubt that it is. Seeing one's group as superior to other groups is both natural to the human mind and propogated by the cultures within which we live.

> "Every group of any kind whatsoever demands that each of its members shall help defend group interests."
> William Graham Sumner

Social Stratification

Sociocentric systems are used in complex societies to justify differential treatment and injustices within the society. This feature of complex social systems has been documented by sociologists who specialize in the phenomenon of social stratification. As virtually all modern societies today are complex, the following characteristics of stratification presumably can be found in all of them. According to Plotnicov and Tuden (1970), every modern society comprises social groups that

1. are ranked hierarchically
2. maintain relatively permanent positions in the hierarchy
3. have differential control of the sources of power, primarily economic and political
4. are separated by cultural and invidious distinctions that also serve to maintain the social distances between the groups
5. are articulated by an overarching ideology that provides a rationale for the established hierarchical arrangements (pp. 4–5)

Given this phenomenon, we should be able to identify where any given group in our society stands in the hierarchy of power, what are its sources of power and control, how the distinctions that indicate status are formulated, how social distances are maintained between the groups, and the overarching ideology that provides the rationale for the way things are. And we should be able to see where we "fit" in the hierarchy.

9.11   *Think for Yourself*

IDENTIFYING SOCIAL STRATIFICATION

Consider the culture with which you are most knowledgeable, and try to construct a hierarchy of the social groups within it. First identify the groups with the most power and prestige. What characteristics do these groups have? Then identify the groups with less and less power, until you reach the groups with the least power. How do the groups with the most power keep their power? To what extent is it possible for groups with less power to increase their power? To what extent do they seem to accept their limited power? To the extent that they accept their limited power, why do you think they do?

Sociocentric Thinking Is Unconscious and Potentially Dangerous

As with egocentric thinking, sociocentric thinking appears in the mind of the person who thinks sociocentrically as reasonable and justified. Similarly, groups often distort the meaning of concepts to pursue their vested interests, but they almost never see themselves doing so. Groups almost always can find problems in the ideologies of other groups, but they rarely are able to find flaws in their own belief systems. And groups usually can identify prejudices that other groups are using against them, but they rarely are able to identify prejudices that they are using against other groups. In short, just as egocentric thinking is self-deceptive, so is sociocentric thinking.

Though the patterns of dysfunctional thinking are similar for egocentric and sociocentric thinking, there is at least one important distinction between the two. We have already pointed out that egocentric thinking is potentially dangerous. Through self-deception, individuals can justify the most egregious actions. But individuals operating alone are usually limited in the amount of harm they can do. Typically, groups engaging in sociocentric thinking can do greater harm to greater numbers of people.

Consider, for example, the Spanish Inquisition, by which the state, controlled by the Catholic Church, executed thousands of reputed heretics. Or consider the Nazis, who tortured and murdered millions of Jews, or the "founders" of the Americas, who enslaved, murdered, or tortured large numbers of Native Americans and Africans.

> Although groups almost always can find problems in the ideologies of other groups, they rarely are able to find flaws in their own belief systems.

In short, throughout history and to the present day, sociocentric thinking has led directly to the pain and suffering of millions of innocent persons. This has happened because groups, in their sociocentric mind-set, use their power in a largely unreflective, and therefore unconscionable, unjust way. Once they have internalized a self-serving ideology, they can act in ways that flagrantly contradict their announced ethical position without noticing any contradictions or inconsistencies.

Sociocentric Uses of Language

Sociocentric thinking is fostered by the way groups use language. Groups justify unjust acts and ways of thinking through their use of concepts or ideas. For example, as William Summer points out, sociocentrism can be exemplified by the very names groups choose for themselves and the ways they differentiate themselves from what they consider lesser groups:

> When Caribs were asked whence they came, they answered, "We alone are people." The meaning of the name *Kiowa* is "real or principal people." The Lapps call themselves "men" or "human beings." The Greenland Eskimo think that Europeans have been sent to Greenland to learn virtue and good manners from the Greenlanders. . . . The Seri of Lower California . . . observe an attitude of suspicion and hostility to all outsiders, and strictly forbid marriage with outsiders. (p. 14)

In the everyday life of sociocentric thinkers, we can find many self-serving uses of language that obscure unethical behavior. During the time when Europeans first inhabited the Americas, they forced Indians into slavery and tortured and murdered them in the name of progress and civilization. By thinking of the Indians as "savages," they could justify this inhumane treatment. At the same time, by thinking of themselves as "civilized," they could see themselves as bringing something precious to the savages, namely "civilization."

Europeans used the words *progress, savagery, civilization*, and *the true religion* as vehicles to exploit the American Indians to gain material wealth and property. The sociocentric thinking of these Europeans obscured the basic humanity of the peoples they exploited, as well as these peoples' rightful ownership of the land they had occupied for thousands of years.

Sumner says that the language social groups use is often designed to ensure that they maintain a special, superior place:

> The Jews divided all mankind into themselves and the Gentiles. They were "chosen people." The Greeks called outsiders "barbarians." . . . The Arabs regarded themselves as the noblest nation and all others as more or less barbarous. . . . In 1896, the Chinese minister of

education and his counselors edited a manual in which this statement occurs: "How grand and glorious is the Empire of China, the middle Kingdom! . . . The grandest men in the world have come from the middle empire." . . . In all the literature of all the states equivalent statements occur. . . . In Russian books and newspapers the civilizing mission of Russia is talked about, just as, in the books and journals of France, Germany, and the United States, the civilizing mission of those countries is assumed and referred to as well understood. Each state now regards itself as the leader of civilization, the best, the freest and the wisest, and all others as their inferior. (p. 14)

Disclose Sociocentric Thinking Through Conceptual Analysis

Concepts are one of the eight basic elements of human thinking. We cannot think without them. They form the classifications, through which we interpret what we see, taste, hear, smell, and touch, and they implicitly express our theories about what we perceive. Our world is a conceptually constructed world. And sociocentric thinking, as argued above, is driven by the way groups use concepts.

If we were to think using the concepts of medieval European serfs, we would experience the world as they did. If we were to think using the concepts of an Ottoman Turk general, we would think and experience the world in the way he did.

In a similar way, if we were to bring an electrician, an architect, a carpet salesperson, a lighting specialist, and a plumber into the same building and ask each to describe what he or she sees, we would end up with a range of descriptions that, in all likelihood, would reveal the special "bias" of the observer.

Or again, if we were to lead a discussion of world problems between representatives of different nations, cultures, and religions, we would discover a range of perspectives not only on potential solutions to the problems but sometimes also as to what should be conceived as a problem in the first place.

One cannot be a skilled critical thinker without being skilled in the analysis of concepts. Conceptual analysis is important in a variety of contexts:

1. It allows us to distinguish among the meanings of words that educated speakers use. As a result, we can identify and accurately analyze distinctions and subtleties in written and spoken language.

2. It allows us to identify the difference between ideological and nonideological uses of words and concepts. That is, we can discern when people are giving special, unjustified meaning to words based on ideology.

3. It allows us to analyze accurately the meanings of words (concepts) that define a discipline or domain of thinking. That is, we can analyze technical terms within disciplines and technical fields.

Many problems in thinking are traceable to a lack of command of words and the concepts they represent. For example, people have problems in their romantic relationships when they are unclear about the following three distinctions: (1) between egocentric attachment and genuine love, (2) between friendship and love, and (3) between misuse of the word *love,* as exemplified by many Hollywood movies, and the true meaning of the word *love,* shared by educated speakers of the English language. The misunderstanding and misuse of these and many other concepts directly results from the indoctrinating nature of sociocentricity.

Reveal Ideology at Work Through Conceptual Analysis

People often have trouble differentiating ideological and nonideological uses of words. They are then unable to use important words such as the following in a nonloaded way: *capitalism, socialism, communism, democracy, oligarchy, plutocracy, patriotism, terrorism.* Let's look at this case in greater detail. When the above words are used ideologically, they are applied inconsistently and one-sidedly. The root meaning of the word is often lost, or highly distorted, while the word is used to put a positive or negative gloss on events, obscuring what is really going on. Hence, in countries in which the reigning ideology extols capitalism, the ideologies of socialism and communism are demonized, democracy is equated with capitalism, and plutocracy is ignored. In countries in which the reigning ideology is communism, the ideology of capitalism is demonized, democracy is equated with communism, and oligarchy is ignored. The groups called "terrorist" by the one are called "patriot" by the other.

> In the everyday life of sociocentric thinkers, we can find many self-serving uses of language that obscure unethical behavior.

If we examine the core meanings of these words and use them in keeping with the core meanings they have in the English language, we can recognize contradictions, inconsistencies, and hypocrisy when any group misuses them to advance its agenda. Let us review the core meanings of these terms as defined by *Webster's New World Dictionary:*

- **Capitalism:** an economic system in which all or most of the means of production and distribution, as land, factories, railroads, etc., are privately owned and operated for profit, originally under fully competitive conditions; it has generally been characterized by a tendency toward concentration of wealth.

- **Socialism:** any of the various theories or systems of the ownership and operation of the means of production and distribution by society or the community rather than by private individuals, with all members of society or the community sharing in the work and the products.

- **Communism:** any economic theory or system based on the ownership of all property by the community as a whole.

- **Democracy:** government in which the people hold the ruling power either directly or through elected representatives; rule by the ruled.

- **Oligarchy:** a form of government in which the ruling power belongs to a few persons.

- **Plutocracy:** (1) government by the wealthy, (2) a group of wealthy people who control or influence a government.

- **Patriotism:** love and loyal or zealous support of one's own country.

- **Terrorism:** use of force or threats to demoralize, intimidate, and subjugate, especially such use as a political weapon or policy.

To this day, countries in which the reigning ideology is capitalism tend to use the words *socialism* and *communism* as if they meant "a system that discourages individual incentive and denies freedom to the mass of people." Countries in which the reigning ideology is socialism or communism, in their turn, tend to use the word *capitalism* to imply the exploitation of the masses by the wealthy few. Both see the use of force of the other as *terrorist* in intent. Both see the other as denying its own members fundamental human rights. Both tend to ignore their own inconsistencies and hypocrisy.

The Mass Media Foster Sociocentric Thinking

The mass media and press in a country tend to present events in the world in descriptive terms that presuppose the correctness of the ideology dominant in their own country. As critical consumers of the mass media, we must learn to recognize when language is being used ideologically (and so violating the basic meanings of the terms themselves). We must learn to recognize sociocentric bias wherever we find it.

Many examples of sociocentric thinking can be found in the mass media. This is true, in part, because the media are an inherent part of the culture within which they function. Because much of the thinking within any given culture is sociocentric in nature, we can expect the sociocentric thinking of the culture to be furthered through the mass media as vehicles of large-scale social communication.

For example, the mass media routinely validate the view that one's own country is "right" or ethical in its dealings in the world. This cultivates one-sided nationalistic thinking. The basic idea is that all of us egocentrically think of ourselves in largely favorable terms. As sociocentric thinkers, we think of our nation and the groups to which we belong in largely favorable terms. It follows, therefore, that the media will present in largely unfavorable terms those nations and groups that significantly oppose us.

For example, most citizens of the United States conceptualize the U.S. as a natural leader of all that is right and good in the world. The mass media largely foster this view. When we look critically at the mainstream mass media of any country, it is easy to document its biases in its representations of important world events.

It follows that the mainstream news media are biased toward their country's allies and prejudiced against its enemies. The media therefore present events that regard the countries of allies in as favorable a light as possible, highlighting positive events while downplaying negative events. As for its enemies, the opposite treatment can be expected. Thus, positive events in the countries of one's enemies are either ignored or given little attention while negative events are highlighted and distorted. The ability of a person to identify this bias in action and mentally rewrite the article or representation more objectively is an important critical thinking skill. In the United States, for example, because Israel is our ally, our media usually ignore or give minor attention to mistreatment of the Palestinians by the Israelis. On the other hand, because Fidel Castro of Cuba is our enemy, mainstream news writers take advantage of every opportunity to present Castro and Cuba in a negative light, ignoring most achievements of the Cuban government (e.g., in the areas of universal education, medical care, and meeting the basic needs of its people).

Let's consider some examples from the news to exemplify this pattern of sociocentric bias in the news.

Article One: "U.S. Releases Files on Abuses in Pinochet Era"

(from *New York Times,* July 1, 1999, p. A11)

Historical background. In 1973 a group of military officers overthrew the government of the democratically elected president of Chile, Salvador Allende. Their announced justification was that Allende was trying to replace democracy with communism. At the time of the coup, the U.S. government repeatedly denied any involvement in the coup and any knowledge of the torture and murder of people considered enemies of the coup leaders and the imposed political structure. Accordingly, the mainstream news media presented the official U.S. position (along with its official explanations) as the truth of the matter. The coup leaders were presented as a positive force against communism. The democratically elected government was presented as a threat to our way of life. The coup, in other words, was presented favorably. Human rights violations were played down.

Contents of article. In this article, written some 27 years after the coup, the mainstream media finally admitted that the United States played a significant role in the Chilean coup. The article states:

> The CIA and other government agencies had detailed reports of widespread human rights abuses by the Chilean military, including the killing and torture of leftist dissidents, almost immediately after a 1973 right-wing coup that the United States supported, according to the once-secret documents released today. . . . The Clinton Administration announced last December that, as a result of the arrest of General Pinochet (who seized power in the coup), it would declassify some of the documents.

Another article in the *New York Times,* dated November 27, 1999 (article entitled "Spanish Judge Is Hoping to See Secret Files in U. S.," p. A14), states, "The Nixon Administration openly favored the coup and helped prepare the climate for the military intervention against the Socialist Government of Salvador Allende Gossens, by backing loans, financing strikes and supporting the opposition press."

Significance. This account illustrates how successfully sociocentric renditions of events are rendered by the news media at the time of their occurrence and for many years thereafter. It also points out, in its failure to suggest—even now—that some significant breach of ethics originally occurred, or that, even worse, breaches of our announced values are common occurences. There is also no criticism of the media for their failure at the time to discover and publish the truth of the U.S. involvement in the coup.

Article Two: "U.S. Order to Kill Civilians in Korea Illegal, Experts Say: Prosecution Seen as Impossible Now"

(from *San Francisco Chronicle,* October 2, 1999, p. A12,
taken from the Associated Press)

Historical background. During the Korean War (1950–53), the news media represented U.S. involvement in the war as a fight, on our side, for the freedom of the South Korean people against a totalitarian government in North Korea (which we presented as dupes of the Chinese communists). That the government we supported in South Korea did not itself function in a democratic fashion and easily could have been represented as our "dupes" was not mentioned in the news coverage of the time. The coverage implied that we were there for humanitarian reasons: to protect the rights of innocent Koreans to have a democratically elected government and universal human rights. The mainstream media also failed to point out any problems with either our involvement in the war or the methods we used to deal with "the enemy."

Contents of article. This article, written 25 years after the events in question, focuses on the killing of civilian refugees by American soldiers during the Korean War:

> The Associated Press reported Wednesday that a dozen veterans of the 1st Cavalry Division said their unit killed a large number of South Korean refugees at a hamlet 100 miles southeast of the Korean capital. . . . The survivors say 400 people were killed in the mass shooting and a preceding U.S. air attack. . . . In the 1st Cavalry Division, the operations chief issued this order: "No refugees to cross the front line. Fire at everyone trying to cross lines."
>
> Such orders are patently illegal, military law experts say today. "I've never heard of orders like this, not outside the orders given by Germans that we heard about during the Nuremberg Trials," said Scott Silliman of Duke University, a retired colonel and Air Force lawyer for 25 years. Yet, "during the 1950–53 war, there were no prosecutions of anything more than individual murders of civilians by U.S. servicemen," the experts note.
>
> In pondering the question: Why were the orders to kill refugees kept quiet all these years?, a retired Colonel who eventually became chief drafter of the Korean armistice agreement commented, "If it was in their unit, then for the sake of the unit they didn't want to report it." He goes on to state that for much of U.S. history, "we've done very badly in not trying these cases. . . . What bothers me most is the fact that the American public seems to take the side of the war criminal if he's an American."

Significance. The significance of this article is that, on the one hand, it again is an example of how successfully the news media render sociocentric events at the time of their occurrence and for many years afterward. What is unusual in this article is the suggestion of a pattern of behavior that goes beyond the events at this particular time ("We've done very badly in not trying these cases. . . . What bothers me most is the fact that the American public seems to take the side of the war criminal if he's an American").

This suggestion of a pattern of American wrongdoing is exceptional, as it diverges from the usual sociocentric tendency of the news. It should be noted, however, that we find this merely in the quote of one individual. The suggestion is not taken up in any follow-up articles. It is not a newsmaker, as was the story of President Clinton's sexual escapades. In this sense, the sociocentrism of the news media is not significantly breached.

Article Three: "Treatment Is New Salvo Fired by Reformers in War on Drugs: Courts, Voters Beginning to Favor Therapy, Not Prisons, to Fight Crack"

(from *San Francisco Chronicle,* June 11, 1999, p. A9, taken from the *New York Times*)

Historical background. Sufficient historical background is given in the contents of the article itself.

Contents of article.

> A dozen years after the national alarm over crack hastened the decline of drug treatment in favor of punitive laws that helped create the world's largest prison system, anti-drug policy is taking another turn. Treatment is making a comeback. . . . In the crack years of the 1980s, treatment programs were gutted while the drug-fighting budget quadrupled. New reports said crack was the most addictive substance known to humanity, and prisons started to fill with people who once might have received help instead. The number of Americans locked up on drug offenses grew from 50,000 in 1980 to 400,000 today. Yet even during the height of the prison boom, when some people were sentenced to life behind bars for possessing small amounts of a drug, a number of treatment centers continued to have success. While not all addicts respond to treatment, these programs showed that crack was less addictive than some other street drugs, or even nicotine, and that many of its users responded to conventional therapy.

> The mass media largely foster sociocentric thinking.

Significance. This article exemplifies the powerful role of the media in feeding social hysteria and thereby affecting social and legal policy. The view advanced by news reports that crack is the most addictive substance known to humanity was the popular view of the day. Also popular in the 1980s was the view that crack users are best dealt with by imprisonment rather than through treatment of the drug abuse problem. The news media reinforced a simplistic Puritanical tradition that is deep in our culture: that the world divides into the good and the evil. According to this social ideology, the good defeat the bad by the use of physical force and superior strength, and the bad are taught a lesson only by severe punishment.

Sometimes an article in the news does not display our sociocentrism but implicitly documents the sociocentrism of another group. For example, the *New York Times,*

9.12   *Think for Yourself*

IDENTIFYING SOCIOCENTRIC BIAS IN THE NEWS I

R ead through the newspaper every day for a week and attempt to locate at least one article revealing sociocentric thinking in the news. One of the best ways to do this is to read carefully any articles about the "friends" or "enemies" of the U.S. power structure. You should be able to identify a bias toward preserving "our" view. Any negative article about one of our friends will play down the negative events and present extenuating excuses for those events. You will rarely find positive articles about our enemies, for in our ideology those who are evil do no good. Use the format we have been using in writing what you have found, including *Historical Background* (if possible), *Contents of the Article,* and *Significance.* It also will be useful if you think through how the article might have been written if it did not reflect a sociocentric bias.

June 20, 1999, included an article entitled "Arab Honor's Price: A Woman's Blood" (p. 1), focusing on the sociocentric thinking of Arab religious groups in Jordan. The facts it covers are that

■ An Arab woman in Jordan was shot and killed by her 16-year-old brother for running away from home after her husband suspected her of infidelity

■ After her husband divorced her, she had run away and remarried

■ Her family had been searching for her for six years in order to kill her. "We were the most prominent family, with the best reputation," said Um Tayseer, the mother. "Then we were disgraced. Even my brother and his family stopped talking to us. No one would even visit us. They would say only, 'You have to kill.'" "Now we can walk with our heads high," said Amal, her 18-year-old sister.

The article goes on to document the way in which traditional Arab culture places greater emphasis on chastity in women than on any other "virtue." The article states:

■ What is honor? Abeer Alla, a young Egyptian journalist, remembered how it was explained by a high-school biology teacher as he sketched the female reproductive system and pointed out the entrance to the vagina. "This is where the family honor lies!" the teacher declared.

■ More than pride, more than honesty, more than anything a man might do, female chastity is seen in the Arab world as an indelible line, the boundary between respect and shame.

■ An unchaste woman, it is sometimes said, is worse than a murderer, affecting not just one victim, but her family and her tribe.

■ It is an unforgiving logic, and its product, for centuries and now, has been murder—the killings of girls and women by their relatives, to cleanse honor that has been soiled.

9.13   *Think for Yourself*

IDENTIFYING SOCIOCENTRIC THINKING IN THE NEWS 2

Locate at least one newspaper article containing evidence of sociocentric thinking on the part of some group. Complete these statements:

1. The article I identified is entitled . . . .
2. A brief summary of the article is as follows:
3. The sociocentric thinking depicted in this article is as follows:
4. If this group had not been thinking sociocentrically, and instead had been thinking rationally, it would have behaved in the following way:

CONCLUSION

The thesis of this chapter is that we can successfully deal with our own egocentric and sociocentric tendencies only by facing, admitting, and understanding them. Without a clear understanding of our egocentric tendencies, we are trapped in a narrow and selfish perspective. Without a clear understanding of our sociocentric tendencies, we are trapped in "group think." Dealing with egocentrism and sociocentrism is no easy matter. Since both function subconsciously, it is difficult to identify them. And though no one will object to our being less selfish (personally), if we significantly and publicly dissent from group beliefs, we face an array of informal—if not formal—penalties.

What is important is that we begin to identify egocentrism and sociocentrism in our thinking and our lives. Every time we become aware of selfishness or narrow rigidity in our thinking, we create an opportunity to lessen those pathologies. Every group to which we belong is a possible place to identify sociocentrism at work in ourselves and others. When we begin to identify the many patterns of self-centeredness and social conformity in our lives, we can begin to break out of those patterns. We need not begin with the beliefs that are most challenging to ourselves or whose denial is most "explosive." Furthermore, we need not make all of what we find a matter of public statement. The key is that we do begin within the privacy of our mind, that we follow through with consistency, and that we give ourselves time to grow progressively into better thinkers and persons. By such inward acts we can become people who think for ourselves and adhere to conscious standards of rationality. By such acts we can develop intellectual integrity and emerge increasingly as fair and just persons.

THE STAGES OF CRITICAL THINKING DEVELOPMENT: *AT WHAT STAGE ARE YOU?*

Most of us arc not what we could be. We are less. We have great capacity, but most of it is dormant; most is undeveloped. Improvement in thinking is like improvement in basketball, ballet, or playing the saxophone. It is unlikely to take place in the absence of a conscious commitment to learn. As long as we take our thinking for granted, we don't do the work required for improvement.

Development in thinking is a gradual process requiring plateaus of learning and just plain hard work. It is not possible to become an excellent thinker by simply taking a beginning course in thinking. Changing one's habits of thought is a long-range process that occurs over years, not weeks or months. The essential traits of a critical thinker, which we examined briefly in Chapter 8, will develop only through long-term commitment.

Here are the stages all of us go through if we aspire to develop as thinkers:

Stage 1   The Unreflective Thinker (we are unaware of significant problems in our thinking)

Stage 2   The Challenged Thinker (we become aware of problems in our thinking)

EXHIBIT 10.1 *Most people live their entire lives as unreflective thinkers. To develop as thinkers requires commitment to daily practice.*

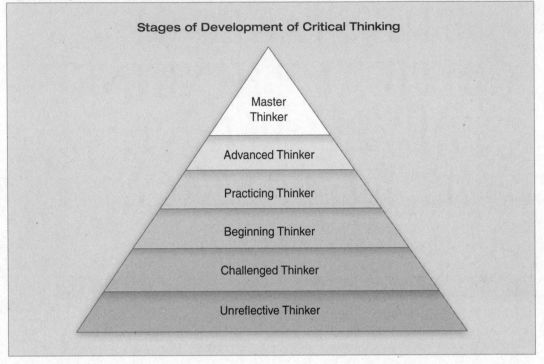

Stage 3	The Beginning Thinker (we try to improve but without regular practice)
Stage 4	The Practicing Thinker (we recognize the necessity of regular practice)
Stage 5	The Advanced Thinker (we advance in accordance with our practice)
Stage 6	The Master Thinker (skilled and insightful thinking become second nature)

In this chapter we will explain the first four stages with the hope that understanding these stages, even at a provisional level, will help you begin to grasp what it means to develop as a thinker. Only through years of advanced practice can one become an "advanced' thinker. Becoming a "master" thinker may serve more as an ideal toward which we can strive than as a practical goal we can reach.*

---

*It is debatable whether any human can become a "master" thinker when no society has as yet adopted critical thinking as a primary social value. For a full description of the stages of critical thinking development, read the article by Elder and Paul, *Developing as Rational Persons: Viewing Our Development in Stages* at www.criticalthinking.org.

STAGE ONE: THE UNREFLECTIVE THINKER

Are You an Unreflective Thinker?

We all are born, and most of us die, as largely unreflective thinkers, fundamentally unaware of the role that thinking is playing in our lives. At this unreflective stage we have no useful conception of what thinking entails. For example, as unreflective thinkers,

- We don't notice that we are continually making assumptions, forming concepts, drawing inferences, and thinking within points of view.
- We don't know how to analyze and assess our thinking.
- We don't know how to determine whether our purposes are clearly formulated, our assumptions justified, our conclusions logically drawn.
- We are unaware of intellectual traits and so are not striving to embody them.
- We are unaware of the fact that many problems in our lives are caused by poor thinking.
- We don't question our beliefs.
- We don't question our decisions.
- We lack intellectual standards and have no idea what such standards might be.
- We lack the intellectual traits but are not aware that we lack them.
- We unconsciously deceive ourselves in many ways.
- We create and maintain pleasant illusions, illusions that often cause problems.

As unreflective thinkers, our beliefs seem reasonable to us, and so we believe them with confidence. We walk about the world with confidence that things really are the way they appear to us. We judge some people to be "good" and some to be "bad." We approve of some actions. We disapprove of others. We make decisions, react to people, go our way in life, without seriously questioning the thinking that largely determines how we live, without questioning the implications of our thinking.

Though we don't realize it, our egocentric tendencies at this stage play a dominant role in our thinking. We lack the skills and the motivation to notice how self-centered and prejudiced we are, how often we stereotype others, how frequently we irrationally dismiss ideas simply because we don't want to change our behavior or our comfortable way of looking at things.

10.1 *Think for Yourself*

REFLECTING ON YOUR KNOWLEDGE OF THINKING

Might you be at the unreflective stage of development? Test yourself by writing your answers to the following:

1. Can you describe the role that thinking is playing in your life? (Be as clear and as detailed as you can.)

2. What was a recent assumption you made (that you should not have made)?

3. What is a recent concept you formed (that you previously lacked)?

4. List five inferences you made in the last hour.

5. Name and explain a point of view that you sometimes use to guide your thinking.

6. Briefly describe how you analyze and assess thinking.

7. Name some intellectual standards you use. Explain how you apply them.

8. Explain the role of egocentric thinking in your life.

9. Take one or two intellectual traits and explain what you are doing to try to embody them.

If you had trouble answering the questions in the last exercise, you may well be at the unreflective stage as a thinker. If so, you do not need to apologize for it or feel badly about it. Most people are at this stage and don't know it. Traditional schooling and the way children are typically reared do not help people become skilled thinkers. Often, parents and teachers themselves are unreflective thinkers. This is the product of a vicious circle. Unreflective persons raise unreflective persons. Once you explicitly recognize that you are at this stage, however, you are ready to move to the next stage. And when you move to the next stage, you may be close to breaking out of the vicious circle of unreflectiveness. To do so requires that we become insightfully *reflective*—that we begin to notice some problems in our thinking, that we begin to recognize that our thinking is often egocentric and irrational, that changes in our own thinking are essential.

> All thinkers, including the best ones, were at one time unreflective thinkers.

Authentic reflectiveness leads to a healthy motivation to change. It is functional and productive. You must not only see problems in your thinking but also have some sense of how those problems might be addressed. You must become reasonably articulate about what you have to do to improve. Motivation is crucial. Without a drive to change, nothing much of significance will happen.

STAGE TWO: THE CHALLENGED THINKER

Are You Ready to Accept the Challenge?

We cannot solve a problem we do not own. We cannot deal with a condition we deny. Without knowledge of our ignorance, we cannot seek the knowledge we lack. Without knowledge of the skills we need to develop, we will not develop those skills.

As we begin to become aware that "normal" thinkers often think poorly, we move into the second stage of critical thinking development. We begin to notice that we often

■ make questionable assumptions.

■ use false, incomplete, or misleading information.

- make inferences that do not follow from the evidence we have.
- fail to recognize important implications in our thought.
- fail to recognize problems we have.
- form faulty concepts.
- reason within prejudiced points of view.
- think egocentrically and irrationally.

We move to the "challenged" stage when we become aware of the way our thinking is shaping our lives, including the recognition that problems in our thinking are causing problems in our lives. We are beginning to recognize that poor thinking can be life-threatening, that it can lead literally to death or permanent injury, that it can hurt others as well as ourselves. For example, we might reflect upon the thinking of

> Even the best thinkers had to recognize at some point the superficiality of their thinking—if they were to grow beyond it.

- the teenager who thinks that smoking cigarettes is sexy.
- the woman who thinks that Pap smears are not important.
- the motorcyclist who reasons that helmets obstruct vision and, therefore, it is safer to ride without one.
- the person who thinks he can drive safely while drunk.
- the person who decides to marry a self centered person with the thought that he or she will "change" after marriage.

We also recognize the difficulty involved in "improving" our thinking. If you are at this stage in your own thinking, you recognize that the problem of changing your habits of thought is an important challenge requiring extensive and difficult changes in your normal routines. Some signs of emerging reflectiveness are that

- you find yourself striving to analyze and assess your thinking.
- you find yourself working with the structures of mind that create thinking or make it possible (for example: concepts, assumptions, inferences, implications, points of view).
- you find yourself thinking about the qualities that make thinking sound—clarity, accuracy, precision, relevance, logic—though you may have only an initial grasp of how these qualities can be achieved.
- you find yourself becoming interested in the role of self-deception in thinking, though your understanding is relatively "abstract" and you may not be able to give many examples from your own life.

At this point in your development, there is a distinct danger of self-deception. Many resist accepting the true nature of the challenge—that their own thinking is a real and significant problem in their life. If you do as many do, you will revert to the unreflective stage. Your experience of thinking about your thinking will fade. Your usual habits of thought will remain as they are. For example, you may find yourself rationalizing in the following way:

My thinking is not that bad. Actually I've been thinking well for quite a while. I question a lot of things. I'm not prejudiced. Besides that, I'm very critical. And I'm not nearly as self-deceived as lots of people I know.

If you reason in this way, you will not be alone. You will join the majority. The view—"if everyone were to think like me, this would be a fine world"—is the dominant view. Those who share this view range from the poorly schooled to the highly schooled. There is no evidence to suggest that schooling correlates with self-reflectivity. Indeed, many college graduates are intellectually arrogant as a result of their schooling. There are unreflective thinkers who did not go beyond elementary school, but there are also unreflective thinkers who have done post-graduate work and now have advanced degrees; unreflective people are found in all socioeconomic classes. They include psychologists, sociologists, philosophers, mathematicians, doctors, senators, judges, governors, district attorneys, lawyers, and indeed people of all professions.

In short, absence of intellectual humility is common among all classes of people, in all walks of life, at all ages. It follows that active or passive resistance to the challenge of critical thinking is the common, not the rare, case. Whether in the form of a careless shrug or outright hostility, most people reject the challenge of critical thinking. That is why some soul-searching is important at this point in the process.

10.2   *Think for Yourself*

DISCUSS THE CHALLENGED THINKER STAGE

Work in groups of three. The person whose first name is earliest in the alphabet will explain the second stage—that of the challenged thinker—to the other two, answering any questions they might have. Then the other two in the group will add any features that the first student missed and elaborate on the points they think are most important.

10.3   *Think for Yourself*

BEGIN TO IDENTIFY PROBLEMS IN YOUR THINKING

See if you can identify any problems in your thinking. The best way to do this is to analyze some behavior you engage in that is somehow creating problems—either for you or others. Look at your personal relationships, your study habits, your interaction patterns. How do you behave when you are upset? How do you act when you don't get your way? Do you expect more of others than you expect of yourself? Consider these questions as beginning places for challenging yourself as a thinker. If you cannot identify any problems in your thinking, think again.

STAGE THREE: THE BEGINNING THINKER

Are You Willing to Begin?

When a person actively decides to take up the challenge to grow and develop as a thinker, that person enters the stage we call "beginning thinker." In this stage of thinking we begin to take thinking seriously. This stage prepares us for the next stages—with the ultimate goal of explicit command of thinking. It is a stage of dawning realizations. It is a stage of developing willpower. It is not a stage of self-condemnation but, rather, of emerging consciousness. It is analogous to the stage in which an alcoholic person recognizes and fully accepts the fact that he or she is an alcoholic. Imagine an alcoholic saying, "I am an alcoholic, and only I can do something about it." Now imagine yourself saying, "I am a weak, undisciplined thinker, and only I can do something about it."

Once people recognize that they are "addicted" to poor thinking, they must begin to recognize the depth and nature of the problem. As beginning thinkers, we should recognize that our thinking is sometimes egocentric. For example, we may notice how little we consider the needs of others and how much we focus on getting what we personally want. We may notice how little we enter the point of view of others and how much we assume the "correctness" of our own. We may even sometimes catch ourselves trying to dominate others to get what we want or, alternatively, acting out the role of submitting to others (for the gains that submissive behavior brings). We may begin to notice the extent to which we uncritically conform to the thinking of others.

> A thinker who has never challenged his own thinking has no right to challenge the thinking of others.

As thinkers thinking about thinking, we are merely beginning to

- analyze the logic of situations and problems
- express clear and precise questions
- check information for accuracy and relevance
- distinguish between raw information and someone's interpretation of it
- recognize assumptions guiding inferences
- identify prejudicial and biased beliefs, unjustifiable conclusions, misused words, and missed implications
- notice when our viewpoint is biased by our selfish interests.

Thus, as beginning thinkers we are becoming aware of how to deal with the structures at work in thinking (purposes, questions, information, interpretations, etc.). We are beginning to appreciate the value of thinking about our thinking in terms of its clarity, accuracy, relevance, precision, logic, justifiability, breadth, depth, and fairness. But we are still at a low level of proficiency in these activities. They feel awkward to us. We have to force ourselves to think in disciplined ways. We are like beginners in ballet. We feel self-conscious adopting the basic positions. We don't feel graceful. We stumble and make mistakes. No one would pay money to watch us perform. We ourselves don't like what we see in the mirror of our minds.

To reach this beginning stage in thinking, our values must begin to shift. We must begin to explore the foundation of our thinking and discover how we have come to think and believe as we do. Let us consider this goal in a little more detail. Reflect now on some of the major influences that have shaped your thinking (and ours):

- You were born into a culture (European, American, African, Asian).
- You were born at some point in time (in some century in some year).
- You were born in some place (in the country, in the city, in the North or South, East or West).
- You were raised by parents with particular beliefs (about the family, personal relationships, marriage, childhood, obedience, religion, politics, schooling).
- You formed various associations (largely based on who was around you— associations with people with a viewpoint, values, and taboos).

If you were to change any one of these influences, your belief system would be different. Suppose you had been born in the Middle Ages as a serf in the fields in France. Can you see that if you had, virtually all of your beliefs would be altered? See if you can perform similar reflective experiments of your own. For example, imagine other changes in these influences and then imaginatively compare some of the beliefs you likely would have with the beliefs you actually do have. You will begin to appreciate how much you, and every other human, are a product of influences over which you, and they, had little or no control. Neither you nor we directed these influences upon us. Their effects, clearly, were both good and bad.

> Our thinking is long shaped by others before we develop any capacity to think for ourselves. Most people never do.

If, for example, we assume that many of these influences engendered false beliefs in us, it follows that in our minds right now there are false beliefs and we are acting on them. Yet, notice that the mind has no mechanism for screening out false beliefs. We all carry around in our minds prejudices from our culture, prejudices from where we were born and raised, prejudices from our parents, and prejudices from our friends and associates. Finding ways to locate those flawed beliefs and replace them with more reasonable ones is part of the agenda of critical thinking.

10.4 *Think for Yourself*

PUTTING YOURSELF IN ANOTHER PLACE AND TIME

Imagine yourself in another place and time. Choose a different century, perhaps a different country, a different gender, a different socioeconomic group—in any case, an altogether different set of circumstances in which you might have lived. Complete the following:

1. The time within which I am imagining that I live is . . .
2. The details of the situation are as follows (be specific):
3. If I had lived in this place and time, I would most likely hold the following beliefs (about religion, my country, sexual conventions and taboos, gender issues, relationships, people of different races, etc.)—again, be specific:

For example, we think within a variety of domains: sociological, philosophical, ethical, intellectual, anthropological, ideological, political, economical, historical, biological, theological, and psychological. We ended up with our particular beliefs because we were influenced to do so in the following ways:

- **Sociological:** our minds are influenced by the social groups to which we belong.

- **Philosophical:** our minds are influenced by our personal philosophy.

- **Ethical:** our minds are influenced by the extent to which we behave in accordance with our obligations and the way we define our obligations.

- **Intellectual:** our minds are influenced by the ideas we hold, by the manner in which we reason and deal with abstractions and abstract systems.

- **Anthropological:** our minds are influenced by cultural practices, conventions, and taboos.

- **Ideological and political:** our minds are influenced by the structure of power and its use by interest groups around us.

- **Economic:** our minds are influenced by the economic conditions under which we live.

- **Historical:** our minds are influenced by our history and by the way we tell our history.

- **Biological:** our minds are influenced by our biology and neurology.

- **Theological:** our minds are influenced by our religious beliefs and attitudes.

- **Psychological:** our minds are influenced by our personality and personal psychology.

Reflections such as these should awaken in us a sense of how little we really know about our own minds. Within each of our minds is a largely unexplored world, an inner world that has been taking shape for the whole of our lives. This inner world is the most important fact about us, for it is where we live. It determines our joy and frustration. It limits what we can see and imagine. It highlights what we do see. It can drive us crazy. It can provide us with solace, peace, and tranquility. If we can appreciate these facts about ourselves, we will find the motivation to take charge of our thinking, to be something more than clay in the hands of others, to become, in fact, the ruling force in our own lives.

10.5   *Think for Yourself*

DISCUSS THE BEGINNING THINKER STAGE

Work in groups of three. The person whose first name is last in the alphabet will explain the third stage—that of the beginning thinker—to the other two, answering any questions they might have. Then the other two in the group will add any features that the first student missed and elaborate on the points they think are most important.

Let's now consider two lurking traps that can derail the beginning thinker:

Trap # 1:   The temptation of *dogmatic absolutism*—believing that truth is acquired not through reasoning and inquiry but, rather, through some predetermined, nonintellectual faith.

Trap # 2:   The temptation of *subjective relativism*—believing that there are no intellectual standards by which to judge anything as true or false.

Both traps promise us easy answers. To advance as a beginning thinker and not fall into one or the other of these traps requires developing confidence in reason as a way of acquiring sound knowledge and insight. These two pathologies are mirror images of each other. If we become either a subjective relativist or a dogmatic absolutist, we will lose our motivation to develop as a critical thinker. As a subjective relativist, we will come to believe that everyone automatically acquires "their own truth" in some inexplicable subjective way. As a dogmatic absolutist, we end up following wherever our "faith" leads us. In both cases, there is no real place for the intellectual work and discipline of critical thinking. Both render it superfluous. Both free us from any intellectual responsibility.

> The best thinkers are neither dogmatic absolutists nor subjective relativists.

If we avoid these traps, if we recognize how we have been shaped by forces beyond our control, if we discover that there are skills that can help us begin to take charge of our minds, if we develop some initial confidence in reason, if we develop some intellectual humility and perseverance, we are ready to begin creating a genuine foundation on which we can rebuild our identity and character as thinkers and persons of integrity.

The key question is *how?* How exactly can we do this? We shall focus on this question for the rest of this chapter. In a sense, it is the most vital goal of the entire book.

10.6   *Think for Yourself*

DISCUSS DOGMATIC ABSOLUTISM AND SUBJECTIVE RELATIVISM

Work in groups of three. The person whose first name is second in the alphabet will explain the distinction between dogmatic absolutism and subjective relativism to the other two, answering any questions they might have. Then the other two in the group will add any features that the first student missed and elaborate on the points they think are most important.

10.7   *Think for Yourself*

BEGINNING TO DEVELOP AS A THINKER

Make a list of some things you can do to begin your development as a disciplined thinker. Review Chapter 8 for ideas. Then answer this question: What do you think the benefits would be if you took this list seriously?

STAGE FOUR: THE PRACTICING THINKER

Good Thinking Can Be Practiced Like Basketball, Tennis, or Ballet

The only way to move from beginning to practicing thinker is to commit yourself to daily practice in thinking well and begin designing your own plan for practice. When you do so, you become what we call a "practicing thinker."

There are many ways to design practice regimens, some better, some worse for you. For example, you might glance through some of the other chapters of this book. Each provides some suggestions for improving your thinking. You can use any of these suggestions as a starting point.

You might review the *Think for Yourself* activities. You might study the elements of thought, the standards for thought, and the traits of mind. Think of it this way: Everything you read in this book represents a resource for you to use in devising a systematic plan for improving your thinking. As you move through the book, routinely ask yourself: What am I learning in this section or chapter that I can actively incorporate into daily practice?

If you are like most people, you can discover some practical starting points. The problem will be in following through on any that you find. This is the problem in most areas of skill development: People do not usually follow through. They do not establish habits of regular practice. They are discouraged by the strain and awkwardness of early attempts to perform well. They are not willing to set aside time for practice.

To develop as a thinker you will have to work out a plan that will work for you, one you can live with, one that will not burn you out or overwhelm you. Ultimately, success comes to those who are persistent and who figure out strategies for themselves.

Still, at this stage you probably don't know for sure what will work for you, only what seems like it might. You have to field-test your ideas. To be realistic, you should expect to experiment with a variety of plans before you find one that moves you forward as a thinker.

What you should guard against is discouragement. You can best avoid discouragement by recognizing from the outset that you are engaged in a process of trial and error. Prepare yourself for temporary failure. Success is to be understood as the willingness to work your way through a variety of relative failures. The logic is analogous to trying on clothes. Many that you try may not fit or look good on you, but you plod on anyway with the confidence that eventually you will find something that fits and looks good on you.

Consider another analogy. If you want to become skilled at tennis, you improve not by expecting yourself to begin as an expert player. You improve not by expecting to win every game you play or by mastering new strokes with little practice. Rather, you improve when you develop a plan that you can modify as you see what improves your "game." Today you may decide to work on keeping your eye on the ball. Tomorrow you may coordinate watching the ball with following through on your swing. Every day you re-think your strategies for improvement. Development of the human mind is quite parallel to the development of the human body. Good theory, good practice, and good feedback are essential.

A "GAME PLAN" FOR IMPROVEMENT

As you begin to take your thinking seriously, you need to think about what you can do consistently every day to improve your thinking. Because excellence in thinking requires a variety of independent skills and traits that work together, you can choose to work on a range of critical-thinking skills at any given point in time. The key is in focusing on fundamentals and on making sure that you don't try to do too much. Choose your point of attack, but limit it. If you overdo it, you will probably give up entirely. But if you don't focus on fundamentals, you will never have them as a foundation in your thought.

Start slowly, and emphasize fundamentals. The race is to the tortoise, not to the hare. Be a good and wise turtle. The solid, steady steps you take every day determine where you ultimately end up.

A GAME PLAN FOR DEVISING A GAME PLAN

We have put together a few ideas to stimulate your thought about a game plan. There is nothing magical about our ideas. No one of them is essential. Nevertheless, each represents a definite point of attack, one way to begin to do something plausible to improve thinking in a regular way. Though you probably can't do all of these at the same time, we recommend an approach in which you experiment with all of these. You can add any others you find in this book or come up with yourself. We will explain how this works after you familiarize yourself with some of the options.

1. Use "wasted" time. All humans waste some time. No one uses all of his or her time productively or even pleasurably. Sometimes we jump from one diversion to another without enjoying any of them. Sometimes we become irritated about matters beyond our control. Sometimes we fail to plan well, causing negative consequences that we easily could have avoided (for example, we spend time unnecessarily trapped in traffic—though we could have left a half hour earlier and avoided the rush). Sometimes we worry unproductively. Sometimes we spend time regretting what is past. Sometimes we just stare off blankly into space.

The key is that the time is "spent," and if we had thought about it and considered our options, we would not have deliberately spent our time in that way. So our idea is this: Why not take advantage of the time you normally waste, by practicing good thinking during that time? For example, instead of sitting in front of the TV at the end of the day flicking from channel to channel in a vain search for a program worth watching, you could spend that time, or at least part of it, thinking back over your day and evaluating your strengths and weaknesses. You might ask yourself questions like these:

- When did I do my worst thinking today?
- When did I do my best thinking?
- What did I actually think about today?
- Did I figure out anything?
- Did I allow any negative thinking to frustrate me unnecessarily?

- If I had to repeat today, what would I do differently? Why?
- Did I do anything today to further my long-term goals?
- Did I act in accordance with my own expressed values?
- If I were to spend every day this way for 10 years, would I at the end have accomplished something worthy of that time?

It is important to take a little time with each question. It would be useful to review these questions periodically, perhaps weekly, to write your answers to them in a journal and in so doing to keep a record of how your thinking is developing.

2. Handle a problem a day. At the beginning of each day (perhaps driving to work or to class), choose a problem to work on when you have free moments. Figure out the logic of the problem by identifying its elements. Systematically think through the questions: What exactly is the problem? How can I put it into the form of a question?

3. Internalize intellectual standards. Each week, study and actively bring into your thinking one of the universal intellectual standards presented in Chapter 3. Focus one week on clarity, the next on accuracy, and so on. For example, if you are focusing on clarity for the week, try to notice when you are being unclear in communicating with others. Notice when others are unclear in what they are saying. When you read, notice whether you are clear about what you are reading. When you write a paragraph for class, ask yourself whether you are clear about what you are trying to say and in conveying your thoughts in writing. In doing this, you will practice four techniques of clarification: (1) stating what you are saying with some consideration given to your choice of words, (2) elaborating on your meaning in other words, (3) giving examples of what you mean from experiences you have had, and (4) using analogies, metaphors, pictures, or diagrams to illustrate what you mean. In clarifying thinking, you should state, elaborate, illustrate, and exemplify your points, and you should regularly ask others to do the same.

4. Keep an intellectual journal. Each week, write out a certain number of journal entries. Use the following format for each important event you write about:
- Describe only situations that are emotionally significant to you (situations you care deeply about).
- Describe only one situation at a time.
- Describe (and keep this separate) how you behaved in the situation, being specific and exact. (What did you say? What did you do? How did you react? To what extent did you think or behave egocentrically?)
- Analyze, in the light of what you have written, what precisely was going on in the situation; dig beneath the surface.
- Assess the implications of your analysis. (What did you learn about yourself? What would you do differently if you could relive the situation?)

5. Reshape your character. Choose one intellectual trait to strive for each month, focusing on how you can develop that trait in yourself. For example, concentrating on intellectual humility, begin to notice when you admit you are wrong. Notice when you refuse to admit you are wrong, even in the face of glaring evidence that you are in fact wrong. Notice when you become defensive when another person tries to point out a deficiency in your work or your thinking. Notice when your arrogance keeps you from learning, when you say to yourself, for example, "I already know everything I need to know about this subject" or, "I know as much as he does. Who does he think he is, forcing his opinions onto me?"

6. Deal with your ego. On a daily basis, begin to observe your egocentric thinking in action by contemplating questions like these: As I reflect upon my behavior today, did I ever become irritable over small things? Did I do or say anything irrational to get my way? Did I try to impose my will upon others? Did I ever fail to speak my mind when I felt strongly about something, and then later feel resentment?

Once you identify egocentric thinking in operation, you can work to replace it with more rational thought through systematic self-reflection. What would a rational person feel in this or that situation? What would a rational person do? How does that compare with what you did? (Hint: If you find that you continually conclude that a rational person would behave just as you behaved, you are probably engaging in self-deception. See Chapter 9 for more ways to identify egocentric thinking.)

7. Redefine the way you see things. We live in a world, both personal and social, in which every situation is defined; it is given a fundamental meaning. How a situation is defined determines not only how we feel about it but also how we act in it and what implications it has for us. Virtually every situation, however, can be defined in more than one way. This fact carries with it tremendous opportunities for all of us to make our life more of what we want it to be. In principle, it lies within your power to make your life much happier and more fulfilling than it is.

Many of the negative definitions that we give to situations in our lives could in principle be transformed into positive definitions. As a result, we can gain when otherwise we would have lost. We can be happy when otherwise we would have been sad. We can be fulfilled when otherwise we would have been frustrated. In this game plan, we practice redefining the way we see things, turning negatives into positives, dead-ends into new beginnings, mistakes into opportunities to learn. To make this game plan practical, we should create some specific guidelines for ourselves. For example, we might make ourselves a list of five to ten recurrent negative situations in which we feel frustrated, angry, unhappy, or worried. We then could identify the definition in each case that is at the root of the negative emotion. Next we would choose a plausible alternative definition for each and then plan for our new responses as well as our new emotions.

Suppose you have a roommate who gets on your nerves by continually telling you about all the insignificant events in his or her life. Your present definition of the situation is, "What a bore! How am I going to last a whole semester listening to that brainless soap opera?" Your response might be: "Since I have to do a required research project for my introduction to psychology class, I will focus my project on the psychology of my roommate." Now instead of sitting passively listening to the daily blow-by-blow description of your roommate's day, you actively question him or her to gather information you can use in your psychology paper. Because you are now directing the conversation, your roommate is not able to bore you with the details of his or her day, and you transform your interactions into a learning experience.

Another possibility is to redefine an "impossibly difficult class" as a "challenge to figure out new fundamental concepts and a new way of thinking." Let's look at another example. You redefine your initial approach to a person who attracts you not in terms of the definition, "His or her response will determine whether I am an attractive person" but, instead, in terms of the definition, "Let me test to see if this person is initially drawn to me—given the way he or she perceives me." With the first definition in mind, you feel personally put down if the person is not interested in you; with the second definition you explicitly recognize that people initially respond not to the way a stranger *is* but, rather, the way the person subjectively *looks* to the other. You therefore do not perceive someone's failure to show interest in you as a defect in you.

8. Get in touch with your emotions. Whenever you feel some negative emotion, systematically ask yourself: What, exactly, is the thinking that leads to this emotion? How might this thinking be flawed? What am I assuming? Should I be making these assumptions? What information is my thinking based on? Is that information reliable? and so on (see Chapter 1).

9. Analyze group influences on your life. Closely analyze the behavior that is encouraged and discouraged in the groups to which you belong. For a given group, what are you required or expected to believe? What are you "forbidden" to do? If you conclude that your group does not require you to believe anything, or that it has no taboos, realize that you have not deeply analyzed that group. To gain insight into the process of socialization and group membership, review an introductory text in sociology (see Chapter 9).

INTEGRATING STRATEGIES ONE BY ONE

When designing strategies, the key point is that you are engaged in an experiment. You are testing strategies in your personal life. You are integrating them and building on them, in light of your actual experience. All strategies have advantages and disadvantages. One plausible way to do this is to work with all of the strategies on the list below in any order of your choosing.

1. Use "wasted" time.
2. Handle a problem a day.
3. Internalize intellectual standards.
4. Keep an intellectual journal.
5. Reshape your character.
6. Deal with your ego.
7. Redefine the way you see things.
8. Get in touch with your emotions.
9. Analyze group influences on your life.

As you begin to design strategies to improve the quality of your life, suppose you find the strategy "Redefine the way you see things" to be intuitive to you, so begin with this strategy. As you focus intently on this idea and apply it in your life, you begin to notice social definitions within groups. You begin to recognize how your behavior is shaped and controlled by group definitions. You begin to see how you, and others, uncritically accept group definitions, rather than creating your own definitions. Notice the definitions embedded in the following statements:

1. "I'm giving a *party.*"
2. "We're going to have a *meeting.*"
3. "Why don't you run for *election?*"
4. "The *funeral* is Tuesday."
5. "Jack is an *acquaintance,* not really a *friend.*"

As you internalize this idea, you begin to see the importance and pervasiveness of social definitions. As you become more insightful about social definitions, you begin to redefine situations in ways that run contrary to commonly accepted social definitions. You then begin to see how redefining situations and relationships enable you to "get in touch with your emotions." You recognize that the way you define things generates the emotions you feel. When you think you are threatened (you define a situation as "threatening"), you feel fear. If you define a situation as a "failure," you may feel depressed. On the other hand, if you define that same situation as a "lesson or opportunity to learn," you feel empowered to learn. When you recognize that you are capable of exercising this kind of control over "definitions" in situations, the two strategies begin to work together and reinforce each other.

You might then begin to integrate strategy #9 ("Analyze group influences on your life") with the two strategies you have already internalized. One of the main ways in which groups control us is by controlling the definitions we are allowed to use. When a group defines some things as "cool" and some as "dumb," members of the group try to appear "cool" and not appear "dumb." When the boss of a business says, "That makes a lot of sense," his subordinates know they are not to say, "No, it is ridiculous." They know this because defining someone as the "boss" gives him or her special privileges to define situations and relationships. As a developing thinker, you begin to decide what groups you allow to influence your thinking and what group influences you reject.

You now have three strategies interwoven: You "redefine the way you see things," "get in touch with your emotions," and "analyze group influences on your life." The three strategies are integrated into one. At this point, you can experiment with any of the other strategies (listed below), looking for opportunities to integrate them into your thinking and your life.

- Use wasted time.
- Handle a problem a day.
- Internalize intellectual standards.
- Keep an intellectual journal.
- Reshape your character.
- Deal with your ego.

10.8 *Think for Yourself*

BEGINNING TO DEVELOP A PLAN FOR YOURSELF

Focusing on the strategies that you have just read, write out a basic plan for beginning your development as a thinker. List the first three strategies you will incorporate into your thinking and how you plan to do this. Be specific and detailed. Then, at the end of each day, revisit your list and see how you are progressing. Add to your list as you internalize previously learned ideas.

If you follow through on a plan, you are going beyond the "beginning thinker" stage; you are becoming a "practicing thinker."

FURTHER EXERCISES IN CLOSE READING AND SUBSTANTIVE WRITING

These exercises supplement those in Chapter 7 and provide further practice in close reading and substantive writing. Directions provided for the first passage should be used for each passage. For the first five passages, we provide a first- and second-level reading. For the last two passages, we provide a first-level reading only.

FIRST-LEVEL READING

Directions: For each reading that follows, test your grasp of the passages by paraphrasing them—putting them into your own words. This can be done either in oral or written form. Then compare your interpretations with the sample interpretations that follow the First-Level Reading: Paraphrasing section.

"THE NINETEENTH-CENTURY AMERICAN"

Background information: This excerpt is from the book *The American Mind* by the distinguished historian Henry Steele Commager (1950).

In one realm the American was a conformist, and that was the realm of morals. Although he did not always observe them, he accepted without question the moral standards of the Puritans, and if a later generation was to find him repressed and inhibited, there is little evidence that he was conscious of his sufferings. . . . Conformity and conventionalism in matters of morals sometimes assumed aggressive form, and the willingness to resign control of the whole field of culture to women combined with the tradition of Puritanism to encourage intolerance and justify censorship. Language was emasculated, literature expurgated, art censored. Piano legs were draped with pantalets, words like *belly* and *breast* dropped from polite conversation, the discussion of sex confined to men and obstetrics to women, while Shakespeare and Fielding joined French writers generally in disrepute. Early in the century a furor was raised when Hiram Powers exhibited his undraped "Greek Slave," and at the end of the century Thomas Eakins, perhaps the greatest of American painters, was driven from the Pennsylvania Academy when he used male models in mixed classes. Dancing, plays, and mixed bathing came under the ban. Censorship of art and literature slid easily into censorship of morals, especially those having to do with love and drinking; modesty degenerated into Comstockery and the temperance movement into prohibition. (pp. 22–23)

First-Level Reading: Paraphrasing

In one realm the American was a conformist, and that was the realm of morals.
Paraphrase:

Although he did not always observe them, he accepted without question the moral standards of the Puritans,
Paraphrase:

and if a later generation was to find him repressed and inhibited, there is little evidence that he was conscious of his sufferings.
Paraphrase:

Conformity and conventionalism in matters of morals sometimes assumed aggressive form, and the willingness to resign control of the whole field of culture to women combined with the tradition of Puritanism to encourage intolerance and justify censorship. Language was emasculated, literature expurgated, art censored.
Paraphrase:

Piano legs were draped with pantalets, words like *belly* and *breast* dropped from polite conversation, the discussion of sex confined to men and obstetrics to women, while Shakespeare and Fielding joined French writers generally in disrepute. Early in the century a furor was raised when Hiram Powers exhibited his undraped "Greek Slave," and at the end of the century Thomas Eakins, perhaps the greatest of American painters, was driven from the Pennsylvania Academy when he used male models in mixed classes.

Paraphrase:

Dancing, plays, and mixed bathing came under the ban. Censorship of art and literature slid easily into censorship of morals, especially those having to do with love and drinking; modesty degenerated into Comstockery and the temperance movement into prohibition.

Paraphrase:

First-Level Reading: Sample Interpretation

In one realm the American was a conformist, and that was the realm of morals.

Paraphrase: Though Americans may have been independent thinkers in some domains of their lives, they did not think independently about social and religious understandings of what is right and wrong.

Although he did not always observe them, he accepted without question the moral standards of the Puritans,

Paraphrase: Though Americans did not always live in accordance with a Puritanical view of right and wrong, they nevertheless did not question the dominant idea that a Puritan outlook was morally correct and obligatory.

and if a later generation was to find him repressed and inhibited, there is little evidence that he was conscious of his sufferings.

Paraphrase: If a historical view now shows the nineteenth-century American to be hampered and inwardly intimidated by these Puritanical rules, there is little proof that he had any awareness of the negative impact that these beliefs were having on him.

Conformity and conventionalism in matters of morals sometimes assumed aggressive form, and the willingness to resign control of the whole field of culture to women combined with the tradition of Puritanism to encourage intolerance and justify censorship. Language was emasculated, literature expurgated, art censored.

Paraphrase: The whole range of "acceptable" behavior significantly narrowed, especially anything having to do with human sexuality or sensuality. The enforcement of a narrow set of norms became militant and warlike. As women increasingly dictated what is and is not "moral" within society, as Puritanism increasingly influenced culture, intolerance and censorship seemed equivalent to standing up for what is right, decent, and just. Freedom of speech and expression were undermined and curtailed. Officials assumed the authority to make sweeping judgments about printed material, movies, and the arts, and to suppress any parts of these materials on the basis of perceived "obscenity" and a threat to security. As a result, books, movies, and the arts considered acceptable were generally those with questionable literary and artistic quality. Conversely, the range of ideas and practices considered "offensive" was greatly expanded.

Piano legs were draped with pantalets, words like *belly* and *breast* dropped from polite conversation, the discussion of sex confined to men and obstetrics to women, while Shakespeare and Fielding joined French writers generally in disrepute. Early in the century a furor was raised when Hiram Powers exhibited his undraped "Greek Slave," and at the end of the century Thomas Eakins, perhaps the greatest of American painters, was driven from the Pennsylvania Academy when he used male models in mixed classes.

Paraphrase: Essentially anything considered overtly, or even subtly, sexual was removed from public viewing and could not be publicly discussed. People who disagreed with Puritanical views were ridiculed and ostracized, if not persecuted or prosecuted. Even piano legs had to be covered because they appeared to the Puritanical mind to be sexually erotic. Many commonly used words were no longer socially acceptable because they seemed crude and vulgar. Women were not allowed to discuss sex, and men were not allowed to discuss childbirth. Writers of classics such as Shakespeare and Fielding were considered vulgar, along with the French writers; and an artist who used nude male models in classes with both genders was banned from an art academy.

Dancing, plays, and mixed bathing came under the ban. Censorship of art and literature slid easily into censorship of morals, especially those having to do with love and drinking; modesty degenerated into Comstockery and the temperance movement into prohibition.

Paraphrase: Due to this religious fervor sweeping the country, dancing, attending plays, and swimming in mixed company were all banned. Disallowing certain ideas to be exhibited in the arts and literature led to the disallowing of personal rights, such as the right to drink alcohol and the freedom to choose one's own behavior within romantic relationships. Being sexually reserved was transformed into obsessive Puritanism and censorship, and prudent drinking of alcohol transformed into laws against all drinking, whether public or private.

SECOND-LEVEL READING

Directions: Complete the following four tasks:

1. State the thesis of the passage in your own words.
2. Elaborate the thesis.
3. Give one or more examples of the thesis.
4. Illustrate the thesis with a metaphor or analogy.

This exercise can be done either in oral or written form.

Second-Level Reading: Thesis of "The Nineteenth-Century American"

Statement of thesis. Nineteenth-century Americans were unquestioning Puritanical conformists, especially the women, who came to dominate a strict conventional sexual morality and impose it on all facets of culture and art.

Elaboration of thesis. In other words, morality was dictated by sexual convention. Violations of sexual conventions were kept secret. Intolerance and censorship were the rule. Dogmatic inflexibility was developed in every dimension of American life. This Puritanical fanaticism led to violations of individual rights.

Exemplification of thesis. For example, "piano legs were draped with pantalets, words like *belly* and *breast* dropped from polite conversation . . . and at the end of the century Thomas Eakins, perhaps the greatest of American painters, was driven from the Pennsylvania Academy when he used male models in mixed classes. . . . Dancing, plays, and mixed bathing came under the ban."

Illustration of thesis. People in nineteenth-century America perceived the world in largely childlike, simplistic terms. As with groups of children, dissent was ridiculed. Those who didn't go along with the group were ostracized. Social hysteria and witch-hunts became common events. A worldview of unsophisticated cowboys versus Indians, good guys versus bad guys became the rule. To this day, American political and social thinking continues to suffer from this same cultural narrowness of mind. Consider U.S. President Bush's recent characterization of the world as dividing into those who are "good" and those who are "evil," and his challenge to all countries in the world to decide, therefore, whether they are "for us or against us," implying that there is no other choice possible. Compare the comment of Alexander Solzhenitsyn, the Nobel laureate, who said, "If only there were evil people somewhere insidiously committing evil deeds and it were necessary only to separate them from the rest of us and destroy them. But the line dividing good and evil cuts through the heart of every human being."

"THE ART OF LOVING"

Background information: These passages are from the book *The Art of Loving* by the distinguished psychologist Erich Fromm (1956).

Is love an art? Then it requires knowledge and effort. Or is love a pleasant sensation, which to experience is a matter of chance, something one "falls into" if one is lucky? This little book is based on the former premise, while undoubtedly the majority of people today believe in the latter.

Not that people think that love is not important. They are starved for it; they watch endless numbers of films about happy and unhappy love stories, they listen to hundreds of trashy songs about love—yet hardly anyone thinks that there is anything that needs to be learned about love.

This peculiar attitude is based on several premises which either singly or combined tend to uphold it. Most people see the problem of love primarily as that of being loved, rather than that of loving, of one's capacity to love. Hence the problem to them is how to be loved, how to be lovable. In pursuit of this aim they follow several paths. One, which is especially used by men, is to be successful, to be as powerful and rich as the social margin of one's position permits. Another, used especially by women, is to make oneself attractive, by cultivating one's body, dress, etc. Other ways of making oneself attractive, used both by men and women, are to develop pleasant manners, interesting conversation, to be helpful, modest, inoffensive. Many of the ways to make oneself lovable are the same as those used to make oneself successful, "to win friends and influence people." As a matter of fact, what most people in our culture mean by being lovable is essentially a mixture between being popular and having sex appeal.

The active character of love becomes evident in the fact that it always implies certain basic elements, common to all forms of love. These are care, responsibility, respect, and knowledge. . . . Love is the active concern for the life and the growth of that which we love. . . . Respect is the ability to see a person as he is, to be aware of his unique individuality. Respect means the concern that the other person should grow and unfold as he is. Respect, thus, implies the absence of exploitation. I want the loved person to grow and unfold for his own sake, and in his own ways, and not for the purpose of serving me. If I love the other person, I feel one with him or her, but with him as he is, not as I need him to be as an object for my use. It is clear that respect is possible only if I have achieved independence; if I can stand and walk without needing crutches, without having to dominate and exploit anyone else. Respect exists only on the basis of freedom: "l'amour est l'enfant de la liberté" as an old French song says; love is the child of freedom, never of domination. . . . To love somebody is not just a strong feeling—it is a decision, it is a judgment, it is a promise.*

First-Level Reading: Paraphrasing

Is love an art? Then it requires knowledge and effort.

Paraphrase:

Or is love a pleasant sensation, which to experience is a matter of chance, something one "falls into" if one is lucky?

Paraphrase:

This little book is based on the former premise, while undoubtedly the majority of people today believe in the latter.

Paraphrase:

Not that people think that love is not important. They are starved for it; they watch endless numbers of films about happy and unhappy love stories, they listen to hundreds of trashy songs about love—yet hardly anyone thinks that there is anything that needs to be learned about love.

Paraphrase:

This peculiar attitude is based on several premises which either singly or combined tend to uphold it. Most people see the problem of love primarily as that of being loved, rather

*Excerpts from pages 1–2, 26, and 28 from *The Art of Loving* by Erich Fromm. Copyright © 1956 by Eric Fromm. Copyright renewed © 1984 by Annis Fromm. Reprinted by permission of HarperCollins Publishers.

than that of loving, of one's capacity to love. Hence the problem to them is how to be loved, how to be lovable.

Paraphrase:

In pursuit of this aim they follow several paths. One, which is especially used by men, is to be successful, to be as powerful and rich as the social margin of one's position permits. Another, used especially by women, is to make oneself attractive, by cultivating one's body, dress, etc.

Paraphrase:

Other ways of making oneself attractive, used both by men and women, are to develop pleasant manners, interesting conversation, to be helpful, modest, inoffensive. Many of the ways to make oneself lovable are the same as those used to make oneself success-ful, "to win friends and influence people." As a matter of fact, what most people in our culture mean by being lovable is essentially a mixture between being popular and hav-ing sex appeal.

Paraphrase:

The active character of love becomes evident in the fact that it always implies certain ba-sic elements, common to all forms of love. These are care, responsibility, respect, and knowledge. . . . Love is the active concern for the life and the growth of that which we love. . . .

Paraphrase:

Respect is the ability to see a person as he is, to be aware of his unique individuality. Re-spect means the concern that the other person should grow and unfold as he is. Respect, thus, implies the absence of exploitation. I want the loved person to grow and unfold for his own sake, and in his own ways, and not for the purpose of serving me. If I love the other person, I feel one with him or her, but with him as he is, not as I need him to be as an object for my use.

Paraphrase:

It is clear that respect is possible only if I have achieved independence; if I can stand and walk without needing crutches, without having to dominate and exploit anyone else. Re-spect exists only on the basis of freedom: "l'amour est l'enfant de la liberté" as an old French song says; love is the child of freedom, never of domination.

Paraphrase:

To love somebody is not just a strong feeling—it is a decision, it is a judgment, it is a promise.

Paraphrase:

First-Level Reading: Sample Interpretation

Is love an art? Then it requires knowledge and effort.

Paraphrase: If love is an art, involving skills and abilities, it requires deep understanding and the motivation to apply that understanding.

Or is love a pleasant sensation, which to experience is a matter of chance, something one "falls into" if one is lucky?

Paraphrase: Or perhaps love is strictly an enjoyable physical feeling, not something requiring skill, but rather an accidental occurrence or coincidence that just happens to people.

This little book is based on the former premise, while undoubtedly the majority of people today believe in the latter.

Paraphrase: The book *The Art of Loving* is based on the assumption that love requires skills and insights that must be developed, as well as commitment, though most people do not see love in this way. Rather, they see it as something that happens by sheer luck.

Not that people think that love is not important. They are starved for it; they watch endless numbers of films about happy and unhappy love stories, they listen to hundreds of trashy songs about love—yet hardly anyone thinks that there is anything that needs to be learned about love.

Paraphrase: Most people value love, at least at some level. In fact, they crave it. We know this because they watch innumerable movies about love and listen to endless vulgar songs about love. Yet, almost no one thinks that the ability to love is something that must be learned.

This peculiar attitude is based on several premises which either singly or combined tend to uphold it. Most people see the problem of love primarily as that of being loved, rather than that of loving, of one's capacity to love. Hence the problem to them is how to be loved, how to be lovable.

Paraphrase: This dysfunctional way in which people tend to think of love is based on one or more beliefs they hold about love. People primarily see the difficulty of love as trying to figure out how to get love from someone else rather than giving love to someone else. They therefore focus their energy on getting others to love them. They try to appear engaging, charming, or adorable to attract a lover.

In pursuit of this aim they follow several paths. One, which is especially used by men, is to be successful, to be as powerful and rich as the social margin of one's position permits. Another, used especially by women, is to make oneself attractive, by cultivating one's body, dress, etc.

Paraphrase: To achieve the goal of "being lovable," men tend to use a different strategy than women use. Men strive to achieve a position of status, which usually involves having as much power and money as they can. Women tend to emphasize making themselves physically attractive to the opposite sex, through adorning their body, attending to their clothing, and the like.

Other ways of making oneself attractive, used both by men and women, are to develop pleasant manners, interesting conversation, to be helpful, modest, inoffensive. Many of the ways to make oneself lovable are the same as those used to make oneself successful, "to win friends and influence people." As a matter of fact, what most people in our culture mean by being lovable is essentially a mixture between being popular and having sex appeal.

Paraphrase: Both men and women strive for appealing manners and a conversational style that renders them attractive and therefore "lovable" to the opposite sex. They try to appear cooperative, supportive, unassuming, and unobjectionable. These same strategies are used to appear successful in others' eyes, to gain friends and win over people. To most people, being lovable is really the same as being sexy and well-liked.

The active character of [genuine] love becomes evident in the fact that it always implies certain basic elements, common to all forms of love. These are care, responsibility, respect, and knowledge. . . . Love is the active concern for the life and the growth of that which we love. . . .

Paraphrase: Certain basic parts of love exist within any form of real love. These are thoughtfulness, dependability, consideration, and understanding. When we love someone, we seek their best welfare. We show our concern for what happens to them.

Respect is the ability to see a person as he is, to be aware of his unique individuality. Respect means the concern that the other person should grow and unfold as he is. Respect, thus, implies the absence of exploitation. I want the loved person to grow and unfold for his own sake, and in his own ways, and not for the purpose of serving me. If I love the other person, I feel one with him or her, but with him as he is, not as I need him to be as an object for my use.

Paraphrase: When we respect others, we don't need to idealize them. We can see them as they really are, as persons with distinctive characteristics. We want them to develop as they want to develop and be what they want to be. We do not treat them as objects to be used for our own selfish interests. When we love others, we feel deeply connected to them as they are, with all their unique qualities.

It is clear that respect is possible only if I have achieved independence; if I can stand and walk without needing crutches, without having to dominate and exploit anyone else. Respect exists only on the basis of freedom: "l' amour est l'enfant de la liberté" as an old French song says; love is the child of freedom, never of domination.

Paraphrase: I can respect another only if I am myself an autonomous person, if I can stand on my own two feet, without the need to lean on others for support, without the need to use others, to control them so that they might serve me. Respect can happen only when people are allowed to be what they want to be, never when they are being forced to live a certain way against their will.

To love somebody is not just a strong feeling—it is a decision, it is a judgment, it is a promise.

Paraphrase: Love is not just a feeling. It is a choice, a resolution, a commitment, a pledge.

Second-Level Reading: Thesis of "The Art of Loving"

Statement of thesis. Loving another person is an art. It requires knowledge, skill, and insight. Genuine love doesn't just happen to people. It must be cultivated through deep commitment. This way of looking at love is very different from the way most people do.

Elaboration of thesis. We need to change the way we think about love. We should abandon images that imply that love is mysterious and beyond our control. We should see it as a form of strength in which we give to others what enhances their well-being. When we are weak, we want others to hold us up, to protect us, to take care of us. Weakness is not a sound basis for giving love. When we truly love others, we want them to develop and grow. We do not use them to serve us.

Exemplification of thesis. In many Hollywood films and soap operas, love is associated with passionate, out-of-control accusations and cruel acts, often followed by apologies and sexual intimacy. Jealousy, envy, and an attempt to control the other are all commonplace in the public image of lovers in action. Genuine love, as a long-term commitment to the well-being of others, does not make for action-packed drama. Portrayals of genuine love are rarely depicted in Hollywood films.

Illustration of thesis. Defective forms of love are like a suffocating vine that attaches itself to a plant and eventually kills it. The vine dominates the plant, requiring the plant to submit to its domination. But genuine love neither dominates nor submits. Genuine love can exist only between relative equals, like two plants growing side by side, sharing the same sunlight and soil nutrients, allowing one another the space to grow as unique individuals.

"MAN'S SEARCH FOR MEANING"

Background information: The following excerpt is taken from Viktor E. Frankl's book *Man's Search for Meaning* (1959). Dr. Frankl, a psychiatrist and neurologist who was imprisoned at Auschwitz and other Nazi prisons, developed a theory of "logotherapy" that "focuses its attention upon mankind's groping for a higher meaning in life."

What man actually needs is not a tensionless state but rather the striving and struggling for some goal worthy of him. What he needs is not the discharge of tension at any cost, but the call of a potential meaning waiting to be fulfilled by him. . . . [People] lack the awareness of a meaning worth living for. They are haunted by the experience of their inner emptiness, a void within themselves; they are caught in that situation which I have called the "existential vacuum." . . . This existential vacuum manifests itself mainly in a state of boredom. . . . Not a few cases of suicide can be traced back to this

> existential vacuum. . . . Sometimes the frustrated will to meaning is vicariously compensated for by a will to power, including the most primitive form of the will to power, the will to money. In other cases, the place of frustrated will to meaning is taken by the will to pleasure. . . . Ultimately, man should not ask what the meaning of life is, but rather must recognize that it is he who is asked. In a word, each meaning is questioned by life; and he can only answer to life by answering for his own life; to life he can only respond by being responsible. (pp. 166–172)

First-Level Reading: Paraphrasing

What man actually needs is not a tensionless state but rather the striving and struggling for some goal worthy of him. What he needs is not the discharge of tension at any cost, but the call of a potential meaning waiting to be fulfilled by him. . . .

Paraphrase:

[People] lack the awareness of a meaning worth living for. They are haunted by the experience of their inner emptiness, a void within themselves; they are caught in that situation which I have called the "existential vacuum." . . .

Paraphrase:

This existential vacuum manifests itself mainly in a state of boredom. . . . Not a few cases of suicide can be traced back to this existential vacuum. . . .

Paraphrase:

Sometimes the frustrated will to meaning is vicariously compensated for by a will to power, including the most primitive form of the will to power, the will to money. In other cases, the place of frustrated will to meaning is taken by the will to pleasure. . . .

Paraphrase:

Ultimately, man should not ask what the meaning of life is, but rather must recognize that it is he who is asked.

Paraphrase:

In a word, each meaning is questioned by life; and he can only answer to life by answering for his own life; to life he can only respond by being responsible.

Paraphrase:

First-Level Reading: Sample Interpretation

What man actually needs is not a tensionless state but rather the striving and struggling for some goal worthy of him. What he needs is not the discharge of tension at any cost, but the call of a potential meaning waiting to be fulfilled by him. . . .

Paraphrase: People should not strive to be without stress and challenge. Rather they should actively seek important purposes. People shouldn't spend their time and energy simply trying to relieve pressure in their lives. Instead they should use their energy seeking out pursuits that are significant and important to them.

[People] lack the awareness of a meaning worth living for. They are haunted by the experience of their inner emptiness, a void within themselves; they are caught in that situation which I have called the "existential vacuum." . . .

Paraphrase: People often do not see that there is anything significant in life. Their minds are not actively pursing anything interesting, anything that gives them deep meaning in their lives. Life seems barren and unfulfilling.

This existential vacuum manifests itself mainly in a state of boredom. . . . Not a few cases of suicide can be traced back to this existential vacuum. . . .

Paraphrase: This lack of significant meaning in one's life often leads to tedium, dullness, apathy, indifference. Even suicide is sometimes caused by a state of "empty existence."

Sometimes the frustrated will to meaning is vicariously compensated for by a will to power, including the most primitive form of the will to power, the will to money. In other cases, the place of frustrated will to meaning is taken by the will to pleasure. . . .

Paraphrase: Sometimes when people fail to pursue important meanings and goals, their energy is used instead in the pursuit of control and domination. Some even resort to the most crude type of power, that of pursuing wealth simply for the sake of wealth. In still other persons, the failure to pursue important objectives is covered over by a vain pursuit of pleasure.

Ultimately, man should not ask what the meaning of life is, but rather must recognize that it is he who is asked. In a word, each meaning is questioned by life; and he can only answer to life by answering for his own life; to life he can only respond by being responsible. . . .

Paraphrase: In the final analysis people should not try to figure out the meaning of life. Instead they should answer the questions: "What meaning can I give to my own life? What important meaning can I create for myself? What goals can I pursue that make my life important?" In short, people have to answer to the world for their actions. Each of us must justify how and why we are living our lives the way we do. And each of us is responsible to pursue important goals, to live in a conscientious way. Each of us is accountable for the life-forming decisions we make. Each of us is responsible for our own well-being.

Second-Level Reading: Thesis of "Man's Search for Meaning"

Statement of thesis. The only way to live a truly meaningful life is to seek important purposes and live in accordance with those purposes.

Elaboration of thesis. Most people have no sense of how to find important meanings for their lives. Instead, they are bored with life. They ask questions like: "What is the meaning of life?" In its place they should ask, "What important meanings can I create for myself?" In short, people tend to look outside themselves for predesigned meaning instead of selecting from a range of challenging and important goals for themselves.

Exemplification of thesis. Rather than seeking objectives that would be truly fulfilling, people often pursue power, money, fun, and excitement. When people pursue power, for example, they funnel their energy into that which enables them to control other people, to see themselves as superior to others. This substitutes for a truly fulfilling meaning in life. But when people develop meaningful, rational purposes, they become much more satisfied with life. Many teenagers lack important purposes. They are looking for instant gratification. They are seeking fun and excitement in superficial relationships and events. Because this lifestyle doesn't lead to any important meaning in their lives, they often turn to drugs and alcohol for cheap thrills. Alternatively, when teenagers pursue activities and goals that are important to them (e.g., sports, photography, writing, political causes, drama), they find true meaning in their lives. They aren't bored with life. They don't need to be accepted by their peer group. They use their energy to create something they see as important to them personally.

Illustration of thesis. Seeking important meanings in life is like seeking a pearl in an oyster. The oyster is like the stuff of life that can keep us from identifying important goals, the stuff that gets in the way of the prize that is worth the seeking. It is the dull, grayish brown substance that easily entraps us. We have to work through the oyster to get to the pearl. We have to work through difficulties to find what is really important to us. But the reward is brilliant and shiny, and true (to who and what we are).

"HISTORY OF THE GREAT AMERICAN FORTUNES"

Background information: In 1909, Gustavus Myers wrote a three-volume history of the great American fortunes. At the time, Myers was attempting to understand and then explain how the wealthiest people in the country obtained their wealth. In his book, he focuses neither on extraordinary ability or hard work on the part of these people, nor does he directly connect this vast wealth to greed or lack of ethics. Rather he contends that "the great fortunes are the natural, logical outcome of a system" . . . [a system producing] "the utter despoilment of the many for the benefit of a few." The result is a "natural" economic and human result. As he put it, "our plutocrats rank as nothing more or less than so many unavoidable creations of a set of processes which must imperatively produce a certain set of results." The following excerpt is from the first chapter of his book *History of the Great American Fortunes* (1907):

The noted private fortunes of settlement and colonial times were derived from the ownership of land and the gains of trading. . . . Throughout the colonies were scattered lords of the soil who had vast territorial domains over which they exercised an arbitrary and, in some portions of the colonies, a feudal sway. . . . Nearly all the colonies were settled by chartered companies, organized for purely commercial purposes and the success of which largely depended upon the emigration which they were able to promote.

These corporations were vested with enormous powers and privileges which, in effect, constituted them as sovereign rulers. . . .

As the demands of commerce had to be sustained at any price, a system was at once put into operation of gathering in as many of the poorer English class as could be impressed upon some pretext, and shipping them over to be held as bonded laborers. Penniless and lowly Englishmen, arrested and convicted for any one of the multitude of offenses then provided for severely in law, were transported as criminals or sold into the colonies as slaves for a term of years. The English courts were busy grinding out human material for the Virginia Plantation. . . . No voice was raised in protest. (pp. 11–12)

First-Level Reading: Paraphrasing

The noted private fortunes of settlement and colonial times were derived from the ownership of land and the gains of trading.

Paraphrase:

. . . Throughout the colonies were scattered lords of the soil who had vast territorial domains over which they exercised an arbitrary and, in some portions of the colonies, a feudal sway. . . .

Paraphrase:

Nearly all the colonies were settled by chartered companies, organized for purely commercial purposes and the success of which largely depended upon the emigration which they were able to promote.

Paraphrase:

These corporations were vested with enormous powers and privileges which, in effect, constituted them as sovereign rulers. . . .

Paraphrase:

As the demands of commerce had to be sustained at any price, a system was at once put into operation of gathering in as many of the poorer English class as could be impressed upon some pretext, and shipping them over to be held as bonded laborers.

Paraphrase:

Penniless and lowly Englishmen, arrested and convicted for any one of the multitude of offenses then provided for severely in law, were transported as criminals or sold into the colonies as slaves for a term of years. The English courts were busy grinding out human material for the Virginia Plantation. . . .

Paraphrase:

No voice was raised in protest.

Paraphrase:

First-Level Reading: Sample Interpretation

The noted private fortunes of settlement and colonial times were derived from the ownership of land and the gains of trading.

Paraphrase: During the time of the early American colonies, the wealthy people got their wealth from owning land and engaging in trade.

. . . Throughout the colonies were scattered lords of the soil who had vast territorial domains over which they exercised an arbitrary and, in some portions of the colonies, a feudal sway. . . .

Paraphrase: Everywhere in the colonies there were people with huge estates so large and powerful, so great, that these land-owners were virtual "lords" who could command almost anything they wanted of the people who lived in their province, as medieval lords could.

Nearly all the colonies were settled by chartered companies, organized for purely commercial purposes and the success of which largely depended upon the emigration which they were able to promote.

Paraphrase: Almost all the people who took over these territories from the Native Americans did so through licensed companies. These companies were concerned with nothing but profit. Their success depended on getting people to come from other lands.

These corporations were vested with enormous powers and privileges which, in effect, constituted them as sovereign rulers. . . .

Paraphrase: The companies so formed had stupendous power and rights that rendered them autonomous and virtually self-governing.

As the demands of commerce had to be sustained at any price, a system was at once put into operation of gathering in as many of the poorer English class as could be impressed upon some pretext, and shipping them over to be held as bonded laborers.

Paraphrase: Because profit was their only ultimate motive and the system they set up required cheap labor, England began the practice of devising excuses that justified forcing poor people to come to the colonies as near slaves.

Penniless and lowly Englishmen, arrested and convicted for any one of the multitude of offenses then provided for severely in law, were transported as criminals or sold into the colonies as slaves for a term of years. The English courts were busy grinding out human material for the Virginia Plantation. . . .

Paraphrase: The English court-system became the economic vehicle that enabled the wealthy colonial companies and their masters to gather and use masses of poor people for their vested interests. The system was set up so that for any number of reasons the poor could be found guilty of any of a number of offenses and punished severely. This punishment often consisted of sending them off to the colonies as slaves for a specified number of years.

No voice was raised in protest.

Paraphrase: Virtually no one objected to this cruel and unethical system.

Second-Level Reading: Thesis of "History of the Great American Fortunes"

Statement of thesis. A minority of persons in the early American colonies acquired vast fortunes, land, and power through the exploitation of poor people in England.

Elaboration of thesis. The dominant form of government in the early American colonies was not democracy but something more like feudal oligarchy. Relatively few wealthy colonists were at the pinnacle of a system of powerful licensed companies that had acquired from the English king complete power and authority to rule a region and the people in it. Profit was the overriding end. The systematic denial of human rights for those manipulated and used by the powerful was standard practice and went virtually unquestioned.

Exemplification of thesis. For example, people were accused and convicted of petty crimes in England for the tacit purpose of providing virtual slaves for the colonies. (These convicts were sentenced into forced labor for the companies authorized by the king.)

Illustration of thesis. To better understand this phenomenon, we might consider the legal institution of slavery in America from the 1600s until the 1800s. Innocent Africans were rounded up and sold into slavery for one explicit purpose—the pursuit of wealth by land-owners. By using free forced labor, the rich got richer and the slaves were denied their most fundamental human rights. The same denial of rights was inherent in the system that sentenced poor people in England to a life of virtual slavery to American land-owners.

"ON LIBERTY"

Background information: The following excerpt is taken from H. L. Mencken's article entitled "On Liberty," published in the December 5, 1923, edition of the *Nation Magazine*. Mencken's work is highly acclaimed by scholars for its literary, social, and political critique. Mencken is arguably the most distinguished journalist in United States history.

I believe in liberty. And when I say liberty, I mean the thing in its widest imaginable sense—liberty up to the extreme limits of the feasible and tolerable. I am against forbidding anybody to do anything, or say anything, or think anything so long as it is at all possible to imagine a habitable world in which he would be free to do, say, and think it. The burden of proof, as I see it, is always upon the policeman, which is to say, upon the lawmaker, the theologian, the right-thinker. He must prove his case doubly, triply, quadruply, and then he must start all over and prove it again. The eye through which I view him is watery and jaundiced. I do not pretend to be "just" to him—any more than a Christian pretends to be just to the devil. He is the enemy of everything I admire and respect in this world—of everything that makes it various and amusing and charming. He impedes every honest search for the truth. He stands against every sort of good-will and common decency. His ideal is that of an animal trainer, an archbishop, a major general in the army. I am against him until the last galoot's ashore.

First Level Reading: Paraphrasing

I believe in liberty. And when I say liberty, I mean the thing in its widest imaginable sense—liberty up to the extreme limits of the feasible and tolerable.

Paraphrase:

I am against forbidding anybody to do anything, or say anything, or think anything so long as it is at all possible to imagine a habitable world in which he would be free to do, say, and think it.

Paraphrase:

The burden of proof, as I see it, is always upon the policeman, which is to say, upon the lawmaker, the theologian, the right-thinker. He must prove his case doubly, triply, quadruply, and then he must start all over and prove it again.

Paraphrase:

The eye through which I view him is watery and jaundiced. I do not pretend to be "just" to him—any more than a Christian pretends to be just to the devil.

Paraphrase:

He is the enemy of everything I admire and respect in this world—of everything that makes it various and amusing and charming. He impedes every honest search for the truth.

Paraphrase:

He stands against every sort of good-will and common decency. His ideal is that of an animal trainer, an archbishop, a major general in the army.

Paraphrase:

I am against him until the last galoot's ashore.
Paraphrase:

First-Level Reading: Sample Interpretation

I believe in liberty. And when I say liberty, I mean the thing in its widest imaginable sense—liberty up to the extreme limits of the feasible and tolerable.

Paraphrase: I believe in freedom. By this I mean that people should be absolutely as free as possible to do what they want, to live life as they choose. The only freedoms people shouldn't have are those that cannot be supported by a civil society (because they deny someone else a fundamental right).

I am against forbidding anybody to do anything, or say anything, or think anything so long as it is at all possible to imagine a habitable world in which he would be free to do, say, and think it.

Paraphrase: I believe that people should be given the right to say what they choose, to think what they choose, to do what they choose, as long as people can at all get along while they have these rights.

The burden of proof, as I see it, is always upon the policeman, which is to say, upon the lawmaker, the theologian, the right-thinker. He must prove his case doubly, triply, quadruply, and then he must start all over and prove it again.

Paraphrase: Anyone arguing against the fundamental rights to say, think, and do as one chooses must prove beyond any doubt that these rights must be denied someone for unquestionable reasons. The burden of proof falls, not on those accused of some wrongdoing, but on accusers, on police officers, politicians who create laws, religious leaders, and righteous people (i.e., people who see themselves as possessing the truth). These accusers must prove unequivocally that one deserves to be denied one's fundamental rights, and they must prove it not only once, but twice, three times, four times, and then yet another time. In other words, they must prove it beyond any doubt whatsoever.

The eye through which I view him is watery and jaundiced. I do not pretend to be "just" to him—any more than a Christian pretends to be just to the devil.

Paraphrase: I am cynical, pessimistic, and skeptical about people who see themselves as possessing the truth and who inflict their righteous views on others. Because they deny people their rights to think and do as they choose, I see them as unjust. Therefore I openly refuse to treat their views equal to views that support fundamental human rights.

He is the enemy of everything I admire and respect in this world—of everything that makes it various and amusing and charming.

Paraphrase: Righteous thinking that would deny someone their basic rights goes against everything that is good in the world, everything I hold in high esteem, everything that is honorable. Without differing views and differing ways of living, life would be boring, uninteresting, dull.

He impedes every honest search for the truth. He stands against every sort of good-will and common decency. His ideal is that of an animal trainer, an archbishop, a major general in the army.

Paraphrase: Because they see themselves as possessing the truth, righteous thinkers get in the way of figuring out what is actually going on in a situation or what makes sense to believe. They don't seek the truth, but rather distort the truth according to their belief systems. They routinely act in bad faith. They lack integrity and are, in sum, unethical. They want to rule and dominate people, and they expect people to accept their domination submissively.

I am against him until the last galoot's ashore.

Paraphrase: I am absolutely against these righteous, holier-than-thou thinkers until the last foolish or uncouth person comes to this country (which will be never, because some foolish and uncouth people will always be arriving).

Second-Level Reading: Thesis of "On Liberty"

Statement of thesis. As long as they are not actually harming others, people should be allowed to say what they want, think what they want, and do what they want. This is what it means to live in a free, civilized society.

Elaboration of thesis. There are many righteous people who believe that the way they think and act are the only correct ways to think and act. These people are narrow-minded in view, and they expect everyone else to see things as they do. They do not allow for autonomous thought. Moreover, these people are often in positions of authority. In order to maintain individual liberties as espoused in a free society, people with authority over others (such as police, judges, social workers, politicians who create laws), when attempting to take away someone's rights, must always prove beyond any doubt that this action is the only reasonable way to deal with the situation. But people in these positions of authority are often self-righteous, unable to look at life from multiple perspectives. They therefore cannot be trusted either to see what is right in a situation or to do what is right.

Exemplification of thesis. For example, some "child protective services" workers profess to be concerned with the well-being of children, while at the same time ignoring information that would help them best serve the child. For instance, in some cases, children have been taken away from their parents simply because the CPS worker thought the parents didn't keep the house as clean as they thought it should be kept. At the same time, children taken into state custody often fare much worse than they would have done if they had stayed with their parents (due to the dismal conditions of many foster care programs). People in positions of authority often use their prejudices to determine what is right in the situation. Without knowing it, they often impose their personal beliefs and value judgments on others, as if their own views were part of the law.

Illustration of thesis. To illustrate the point that Mencken makes in this passage, imagine a bird soaring through the air, free to go wherever it chooses, whenever it chooses. Then imagine that bird harnessed, entrapped, caged in by those more powerful. People, like birds, are meant to fly free, to live according to their own desires, to develop unique thoughts, to pursue personal ideals. Our distinctive and individual ways of taking flight, our varying destinations, our alternative viewpoints are what make living interesting. When this natural freedom is denied us, we, like the trapped bird, find ourselves in a cage, everyone unable to fly, all expected to act in the same narrow-minded, judgmental way.

"CORN-PONE OPINIONS"

Background information: This excerpt, written by the distinguished novelist and social critic Mark Twain, is found in *The Portable Mark Twain*. By "corn-pone opinions" Twain meant the tendency of people to abandon any view or belief "which might interfere with their bread and butter. . . . In matters of large moment, like politics and religion, he must think and feel with the bulk of his neighbors or suffer damage in his social standing and in his business prosperity."

I am persuaded that a coldly-thought-out and independent verdict upon a fashion in clothes, or manners, or literature, or politics, or religion, or any other matter . . . is a most rare thing—if it has indeed ever existed. . . . Mohammedans are Mohammedans because they are born and reared among that sect, not because they have thought it out and can furnish sound reasons for being Mohammedans; we know why Catholics are Catholics; why Presbyterians are Presbyterians, why Baptists are Baptists, why Mormons are Mormons, why thieves are thieves, why monarchists are monarchists, why Republicans are Republicans and Democrats, Democrats. . . . Men think they think upon great political questions, and they do; but they think with their party, not independently; they read its literature but not that of the other side; they arrive at convictions but they are drawn from a partial view of the matter in hand and are of no particular value. . . . We all do no end of feeling and we mistake it for thinking. And out of it we get an aggregation which we consider a boon. Its name is Public Opinion. It is held in reverence. It settles everything. Some think it the Voice of God. (pp. 573, 576, 577, 578)

For this and the next passage we provide a first-level reading only.

First-Level Reading: Paraphrasing

I am persuaded that a coldly-thought-out and independent verdict upon a fashion in clothes, or manners, or literature, or politics, or religion, or any other matter . . . is a most rare thing—if it has indeed ever existed. . . .

Paraphrase:

Mohammedans are Mohammedans because they are born and reared among that sect, not because they have thought it out and can furnish sound reasons for being Mohammedans; we know why Catholics are Catholics; why Presbyterians are Presbyterians, why Baptists are Baptists, why Mormons are Mormons, why thieves are thieves, why monarchists are monarchists, why Republicans are Republicans and Democrats, Democrats. . . .

Paraphrase:

Men think they think upon great political questions, and they do; but they think with their party, not independently; they read its literature but not that of the other side; they arrive at convictions but they are drawn from a partial view of the matter in hand and are of no particular value. . . .

Paraphrase:

We all do no end of feeling and we mistake it for thinking. And out of it we get an aggregation which we consider a boon. Its name is Public Opinion. It is held in reverence. It settles everything. Some think it the Voice of God.

Paraphrase:

First-Level Reading: Sample Interpretation

I am persuaded that a coldly-thought-out and independent verdict upon a fashion in clothes, or manners, or literature, or politics, or religion, or any other matter . . . is a most rare thing—if it has indeed ever existed. . . .

Paraphrase: People do not think independently, but rather as part of a mass. I firmly believe, based on the evidence I have seen, that people rarely, if ever, think autonomously and rationally about the clothes they wear, the social rules to which they adhere, the books they choose to read, the political or religious views they hold, indeed about anything whatsoever.

Mohammedans are Mohammedans because they are born and reared among that sect, not because they have thought it out and can furnish sound reasons for being Mohammedans; we know why Catholics are Catholics; why Presbyterians are Presbyterians, why Baptists are Baptists, why Mormons are Mormons, why thieves are thieves, why monarchists are monarchists, why Republicans are Republicans and Democrats, Democrats. . . .

Paraphrase: People maintain their ideological and belief systems because they were raised within those systems, not because they have critically analyzed their beliefs. This truth is exemplified by the fact that people belong to the same religious groups within which they were born. The same sort of indoctrination occurs within any social system, religious, political, or otherwise.

Men think they think upon great political questions, and they do; but they think with their party, not independently; they read its literature but not that of the other side; they arrive at convictions but they are drawn from a partial view of the matter in hand and are of no particular value. . . .

Paraphrase: People see themselves as thinking through important political questions, and they do think about those questions. But rather than think autonomously, they think within the perspectives of their political party. They read to understand their own party's views, but they do not read dissenting views. People hold fast to their views, but because those views are so narrow in focus, they are essentially worthless.

We all do no end of feeling and we mistake it for thinking. And out of it we get an aggregation which we consider a boon. Its name is Public Opinion. It is held in reverence. It settles everything. Some think it the Voice of God.

Paraphrase: People often come to situations with a lot of emotional energy, but that energy is mistaken for rational thought. Collectively we validate our group's beliefs, and we get more emotional energy from sharing group goals and perspectives. We feel more powerful. We call these collective beliefs "public opinion." We worship our group ideology. We see it as "the truth." Some even see it as divine truth from God.

"THE IDEA OF EDUCATION"

Background information: In 1851, John Henry Newman wrote his famous set of lectures, "Discourses on the Scope and Nature of University Education," which in 1952 became *The Idea of a University.* This book focuses on Newman's vision of education.

All I say is, call things by their right names, and do not confuse together ideas which are essentially different. A thorough knowledge of one science and a superficial acquaintance with many are not the same thing; a smattering of a hundred things or a memory for detail, is not a . . . comprehensive view. . . . Do not say, the people must be educated, when, after all, you only mean amused, refreshed, soothed, put into good spirits and good humor, or kept from vicious excesses. . . . Education is a high word; it is the preparation for knowledge, and it is the imparting of knowledge in proportion to that preparation. . . . It is education which gives a man a clear conscious view of his own opinions and judgments, a truth in developing them, an eloquence in expressing them, and a force in urging them. It teaches him to see things as they are, to go right to the point, to disentangle a skein of thought, to detect what is sophistical, and to discard what is irrelevant. . . . It shows him how to accommodate himself to others, how to throw himself into their state of mind, how to bring before them his own, how to influence them, how to come to an understanding with them, how to bear with them. . . . He knows when to speak and when to be silent; he is able to converse, he is able to listen; he can ask a question pertinently, and gain a lesson seasonably, when nothing to impart himself.

First-Level Reading: Paraphrasing

All I say is, call things by their right names, and do not confuse together ideas which are essentially different.

Paraphrase:

A thorough knowledge of one science and a superficial acquaintance with many are not the same thing;

Paraphrase:

A smattering of a hundred things or a memory for detail, is not . . . a comprehensive view. . . .

Paraphrase:

Do not say, the people must be educated, when, after all, you only mean amused, refreshed, soothed, put into good spirits and good humor, or kept from vicious excesses. . . .

Paraphrase:

Education is a high word; it is the preparation for knowledge, and it is the imparting of knowledge in proportion to that preparation. . . .

Paraphrase:

It is education which gives a man a clear conscious view of his own opinions and judgments, a truth in developing them, an eloquence in expressing them, and a force in urging them.

Paraphrase:

It teaches him to see things as they are, to go right to the point, to disentangle a skein of thought, to detect what is sophistical, and to discard what is irrelevant. . . .

Paraphrase:

It shows him how to accommodate himself to others, how to throw himself into their state of mind, how to bring before them his own, how to influence them, how to come to an understanding with them, how to bear with them. . . .

Paraphrase:

He knows when to speak and when to be silent; he is able to converse, he is able to listen; he can ask a question pertinently, and gain a lesson seasonably, when nothing to impart himself.

Paraphrase:

First-Level Reading: Sample Interpretation

All I say is, call things by their right names, and do not confuse together ideas which are essentially different.

Paraphrase: My main point is that people should choose their words carefully so that they clearly distinguish ideas that are different from each other.

A thorough knowledge of one science and a superficial acquaintance with many, are not the same thing;

Paraphrase: Having deep understanding and command of one subject or discipline, and knowing a little bit about a lot of subjects are very different things and should not be confused with one another.

A smattering of a hundred things or a memory for detail, is not a . . . comprehensive view. . . .

Paraphrase: Knowing a little about a lot of things or being adept at remembering specifics is not the same as being able to think abstractly about important topics. Nor is it the same as having a broad perspective.

Do not say, the people must be educated, when, after all, you only mean amused, refreshed, soothed, put into good spirits and good humor, or kept from vicious excesses. . . .

Paraphrase: Do not confuse education with enjoyment or entertainment, or with being rejuvenated or energized. Do not confuse education with being made comfortable or content. And don't say that a person is educated merely because he or she avoids immoderate or unrestrained behavior.

Education is a high word; it is the preparation for knowledge, and it is the imparting of knowledge in proportion to that preparation. . . .

Paraphrase: The concept of education has deep and significant meaning. It is not to be taken lightly, nor applied lightly. Education prepares the mind to understand and to learn important ideas. It enables one to take possession of knowledge and apply it.

It is education which gives a man a clear conscious view of his own opinions and judgments, a truth in developing them, an eloquence in expressing them, and a force in urging them.

Paraphrase: Through education one comes to know truly and deeply what one believes and why one believes it. It brings integrity to the process of belief, and it enables one to express what one believes with grace, style, and power.

It teaches him to see things as they are, to go right to the point, to disentangle a skein of thought, to detect what is sophistical, and to discard what is irrelevant. . . .

Paraphrase: Education fosters the ability to see what is actually true in a situation, to see through what is irrelevant in order to focus on what is important and relevant. When people are educated, they cannot be manipulated by people who use language in deceptive ways, people who say one thing and mean another.

It shows him how to accommodate himself to others, how to throw himself into their state of mind, how to bring before them his own, how to influence them, how to come to an understanding with them, how to bear with them. . . .

Paraphrase: Education enables people to think within multiple viewpoints, to empathize with the views of others in order to understand them. It enables people to rationally present their own arguments, using good reasons to persuade others of their views. It enables people to take into account reasonable viewpoints and arguments, and change their own views when faced with more reasonable views. It enables them to listen carefully and comprehend the views of others and be patient with those who are not patient themselves.

He knows when to speak and when to be silent; he is able to converse, he is able to listen; he can ask a question pertinently, and gain a lesson seasonably, when nothing to impart himself.

Paraphrase: Educated persons realize when it makes sense to state their views aloud and when it makes sense to be quiet and listen to others. They know how to discuss ideas effectively with others. They are good listeners. They are good at asking questions that facilitate discussion. They are skilled learners, even when they have nothing to add to a conversation or situation themselves.

SAMPLE ANALYSIS OF THE LOGIC OF . . .

EXHIBIT B.1   *The logic of love.*

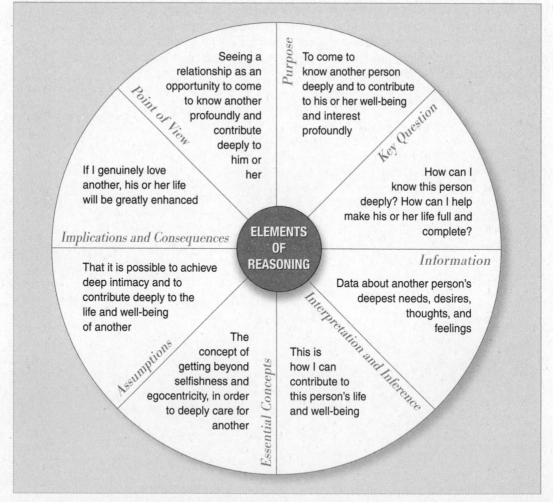

EXHIBIT B.2   *The logic of fear.*

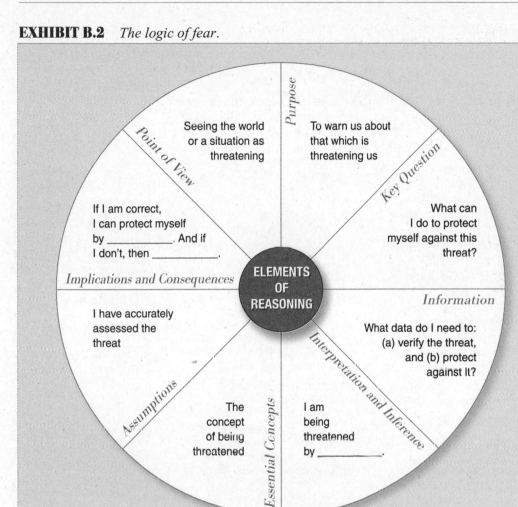

EXHIBIT B.3   *The logic of anger.*

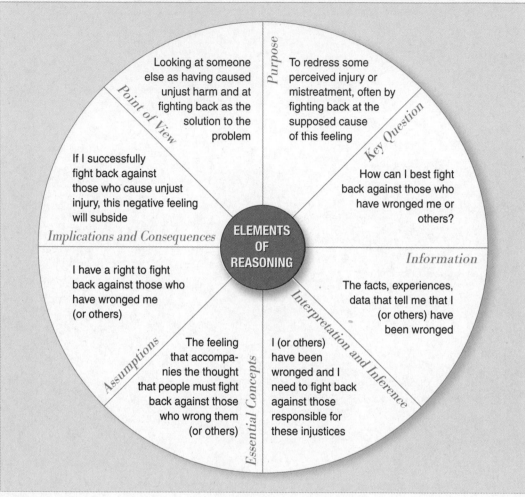

EXHIBIT B.4   *The logic of Christianity.*

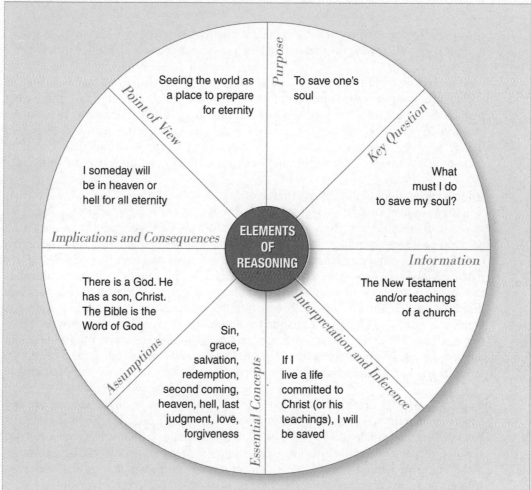

Purpose — To save one's soul

Key Question — What must I do to save my soul?

Information — The New Testament and/or teachings of a church

Interpretation and Inference — If I live a life committed to Christ (or his teachings), I will be saved

Essential Concepts — Sin, grace, salvation, redemption, second coming, heaven, hell, last judgment, love, forgiveness

Assumptions — There is a God. He has a son, Christ. The Bible is the Word of God

Implications and Consequences — I someday will be in heaven or hell for all eternity

Point of View — Seeing the world as a place to prepare for eternity

ELEMENTS OF REASONING

THE LOGIC OF ECONOMICS

Purpose: To develop theories that explain the distribution of goods and services within a society, as well as theories that define how goods and services should be distributed.

Key questions: How are goods and services produced, distributed, and consumed within any given society? How should they be? What is the best way to determine what people should get and how they should be allowed to get it? For example, to what extent should people be encouraged to pursue wealth and power principally for their own benefit? To what extent should society try to provide equal access to education, wealth, and power? What are the strengths and weaknesses of competing economic theories?

Information: Economists from differing schools of thought disagree on the information they use in reasoning through economic problems. Those who favor capitalism, for example, focus on information about supply of products versus demand, consumer preferences, consumer spending, business investments, and government support of business. In solving economic problems, they emphasize information about how to keep aggregate demand high. Those who favor socialism focus on information that reveals the impact of the distribution of wealth on the well-being of everyone, especially the poor and disadvantaged. Their ideal is to distribute wealth so that resources are made available as equally as possible, taking into account the crucial problem of how to motivate people to contribute to the well-being of others as well as themselves. The information that economists use is ultimately determined by the way they conceptualize ideal economic systems and the questions implied by the economic theories that guide their thinking.

Key concepts: Economics is the study of how goods, services, and resources are and should be distributed and used within human societies. Leading economic concepts have evolved, especially through the last 200 years. Some of them are: the principle of competition, law of supply and demand, utilitarianism, capitalism, socialism, communism, Marxism, exploitation, class conflict between economic strata (especially between workers and employers), private property, free markets, self-interest, psychological variables influencing economic behavior, assumption of scarcity, law of diminishing returns, principles of marginal utility and productivity, aggregate demand, labor theory of value, Malthusian population doctrine, and Keynesian economics.

Assumptions: By economists studying the ways and means for distributing goods and services, economic systems can become more stable and more fair to the people who vie for resources within those systems. Beyond this shared assumption, economists' assumptions differ according to their philosophies, values, and theories. Those who favor capitalism assume that humans are fundamentally selfish and that only a system that utilizes the driving force of human selfishness will be realistic. Socialists, in contrast, assume that education can be used to shift the emphasis in human activity from self-aggrandizement to altruism.

Inferences: Economists make inferences about how best to stabilize and enhance the distribution, production, and use of goods and services. They make these inferences in accordance with their economic philosophies, considering trends and patterns of individual business and government spending, economic health, and distribution of wealth.

Implications: The implications that economic theories generate vary from theory to theory. Which of the theoretical implications become actual consequences is a matter of continual debate. The debate focuses on what actual consequences seem to be accounted for by this or that economic theory and what consequences (good or bad) result from variables other than those postulated by a given theory. For example, did the Great Depression of the 1930s result from a deep flaw in capitalist theory, or did it result from a failure to practice the theory thoroughly enough?

Point of view: Economists look at the distribution of goods and services within a society, along with the distribution of power that distribution entails, as a crucial object of systematic study.

THE LOGIC OF SCIENCE

Goals scientists pursue: Scientists seek to figure out how the physical world operates through systematic observation, experimentation, and analysis. By analyzing the physical world, they seek to formulate principles, laws, and theories useful in explaining natural phenomena and in guiding further scientific study.

Questions scientists ask: How does the physical world operate? What are the best methods for figuring things out about the physical world? What are the barriers to figuring things out about the physical world? How can we overcome those barriers?

Information scientists use: Scientists use virtually any type of information that can be gathered systematically through observation and measurement, though most specialize in analyzing specific kinds of information. To name just some of the information scientists use, they observe and examine plants, animals, planets, stars, rocks, rock formations, minerals, bodies of water, fossils, chemicals, phenomena in the earth's atmosphere, and cells. They also observe interactions between phenomena.

Judgments scientists make: Scientists make judgments about the physical world based on observations and experimentation. These judgments lead to systematized knowledge, theories, and principles helpful in explaining and understanding the world.

Concepts that guide scientists' thinking: The most fundamental concepts that guide the thinking of scientists are (1) physical world (of nature and all matter); (2) hypothesis (an unproved theory, proposition, or supposition tentatively accepted to explain certain facts or to provide a basis for further investigation); (3) experimentation (a systematic and operationalized process designed to figure out something about the physical world); and (4) systematic observation (the act or practice of noting or recording facts or events in the physical world). Other fundamental concepts in science include: theory, law, scientific method, pure sciences, and applied sciences.

Key assumptions scientists make: (1) There are laws at work in the physical world that can be figured out through systematic observation and experimentation; (2) much about the physical world is still unknown; (3) through science, the quality of life on Earth can be enhanced.

Implications of science: Many important implications and consequences have resulted from scientific thinking, some of which have vastly improved the quality of life on Earth, others of which have resulted in decreased quality of life (the destruction of the Earth's forests, oceans, natural habitats, etc.). One important positive implication of scientific thinking is that it enables us to replace mythological thinking with theories and principles based in scientific fact.

The scientific point of view: Scientists look at the physical world and see phenomena best understood through careful observation and systematic study. They see scientific study as vital to understanding the physical world and replacing myth with scientific knowledge.

THE LOGIC OF ECOLOGY

Goals of ecologists: Ecologists seek to understand plants and animals as they exist in nature, with emphasis on their interrelationships, interdependence, and interactions with the environment. They work to understand all the influences that combine to produce and modify an animal or given plant, and thus to account for its existence and peculiarities within its habitat.

Questions that ecologists ask: How do plants and animals interact? How do animals interact with each other? How do plants and animals depend on one another? How do the varying ecosystems function within themselves? How do they interact with other ecosystems? How are plants and animals affected by environmental influences? How do animals and plants grow, develop, die, and replace themselves? How do plants and animals create balances between each other? What happens when plants and animals become unbalanced?

Information that ecologists use: The primary information used by ecologists is gained through observing plants and animals themselves, their interactions, and how they live within their environments. Ecologists note how animals and plants are born, how they reproduce, how they die, how they evolve, and how they are affected by environmental changes. They also use information from other disciplines including chemistry, meteorology, and geology.

Judgments that ecologists make: Ecologists make judgments about how ecosystems naturally function, about how animals and plants within them function, and about why they function as they do. They make judgments about how ecosystems become out of balance and what can be done to bring them back into balance. They make judgments about how natural communities should be grouped and classified.

Concepts that guide ecologists' thinking: One of the most fundamental concepts in ecology is *ecosystem,* defined as a group of living things that are dependent on one another and living in a particular habitat. Ecologists study how differing ecosystems function. Another key concept in ecology is *ecological succession,* the natural pattern of change occurring within every ecosystem when natural processes are undisturbed. This pattern includes the birth, development, death, and then replacement of natural communities. Ecologists have grouped communities into larger units called *biomes,* regions throughout the world classified according to physical features, including temperature, rainfall, and type of vegetation. Another fundamental concept in ecology is *balance of nature,* the natural process of birth, reproduction, eating, and being eaten, which keeps animal/plant communities fairly stable. Other key concepts include imbalances, energy, nutrients, population growth, diversity, habitat, competition, predation, parasitism, adaptation, co-evolution, succession and climax communities, and conservation.

Key assumptions that ecologists make: Patterns exist within animal/plant communities; these communities should be studied and classified; animals and plants often depend on one another and modify one another; balances must be maintained within ecosystems.

Implications of ecology: The study of ecology leads to numerous implications for life on Earth. By studying the balance of nature, for example, we can see when nature is out of balance, as in the current population explosion. We can see how pesticides, designed to kill pests on farm crops, also lead to the harm of mammals and birds, either directly or indirectly through food webs. We can also learn how over-farming causes erosion and depletion of soil nutrients.

Point of view of ecologists: Ecologists look at plants and animals and see them functioning in relationship with one another within their habitats, and needing to be in balance for the Earth to be healthy and sustainable.

THE LOGIC OF ASTRONOMY

Goals of astronomers: Astronomers study the universe in order to better understand what it is comprised of and how celestial bodies and energy function within it. Astronomers seek to understand the origins, evolution, composition, motions, relative positions, size, and movements of celestial bodies, including planets and their satellites, comets and meteors, stars and interstellar matter, galaxies and clusters of galaxies, black holes and magnetic fields, etc.

Questions astronomers ask: How did matter and energy in the universe ever come to be? How is the universe structured? What energy forces exist in the universe and how do they function? Will the universe continue to expand forever? How are celestial bodies born? How do they function? How do they evolve? How do they die? Do planets similar to Earth exist in the universe? What questions remain to be asked about the universe?

Information astronomers use: Astronomers gather information about celestial bodies and energy through direct observation and indirect measurements. Developing methods for gathering information about the universe is a key ongoing focus of astronomers' work. For example, they use telescopes, as well as images taken from balloons and satellites. They gather information about the radiation of bodies in the universe through the electromagnetic spectrum, including radio waves, ultraviolet and infrared radiation, X-rays, and gamma rays. Telescopes placed on orbiting satellites gather information about radiation blocked by the atmosphere. Astronomers rely on computers with image processing software that notes the power and shape of light. They also use the interferometer, a series of telescopes that collectively have tremendous power.

Judgments astronomers make: Astronomers make judgments about the universe and how it functions. Using the instruments they design and continually seek to refine, they make judgments about suns, stars, satellites, moons, nebulae and galaxies, black holes, magnetic fields, gas clouds, comets, and so forth. They make judgments about the distances, brightness, and composition of celestial bodies and their temperature, radiation, size, and color. From a practical perspective, astronomers make judgments that include making astronomical tables for air and sea navigation, and determining the correct time.

Concepts that guide astronomers' thinking: The universe is the most fundamental concept in astronomy. The universe is the total of all bodies and energy in the cosmos that function as a harmonious and orderly system. Other important concepts in astronomy include: gravity, electromagnetism, nuclear forces (strong and weak), and quantum theory.

Key assumptions astronomers make: (1) There are laws governing the universe, though we don't yet know them all; (2) the universe is largely unexplored and at present unexplained; (3) we need to develop better instruments of observation and measurement to understand the universe; (4) judgments in astronomy are limited by the observational instruments and research methods currently available.

Implications of astronomy: One important implication of astronomy is that, as we improve our understanding of the universe, based on scientific observations and conclusions, we improve our understanding of life as an organic process, and we therefore rely less on myth to explain the universe. Furthermore, advances in astronomy help us see the Earth as a minuscule body within a vast, expanding universe, rather than the Earth (and therefore humans) as the center of the universe.

The point of view of astronomers: Astronomers look at the universe and see a vast system of systems and a hugely unexplored space waiting to be discovered and understood.

WHAT DO WE MEAN BY "THE BEST THINKERS"?

Throughout this book we use the construct "the best thinkers." We derive it not from empirical study of any given list of potential "best thinkers." Rather, we derive it from the strategies, skills, and insights inherent in a substantive concept of critical thinking. In other words, we believe it captures the intellectual ideal of "the critical thinker."

Though it behooves us to strive toward being the ideal thinker, in fact, there is no perfect thinker. By the same token, there is no perfect dancer, tennis player, or scientist. Nevertheless, it is possible to think through any field and extrapolate the traits, abilities, and insights that explain why some people, rather than others, are to be included in the categories of "the best dancers," "the best tennis players," and "the best scientists." This is precisely what we have attempted to do with the concept "the best thinker."

It is possible to talk of the "best thinkers" because it is possible to delineate what the goals and purposes of thought are—to understand accurately, communicate successfully, and apply ideas effectively—and what it takes to achieve those goals and fulfill those purposes. Review the chapters on the elements of thought and the standards for thought for examples. And notice how we have deduced skills and abilities by combining elements with standards.

To conceptualize the best thinkers, it is useful to conceptual their opposites—the worst thinkers. Consider the following practices of the "worst" thinkers (and note how common it is for people to think in these ways).

The worst thinkers commonly:

- are unclear, muddled, or confused.
- jump to conclusions.
- fail to think through implications.

- lose track of their goal.
- are unrealistic.
- focus on the trivial.
- fail to notice contradictions.
- use inaccurate information in their thinking.
- ask vague questions.
- give vague answers.
- ask loaded questions.
- ask irrelevant questions.
- confuse questions of different types.
- answer questions they are not competent to answer.
- come to conclusions based on inaccurate or irrelevant information.
- use only the information that supports their view.
- make inferences not justified by their experience.
- distort data and represent data inaccurately.
- fail to notice the inferences they make.
- come to unreasonable conclusions.
- fail to notice their assumptions.
- make unjustified assumptions.
- miss key ideas.
- use irrelevant ideas.
- form confused ideas.
- form superficial concepts.
- misuse words.
- ignore relevant viewpoints.
- fail to see issues from points of view other than their own.
- confuse issues of different types.
- lack insight into their prejudices.
- think narrowly.
- think imprecisely.
- think illogically.
- think one-sidedly.
- think simplistically.
- think hypocritically.
- think superficially.
- think ethnocentrically.
- think egocentrically.

- think irrationally.
- cannot solve problems they face.
- make poor decisions.
- lack insight into their own ignorance.

We can now construct a list of "best thinking" practices by attributing to them the *opposite* characteristics to those above. For example, when people are thinking well, they commonly:

- are clear in their thinking.
- avoid jumping to conclusions.
- think through implications carefully.
- keep track of their goal.
- are realistic.
- focus on what is most important.
- notice contradictions.
- use accurate and relevant information.
- ask clear and precise questions.
- give clear and precise answers.
- ask questions that are not loaded.
- ask relevant and important questions.
- ask live and stimulating questions.
- distinguish between questions of different types.
- answer only those questions they are competent to answer.
- come to conclusions based on accurate and relevant information.
- consider and weigh information whether or not it supports their view.
- make inferences justified by their experience.
- formulate and represent data accurately.
- notice the inferences they make.
- come to reasonable conclusions.
- notice their assumptions.
- make justified assumptions.
- identify key ideas.
- use relevant ideas.
- form clear ideas.
- form deep concepts.
- use words in keeping with established usage.
- consider relevant viewpoints.
- see issues from points of view other than their own.
- differentiate between issues of different types.

- develop insight into their prejudices.
- think widely.
- think precisely.
- think logically.
- think within multiple viewpoints.
- think with integrity.
- think deeply.
- think nonparochially.
- think rationally.
- are skilled in problem recognition and problem solving.
- make sound and wise decisions.
- develop insight into their own ignorance.

One way to see the force behind this conceptualization is to think through the implications of a thinker lacking one of these abilities. When you identify those implications, we believe that you will discover two things:

1. that anyone who lacks one of these qualities will probably, as a result, lack others as well; and

2. that, given those consequences, such a thinker should not properly be considered a "best" thinker.

By the way, we do not consider our analysis of the qualities and skills of the best thinkers exhaustive. We are more than open to entertain further qualities and skills. The key is the practical implications of the concept "best thinker"—to provide us with important ideals toward which we can strive in our development as thinkers. Foundational critical-thinking tools are foundational tools for the best thinkers simply because anyone violating basic critical-thinking principles would not pass the test of "good" thinking, let alone that of the "best" thinking.

Moreover, if we add traits of mind to our list of skills and abilities above, we get a deeper sense of the concept "best thinker." (These traits are the focus of Chapter 8.) It is clear that one cannot be a "good" thinker if one is intellectually arrogant, intellectually lazy, intellectually hypocritical, intellectually conformist, intellectually self-centered, possessed of an intellectual disregard for justice, or distrustful of reason and evidence. With traits such as these, one can hardly be considered a candidate for the label "good" thinker, let alone "best" thinker. Thus we can conclude that being intellectually humble, perseverant, independent, and so forth are necessary conditions of being included in the category of "best" thinker.

As we have said, the ideal thinker does not and cannot exist, for the ideal thinker is the perfect thinker, the thinker who never makes mistakes, who is never irrational or egocentric, who is all-knowing. However, each of us can strive to be a "best thinker," to keep improving our thinking one day at a time, one idea at a time, one skill at a time. By having a rich concept in mind of the "best thinker," we have clear direction for our thinking. Whether we take that direction is an individual choice.

GLOSSARY

A GUIDE TO CRITICAL-THINKING TERMS AND CONCEPTS

ACCURATE   Free from errors, mistakes, or distortion. *Accurate* implies a positive exercise of care to obtain conformity with fact or truth. By comparison, *correct* connotes little more than absence of error; *exact* stresses perfect conformity to fact, truth, or some standard; *precise* suggests minute accuracy of detail. Accuracy is an important goal in critical thinking, though it is almost always a matter of degree. It is also important to recognize that making mistakes is an essential part of learning and that it is far better that students make their own mistakes than that they parrot the thinking of the text or teacher. It also should be recognized that some distortion usually results whenever we think within a point of view or frame of reference. Students should think with this awareness in mind, with some sense of the limitations of their own, the text's, the teacher's, and the subject's perspective. *See also* perfections of thought.

AMBIGUOUS   Having two or more possible meanings. Sensitivity to ambiguity and vagueness in writing and speech is essential to good thinking. A continual effort to be clear and precise in language usage is fundamental to education. Ambiguity is a problem more of sentences than of individual words. Furthermore, not every sentence that can be construed in more than one way is problematic and deserving of analysis. Many sentences are clearly intended one way; any other construal is obviously absurd and not meant. For example, "Make me a sandwich" is never seriously intended to request metamorphic change. It is a poor example for teaching genuine insight into critical thinking. For an example of a problematic ambiguity, consider the statement, "Welfare is corrupt." Among the possible meanings of this sentence are the following: (1) Those who administer welfare programs take bribes to administer welfare policy unfairly. (2) Welfare policies are written in such a way that much

of the money goes to people who don't deserve it rather than to those who do. (3) A government that gives money to people who haven't earned it corrupts both the giver and the recipient. The first makes moral claims about administrators. The second makes legal claims about policy. The third questions the very principle of welfare. If two people are arguing about whether welfare is corrupt but interpret the claim differently, they can make little or no progress; they aren't arguing about the same point. Evidence and considerations relevant to one interpretation may be irrelevant to others. Therefore, before taking a position on an issue or arguing a point, it is essential to be clear about the issue at hand. *See also* clarify.

ANALYZE   To break up a whole into its parts; to examine in detail so as to determine the nature of; to look more deeply into an issue or situation. All learning presupposes some analysis of what we are learning, if only by categorizing or labeling things in one way rather than another. Students should routinely be asked to analyze their own ideas, claims, experiences, interpretations, judgments, and theories, and those they hear and read. *See also* elements of thought.

ARGUE   (1) To engage in a quarrel; bicker; (2) to persuade by giving reasons. As developing critical thinkers, we strive to move from the first sense of the word to the second; that is, we try to focus on giving reasons to support our views without becoming egocentrically involved in the discussion. This is a fundamental problem in human life. To argue in the critical-thinking sense is to use logic and reason and to bring forth facts to support or refute a point. It is done in a spirit of cooperation and good will.

ARGUMENT   A reason or reasons offered for or against something; the offering of such reasons; a discussion in which there is disagreement, suggesting using logic and bringing forth facts to support or refute a point.

ASSUME   Take for granted or presuppose. Critical thinkers make their assumptions explicit, assess them, and correct them. Assumptions can vary from the mundane to the problematic: I heard a scratch at the door. I got up to let the cat in. I assumed that only the cat makes that noise, and that he makes it only when he wants to be let in. Someone speaks gruffly to me. I feel guilty and hurt. I assume she is angry at me, that she is angry at me only when I do something bad, and that if she's angry at me, she dislikes me. People often equate making assumptions with making *false* assumptions. When people say, "Don't assume," this is what they mean. But we cannot avoid making assumptions, and some are justifiable. (For instance, we have assumed that people who buy this book can read English.) Rather than saying "Never assume," we say, "Be aware of and careful about the assumptions you make, and be ready to examine and critique them." *See also* assumption, elements of thought.

ASSUMPTION   A statement accepted or supposed as true without proof or demonstration; an unstated premise or belief. All human thought and experience are based on assumptions. Our thought must begin with something we take to be true in a particular context. We are typically unaware of what we assume and therefore rarely question our assumptions. Most of our assumptions are unconscious. They operate in our thinking without our knowing it. Much of what is wrong with human thought can be found in the uncritical or unexamined assumptions that underlie it. All of our prejudices, biases, and preconceived generalizations lie in the form of assumptions. We often experience the world in such a way as to assume that we are observing things just as they are, as though we were seeing the world without the filter of a point of view. People we disagree with, of course, we recognize as having a point of view. One of the key dispositions of critical thinking is the ongoing sense that, as humans, we always think within a perspective, that we almost never experience things totally and absolutistically. There is a connection, therefore, between thinking so as to be aware of our assumptions and being intellectually humble.

By "reasoning based on assumptions," we mean "whatever we take for granted as true" to figure out something else. Thus, if you infer that because a candidate is a Republican, he or she will support a balanced budget, you assume that all Republicans support a balanced budget. If you infer that foreign leaders presented in the news as "enemies" or "friends" are in fact enemies or friends, you assume that the news is always accurate in its presentation of the character of foreign leaders. If you infer that someone who invites you to his or her apartment after a party "to continue this interesting conversation" is really interested in you romantically or sexually, you assume that the only reason for going to someone's apartment late at night after a party is to pursue a romantic or sexual relationship. All reasoning has some basis in the assumptions we make (but usually do not express openly).

AUTHORITY   (1) The power or supposed right to give commands, enforce obedience, take action, or make final decisions; (2) a person with much knowledge and expertise in a field, and hence reliable. Critical thinkers recognize that ultimate authority rests with reason and evidence, as it is only on the assumption that purported experts have the backing of reason and evidence that they rightfully gain authority. Much instruction discourages critical thinking by encouraging students to believe that whatever the text or teacher says is true. As a result, students do not learn how to assess authority. *See also* knowledge.

BIAS   (1) A mental leaning or inclination; (2) partiality, prejudice. We must clearly distinguish two different senses of the word "bias." One is neutral, the other negative. In the neutral sense, because of one's point of view, one notices some things rather than others, emphasizes some points rather than others, and thinks in one direction rather than others. This is not in itself a criticism because thinking within a point of view is unavoidable. In the negative sense, we are implying blindness or irrational resistance to weaknesses within one's own point of view or to the strength or insight within a point of view one opposes. Fair-minded critical thinkers try to be aware of their bias (in the first sense) and try hard to avoid bias (in the second sense). Many people confuse these two senses. Many confuse bias with emotion or with evaluation, perceiving any expression of emotion or any use of evaluative words to be biased (the second sense). Evaluative words that can be justified by reason and evidence are not biased in the negative sense. *See also* criteria, evaluate, judgment, opinion.

CLARIFY   To make easier to understand, to free from confusion or ambiguity, to remove obscurities. *Clarity* is a fundamental perfection of thought, and *clarification* is a fundamental aim in critical thinking. It is important that students see why it is important to write and speak clearly, why it is important to say what they mean and mean what they say. The key to clarification is concrete, specific examples. *See also* accurate, ambiguous, logic of language, vague.

CONCEPT   An idea or thought, especially a generalized idea of a thing or of a class of things. Humans think within concepts or ideas. We cannot achieve command over our thoughts unless we learn how to achieve command over our concepts or ideas. Thus, we must learn how to identify the concepts or ideas we are using, contrast them with alternative concepts or ideas, and clarify what we include and exclude by means of them. In this book, the concepts of critical thinking and uncritical thinking are important ideas. Everything written in this book can be classified as an attempt to explain one or the other of these two ideas. Each of these ideas is explained, in turn, by means of other ideas. Thus, the concept of *thinking critically* is explained by reference to yet other concepts such as *intellectual standards for thought*. Each discipline develops its own set of concepts or technical vocabulary to facilitate its thinking. All sports develop a vocabulary of concepts that enables those who are trying to understand or master the game to make sense of it. One cannot understand ethics without a clear concept of justice, kindness, cruelty, rights, and obligations.

People are often unclear about the concepts they are using. For example, most people say they believe strongly in democracy, but few can clarify with examples what that word does and does not imply. Most people confuse the meaning of words with cultural associations, with the result that *democracy,* to many, means whatever we do in running our government, and any country that is different from ours is undemocratic. We must distinguish the concepts implicit in the English language from the psychological associations surrounding those concepts in a given social group or culture. The failure to develop this ability is a major cause of uncritical thought and selfish critical thought. *See also* logic of language.

CONCLUDE/CONCLUSION   To decide by reasoning, to infer, to deduce; the last step in a reasoning process; a judgment, decision, or belief formed after investigation or reasoning. All beliefs, decisions, and actions are based on human thought, but seldom as the result of conscious reasoning or deliberation. All that we believe is, one way or another, based on conclusions that we have come to during our lifetime. By "coming to conclusions," we mean taking something we believe we know and figuring out something else on the basis of it. When we do this, we make inferences. For example, if you walk right by me without saying hello, I might come to the conclusion (make the inference) that you are angry with me. If the water kettle on the stove begins to whistle, I come to the conclusion (make the inference) that the water in it has started to boil.

In everyday life, we continually are making inferences (coming to conclusions) about the people, things, places, and events in our lives. Yet, we rarely monitor our thought processes, and we don't critically assess the conclusions we come to, to determine whether we have sufficient grounds or reasons for accepting them. We seldom recognize when we have come to a conclusion—confusing our conclusions with evidence—and so cannot assess the reasoning that took us from evidence to conclusion. Recognizing that human life is inferential, that we continually come to conclusions about ourselves and the things and persons around us, is essential to think critically and reflectively.

CONSISTENCY   Thinking, acting, or speaking that is in agreement with what already has been thought, done, or expressed; intellectual or moral integrity. Human life and thought are filled with inconsistency, hypocrisy, and contradiction. We often say one thing and do another, judge ourselves and our friends by one standard and our antagonists by another, lean over backward to justify what we want or negate what does not serve our interests. Similarly, we often confuse desires with needs, treating our desires as equivalent to needs, putting what we want above the basic needs of others. Logical and moral consistency are fundamental values of fair-minded critical thinking. Social conditioning and native egocentrism often obscure social contradictions, inconsistency, and hypocrisy. *See also* personal contradiction, social contradiction, intellectual integrity, human nature.

CONTRADICT/CONTRADICTION   To assert the opposite of; to be contrary to, go against; a statement in opposition to another; a condition in which things tend to be contrary to each other; inconsistency; discrepancy; a person or thing containing or composed of contradictory elements. *See also* personal contradiction, social contradiction.

CRITERION (CRITERIA, pl.)   A standard, rule, or test by which something can be judged or measured. Human life, thought, and action are based on human values. Criteria are the standards by which we determine whether those values are achieved in any situation. Critical thinking depends upon making explicit the standards or criteria for rational or justifiable thinking and behavior. *See also* evaluate.

CRITICAL LISTENING   A mode of monitoring how we are listening to maximize our accurate understanding of what another person is saying. By understanding the logic of human communication—that everything spoken expresses point of view, uses some ideas and not others, has implications, and so on—critical thinkers can listen so as to enter empathically and analytically into the perspective of others. *See also* critical reading, critical writing, elements of thought, intellectual empathy.

CRITICAL PERSON   One who has mastered a range of intellectual skills and abilities. If that person generally uses those skills to advance his or her own selfish interests, that person is a critical thinker only in a weak or qualified sense. If that person generally uses those skills fair-mindedly, entering empathically into the points of view of others, he or she is a critical thinker in the strong or fullest sense. *See also* critical thinking.

CRITICAL READING   An active, intellectually engaged process in which the reader participates in an inner dialogue with the writer. Most people read uncritically and so miss some part of what is expressed and distort other parts. Critical readers realize the way in which reading, by its very nature, means entering into a point of view other than our own, the point of view of the writer. Critical readers actively look for assumptions, key concepts and ideas, reasons and justifications, supporting examples, parallel experiences, implications and consequences, and any other structural features of the written text, to interpret and assess it accurately and fairly. Critical readers do not evaluate written pieces until they accurately understand the author's viewpoint. *See also* elements of thought.

CRITICAL SOCIETY   A culture that rewards adherence to the values of critical thinking and hence does not use indoctrination and inculcation as basic modes of learning. Instead, it rewards reflective questioning, intellectual independence, and reasoned dissent. Socrates is not the only thinker to imagine a society in which independent critical thought becomes embodied in the concrete, day-

to-day life of individuals. William Graham Sumner, North America's distinguished anthropologist, explicitly formulated the ideal:

The critical habit of thought, if usual in a society, will pervade all its mores, because it is a way of taking up the problems of life. Men educated in it cannot be stampeded by stump orators and are never deceived by dithyrambic oratory. They are slow to believe. They can hold things as possible or probable in all degrees, without certainty and without pain. They can wait for evidence and weigh evidence, uninfluenced by the emphasis or confidence with which assertions are made on one side or the other. They can resist appeals to their dearest prejudices and all kinds of cajolery. Education in the critical faculty is the only education of which it can be truly said that it makes good citizens. (Folkways, 1906)

Until critical habits of thought pervade our society, however, schools as social institutions will tend to transmit the prevailing world view more or less uncritically, to transmit it as reality, not as a picture of reality. Education for critical thinking, then, requires that the school or classroom become a microcosm of a critical society. *See also* didactic instruction, dialogical instruction, intellectual virtues, knowledge.

CRITICAL THINKING   (1) Disciplined, self-directed thinking that exemplifies the perfections of thinking appropriate to a specific mode or domain of thinking; (2) thinking that displays mastery of intellectual skills and abilities; (3) the art of thinking about one's thinking while thinking, to make one's thinking better: more clear, more accurate, or more defensible; (4) thinking that is fully aware of and continually guards against the natural human tendency to self-deceive and rationalize to selfishly get what it wants. Critical thinking can be distinguished into two forms: (1) "selfish" or "sophistic," on the one hand, and (2) "fair-minded," on the other. In thinking critically, we use our command of the elements of thinking and the universal intellectual standards to adjust our thinking successfully to the logical demands of a type or mode of thinking. *See also* critical person, critical society, critical reading, critical listening, critical writing, perfections of thought, elements of thought, domains of thought, intellectual virtues.

CRITICAL WRITING   To express ourselves in written language requires that we arrange our ideas in some relationship to each other. When accuracy and truth are at issue, we must understand what our thesis is, how we can be support it, how we can elaborate it to make it intelligible to others, what objections to it can be raised from other points of view, what the limitations are to our point of view, and so forth. Disciplined writing requires disciplined thinking; disciplined thinking is enhanced by disciplined writing. *See also* critical listening, critical reading, logic of language.

CRITIQUE   An objective judging, analysis, or evaluation of something. The purpose of critique is the same as the purpose of critical thinking—to appreciate strengths as well as weaknesses, virtues as well as failings. Critical thinkers critique in order to redesign, remodel, and make better.

CULTURAL ASSOCIATION   Personal and cultural ideas about relationships and linkages absorbed or uncritically formed. If a person who treated me cruelly as a child had a certain tone of voice, I may find myself disliking other persons with the same tone of voice. Media advertising juxtaposes and joins logically unrelated things to influence our buying habits. When we grow up in a particular country or within a certain group within it, we form mental links that, if they remain unexamined, unduly influence our thinking. *See also* concept, critical society.

CULTURAL ASSUMPTION   An unassessed, often implicit belief adopted by virtue of upbringing in a society. We unconsciously take on our society's point of view, values, beliefs, and practices. At the root of each of these are many kinds of assumptions. Not knowing that we perceive, conceive, think, and experience within assumptions we have taken in, we take ourselves to be perceiving things as they are, not things as they appear from a cultural vantage point. Becoming aware of our cultural assumptions so we might critically examine them is a crucial dimension of critical thinking. This dimension, however, is almost totally absent from schooling. Although lip service to this ideal is common enough, a realistic emphasis is virtually unheard of. *See also* ethnocentricity, prejudice, social contradiction.

DATA   Facts, figures, or information from which conclusions can be inferred, or upon which interpretations or theories can be based. Critical thinkers must make certain to distinguish hard data from the inferences or conclusions drawn from them.

DIALECTICAL THINKING   Thinking within more than one perspective (dialogical thinking), conducted to test the strengths and weaknesses of opposing points of view. (Court trials and debates are, in a sense, dialectical.)

When thinking dialectically, reasoners pit two or more opposing points of view in competition with each other, developing each by providing support, raising objections, countering those objections, raising further objections, and so on. Dialectical thinking or discussion can be conducted so as to win by defeating the positions one disagrees with—using critical insight to support one's own view and point out flaws in other views (associated with critical thinking in the restricted or weak sense), or fair-mindedly, by conceding points that don't stand up to critique, trying to integrate or incorporate strong points found in other views, and using critical insight to develop a fuller and more accurate view (associated with critical thinking in the fuller or strong sense). *See also* multilogical problems, strong-sense critical thinkers, weak-sense critical thinkers.

DIALOGICAL THINKING   Thinking that involves a dialogue or extended exchange between different points of view or frames of reference. Students often learn effectively in dialogical situations, in circumstances in which they continually express their views to others and try to fit others' views into their own. *See also* Socratic questioning, monological thinking, multilogical thinking, dialectical thinking.

DIDACTIC INSTRUCTION   Teaching by telling. In didactic instruction, the teacher directly tells the student what to believe and think about a subject. The student's task is to remember what the teacher said and reproduce it on demand. In its most common form, this mode of teaching falsely assumes that one can give a person knowledge directly without that person having to think his or her way to it. It falsely assumes that knowledge can be separated from understanding and justification. It confuses the ability to state a principle with understanding it, the ability to supply a definition with knowing a word, and the act of saying that something is important with recognizing its importance. *See also* critical society, knowledge.

DOMAINS OF THOUGHT   Different modes of thinking determined by their fundamental purposes and agendas. Critical thinkers learn to discipline their thinking to take into account the nature of the issue or domain. We see this most clearly when we consider the difference between issues and thinking within different academic disciplines or subject areas. Hence, mathematical thinking is quite different from, say, historical thinking. Mathematics and history, we can say then, represent different domains of thought. *See also* logic of questions.

DOMINATING EGO   The irrational tendency of the mind to seek what it wants through the irrational use of direct control or power over people. Dominating strategies are an inherent part of one mode of egocentric thinking. This from of thinking seeks to gain advantage by irrationally wielding power over another. It is contrasted with *submissive* egocentric thinking, in which one irrationally seeks to gain some end by submitting to a person with power. Domination may be overt or covert. On the one hand, dominating egocentrism can involve harsh, dictatorial, tyrannical, or bullying behavior (e.g., a physically abusive spouse). On the other hand, it might involve subtle messages and behavior that imply the use of control or force if "necessary" (e.g., a supervisor reminding a subordinate, by quiet innuendo, that his or her employment is contingent upon unquestioning loyalty to the organization). Human irrational behavior is always some combination of dominating and submissive acts. No one's irrational acts are exclusively one or the other. In the ideal of a Fascist society, for example, everyone except the dictator is submissive to everyone above him and dominating to everyone below him. Opposite is *submissive ego.*

EGOCENTRICITY   A tendency to view everything in relationship to oneself, to confuse immediate perception (how things seem) with reality; the tendency to be self-centered, or to consider only oneself and one's own interests; selfishness. One's desires, values, and beliefs (seeming to be self-evidently correct or superior to those of others) are often uncritically used as the norm of all judgment and experience. Egocentricity is one of the fundamental impediments to critical thinking. As one learns to think critically in a strong sense, one learns to become more rational and less egocentric. *See also* human nature, strong-sense critical thinkers, ethnocentricity, sociocentricity, personal contradiction.

ELEMENTS OF THOUGHT   A universal set of components of thinking, each of which can be monitored for quality. They are: purpose, question, point of view, assumptions, inferences, implications, concepts, and information. When we understand the elements of thought, we have a powerful set of tools for analyzing thinking. We can ask questions such as: Are we clear about our purpose or goal? About the problem or question at issue? About our point of view or frame of reference? About our assumptions? About the claims we are making? About the reasons or evidence upon which we are basing our claims? About our inferences and line of reasoning? About the implications and consequences that follow from our reasoning? Critical thinkers develop skills of identifying and assessing these elements in their thinking and in the thinking of others.

EMOTION   A feeling aroused to the point of awareness, often a strong feeling or state of excitement. Our emotions are integrally related to our thoughts and desires. These three mental structures—thoughts, feelings, and desires—are continually influencing one another in reciprocal ways. We experience negative *feelings* for example, when we *think* things are not going well for us. Moreover, at any given moment, our thoughts, feelings, and desires are under the influence of either our rational faculties or our native irrational tendencies. When our *thinking* is irrational, or egocentric, irrational *feeling* states emerge. When this happens, we are excited by (what is at base) infantile anger, fear, and jealousy, and our objectivity and fair-mindedness decrease. Critical thinkers strive to recognize when dysfunctional thinking is leading to inappropriate or unproductive feeling states. They use their rational passions (for example, the passion to be fair) to reason themselves into feelings appropriate to the situation as it really is, rather than egocentrically reacting to distorted views of reality. Thus, emotions and feelings are not in themselves irrational; they are irrational only when they arise from egocentric thoughts. Strong-sense critical thinkers are committed to living a life in which rational emotions predominate and egocentric feelings are reduced to a minimum. *See also* rational emotions/passions, intellectual virtues, strong-sense critical thinkers.

EMPIRICAL   Relying or based on experiment, observation, or experience rather than on theory or meaning. It is important to continually distinguish considerations based on experiment, observation, or experience from those based on the meaning of a word or concept or implications of a theory. Uncritical thinkers often distort facts or experience to preserve a preconceived meaning or theory. For example, uncritical conservatives may distort the facts that support a liberal perspective to prevent empirical evidence from counting against a theory of the world that he or she holds rigidly; uncritical liberals return the favor by a parallel distortion of facts that support a conservative perspective. Indeed, within all perspectives and belief systems many will distort the facts rather than admit to a weakness in their favorite theory or belief. *See also* data, fact, evidence.

EMPIRICAL IMPLICATION   That which follows from a situation or fact, not resulting from the logic of language but, rather, from experience or scientific law. The redness of the coil on the stove empirically implies a high level of heat.

ETHICAL REASONING   Thinking through ethical problems and issues. Despite popular beliefs to the contrary, ethical reasoning is to be analyzed and assessed in the same way as any other domain of reasoning. Ethical reasoning involves the same elements and is to be assessed by the same standards of clarity, accuracy, precision, relevance, depth, breadth, logic, and significance. Ethical thinking, when reasonable, is ultimately driven by ethical concepts (for example, fairness) and principles (for example, "Like cases must be treated in a like manner"), as well as sound principles of critical thought. Understanding ethical principles is as important to sound ethical reasoning as understanding principles of math and biology is to mathematical and biological reasoning.

Ethical principles are guides for human conduct and imply what contributes to good or harm and what one is either obligated to do or obligated not to do. They enable us to determine the ethical value of a behavior even when that behavior is not, strictly speaking, an obligation. Ethical questions, like questions in any domain of thought, can be either questions with a clear-cut answer or questions with competing reasonable answers, matters about which we must strive to exercise our best judgment. They are *not* matters of personal preference. It makes no sense to say, "Oh, you prefer to be fair. Well, I prefer to be unfair!"

ETHNOCENTRICITY   A tendency to view one's own race or culture as privileged, based on the deep-seated belief that one's own group is superior to all others. Ethnocentrism is a form of egocentrism extended from the self to the group. Much uncritical or selfish critical thinking is either egocentric or ethnocentric in nature. (*Ethnocentrism* and *sociocentrism* are used synonymously, for the most part, though sociocentricity is broader, relating to any social group, including, for example, sociocentricity regarding one's profession.)

The "cure" for ethnocentrism or sociocentrism is empathic thought (thinking within the perspective of opposing groups and cultures). Empathic thought is rarely cultivated. Instead, many give lip service to tolerance while privileging the beliefs, norms, and practices of their own culture.

Critical thinkers are aware of the sociocentric nature of virtually all human groups and resist the pressure of group-think that emerges from in-group thinking. They realize that universal ethical standards supersede group expectations and demands when questions of an ethical nature are at issue. They do not assume that the groups to which they belong are inherently superior to other groups. Instead, they attempt to critique every group accurately, seeking to determine its strengths and weaknesses. Their loyalty to a country is critically based on the principles and ideals of the country and is not based on uncritical loyalty to person, party, or national traditions.

EVALUATE   To judge or determine the worth or quality of. Evaluation has a logic and should be carefully distinguished from mere subjective preference. The elements of its logic may be put in the form of questions that may be asked whenever an evaluation is to be carried out: (1) Do we clearly understand what we are evaluating? (2) Are we clear about our purpose? Is our purpose legitimate? (3) Given our purpose, what are the relevant criteria or standards for evaluation? (4) Do we have sufficient information about that which we are evaluating? Is that information relevant to the purpose? (5) Have we applied our criteria accurately and fairly to the facts as we know them? Uncritical thinkers often treat evaluation as mere preference or treat their evaluative judgments as direct observations not admitting of error.

EVIDENCE   The data on which a judgment or conclusion might be based or by which proof or probability might be established. Critical thinkers distinguish the evidence or raw data upon which they base their interpretations or conclusions from the inferences and assumptions that connect data to conclusions. Uncritical thinkers treat their conclusions as something given to them in experience, as something they directly observe in the world. As a result, they find it difficult to see why anyone might disagree with their conclusions. After all, the truth of their views, they believe, is right there for everyone to see! These people find it difficult or even impossible to describe the evidence or experience without confusing that description with their interpretation.

EXPLICIT   State openly and directly; distinctly expressed; definite. The term *explicit* is applied to that which is so clearly stated or distinctly set forth that there is no doubt as to its meaning. What is explicit is exact and precise, suggesting that which is made unmistakably clear. Critical thinkers strive to make explicit what is implicit in their thinking when that practice enables them to assess the thinking. They realize that problems in thinking often occur when thinking is unclear, vague, or ambiguous.

FACT   What actually happened, what is true; what is verifiable by empirical means; what is distinguished from interpretation, inference, judgment, or conclusion; the raw data. There is a range of distinct senses of the word *factual*. For example, sometimes it means simply "true" as opposed to "claimed to be true," or "empirical" as opposed to "conceptual" or "evaluative." Sometimes it means "that which can be verified or disproved by observation or empirical study." People often confuse these two senses, even to the point of accepting as true a statement that merely seems factual—for example, the scientific-sounding claim, "29.23 percent of Americans suffer from depression." Purported facts should be assessed for their accuracy, completeness, and relevance to the issue. Sources of purported facts should be assessed for their qualifications, track record, and impartiality. *See also* intellectual humility, knowledge.

FAIR   Treating both or all sides alike without reference to one's own feelings or interests; implies adherence to a standard of rightness or lawfulness without reference to one's own inclinations. *Impartial* and *unbiased* both imply freedom from prejudice for or against any side; *dispassionate* implies the absence of passion or strong emotion—hence, disinterested judgment; *objective* implies viewing persons or things without reference to oneself or one's interests.

FAIR-MINDEDNESS   A cultivated disposition of mind that enables the thinker to treat all perspectives relevant to an issue in an objective manner. It implies being conscious of the need to treat all viewpoints alike without reference to one's own feelings or selfish interests, or the feelings or selfish interests of one's friends, community, or nation. It implies adherence to intellectual standards without reference to one's own advantage or the advantage of one's group.

FAITH   (1) Blind belief that does not require proof or evidence; (2) complete confidence, trust, or reliance. A critical thinker does not accept faith in the first sense, "blind" faith, for every belief is reached on the basis of some thinking, which therefore may be assessed. Critical thinkers have faith or confidence in reason, but this confidence is not "blind." They recognize that reason and reasonability have proved their worth in the acquisition of knowledge. Ask yourself what it would be not to have faith in evidence, not to have faith in accuracy, or relevance.

FAITH IN REASON   Confidence that in the long run one's own higher interests and those of humankind at large will best be served by giving the freest play to reason—by encouraging people to come to their own conclusions through a process of developing their own rational faculties; confidence that, with proper encouragement and cultivation, people can learn to think for themselves, form rational viewpoints, draw reasonable conclusions, think coherently and logically, persuade each other by reason, and become reasonable, despite the deep-seated obstacles in the native character of the human mind and in society. Confidence in reason is developed through experiences in which one reasons one's way to insight, solves problems through reason, uses reason to persuade, and is persuaded by reason. Confidence in reason is undermined when one is expected to perform tasks without understanding why, to repeat statements without having verified or justified them, to accept beliefs on the sole basis of authority or social pressure.

FALLACY/FALLACIOUS   An error in reasoning, a flaw or defect in argument; an argument that doesn't conform to rules of good reasoning (especially one that appears to be sound); containing or based on a fallacy; deceptive in appearance or meaning; misleading; delusive.

HIGHER-ORDER LEARNING   Learning by thinking through the logic of disciplines, by thinking through the foundations, justification, implications, and value of facts, principles, skills, concepts, issues; learning so as to understand deeply. One can learn in keeping with the rational capacities of the human mind or in keeping with its irrational propensities, cultivating the capacity of the human mind to discipline and direct its thought through commitment to intellectual standards; or one can learn through mere association. Education for critical thought produces higher-order learning by helping students actively think their way to conclusions; discuss their thinking with other students and the teacher; entertain a variety of points of view; analyze concepts, theories, and explanations in their own terms; actively question the meaning and implications of what they learn; compare what they learn to what they have experienced; take seriously what they read and write; solve nonroutine problems; examine assumptions; and gather and assess evidence. When students are engaged in thinking within a subject—when they are learning to think historically, to think mathematically—they are developing higher-order thinking skills. *See also* dialogical thinking, lower-order learning, critical society, knowledge, principle, domains of thought.

HUMAN NATURE   The qualities common to all people. People have both a primary and a secondary nature. Our primary nature is spontaneous, egocentric, and strongly prone to the formation of irrational belief. It is the basis for our instinctual thought. People need no training to believe what we want to believe: what serves our immediate interests, what preserves our sense of personal comfort and righteousness, what minimizes our sense of inconsistency, and what presupposes our own correctness. People need no special training to believe what those around us believe: what our parents and friends believe, what is taught to us by religious and school authorities, what is repeated often by the media, and what is commonly believed in the nation in which we grow up.

People need no training to think that those who disagree with us are wrong and probably prejudiced. People need no training to assume that our own most fundamental beliefs are self-evidently true or easily justified by evidence. People naturally and spontaneously identify with their own beliefs. We experience most disagreements as personal attacks. The resulting defensiveness interferes with our capacity to empathize with or enter into other points of view. On the other hand, we need extensive and systematic practice to develop our secondary nature, our implicit capacity to function as rational persons. We need extensive and systematic practice to recognize the tendencies we have to form irrational beliefs. We need extensive practice to develop a dislike of inconsistency, a love of clarity, a passion to seek reasons and evidence and to be fair to points of view other than our own. We need extensive practice to recognize that we indeed have a point of view, that we live inferentially, that we do not have a direct pipeline to reality, that it is perfectly possible to have an overwhelming inner sense of the correctness of our views and still be wrong. *See also* intellectual virtues.

IDEA (CONCEPT, CATEGORY)   Anything existing in the mind as an object of knowledge or thought; *concept* refers to a generalized idea of a class of objects, based on knowledge of particular instances of the class. Critical thinkers are aware of the ideas (or concepts) they are using in their thinking. They recognize that all disciplines are driven by key concepts. They recognize that all thinking presupposes concepts in use. They seek to identify irrational ideas. They seek to use words (expressive of ideas) in keeping with educated usage. *See also* clarify, concept, logic, logic of language.

IMPLICATION   A claim or truth that follows from other claims or truths. By the "implications of reasoning," we mean that which follows from our thinking. It means that to which our thinking is leading us. If you say to someone that you "love" him or her, you imply that you are concerned with the person's welfare. If you make a promise, you imply that you intend to keep it. If you call a country a democracy, you imply that the political power is in the hands of the people at large (instead of a powerful minority). If you call yourself a feminist, you imply that you are in favor of political, social, and economic equality of the sexes. We often test the credibility of a person by seeing if he or she is true to the implications of his or her own words. "Say what you mean and mean what you say" is a sound principle of critical thinking (and of personal integrity as well, for that matter).

One of the most important skills of critical thinking is the ability to distinguish between what a statement or situation actually implies and what people may carelessly infer. Critical thinkers try to monitor their inferences to keep them in line with what is actually implied by what they know. When speaking, critical thinkers try to use words that imply only what they can legitimately justify. They recognize that there are established word usages that generate established implications. *See also* clarify, precision, logic of language, critical listening, critical reading, elements of thought.

INFERENCE   A step of the mind, an intellectual act by which one concludes that something is so in light of something else's being so, or seeming to be so. If you come at me with a knife in your hand, I probably would infer that you mean to cause me harm. Inferences can be accurate or inaccurate, logical or illogical, justified or unjustified. Inferences are based upon assumptions. *See also* implication.

INFORMATION   Statements, statistics, data, facts, and diagrams gathered in any way, as by reading, observation, or hearsay. Information itself does not imply validity or accuracy. By "using information in our reasoning," we mean using some set of facts, data, or experiences to support our conclusions. Whenever someone is reasoning, it makes sense to ask, "What facts or information are you basing your reasoning on?" The informational basis for reasoning is always important and often crucial. For example, in deciding whether to support capital punishment, we need factual information to support our side of the argument. Statements representing information that one might present to support the position that capital punishment is unjustified might be:

- "Since the death penalty was reinstated by the Supreme Court in 1976, for every seven prisoners who were executed, one prisoner awaiting execution was found to be innocent and released."

- "At least 381 homicide convictions have been overturned since 1963 because prosecutors concealed evidence of innocence or presented evidence they knew to be false."

- "A study by the U.S. General Accounting Office found racial prejudice in death sentencing. . . . Killers of whites were proportionally more likely to be executed than were killers of blacks."

- "Since 1984, 34 mentally retarded people have been executed."*

A separate question is whether the information presented is accurate. Also, we should recognize that the other side has information to back it as well.

INSIGHT   The ability to see and understand clearly and deeply the inner nature of things. Instruction for critical thinking fosters insight rather than mere performance. It cultivates the achievement of deeper knowledge and understanding through insight. Thinking one's way into and through a subject leads to insights as one synthesizes what one is learning, relating one subject to other subjects and all subjects to personal experience. Rarely is insight formulated as a goal in present curricula and texts. *See also* dialogical instruction, higher-order learning, lower-order learning, didactic instruction, intellectual humility.

INTELLECTUAL AUTONOMY   Having rational control of one's beliefs, values, and inferences. The ideal of critical thinking is to learn to think for oneself, to gain command over one's thought processes. Intellectual autonomy does not entail willfulness, stubbornness, or rebellion. It entails a commitment to analyzing and evaluating beliefs on the basis of reason and evidence, to questioning when it is rational to question, to believing when it is rational to believe, and to conforming when it is rational to conform. *See also* know, knowledge.

INTELLECTUAL CIVILITY   A commitment to take others seriously as thinkers, to treat them as intellectual equals, to grant respect and full attention to their views—a commitment to persuade rather than browbeat. It is distinguished from intellectual rudeness: verbally attacking others, dismissing them, stereotyping their views. Intellectual civility is not a matter of mere courtesy but, instead, arises from a sense that communication itself requires honoring others' views and their capacity to reason.

INTELLECTUAL COURAGE   Willingness to face and fairly assess ideas, beliefs, or viewpoints to which we have not yet given a serious hearing, regardless of our strong negative reactions to them; arises from the recognition that ideas considered dangerous or absurd are rationally justified sometimes, in whole or in part, and that conclusions or beliefs that those around us espouse or inculcate in us are sometimes false or misleading. To determine for ourselves which is which, we must not passively and uncritically accept what we have learned. Intellectual courage comes into play here because inevitably we will come to see truth in some ideas considered dangerous and absurd and distortion or falsity in some ideas strongly held in our social group. It takes courage to be true to our own thinking in these circumstances. Examining cherished beliefs is difficult, and the penalties for nonconformity are often severe.

INTELLECTUAL CURIOSITY   A strong desire to understand deeply, to figure out things, to propose and assess useful and plausible hypotheses and explanations, to learn, to find out. People do not learn well, do not gain knowledge, unless they want knowledge—deep, accurate, complete understanding. When people lack passion for figuring out things—have intellectual apathy—they tend to settle for an incomplete, incoherent, sketchy sense of things incompatible with a critically developed, richer, fuller conception. Intellectual curiosity can flourish only when it is allowed and encouraged, when people are able to pose and pursue questions of interest to them, and when their intellectual curiosity pays off in increasing understanding.

INTELLECTUAL DISCIPLINE   The trait of thinking in accordance with intellectual standards, intellectual rigor, carefulness, order, conscious control. Undisciplined thinkers do not recognize when they come to unwarranted conclusions, confuse ideas, fail to consider pertinent

---

*Moratorium Now, *New York Times,* Nov. 22, 1999.

evidence, and so on. Thus, intellectual discipline is at the very heart of becoming a critical person. It takes discipline of mind to stay focused on the intellectual task at hand, to locate and carefully assess needed evidence, to systematically analyze and address questions and problems, to hold one's thinking to intellectual standards such as clarity, precision, completeness, and consistency. Intellectual discipline is achieved slowly, bit by bit, and only through deep commitment.

INTELLECTUAL EMPATHY   Understanding the need to put oneself imaginatively in the place of others to genuinely understand them. We must recognize our egocentric tendency to identify truth with our immediate perceptions or longstanding beliefs. Intellectual empathy correlates with the ability to reconstruct accurately the viewpoints and reasoning of others and to reason from premises, assumptions, and ideas other than our own. This trait also requires that we remember occasions when we were wrong, despite an intense conviction that we were right, and consider that we might be similarly deceived in a case at hand.

INTELLECTUAL HUMILITY   Awareness of the limits of one's knowledge, including sensitivity to circumstances in which one's native egocentrism is likely to function self-deceptively; sensitivity to bias and prejudice in, and limitations of, one's viewpoint. Intellectual humility is based on the recognition that no one should claim more than he or she actually knows. It does not imply spinelessness or submissiveness. It implies the lack of intellectual pretentiousness, boastfulness, or conceit, combined with insight into the strengths or weaknesses of the logical foundations of one's beliefs.

INTELLECTUAL INTEGRITY   Recognition of the need to be true to one's own thinking, to be consistent in the intellectual standards one applies, to hold oneself to the same rigorous standards of evidence and proof to which one holds one's antagonists, to practice what one advocates for others, and to honestly admit discrepancies and inconsistencies in one's own thought and action. This trait develops best in a supportive atmosphere in which people feel secure and free enough to honestly acknowledge their inconsistencies and can develop and share realistic ways of ameliorating them. It requires honest acknowledgment of the difficulties in achieving greater consistency.

INTELLECTUAL PERSEVERANCE   Willingness and consciousness of the need to pursue intellectual insights

and truths despite difficulties, obstacles, and frustrations; firm adherence to rational principles despite irrational opposition from others; a sense of the need to struggle with confusion and unsettled questions over an extended time to achieve deeper understanding or insight.

INTELLECTUAL RESPONSIBILITY   A sense of obligation to fulfill one's duties in intellectual matters. Intellectually responsible people feel strongly obliged to achieve a high level of precision and accuracy in their reasoning and are deeply committed to gathering complete, relevant, adequate evidence. This sense of obligation arises when people recognize the need for meeting the intellectual standards required by rational, fair-minded thought.

INTELLECTUAL SENSE OF JUSTICE   Willingness and consciousness of the need to entertain all viewpoints sympathetically and to assess them with the same intellectual standards, without reference to one's own feelings or vested interests, or the feelings or vested interests of one's friends, community, or nation; implies adherence to intellectual standards without reference to one's own advantage or the advantage of one's group.

INTELLECTUAL STANDARD   Some measure, principle, or model by which things of the same class are compared, to determine their quality or value. Intellectual standards are concepts and principles by which reasoning should be judged to determine its quality or value. Because their contextualized application generates the specific criteria by which reasoning is assessed, intellectual standards are fundamental to critical thinking. Critical thinkers are able to take apart their thinking (focusing on the elements of reasoning) and assess the parts of thinking based on intellectual standards. The most important intellectual standards for thinking are clarity, accuracy, relevance, precision, breadth, depth, logic, significance, consistency, fairness, completeness, plausibility, probability, and reliability.

INTELLECTUAL VIRTUES   The traits of mind and intellectual character traits necessary for right action and thinking; the traits essential for fair-mindedness. They distinguish the narrow-minded, self-serving critical thinker from the open-minded, truth-seeking critical thinker. Intellectual traits are interdependent, each developing simultaneously in conjunction with the others. They cannot be imposed from without; they must be developed from within. The intellectual virtues include intellectual sense of justice, intellectual perseverance, intellectual integrity, intellectual humility, intellectual empathy, intellectual courage, intellectual confidence in reason, and intellectual autonomy.

INTERPRET   To give one's own conception of, to place in the context of one's own experience, perspective, point of view, or philosophy. Interpretations should be distinguished from the facts, the evidence, the situation. (I may interpret someone's silence as an expression of hostility toward me. This interpretation may or may not be correct. I may have projected my patterns of motivation and behavior onto that person, or I may have accurately noticed this pattern in the other.) The best interpretations take the most evidence into account. Critical thinkers recognize their interpretations, distinguish them from evidence, consider alternative interpretations, and reconsider their interpretations in the light of new evidence. All learning involves personal interpretation, because whatever we learn we must integrate into our own thinking and action. What we learn we must give a meaning to. It must be meaningful to us, and hence involves interpretive acts on our part. *Didactic instruction,* in attempting to implant knowledge directly in students' minds, typically ignores the role of personal interpretation in learning.

INTUITION   The direct knowing or learning of something without the conscious use of reasoning. We sometimes seem to know or learn things without recognizing how we came to that knowledge. When this occurs, we experience an inner sense that what we believe is true. The problem is that sometimes we are correct (and have genuinely experienced an intuition) and sometimes we are incorrect (having fallen victim to one of our prejudices). Critical thinkers do not blindly accept what they think or believe but cannot prove as true. They realize how easily they confuse intuitions and prejudices. Critical thinkers may follow their inner sense that something is so, but only with a healthy sense of intellectual humility.

A second sense of intuition that is important for critical thinking is suggested in the following sentence: "To develop your critical-thinking abilities, it is important to develop your critical-thinking intuitions." We can learn concepts at various levels. If we learn nothing more than an abstract definition for a word and do not learn how to apply it effectively in a wide variety of situations, we end up with no intuitive basis for applying it. We lack the insight into how, when, and why it applies. We develop critical-thinking intuitions when we gain the practical insights necessary for a ready and swift application of concepts to cases in a large array of circumstances. We want critical thinking to be intuitive to us, ready and available for immediate translation into everyday thought and experience.

IRRATIONAL/IRRATIONALITY   (1) Lacking the power to reason; (2) contrary to reason or logic; (3) senseless, absurd. Uncritical thinkers have failed to develop the ability or power to reason well. Their beliefs and practices, then, are often contrary to what is reasonable, sensible, and logical and are sometimes blatantly absurd. The terms can be applied to persons, acts, emotions, policies, laws, social practices, belief systems, even whole societies—to virtually any human construct. *See also* reason, rationality, logic.

IRRATIONAL LEARNING   Learning that is not based on rational assent. Not all learning is automatically or even commonly rational. Much that we learn in everyday life is quite distinctively irrational. It is quite possible—and indeed the bulk of human learning is unfortunately of this character—to come to believe any number of things without knowing how or why. We believe for irrational reasons—because those around us believe, because we are rewarded for believing, because we are afraid to disbelieve, because our vested interest is served by belief, because we are more comfortable with belief, or because we have ego-identified ourselves, our image, or our personal being with belief. In all of these cases, our beliefs are without rational grounding, without good reason and evidence, without the foundation a rational person demands. Conversely, we become rational to the extent that our beliefs and actions are grounded in good reasons and evidence; to the extent that we recognize and critique our own irrationality; to the extent that we are not moved by bad reasons and a multiplicity of irrational motives, fears, and desires; to the extent that we have cultivated a passion for clarity, accuracy, and fair-mindedness. These global skills, passions, and dispositions, integrated into behavior and thought, characterize the rational, the educated, and the critical person. *See also* higher-order learning, lower-order learning, knowledge, didactic instruction.

JUDGMENT   (1) The act of deciding; (2) understanding and good sense. A person has good judgment when he or she typically judges and decides on the basis of understanding and good sense. Whenever we form a belief or opinion, make a decision, or act, we do so on the basis of implicit or explicit judgments. All thought presupposes making judgments concerning what is so and what is not so, what is true and what is not. To cultivate people's ability to think critically is to foster their judgment, to help them develop the habit of judging on the basis of reason, evidence, logic, and good sense. Good judgment is developed not by merely learning about principles of good judgment but by frequent practice in judging and assessing judgments.

JUSTIFY/JUSTIFICATION   To show a belief, opinion, action, or policy to be in accord with reason and evidence; ethical acceptability. Education should foster reasonability in students. This goal requires that teachers and students develop the disposition to ask for and give justifications for beliefs, opinions, actions, and policies. Asking for a justification should not be viewed as an insult or attack but, rather, as a normal act of a rational person.

KNOW   To have a clear perception or understanding of, to be sure of, to have a firm mental grasp of. *Information* applies to data gathered in any way, as by reading, observation, or hearsay, and does not necessarily connote validity; *knowledge* applies to any body of facts gathered by study or observation, and to the ideas inferred from these facts, and connotes an understanding of what is known. Critical thinkers distinguish knowledge from opinion and belief. *See also* knowledge.

KNOWLEDGE   A clear and justifiable grasp of what is so or of how to do something. Knowledge is based on understanding or skill, which in turn is based on thought, study, and experience. "Thoughtless knowledge" is a contradiction. "Blind knowledge" is a contradiction. "Unjustifiable knowledge" is a contradiction. Knowledge implies justifiable belief or skilled action. Hence, when students blindly memorize and are tested for recall, they are not being tested for knowledge.

In present-day schooling, knowledge is continually confused with mere recall. This confusion is a deep-seated impediment to the integration of critical thinking into schooling.

Genuine knowledge is inseparable from thinking minds. We often wrongly talk of knowledge as if it could be divorced from thinking, as though it could be gathered by one person and given to another in the form of a collection of sentences to remember. When we talk in this way, we forget that knowledge, by its very nature, depends on thought. Knowledge is produced by thought, analyzed by thought, comprehended by thought, organized, evaluated,

maintained, and transformed by thought. Knowledge can be acquired only through thought. Knowledge exists, properly speaking, only in minds that have comprehended and justified it through thought. Knowledge is not to be confused with belief or with symbolic representation of belief. Humans easily and frequently believe things that are false or believe things to be true without knowing them to be so. A book contains knowledge only in a derivative sense, only because minds can read it thoughtfully and through that process gain knowledge.

LOGIC   (1) Correct reasoning or the study of correct reasoning and its foundations; (2) the relationships between propositions (supports, assumes, implies, contradicts, counts against, is relevant to); (3) the system of principles, concepts, and assumptions that underlies any discipline, activity, or practice; (4) the set of rational considerations that bear upon the truth or justification of any belief or set of beliefs; (5) the set of rational considerations that bear upon the settlement of any question or set of questions.

The word "logic" covers a range of related concerns all bearing upon the question of rational justification and explanation. All human thought and behavior are based to some extent on logic rather than instinct. Humans try to figure things out using ideas, meanings, and thought. This intellectual behavior inevitably involves logic or considerations of a logical sort—some sense of what is relevant and irrelevant, of what supports and what counts against a belief, of what we should and should not assume, of what we should and should not claim, of what we do and do not know, of what is and is not implied, of what does and does not contradict, of what we should or should not do or believe.

Concepts have a logic in that we can investigate the conditions under which they do and do not apply, of what is relevant or irrelevant to them, of what they do or don't imply. Questions have a logic in that we can investigate the conditions under which they can be settled. Disciplines have a logic in that they have purposes and a set of logical structures that bear upon those purposes: assumptions, concepts, issues, data, theories, claims, implications, consequences.

The concept of logic is a seminal notion in critical thinking. It takes considerable time, however, before most people become comfortable with its many uses. In part, this stems from our failure to monitor our own thinking in keeping with the standards of reason and logic. This is not to deny, of course, that logic is involved in all human thinking. Rather, it is to say that the logic we use is often implicit and unexpressed, and sometimes contradictory. *See also* knowledge, higher-order thinking, logic of a discipline, logic of language, logic of questions, lower-order learning.

LOGIC OF A DISCIPLINE   The notion that every technical term has logical relationships with other technical terms, that some terms are logically more basic than others, and that every discipline relies on concepts, assumptions, and theories; makes claims; gives reasons and evidence; avoids contradictions and inconsistencies; and has implications and consequences. Though all students study disciplines, most are ignorant of the logic of the disciplines they study. This severely limits their ability to grasp the discipline as a whole, to think independently within it, to compare and contrast it with other disciplines, and to apply it outside the context of academic assignments.

Typically, students do not look for seminal terms as they study an area. They do not strive to translate technical terms into analogies and ordinary words they understand, or to distinguish technical from ordinary uses of terms. They do not look for the basic assumptions of the disciplines they study. On the whole, they do not know what assumptions are or why it is important to examine them. What they have in their heads exists like so many BBs in a bag. Whether one thought supports or follows from another, whether one thought elaborates another, exemplifies, presupposes, or contradicts another, are matters that students have not learned to think about. They have not learned to use thought to understand thought—another way of saying that they have not learned how to use thought to gain knowledge.

Instruction for critical thinking cultivates students' ability to make explicit the logic of what they study. This emphasis gives depth and breadth to study and learning. It lies at the heart of the differences between lower-order and higher-order learning. *See also* knowledge.

LOGIC OF LANGUAGE   For a language to exist and be learnable by persons from a variety of cultures, it is necessary that words have definite uses and defined concepts that transcend any culture. The English language, for example, is learned by many peoples of the world who are unfamiliar with English or North American cultures. Critical thinkers must learn to use their native language with precision, in keeping with educated usage.

Many students do not understand the significant relationship between precision in language use and precision in thought. Consider, for example, how most students relate to their native language. Questioned about the meanings of words, they often say that people have their own meanings for all the words they use. If this were true, we could not understand each other. Students often speak and write in vague sentences because they do not have rational criteria for choosing words; they simply write whatever words pop into their heads. They do not realize that every language has a highly refined logic that one must learn in order to express oneself precisely. They do not realize that even words similar in meaning typically have different implications.

Consider, for example, the words *explain, expound, explicate, elucidate, interpret,* and *construe. Explain* implies the process of making clear and intelligible something not understood or known. *Expound* implies a systematic and thorough explanation, often by an expert. *Explicate* implies a scholarly analysis developed in detail. *Elucidate* implies shedding light by clear and specific illustration or explanation. *Interpret* implies bringing out meanings not immediately apparent. *Construe* implies forming a specific interpretation of something whose meaning is ambiguous. *See also* clarify, concept.

LOGIC OF QUESTIONS   The range of rational considerations that bear upon settlement of a given question or group of questions. Critical thinkers are adept at analyzing questions to determine what, precisely, a question asks and how to go about rationally settling it. Critical thinkers recognize that different kinds of questions often call for different modes of thinking, different kinds of considerations, and different procedures and techniques. Uncritical thinkers often confuse distinct questions and use considerations irrelevant to an issue while ignoring relevant ones.

LOWER-ORDER LEARNING   Learning by rote memorization, association, and drill. Schools use a variety of forms of lower-order learning that we can identify by understanding the relative lack of logic informing them. Because lower-order learning is learning by sheer association or rote, students come to think of history class, for example, as a place where they hear names, dates, places, events, and outcomes, where they try to remember them and state them on tests. Math comes to be thought of as numbers, symbols, and formulas—mysterious things they mechanically manipulate as the teacher told them, to get the right answer. Literature is often thought of as uninteresting stories to remember, along with what the teacher said is important about them.

Consequently, these students leave with a jumble of undigested fragments, scraps left over after they have forgotten most of what they stored in their short-term memory for tests. They do not grasp the logic of what they learn. Rarely do they relate what they learn to their own experience or critique each by means of the other. Rarely do they try to test what they learn in everyday life. Rarely do they ask, "Why is this so? How does this relate to what I already know? How does this relate to what I am learning in other classes?"

In a nutshell, few students think of what they are learning as worthy of being arranged logically in their mind or have the slightest idea of how to do so. *See also* didactic instruction, monological problems, multilogical problems, multilogical thinking.

MONOLOGICAL PROBLEMS   One-dimensional problems that can be solved by reasoning exclusively within one point of view or frame of reference. Consider the following problems: (1) Ten full crates of walnuts weigh 410 pounds, whereas an empty crate weighs 10 pounds. How much do the walnuts alone weigh? and (2) In how many days of the week does the third letter of the day's name immediately follow the first letter of the day's name in the alphabet? We call these problems, and the means by which they are solved, *monological*. They are settled within one frame of reference with a definite set of logical moves. When the right set of moves is performed, the problem is settled. The answer or solution proposed can be shown by standards implicit in the frame of reference to be the right answer or solution.

Most important human problems are multilogical rather than monological. They are non-atomic problems inextricably joined to other problems, with some conceptual messiness to them, often with important values lurking in the background. When the problems have an empirical dimension, that dimension tends to have a controversial scope. In multilogical problems, it is often arguable how some facts should be considered and interpreted and how their significance should be determined. When they have a conceptual dimension, the concepts usually can be pinned down in different ways. While life presents us with predominantly multilogical problems, schooling

today overemphasizes monological problems. Worse, present instructional practices frequently treat multilogical problems as though they were monological. The posing of multilogical problems and their consideration from multiple points of view play an important role in the cultivation of critical thinking and higher-order learning.

MONOLOGICAL THINKING   One-dimensional thought conducted exclusively within one point of view or frame of reference—figuring out how much this $67.49 pair of shoes with a 25 percent discount will cost me; learning what signing this contract obliges me to do; finding out what year Kennedy was elected president. A person can think monologically whether the question is or is not genuinely monological. (For example, if one considers the question "Who caused the Civil War?" only from a Northerner's perspective, one is thinking monologically about a multilogical question.) Strong-sense critical thinkers avoid monological thinking when the question is multilogical. Moreover, higher-order learning requires multilogical thought even when the problem is monological (for example, learning a concept in chemistry), as students must explore and assess their original beliefs to develop insight into new ideas.

MULTILOGICAL PROBLEMS   Multidimensional problems that can be analyzed and approached from more than one (often from conflicting) points of view or frames of reference. For example, many ecological problems have a variety of dimensions to them—historical, social, economic, biological, chemical, moral, political. A person who is comfortable thinking through multilogical problems is comfortable thinking within multiple perspectives, engaging in dialogical and dialectical thinking, practicing intellectual empathy, thinking across disciplines and domains. *See also* monological problems, logic of questions, logic of disciplines, intellectual empathy, dialogical instruction.

MULTILOGICAL THINKING   Thought that empathically enters, considers, and reasons within multiple points of view. *See also* multilogical problems, dialectical thinking, dialogical instruction.

NATIONAL BIAS   Prejudice in favor of one's country, its beliefs, traditions, practices, image, and world view; a form of sociocentrism or ethnocentrism. It is natural, if not inevitable, for people to be favorably disposed toward the beliefs, traditions, practices, and world view within which they grew up. This favorable inclination commonly becomes a form of prejudice—a more or less rigid, irrational ego-identification that significantly distorts one's view of one's own nation and the world at large. It is manifested in a tendency to mindlessly take the side of one's own government, to uncritically accept governmental accounts of the nature of disputes with other nations, to uncritically exaggerate the virtues of one's own nation while playing down the virtues of enemy nations.

National bias is reflected in the press and media coverage of every nation of the world. Events are included or excluded according to what seems significant within the dominant world view of the nation, and are shaped into stories to validate that view. Though constructed to fit into a certain view of the world, the news stories are presented as neutral, objective accounts, and are uncritically accepted as such because people tend to assume uncritically that their own view of things is the way things really are.

To become responsible, critically thinking citizens and fair-minded people, students must practice identifying national bias in the news and in their texts, and broaden their perspective beyond that of uncritical nationalism. *See also* ethnocentricity, sociocentricity, bias, prejudice, world view, intellectual empathy, critical society, dialogical instruction, knowledge.

OPINION   A belief, typically one open to dispute. Sheer unreasoned subjective opinion or preference should be distinguished from reasoned judgment—beliefs formed on the basis of careful reasoning. *See also* evaluation, judgment, justify, know, knowledge, reasoned judgment.

PERFECTIONS OF THOUGHT   A natural excellence or fitness to thinking, viewed in an attempt to understand or make sense of the world. This excellence is manifest in its clarity, precision, specificity, accuracy, relevance, consistency, logic, depth, completeness, significance, fairness, and adequacy. These perfections are general achievements of thought. Their absence represents legitimate concerns irrespective of the discipline or domain of thought.

To develop one's mind and discipline, one's thinking with respect to these standards requires regular practice and long-term cultivation. Of course, achieving these standards is a relative matter and varies to some degree among domains of thought. Being precise while doing mathematics is not the same as being precise while writing a poem, describing an experience, or explaining a historical event.

What is more, skilled propaganda, skilled political debate, skilled defense of a group's interests, skilled deception of one's enemy may require the violation or selective application of any of the above standards. Perfecting one's thought as an instrument for success in a world based on power and advantage differs from perfecting one's thought for the apprehension and defense of fair-minded, balanced truthfulness. To develop one's critical thinking skills merely to the level of adequacy for social success is to sacrifice the higher perfections of thought for pragmatic gain and generally involves more than a little self-deception.

PERSONAL CONTRADICTION   An inconsistency in life wherein people say one thing and do another, or use a double standard, judging themselves and their friends by an easier standard than that used for people they don't like; typically a form of hypocrisy accompanied by self-deception. Most personal contradictions remain unconscious. People too often ignore the difficulty of becoming intellectually and morally consistent, preferring instead merely to admonish others. Personal contradictions are more likely to be discovered, analyzed, and reduced in an atmosphere in which they can be openly admitted and realistically considered without excessive penalty. *See also* egocentricity, intellectual integrity.

POINT OF VIEW   Perspective. Human thought is relational and selective. It is impossible to understand any person, event, or phenomenon from every vantage point simultaneously. Our purposes often control how we see things. Critical thinking requires that we take this into account when analyzing and assessing thinking. This is not to say that human thought is incapable of truth and objectivity, but only that human truth, objectivity, and insight are limited and partial, not total and absolute. By reasoning within a point of view, then, we mean that our thinking inevitably has some comprehensive focus or orientation. Our thinking is focused *on* something *from* some angle.

We can change either what we are focusing on or the angle of our focus. We often give names to the angle from which we are thinking about something. For example, we could look at something politically or scientifically, poetically or philosophically. We might look at something conservatively or liberally, religiously or secularly. We might look at something from a cultural or a financial perspective, or both. Once we understand how someone is approaching a question or topic (the person's comprehensive perspective), we usually are much better able to understand the logic of the person's thinking as an organized whole.

PRECISION   The quality of being accurate, definite, and exact. The standards and modes of precision vary according to subject and context. *See also* logic of language, elements of thought.

PREJUDICE   A judgment, belief, opinion, or point of view—favorable or unfavorable—formed before the facts are known, resistant to evidence and reason, or in disregard of facts that contradict it. Self-announced prejudice is rare. Prejudice almost always exists in obscured, rationalized, socially validated, functional forms. It enables people to sleep peacefully at night even while flagrantly abusing the rights of others. It enables people to get more of what they want, or to get it more easily. It is often sanctioned with a superabundance of pomp and self-righteousness. Unless we recognize these powerful tendencies toward selfish thought in our social institutions, even in what seem to be lofty actions and moralistic rhetoric, we will not face squarely the problem of prejudice in human thought and action.

Uncritical and selfishly critical thought are often prejudiced. Most instruction in schools today, because students do not think their way to what they accept as true, tends to give students prejudices rather than knowledge. For example, partly as a result of schooling, people often accept as authorities those who sprinkle their statements liberally with numbers and intellectual-sounding language, however irrational or unjust their positions. This prejudice toward pseudo-authority impedes rational assessment. *See also* insight, knowledge.

PREMISE   A proposition upon which an argument is based or from which a conclusion is drawn. A starting point of reasoning. For example, in commenting on someone's reasoning, one might say, "You seem to be reasoning from the premise that everyone is selfish in everything they do. Do you hold this belief?"

PRINCIPLE   A fundamental truth, law, doctrine, value, or commitment upon which others are based. Rules, which are more specific than principles, and often superficial and arbitrary, are based on principles. Rules are more algorithmic; they needn't be understood to be followed. Principles must be understood to be applied or followed appropriately. One important type of principles is ethical principles, which are guides for human conduct. Critical thinking is dependent on principles, not rules and procedures. Critical thinking is principled, not procedural thinking. Principles must be practiced and applied to be internalized. *See also* higher-order learning, lower-order learning, judgment.

PROBLEM   A question, matter, situation, or person that is perplexing or difficult to figure out, handle, or resolve. Problems, like questions, can be divided into many types. Each has a certain logic. *See also* logic of questions, monological problems, multilogical problems.

PROBLEM SOLVING   The process of reaching solutions. Whenever a problem cannot be solved formulaically or robotically, critical thinking is required—first, to determine the nature and dimensions of the problem, and then, in the light of the first, to determine the considerations, points of view, concepts, theories, data, and reasoning relevant to its solution. Extensive practice in independent problem solving is essential to developing critical thought. Problem solving is rarely best approached procedurally or as a series of rigidly followed steps. For example, problem solving schemas typically begin, "State the problem." Rarely can problems be stated precisely and fairly prior to analysis, gathering of evidence, and dialogical or dialectical thought wherein several provisional descriptions of the problem are proposed, assessed, and revised.

PROOF   Evidence or reasoning so strong or certain as to demonstrate the truth or acceptability of a conclusion beyond a reasonable doubt. How strong evidence or reasoning has to be to demonstrate what it purports to prove varies from context to context, depending on the significance of the conclusion or the seriousness of implications following from it. *See also* domains of thought.

PURPOSE   Object, aim, goal, end in view; something one intends to get or do. By reasoning having a purpose, we mean that when humans think about the world, we do not do so randomly but, rather, in line with our goals, desires, needs, and values. Our thinking is an integral part of a patterned way of acting in the world, and we act, even in simple matters, with some set of ends in view. To understand someone's thinking—including our own—we must understand the functions it serves, what it is about, the direction it is moving, the ends that make sense of it. Most of what we are after in our thinking is not obvious to us. Raising human goals and desires to the level of conscious realization is an important part of critical thinking.

QUESTION   A problem or matter open to discussion or inquiry, something that is asked, as in seeking to learn or gain knowledge. By reasoning upon some question, issue, or problem, we mean that when we think about the world in line with our goals, desires, needs, and values, we often come up against questions we need to answer, problems we need to solve, issues we need to resolve. Therefore, when we find ourselves facing a difficulty, it makes sense to say, "What is the question we need to answer?" or, "What is the problem we need to solve?" or, "What is the issue we need to resolve?" To improve our ability to think well, it is important to learn how to put the questions, problems, and issues we need to deal with in a clear and distinct way. If you change the question, you change the criteria you have to meet to settle it. If you modify the problem, you need to modify how you are going to solve the problem. If you shift the issue, new considerations become relevant to its resolution.

RATIONAL/RATIONALITY   That which conforms to principles of good reasoning, is sensible, shows good judgment, is consistent, logical, complete, and relevant. When we refer to something or someone as rational, we have in mind the quality of being based on or informed by sound reasoning or justified evidence. Rationality is a summary term such as *virtue* or *goodness*. It is manifested in an unlimited number of ways and depends on a host of principles. There is some ambiguity in it, depending on whether one considers only the consistency and effectiveness by which one pursues one's ends, or whether it includes the assessment of ends themselves. There is also ambiguity in whether one considers selfish ends to be rational, even when they conflict with what is just. Does a rational person have to be just or only skilled in pursuing his or her interests? Is it rational to be rational in an irrational world? *See also* perfections of thought, irrational/irrationality, logic, intellectual virtues, weak-sense critical thinkers, strong-sense critical thinkers.

RATIONAL EMOTIONS/PASSIONS   The affective side of reason and critical thought. R. S. Peters (1973) explained the significance of "rational passions" as follows:

There is, for instance, the hatred of contradictions and inconsistencies, together with the love of clarity and hatred of confusion without which words could not be held to relatively constant meanings and testable rules and generalizations stated. A reasonable man cannot, without some special explanation, slap his sides with delight or express indifference if he is told that what he says is confused, incoherent, and perhaps riddled with contradictions.

Reason is the antithesis of arbitrariness. In its operation it is supported by the appropriate passions which are mainly negative in character—the hatred of irrelevance, special pleading, and arbitrary fiat. The more developed emotion of indignation is aroused when some excess of arbitrariness is perpetuated in a situation where people's interests and claims are at stake. The positive side of this is the passion for fairness and impartial consideration of claims. . . . A man who is prepared to reason must feel strongly that he must follow the arguments and decide things in terms of where they lead. He must have a sense of the impersonality of such considerations. Insofar as thoughts about persons enter his head, they should be tinged with the respect which is due to another who, like himself, may have a point of view which is worth considering, who may have a glimmering of the truth which has so far eluded himself. A person who proceeds in this way, who is influenced by such passions, is what we call a reasonable man.

RATIONALIZE   To devise socially plausible explanations or excuses for one's actions, desires, and beliefs, when these are not one's actual motives. To rationalize is to give reasons that sound good but are not honest and accurate. Rationalization is often used in situations in which one is pursuing one's vested interests while trying to maintain the appearance of high moral purpose. Politicians, for instance, are continually rationalizing their actions, implying that they are acting from high motives when they usually are acting as they are because they have received large donations from vested interest groups that profit from the action taken. Those who held slaves often rationalized that slavery was justified because the slaves were like children and had to be taken care of. Rationalization is a defense mechanism the egocentric mind uses to enable people to get what they want without having to face the reality that their motives are selfish or their behavior unconscionable. Rationalizations enable us to keep our actual motives beneath the level of consciousness. We then can sleep peacefully at night while we behave unethically by day.

RATIONAL SELF   Human character and nature to the extent that we seek to base our beliefs and actions on good reasoning and evidence. Who we are, what our true character is and our predominant qualities are, are typically different from who we think we are. Human egocentrism and accompanying self-deception often stand in the way of our gaining more insight into ourselves. We can develop a rational self, become a person who gains significant insight into what our true character is, only by reducing our egocentrism and self-deception. Critical thinking is essential to this process.

RATIONAL SOCIETY   *See* critical society.

REASONED JUDGMENT   Any belief or conclusion reached on the basis of careful thought and reflection, distinguished from mere or unreasoned opinion on the one hand and from sheer fact on the other. Few people have a clear sense of which of their beliefs are based on reasoned judgment and which on mere opinion. Moral or ethical questions, for example, are questions that usually require reasoned judgment. One way of conceiving subject-matter education is as developing students' ability to engage in reasoned judgment in accordance with the standards of each subject.

REASONING   The mental processes of those who reason; especially the drawing of conclusions or inferences from observations, facts, or hypotheses; the evidence or arguments used in this procedure. By reasoning, we mean making sense of something by giving it some meaning in your mind. Almost all thinking is part of our sense-making activities. We hear scratching at the door and think, "It's the dog." We see dark clouds in the sky and think, "It looks like rain." Some of this activity operates at a subconscious level (for example, all of the sights and sounds about me have meaning for me without my explicitly noticing that they do). Most of our reasoning is quite unspectacular. Our reasoning tends to become explicit to us only when it is challenged by someone and we have to defend it. ("Why do you say that Jack is obnoxious? I thought he was quite pleasant.") Critical thinkers try to develop the capacity to transform thought into reasoning at will or, rather, the ability to make their inferences explicit, along with the assumptions or premises upon which those inferences are based. Reasoning is a form of explicit inferring, usually involving several steps.

RECIPROCITY   Entering empathically into the point of view or line of reasoning of others; learning to think as others do and that means sympathetically assessing that thinking. (Reciprocity requires creative imagination as well as intellectual skill and a commitment to fair-mindedness.)

RELEVANT   Bearing upon or relating to the matter at hand. *Relevant* implies a close logical relationship with, and importance to, the matter under consideration. By comparison, *germane* implies such a close natural connection as to be highly appropriate or fit; *pertinent* implies an immediate and direct bearing on the matter at hand (e.g., a pertinent suggestion); *applicable* refers to that which can be brought to bear upon a particular matter or problem. People often have problems sticking to an issue and distinguishing information that bears upon a problem from information that does not.

Merely reminding people to limit themselves to relevant considerations fails to solve this problem. Sensitivity to (ability to judge) relevance can be developed only with continual practice—practice distinguishing relevant from irrelevant data, evaluating or judging relevance, arguing for and against the relevance of facts.

SELF-DECEPTION   Deceiving oneself about one's true motivations, character, or identity. The human species might well be called the self-deceiving animal! Self-deception is a fundamental problem in human life and the cause of much human suffering. Overcoming self-deception through self-critical thinking is a fundamental goal of strong-sense critical thinking. *See also* egocentricity, rational self, personal contradiction, social contradiction, intellectual virtues.

SELFISH INTEREST   What is perceived to be useful to oneself without regard for the rights and needs of others. To be selfish is to seek what one desires without due consideration for others. Being interested in one's own welfare is one thing; trampling on the rights of others while one pursues desires unrelated to human needs is another. As fundamentally egocentric creatures, humans are naturally given to pursue our selfish interests, using rationalization and other forms of self-deception to disguise our true motives and the true character of what we are doing. To develop as fair-minded critical thinkers is to work actively to diminish the power of one's native selfishness without sacrificing any legitimate concerns for one's welfare and long-term good. *See also* self-deception, rationalization, egocentricity, fair-mindedness, vested interest.

SOCIAL CONTRADICTION   An inconsistency between what a society preaches and what it practices. Every society has some degree of inconsistency between its image of itself and its actual character. Social contradiction typically correlates with human self-deception on the social or cultural level. Critical thinking is essential for the recognition of inconsistencies, and recognition is essential for reform and eventual integrity.

SOCIOCENTRICITY   The assumption that one's own social group is inherently and self-evidently superior to all others. When a group or society sees itself as superior, and so considers its views as correct or as the only reasonable or justifiable views, and all its actions as justified, it has a tendency to presuppose this superiority in all of its thinking and, thus, to think closed-mindedly. Dissent and doubt are considered disloyal and are rejected. Few people recognize the sociocentric nature of much of their thought. *See also* ethnocentricity.

SOCRATIC QUESTIONING   A mode of questioning that deeply probes the meaning, justification, or logical strength of a claim, position, or line of reasoning. Socratic questioning can be carried out in a variety of ways and adapted to many levels of ability and understanding. *See also* elements of thought, dialogical instruction, knowledge.

SPECIFY/SPECIFIC   To mention, describe, or define in detail; limiting or limited; precise; definite. Much human thinking, speech, and writing tends to be vague, abstract, and ambiguous rather than specific, concrete, and clear. Learning how to state one's views specifically is essential to learning how to think clearly, precisely, and accurately. *See also* perfections of thought.

STRONG-SENSE CRITICAL THINKERS   Those who are characterized predominantly by the following traits: (1) an ability to question deeply one's own framework of thought; (2) an ability to reconstruct empathically and imaginatively the strongest versions of points of view and frameworks of thought opposed to one's own; and (3) an ability to reason dialectically (multilogically) in such a way as to determine when one's own point of view is at its weakest and when an opposing point of view is at its strongest.

Strong-sense critical thinkers are not routinely blinded by their own viewpoints. They know they have points of view and therefore recognize the framework of assumptions and ideas upon which their own thinking is based. They realize the necessity of putting their own assumptions and ideas to the test of the strongest objections that can be leveled against them.

Teaching for critical thinking in the strong sense is teaching so that students explicate, understand, and critique their own deepest prejudices, biases, and misconceptions, thereby discovering and contesting their own egocentric and sociocentric tendencies. Only if we contest our inevitable egocentric and sociocentric habits of thought can we hope to think in a genuinely rational fashion. Only dialogical thinking about basic issues that genuinely matter to the individual provides the kind of practice and skill essential to strong-sense critical thinking. People need to develop critical-thinking skills in dialogical settings to achieve genuine fair-mindedness. If critical thinking is taught simply as atomic skills separate from the empathic practice of entering into points of view that students are fearful of or hostile toward, the students will simply find additional means of rationalizing prejudices and preconceptions, or of convincing people that their point of view is the correct one. They will be transformed from vulgar to sophisticated (but not to strong-sense) critical thinkers. Opposite is *weak-sense critical thinkers*. *See also* fair-mindedness.

SUBMISSIVE EGO   The irrational tendency of the mind to psychologically join and serve people it deems as more powerful, to get what it wants. Humans are naturally concerned with their interests and are motivated to satisfy their desires. In a world of psychological power and influence, one can succeed in two basic ways: to psychologically conquer or intimidate (subtly or openly) those who stand in one's way, or, alternatively, to psychologically join and serve more powerful others, who then: (1) give one a sense of personal importance, (2) protect one, and (3) share with one some of the benefits of their success. The irrational person uses both techniques, though not to the same extent.

Those who seem to be more successful in submitting to more powerful others have what has been called a submissive ego. Those who seem to be more successful in using overt force and control have what might be called a dominating ego. This behavior can be seen publicly in the relationship of rock stars or sport stars to their admiring followers. Most social groups have an internal "pecking order," with some members playing roles of leader and most playing roles of followers. A fair-minded rational person seeks neither to dominate nor to blindly serve someone else who dominates. Opposite is *dominating ego*.

TEACH   To impart knowledge or skills. Teaching usually connotes some individual attention to the learner. By comparison, *instruct* implies systematized teaching, usually in a specific subject; *educate* stresses the development of latent faculties and powers by formal, systematic teaching, especially in institutions of higher learning; *train* implies the development of a certain faculty or skill or instruction toward a specific occupation, as by methodical discipline or exercise. *See also* knowledge.

THEORY   A systematic statement of principles involved in a subject; a formulation of apparent relationships or underlying principles of certain observed phenomena that have been verified to some extent. Often without realizing it, we form theories that help us make sense of the people, events, and problems in our lives. Critical thinkers put their theories to the test of experience and give due consideration to the theories of others. Critical thinkers do not take theories to be facts.

THINK   To exercise the mental faculties so as to form ideas and arrive at conclusions. By comparison, *reason* implies a logical sequence of thought, starting with what is known or assumed and advancing to a definite conclusion through the inferences drawn; *reflect* implies a turning back of one's thoughts on a subject and connotes deep or quiet continued thought; *speculate* implies reasoning on the basis of incomplete or uncertain evidence and therefore stresses the conjectural character of the opinions formed; *deliberate* implies careful and thorough consideration of a matter to arrive at a conclusion. Though everyone thinks, few people think critically. We don't need instruction to think; we think spontaneously. We need instruction to learn how to discipline and direct our thinking on the basis of sound intellectual standards. *See also* elements of thought, perfections of thought.

TRUTH   Conformity to knowledge, fact, actuality, or logic; a statement proven to be or accepted as true, not false or erroneous. Most people uncritically assume their views to be correct and true; they assume themselves to possess the truth. Critical thinking is essential to avoid this, if for no other reason.

UNCRITICAL PERSON   One who has not developed intellectual skills; is naive, conforming, easily manipulated, dogmatic, easily confused, unclear, closed-minded, narrow-minded, careless in word choice, inconsistent, unable to distinguish evidence from interpretation. Uncriticalness is a fundamental problem in human life, for when we are uncritical, we nevertheless think of ourselves as critical. The first step in becoming a critical thinker consists of recognizing that we are uncritical.

VAGUE   Not clearly, precisely, or definitely expressed or stated; not sharp, certain, or precise in thought, feeling, or expression. Vagueness of thought and expression is a major obstacle to the development of critical thinking. We cannot begin to test our beliefs until we recognize clearly what they are. We cannot disagree with what someone says until we are clear about what he or she means. Students need much practice in transforming vague thoughts into clear ones. *See also* ambiguous, clarify, concept, logic, logic of questions, logic of language.

VERBAL IMPLICATION   That which follows, according to the logic of the language. If I say, for example, that someone used flattery on me, I imply that the compliments were insincere and given only to make me feel positively toward that person, to manipulate me against my reason or interest for some end. *See also* implication, inference, empirical implication, elements of thought.

VESTED INTEREST   (1) Involvement in promoting personal advantage, usually at the expense of others; (2) people functioning as a group to pursue collective selfish goals and exerting influences that enable them to profit at the expense of others. Many groups that lobby Congress do so to gain money, power, and advantage for themselves by provisions in law that specially favor them. The term *vested interest* classically contrasts with the term *public interest*. A group that lobbies Congress in the public interest is not seeking to gain special advantage for a comparative few but, rather, protection for all or the large majority. Preserving the quality of the air is a public interest. Building cheaper cars by including fewer safety features is a vested interest (it makes more money for car manufacturers). *See also* selfish interest.

WEAK-SENSE CRITICAL THINKERS   (1) Those who do not hold themselves or those with whom they ego-identify to the same intellectual standards to which they hold opponents; (2) those who have not learned how to reason empathically within points of view or frames of reference with which they disagree; (3) those who tend to think monologically (within one narrow perspective); (4) those who do not genuinely accept, though they may verbally espouse, the values of critical thinking; (5) those who use the intellectual skills of critical thinking selectively and self-deceptively to foster and serve their selfish interests at the expense of truth; (6) those who use critical-thinking skills to identify flaws in the reasoning of others and sophisticated arguments to refute others' arguments before giving those arguments due consideration; (7) those who are able to justify their irrational thinking with highly skilled rationalizations. Opposite is *strong-sense critical thinkers. See also* monological thinking, rationalization, irrational/irrationality.

WORLD VIEW   A way of looking at and interpreting the world. As schooling now stands, little is done to help students grasp how they are viewing the world and how those views determine the character of their experience, their interpretations, their conclusions about events and persons. In learning critical thinking in a strong sense, we make it a priority to discover our own world view and experience other people's world views. *See also* bias, interpret.

REFERENCES

Campbell, S. (Ed.) (1976). *Piaget Sampler: An Introduction to Jean Piaget Through His Own Words.* New York: John Wiley & Sons.

Campbell, T. (1994). *Beware the Talking Cure: Psychotherapy May Be Hazardous to Your Mental Health.* Boca Raton, FL: Social Issues Resources Series.

Chaplin, J. P. (1985). *Dictionary of Psychology.* New York: Dell.

Clark, R. *Albert Einstein: The Life and Times.* New York: Avon Books.

Coleman, L. (1984). *Reign of Error.* Boston: Beacon Press.

Commager, H. S. (1950). *The American Mind.* New Haven, CT: Yale University Press, pp. 22, 23.

Darwin, F. (1958). *The Autobiography of Charles Darwin.* New York: Dover.

Ennis, R. (1985). *Goals for Critical Thinking/Reasoning Curriculum.* Illinois Critical Thinking Project. Champaign: University of Illinois.

Esterle, J. & Cluman, D. (Eds.) (1993). *Conversations with Critical Thinkers.* San Francisco: Whitman Institute.

Frankl, V. E. (1959). *Man's Search for Meaning.* New York: Washington Square Press.

Fromm, Erich. (1956). *The Art of Loving.* New York: Harper & Row, pp. 1–2, 23–24, 47.

Guralnik, D. B. (Ed.) (1986). *Webster's New World Dictionary.* New York: Prentice Hall.

Jevons, F. R. (1964). *The Biochemical Approach to Life.* New York: Basic Books.

Lipman, M. (1988, March). Critical thinking and the use of criteria. *Inquiry: Newsletter of the Institute for Critical Thinking.* Montclair State College, Upper Montclair, NJ.

Mann, H. (1838). *Lincoln Library of Essential Information.* (1940). Buffalo, NY: The Frontier Press, p. 1633.

Markham, F. (1967). *Oxford.* Holland: Reynal & Co.

McWilliams, P. (1996). *Ain't Nobody's Business If You Do: The Absurdity of Consensual Crimes in Our Free Country.* Los Angeles: Prelude Press, pp. 3, 7.

Mencken, H. L. (1923, Dec. 5). On Liberty *Nation Magazine.*

Milgram, S. (1974). *Obedience to Authority.* New York: Harper & Row.

Myres, Gustavus. (1907). *History of the Great American Fortunes.* Chicago: Charles H. Kerr.

Newman, J. H. (1912). *The Idea of a University.* New York: Longman's Green & Co. (The lectures that formed this book were originally given in 1852.)

New York Times (1998, Oct. 5). Amnesty finds "widespread pattern" of U.S. rights violations.

New York Times (1998, Dec. 28). Iraq is a pediatrician's hell: No way to stop the dying.

New York Times (1999, March 6). Testing the limits of tolerance as cultures mix: Does freedom mean accepting rituals that repel the West?

New York Times (1999, June 12). Beautiful beaches and bronzed men, but no bathing belles.

New York Times (1999, June 20). Arab honor's price: A woman's blood.

New York Times (1999, July 1). U.S. releases files on abuses in Pinochet era, p. A11.

New York Times (1999, Oct. 21). Boy, 11, held on incest charge, and protests ensue.

New York Times (1999, Nov. 22). Moratorium now.

New York Times (1999, Nov. 27). Spanish judge is hoping to see secret files in U. S., p. A14.

New York Times (1999, Nov. 29). Advertisement by the Turning Point Project entitled "Invisible government."

New York Times (1999, Nov. 30). Group asking U.S. for vigilance in patient safety: Wants a federal agency: Academy of Sciences asserts that rate of medical errors is "stunningly high."

New York Times (2004, Feb. 25). Prosecutorial misconduct leads justices to overturn death sentence in Texas.

New York Times (2004, April 4). Convicted of killing his parents, but calling a detective the real bad guy.

Ofshe, R. & Watters, E. (1996). *Making Monsters: False Memories, Psychotherapy, and Sexual Hysteria.* Berkeley, CA: University of California Press.

Paul, R. (1995). *What Every Student Needs to Survive in a Rapidly Changing World.* Dillon Beach, CA: The Foundation for Critical Thinking.

PETA. (1999). 501 Front St., Norfolk, VA 23510, www.peta.com.

Peters, R. S. (1973). *Reason and Compassion.* London: Routledge & Kegan Paul.

Plotnicov, L. & Tuden, A. (Eds.) (1970). *Essays in Comparative Social Stratification.* Pittsburgh: University of Pittsburgh Press.

San Francisco Chronicle (1999, Feb. 6). First Philippine execution in 23 years: Lethal injection for man who raped his stepdaughter, 10.

San Francisco Chronicle (1999, June 11). Treatment is new salvo fired by reformers in war on drugs: Courts, voters beginning to favor therapy, not prisons, to fight crack, p. A9. (Article taken from the *New York Times.*)

San Francisco Chronicle (1999, Oct. 2). U.S. order to kill civilians in Korea illegal, experts say: Prosecution seen as impossible now, p. A12. (Article taken from the Associated Press.)

Siegel, H. (1988). *Educating Reason: Rationality, Critical Thinking, and Education.* New York: Routledge Chapman Hall.

Singer, M. & Lalich, J. (1996). *Crazy Therapies: What Are They? Do They Work?* San Francisco: Jossey-Bass.

Snow, C. P. (1967). *A Variety of Men.* New York: Charles Scribner & Sons.

Stebbing, S. (1952). *Thinking to Some Purpose.* London: Penguin Books.

Sumner, W. G. (1940). *Folkways: A Study of the Sociological Importance of Usages, Manners, Customs, Mores, and Morals.* New York: Ginn and Co.

Thoreau, Henry David. (1937). *Walden and Other Writings.* New York: Modern Library, pp. 635, 636–637, 644.

Twain, M. (1946). *The Portable Mark Twain.* New York: The Viking Press, pp. 573, 576, 577, 578.

Westfall, R. (1993). *The Life of Isaac Newton.* New York: Cambridge University Press.

Zinn, H. (1995). *A People's History of the United States 1492–Present.* New York: HarperCollins.

INDEX

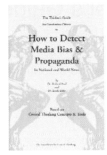

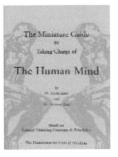

Foundations of Ethical Reasoning – Provides insights into the nature of ethical reasoning, why it is so often flawed, and how to avoid those flaws. It lays out the function of ethics, its main impediments, and its social counterfeits. (1-24 copies $6.00 each; 24-199 copies $4.00 each; 200-499 copies $2.50 each)

How to Detect Media Bias and Propaganda – Designed to help readers come to recognize bias in their nation's news, to detect ideology, slant, and spin at work, and to recognize propaganda when exposed to it, so that they can reasonably determine what media messages need to be supplemented, counter-balanced, or thrown out entirely. It focuses on the internal logic of the news as well as societal influences on the media. (1-24 copies $6.00 each; 25-199 copies $4.00 each; 200-499 copies $2.50 each)

The Human Mind – Designed to give the reader insight into the basic functions of the human mind and into how knowledge of these functions (and their interrelations) can enable one to use one's intellect and emotions more effectively. (1-24 copies $5.00 each; 25-199 copies $2.50 each; 200-499 copies $1.75 each)

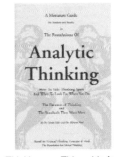

Active & Cooperative Learning – Provides 27 simple ideas for the improvement of instruction. It lays the foundation for the ideas found in the mini-guide How to Improve Student Learning (1-24 copies $3.00; 25-199 copies $1.50 each; 200-499 copies $1.25 each)

How to Improve Student Learning – Provides 30 practical ideas for the improvement of instruction based on the guide Critical Thinking: Concepts and Tools It integrates critical thinking teaching strategies with active and cooperative learning. (1-24 copies $6.00; 25-199 copies $4.00 each; 200-499 copies $2.50 each)

Analytic Thinking – This guide focuses on the intellectual skills that enable one to analyze anything one might think about—questions, problems, disciplines, subjects, etc. It provides the common denominator between all forms of analysis. (1-24 copies $6.00 each; 25-199 copies $4.00 each; 200-499 copies $2.50 each)

For more information or to place an order, contact the Foundation For Critical Thinking at www.criticalthinking.org   or 707-878-9100.

The Thinker's Guide Library

The Thinker's Guide Library provides convenient, inexpensive, portable references you can use to improve the quality of your learning. Their compactness enables you to keep them at hand whenever you are working in or out of class. Their succinctness serves as a continual reminder of the most basic principles of critical thinking.

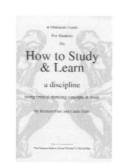

Miniature Guide to Critical Thinking – The essence of critical thinking concepts and tools distilled into a 19-page pocket-size guide. (1-24 copies $4.00 each; 25-199 copies $2.00 each; 200-499 copies $1.75 each)

How to Study & Learn – A variety of strategies—both simple and complex—for becoming not just a better student, but also a master student. (1-24 copies $6.00 each; 25-199 copies $4.00 each; 200-499 copies $2.50 each)

Critical Thinking for Children – Focuses on explaining basic critical thinking principles to young children using cartoon characters. (1-24 copies $5.00 each; 25-199 copies $2.50 each; 200-499 copies $1.75 each)

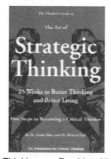

Asking Essential Questions – Introduces the art of asking essential questions. It is best used in conjunction with the Miniature Guide to Critical Thinking and the How to Study & Learn mini-guide. (1-24 copies $6.00 each; 25-199 $4.00 each; 200-499 copies $2.50 each)

Strategic Thinking – Provides 25 "big ideas" to be internalized over a 25-week period. Helps the thinker begin to think strategically about improving one's life through improving one's thinking. (1-24 copies $6.00 each; 25-199 copies $4.00 each; 200-499 copies $2.50 each)

Scientific Thinking – The essence of scientific thinking concepts and tools. It focuses on the intellectual skills inherent in the well-cultivated scientific thinker. (1-24 copies $6.00 each; 24-199 copies $4.00 each; 200-499 copies $2.50 each)

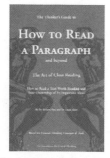

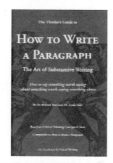

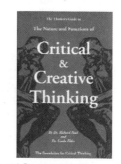

How to Read a Paragraph – This guide provides theory and activities necessary for deep comprehension. Imminently practical for students. (1-24 copies $6.00 each; 25-199 copies $4.00 each; 200-499 copies $2.50)

How to Write a Paragraph – Focuses on the art of substantive writing. How to say something worth saying about something worth saying something about. (1-24 copies $6.00 each; 24-199 copies $4.00 each; 200-499 copies $2.50 each)

Critical and Creative Thinking – Focuses on the interrelationship between critical and creative thinking through the essential role of both in learning. (1-24 copies $6.00 each; 25-199 copies $4.00 each; 200-499 copies $2.50 each)